Tackling Giants
The Life Story of Berkley Bedell
By Larry Ramey and Daniel Haley

Cover by Larry Ramey

ISBN# 0-9768200-0-5
Library of Congress Control Number: 2005925559

Published by:
The National Foundation for Alternative Medicine
22167 C. Street
Winfield, Kansas 67156

Printed in the United States of America

Third Printing

Tackling Giants

The Life Story

of Berkley Bedell

By Larry Ramey and Daniel Haley

Introduction by former Congressman Dr. Bob Edgar, General Secretary, National Council of Churches USA

Dedication

This book is dedicated to former Senator Paul Simon. It would not have been written if it not been for the constant encouragement of Senator Simon. He reviewed it word for word several times. The first time, there must have been an average of at least six recommended changes per page.

His death in 2003 came as a terrible shock. While we were in Congress together, Paul and his wife, Jeanne, were two of our closest friends. They visited us in Naples, Florida, shortly before Jeanne died of brain cancer. As this book points out, I also was his Iowa chairman when he ran for President. I talked with Paul while he was in the hospital waiting for his heart surgery. I was quite heavily involved in Howard Dean's campaign for President, and Paul had endorsed Governor Dean from his hospital bed. The fact that he failed to survive that heart surgery motivates me all the more to try to find better treatments for heart disease and other diseases.

Berkley Bedell

Preface

If there is one thing that my life shows, one message that I would like to communicate from my story, it is: A person should not shrink from challenges.

Time after time, in business, in politics, and in my personal life, I have faced situations where it looked like there might not be any chance of success. But I found that by properly applying myself I could overcome those odds.

In my early life, my mother impressed upon me the importance of success. As a result, perhaps I have been too much obsessed with being successful in everything that came about.

As a young boy, my mother dressed me in short pants and a pretty little suit while my friends were wearing grubby clothes. Because of my dress and my small stature I was cast as little Georgie Bassett in our fourth grade play, "Penrod." I hated it. Because of my determination not to be considered a sissy, I was elected captain of our high school basketball team by a unanimous vote of my team members. Weighing only 120 pounds, I had no business playing football, but because of my determination I made the varsity team for two years. By the time I graduated from high school, I am sure nobody viewed me as a sissy.

I was so obsessed with succeeding in my business that even my own health took a back seat. The odds against being able to build a successful business, starting with only $50 from my newspaper route-were pretty substantial.

However, my grandmother had a saying, "You can do almost anything within reason if you will only put your mind to it."

Her saying is the main message of my life:

• As a teenager, I started a business in my parents' home selling fishing leaders that I did not yet know how to make.

- Although my business operated out of a few rented spaces in the small town of Spirit Lake, Iowa, we decided to compete with one of the biggest corporations in the world. We not only had to figure out how to manufacture a better product, we had to beat DuPont in court for the right to do it.

- We created a company dedicated to treating employees as empowered and successful co-workers, at a time when management and labor fought bitterly in other places and other industries.

- I ran for Congress as a Democrat against a popular Republican incumbent in a predominantly Republican district that consistently voted overwhelmingly for Ronald Reagan – and served six consecutive terms.

- Our Congressional class redefined Congress as a community of colleagues operating on the merit of the issues and the people involved, after a period when the seniority system promoted fiefdoms and political paybacks.

- I succeeded in bringing reforms in military spending through a campaign against a process that created waste and fraud.

- My son, Tom, despite having no previous experience in manufacturing or selling fishing tackle, built Berkley and Company into the largest fishing tackle company in the nation.

- My wife, Elinor, and I have raised three highly motivated children to value and work for peace in a world of competition and conflict.

- I have lived through two potentially fatal health conditions: Lyme disease and prostate cancer, with the help of alternative medical treatments.

- Elinor and I have given away more than half of our income in recent years, and still live a comfortable life.

- Though few people thought it possible, I helped our Iowa Lakes region raise millions of dollars for community projects.

• Ignoring the power of the allopathic medical monopoly, Elinor and I started a foundation to promote research of alternative medical treatments.

There is a tendency for people to hesitate to take on challenges because of concern about failure. The reality is that it is better to give it a try and fail than to shrink from the challenge simply because it seems impossible.

My grandmother probably made a mistake by including "within reason" in her saying, because many things I have done were not very reasonable.

My hope is that you will find something in this biography that will help you take on the challenges of your life, however difficult and unreasonable solutions might seem.

Berkley Bedell

About the Authors

Larry Ramey

Larry Ramey, who wrote the first 29 chapters of the book, is a journalist and faith-based media producer in Dayton, Ohio, with a passion for exploring people's quest for meaning in life. He won state and national awards for feature stories and series as a newspaper reporter and editor in Lorain, Ohio, then studied and taught classes in religious communication at United Theological Seminary in Dayton. He has worked in faith-oriented organizations as a writer, editor, electronic media producer and consultant with churches and non-profit organizations. He has edited and published 10 books and has produced videos and print media on social justice, evangelism and missions. He has both a focus on urban social ministry and fond affection for the smalltown and rural life of his young childhood and that of his mother and late father, an avid outdoorsman.

Daniel Haley

Daniel Haley, who wrote the final chapter, served in the New York assembly from 1970 to 1976 representing St. Lawrence County. To date he is the only Democrat ever elected to the Assembly to represent that district.

In the Assembly he chaired the Legislature's Joint Commission on energy, emphasizing the need to develop alternative energy resources. He authored the Safe Energy Act of 1975. This legislation established the New York State Energy Research and Development Authority, which is directed by statute to focus on renewable energy resources.
Before entering politics, Haley was an international businessman in Brazil. After managing the Mosler Safe Co's Brazilian subsidy, he assembled the beach real estate project, which became the Rio de Janeiro Sheraton. This followed service in the U.S. Air Force as an intelligence officer in Korea, the Philippines and Japan. He graduated from Harvard College cum laude. Haley spent 1997-1999 inclusive writing *Politics in Healing, the Suppression and Manipulation of American Medicine.*

Dan Haley update

As this book was going to press Dan Haley, who authored the last part of the book, had a serious stroke. He lives alone. In the night he awoke to go to the bathroom. He fell and was unable to move the left side of his body. It was several hours before he was discovered. His whole left side was completely paralyzed and without feeling. The prognosis was that he would have to spend the rest of his life in bed, as did my grandmother after her stroke.

Fortunately, Dan's mind was not affected. He refused to accept his gloomy forecast and turned to a number of alternative treatments. After only four weeks, DAN HALEY IS UP AND WALKING. Praise the Lord!

Table of Contents

Introduction

A Great Fisherman

I met Berkley Bedell in November 1974, after we both won surprise elections to the United States House of Representatives. In the wake of Watergate, we joined a host of Democrats and a few Republicans who were elected to attempt to bring integrity and civility back to political life.

Berk was an extraordinarily uncommon and uniquely prepared individual, who brought his homespun Iowa gentleness and business curiosity to the halls of Congress. Speaking quietly, looking like an economy-sized Abraham Lincoln, and carrying a resume that makes Horatio Alger look like the manager of your local mini-market, Berk is perhaps the kindest and friendliest person I have ever known. His demeanor makes him an easy man to underestimate, but legislators did so at their peril. One of the first things I noticed about Berk was his ability to ask the right question at the "wrong" time or the "wrong" question at the right time.

His biography is just as plainspoken, straightforward and uncompromising as the man whose story it tells. Perhaps it is the discipline that comes from a lifetime of fishing. As a confirmed fishing zealot myself, I keep hoping that if I fish enough, I will achieve Berk's ability to speak truth to power.

In Congress, I was regularly amazed at his capacity to cut through the technical jargon and rhetoric, which abound in that institution, and to find the simple truth under a pile of oratory that droned on and on: "Would the distinguished gentleman from the state of Ohio yield to the gentleman from Pennsylvania and describe what is the legislative intention under sub-paragraph VI: Section III: page 3394 of the IRS code," etc. He regularly cut through the arcane ways in which obfuscation takes place in Washington.

Having discovered an important fact about an issue, Berk was absolutely fearless in pointing out in plain English that the emperor was naked. Simple as that! I remember Berk, in his search for the truth, walking out of the Capitol and going down to one of the many government agencies along the Mall in Washington. He would enter the building, take the elevator to the appropriate floor, walk the halls of the agency, and ask government employees to verify some statistic or concept. You can imagine how surprised these employees were to find out that this strange man was a member of Congress. They didn't understand why he was "fishing for facts" out side the sterile Committee Hearing Room format.

Berk would then return to the House floor with information that no other member of Congress and/or their staff had thought to seek. Often, he won his point by his ability to explore, to enquire, or to personalize the legislative process with stories and illustrations of his firsthand fact-finding.

I came to Washington as a campus minister, community organizer and urban activist. It was fun befriending a successful businessman, passionate humanitarian and thoughtful questioner who was dedicated to improving the world around him. No challenge seems too difficult for Berk. In his fights against pork-barreling and government waste, he made clear his passion for doing what is right. In his current work on alternative medicine, he leaves no stones unturned and no "half-baked" idea out of his hope for medical cures. He thinks that if there is a half-baked medical cure, the other half of the baking might save lives in the future, so let's take a look.

I have heard some of the stories in this book from the author's lips and from his wife, Elinor, and family. It is a delight to have them brought together in a compelling, clearly written and unvarnished book. In an era in which politicians are all too often less than the sum of their barber, clothing manufacturer, speechwriter and spin doctors, it is wonderfully refreshing to work with a man who is just plain Berkley Bedell: A man on a mission and a man who takes very seriously the admonition that we should leave the world better than we found it. With the possible exception of God's creature the fish, all of God's creation can celebrate and enjoy a better world because Berkley Bedell has been an active and engaged part of it for more than 80 years.

I commend this book to anyone who doubts that one man or woman can make a difference in their community, their nation, and their world. It was Bobby Kennedy in 1966, who said the following:

"Let no one be discouraged by the belief that there is nothing that one man or one woman can do against the enormous array of the world's ills: against misery or ignorance, injustice or violence. Few will have the greatness to bend history to itself. But each of us can work to change a small portion of events so that in the total of all those acts will be written the history of our generation."

I am honored that Berk has been a part of my history.

He set out to make a difference. The ultimate judgment is in the hands of the Lord but, as a person of faith, I am willing to go on record as a member in good standing of the Berkley Bedell fan club. You will be, too, when you read this book.

Dr. Bob Edgar, General Secretary
National Council of Churches USA
July 2004

Chapter One

Spirit of the Lakes

*The afternoon that changed
the future of Berkley Bedell, Spirit Lake, Iowa,
and the fishing tackle industry*

Fifteen-year-old Berkley Bedell pedaled up the gravel driveway and leaned his bike against the rickety, one-and-a-half story wood-plank building where Frank Marnette lived and operated a bait shop.

The shop stood alongside the tiny creek that bisected the narrow isthmus between two lakes: saucer-dish Big Spirit Lake to the north, boomerang-shaped East Okoboji Lake to the south. Berkley had ridden his bike a mile north from his house in the town of Spirit Lake.

"Mr. Mar-NETTE? Mr. Mar-NETTE?"

Berkley Bedell needed some white buck tail streamers if he and his dad were to get in any fly-fishing before sunset.

The Spirit Lake area had become Iowa's fishing paradise with 18 glacier-scooped lakes near the southern border of Minnesota.

Berkley, a child of the lakes, had heard their call as clearly as the Native Americans who came to fish and hunt there for centuries. He inherited the determination of the people who settled the land in the wake of the 1857 Spirit Lake massacre, when a band of renegade Sioux Indians plundered and killed most of the families who had come to the area and built their log cabins.

The Iowa
Great Lakes Region

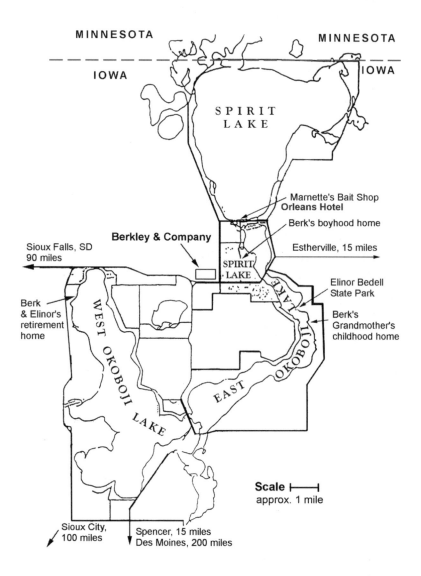

MINNESOTA   MINNESOTA

IOWA   IOWA

SPIRIT
LAKE

Marnette's Bait Shop
Orleans Hotel

Berk's boyhood home

Berkley & Company

Sioux Falls, SD
90 miles

Estherville, 15 miles

SPIRIT
LAKE

Elinor Bedell
State Park

Berk
& Elinor's
retirement
home

WEST OKOBOJI LAKE

Berk's
Grandmother's
childhood home

EAST OKOBOJI LAKE

Scale ⊢——⊣
approx. 1 mile

Sioux City,
100 miles

Spencer, 15 miles
Des Moines, 200 miles

They were followed by people who cleared farmland in the blazing summer heat, endured the lake-freezing winters, and created a resort area in the wilderness.

Berkley grew up during the post-war, pre-Depression optimism of the 1920s, playing in the woods, on the lakes, and in the streets, with happy go-lucky neighborhood children.

But more than anything, he grew up with more fishing lakes than a boy could count, just a short walk or bike ride away. He believed that every day might be a fishing day, with waters upon which he could cast a line. He treated every cast as a leap into a new future with its own set of known and unknown circumstances worthy of its own dream of success.

Next to Marnette's bait shop stood a ghost from the grand history and great dreams of the area – the remains of the once-magnificent Orleans Hotel, built in 1883. In its turn-of-the-century glory, stylish parties of vacationers rode trains from all over Iowa and the Minnesota-South Dakota-Nebraska region to its front door. The grand ballroom overlooked the south shore of Big Spirit Lake. People spread out blankets on the beach or boarded boats to fish or relax. A giant water slide provided a high-speed splash into the lake.

The Orleans Hotel's golden era had long since passed by the time Berkley pedaled his bicycle up to Marnette's bait shop in 1936. It was the middle of the Great Depression and the hotel had been reduced to a shell of its former grandeur.

People still came from all over the region, but they stayed in rustic cottages and motor lodges. The local economy went up and down with tourism, which in those days consisted of low-paying jobs taking care of Depression-thrifty tourists. The town still had more gravel streets than paved ones.

At 15, Berkley Bedell had one foot in his childhood and one foot in his future. In the 1930s, Berkley lived a carefree life fishing and hunting in the Spirit Lake area. But the adult community found it hard to make a living.

No one could even envision a successful future when some of the best jobs in town were with the Works Projects Administration or the Civilian Conservation Corps.

Frank Marnette didn't worry about the economy, or the unrest over Hitler and Mussolini in Europe. What mattered to him was that his back door was 150 feet from some of the best fishing in the Midwest and he knew how to fish with the best of them. He made the best split bamboo fly rods in Iowa and southern Minnesota. His bait shop carried the hand-tied flies Berkley's father and mother loved.

Berkley's dad, attorney Walter Bedell, loved to come home after a day in court, grab his fly rod and a pair of rubber hip boots and wade into the water for an hour before dinner. Berkley's mother, Virginia, who had worked her way from law clerk to attorney, loved to fish as much as Walt. Walt and Ginny took Berkley and his younger brother, Jack, fishing with them as soon as they were big enough to slide a bluegill onto a stringer.

Berkley pulled open Marnette's weathered wooden door and wandered into the dingy shop.

"Mr. Mar-NETTE?" Berk called again as he ventured inside, stepping around a foot-wide hole in the rotting floorboards. He scanned the glass display case strewn with bobbers, poppers, and jigs. "Mr. Mar-NETTE?"

Marnette appeared through the back door, fishing rod in hand.

"Do you have any buck tail streamers, Mr. Marnette?" asked Berkley. Berkley, who had grown to about his father's height in the last year, a slim 5 feet 6 inches tall, looked up into the lean, unshaven face of the master angler.

"Well, if we don't have any in the case, I s'pose we could tie up a couple right quick," Marnette replied. "Pull up a stool."

Marnette wiped his wind-worn hands on his flannel shirt and pulled a small paper sack from the shelf. He drew from it a small tuft of fur he had gathered from a deer's whitetail. He sorted through a hook tray for the hook he wanted and then cut off 24 inches of black thread from a spool mounted on a nail on his workbench. His fish-worn fingers slid the hook into a vice and cranked the vice tight. He wrapped the buck tail hair onto the hook and in a few minutes, had tightly wound the line.

"Simple enough," thought Berkley. Ever since he could remember, Berkley had loved to figure out how to make things like the iceboat that he and young Jack had built the autumn before from scrap lumber and metal.

"Mr. Marnette, do you suppose I could try to tie one?"

"I don't see why not."

Marnette slid the basic ingredients across the counter toward the teen-ager. He watched the determined focus of the young man as he hand-tied his first fly.

"Say, do you suppose I could tie some more of these with you sometime?"

Marnette had grown up knowing Berkley's grandfather, Charlie Price, as one of the town's true wise men and justice of the peace. He knew the legendary spunk of Berk's grandmother, Mamie, and had grown up knowing Berk's mother, Ginny, as the brightest student in school.

Walt and Ginny had become some of his best customers and they were raising two of the smartest, most energetic boys in town. Berk and Jack not only loved to fish and hunt, but they also arose before daylight every day to deliver the *Des Moines Register* newspaper and did odd jobs around town to make money.

"Why don't you come back tomorrow and I'll show you a few tricks of the trade?"

"Thanks!" Berkley placed two dimes on the countertop for the flies. "I'll be here after school!"

He tucked the buck tails into his jacket pocket, stepped around the floor hole, and out the door to his bike.

"If I could learn how to tie flies, I wouldn't have to ride all the way out here every time we lost one," he thought. "Dad and Mother could have all the flies they wanted."

Berkley began thinking to himself. He loved the adventure of fishing, but had never tried the business of fishing.

He started figuring in his head. He could buy small sacks of hooks at the hardware store, and tying line by the spool. He could find animal hair anywhere in the woods.

People could get most of their fishing supplies at the hardware store downtown, but Berkley knew that serious fishermen in the area were always yearning for Marnette's hand-tied flies. Every summer, when the resort crowds swarmed into the area, Marnette could sell flies faster than he could tie them.

"What if I tied flies for you to sell at your bait shop?" Berkley asked, during his next fly-tying lesson.

"Let's just see how you do," Marnette replied. "Let's just see."

Within a couple of months, Berkley was tying flies in his bedroom and selling them for a nickel or a dime apiece, first to Marnette, then to other stores in the area. It started out as sort of a hobby, but he was 15 years old, determined to become a success, and he was looking for ways he could build his budding business.

Before long, he had long strings of fishing flies hanging from a wire stretched from wall to wall across the bedroom he shared with Jack. Berkley and Co. was born in that house, and would be built by Berkley and his friends and schoolmates. The teen-agers' bedroom became home to shoe boxes of feathers, thread, animal hair, and hooks. It became a laboratory, a business office, and a production center.

Berkley had never envisioned that his fly-tying lesson with Marnette – in a tiny, rundown bait shop in a small town far from the major manufacturing and marketing centers – would turn his childhood adventures into the largest fishing tackle manufacturing company in the nation.

But from the first day he could remember, he never considered anything impossible.

For his "can-do spirit," he could thank his grandmother.

To understand that spirit, one must go back to the beginning.

Chapter Two

Child of the Lakes

Aunt Mary hurried down the stairs of Charlie and Sarah Price's home.

"It's a boy! It's a boy!" she announced to the rest of the family waiting patiently in the living room. On March 5, 1921, Berkley Warren Bedell was the first of two boys born to Walter and Virginia Bedell.

He was born in the house of his maternal grandparents, only two blocks from his parents' home in Spirit Lake, Iowa. Virginia's brother-in-law, Dr. Frank Roberts, an osteopath at the time, delivered her sons, as he would deliver her nieces in years to come. In later years, Frank moved his family to Iowa City, and attended medical school to become an M.D. Berkley and his brother, Jack, loved to visit Uncle Frank, Aunt Mary, and their daughters Mary (known as "Bobs") and Velma, in Iowa City – a family with so little money that they became excited to have even a few fresh peaches in their little apartment.

Berkley grew up in a family and community where people built their livelihood around being hospitable to those who came to harvest fish-filled lakes and duck-filled skies. In the town of Spirit Lake, folks could – and some did – go fishing or hunting on their lunch breaks.

Berkley's maternal grandparents were children of the harsh Midwest pioneer life, of a water-glazed land more like glacier-lake Minnesota than grassland Iowa – with a history of blizzards, natural plagues, and the most infamous massacre in Iowa history.

Before 1857, the lakes area had been a favorite fishing and fowl-hunting encampment for American Indians, including at various times the tribes of Iowa, Omaha, Sauk and Fox. During the 1700s, the Sioux people had been pushed westward into the plains region from the forests of Wisconsin and Minnesota.

Despite an 1853 treaty, some Sioux resented encroachment into an area they deemed sacred. Settlers built six cabins in the lakes region in 1856. After enduring a winter of blinding, sub-zero degree blizzards, a harsher fate befell them in March 1857. A renegade band of 50 to 100 Sioux Indians led by a red headed chief named Inkpaduta came into the area. They came to avenge the murder of one of their band by an angry pioneer and to stem the incursion into their territory by the white man. They brutally murdered 40 settlers: Adults were shot or killed with an ax; one was beheaded. They killed children by banging their heads against a tree. The cabins were looted and most of them burned. Three young women and 14-year old Abigail Gardner were taken captive. Two of the women were later killed, but Abigail and another woman were ransomed and escaped.

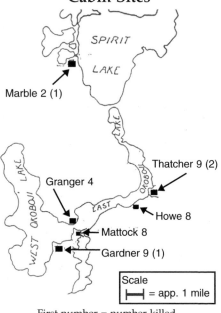

Spirit Lake Massacre of 1857 Cabin Sites

First number = number killed.
( ) = number taken captive

The Indian name for the deepest lake of the area was "Minnetonka," meaning "great water." They held a reverential awe for the widest lake, the one they called "Minnewaukon," translated "spirit water" or "lake of evil spirits." The long and narrow lake that connected these two larger lakes was "Okoboji," meaning "place of rest," "place of peace," or "place of rushes (reeds)." (Minnetonka later became known as West Okoboji, to avoid confusion with a lake in Minnesota.) Early French trappers told the 1804 Lewis and Clark expedition of this lakes region, which they called Lac d'Esprit (*A History of Dickinson County, Iowa,* by R.A. Smith).

In the wake of the Spirit Lake Massacre, federal troops secured the area and built a fort there in June 1857. But as the Civil War consumed the country, only about 200 people had moved to Dickinson County by 1865 – an area about 24 miles wide and 17 miles from north to south.

Berkley's maternal grandparents, Sarah Thomas and Charlie Price, came to this newly settled area in 1870. Sarah Thomas was born on a farm near East Okoboji Lake, Iowa on October 3, 1870. Charlie had been born in September 1868, near Humboldt, Iowa and moved to Spirit Lake as a tot.

Sarah grew up determined to shape a happy adulthood out of a childhood full of natural hazards, family tragedy, and a coldhearted stepmother.

Her family endured winter's deadly blizzards and summer's blistering heat, hordes of mosquitoes and crop-crippling grasshopper plagues. In June 1873, an army of grasshoppers (also known as Rocky Mountain locusts) swarmed the area in what seemed like a huge black cloud that eclipsed the sun. The locusts devoured the grain fields for miles, but Sarah and Charlie's staunch families held fast – even when a larger grasshopper invasion in 1876 drove about one-fourth of the destitute farmers from the area.

While Sarah and Charlie were children, skirmishes with Native Americans had ceased in the Iowa lakes region, but the Sioux wars were raging in the Dakota territories just west of Iowa, including the Battle of Little Big Horn in 1876. When Sarah was a small girl, her pregnant mother, Mary Ann, was kicked by a cow, and died as a result. Sarah grew up yearning for the tenderness of a mother's love, but knew only the stern hand of the stepmother whom her father, Web, married.

Sarah's playful spirit bore her through the hard work and cold of frontier life. She came to believe that she could overcome any obstacle, and often have fun doing it.

She and other pupils in her rural school dreaded fetching water from a nearby pond, not because of the heavy load of the wooden bucket, but because the pond was full of frogs. When the teacher told them that the frogs purified the water, Sarah brought back a pail with frogs in the water!

Sarah Thomas knew she had found her match in schoolmate Charlie Price, a tall, stern boy. He didn't waste words, but loved to tell or hear a good story. He was serious, but not dour; he didn't smile and laugh as much as Sarah, but he liked to play games and loved the outdoors. Charlie also loved history, loved to hunt, and had a keen sense of right and wrong. Their families knew each other well in the close-knit Dickinson County community and before long, among the four Thomas children and four Price children there were three Thomas-Price marriages.

By the time Sarah and Charlie finished their schooling, one of their teachers was actually younger than Charlie, a maiden named Miss Mary Chisholm. She would also live to teach three of Sarah and Charlie's children, and four of their six grandchildren, including Berkley and Jack. Despite being in a wheelchair, due to both legs being amputated from diabetes complications, Miss Chisholm left a keen impression on Berkley. The last time Berkley saw her, when he and Elinor came home on furlough during World War II, she proceeded to tell them what a wonderful life she had had, and how wonderful God is, as she sat in that wheelchair without any legs. Berkley carried her lesson of hope with him all his life.

Sarah attended school for only a few years before she ran away from home and got a job as a cook and housekeeper. She and Charlie married on November 17, 1890; ready to handle whatever challenges they met in life.

By the time Sarah and Charlie married, Spirit Lake had evolved into a different place to raise a family. The lakes region had become a vacation destination for people living in the lakeless part of Iowa. By 1876, people came from near and far to fish the lakes in the spring and summer, hunt waterfowl along its migration flyway during the autumn, and erect ice-fishing shanties on the frozen lakes in the winter.

One outdoorsman claimed he and his friends shot 350 ducks – Canvasbacks, Redheads, and Mallards – in a day-and-a-half in the fall of 1878. Joseph W. Wadsworth, of Algona, Iowa said that in the spring of 1883, he and a fishing partner caught 112 pike in less than two hours on Big Spirit Lake.

When the railroads connected the region to the outside world in 1880, townspeople began to build inns and cottages to accommodate the growing numbers of visitors. The grand Orleans Hotel, built on the isthmus between Big Spirit Lake and East Okoboji Lake in 1883, added the attraction of a stylish vacation resort to the still-thriving wildlife recreation destination.

In 1893, Charlie Price was accidentally shot while hunting. As a result, the doctor had to saw off his leg below his knee. A fitted wooden prosthetic served as his lower leg for the rest of his life.

"He never whimpered about his physical impairment," his grandson, and Berkley's brother, Jack Bedell recalled. "He had an office downtown. He would walk there every morning, walk home for lunch and back, and then return home at the end of the day, every day."

Every night at dinner, Charlie had a story or a joke to tell, often drawing upon his considerable knowledge and love of history. He taught at his old one-room schoolhouse for a brief time, served as Dickinson County Recorder, Mayor of Spirit Lake, and Justice of the Peace until 1942.

"He knew more history than any history teacher I ever had," recalled Jack Bedell. "He read history constantly; could recite dates, battles, generals ... He knew more about American history than anybody I've ever known in my life."

Charlie and Sarah raised their three daughters, Myrtle, Mary, and Virginia, in the growing town of Spirit Lake, full of the games and fun that Mamie (Berkley's name

House on the farm where Berkley's grandmother, Sarah, grew up, about a quarter-mile south of present-day Elinor Bedell State Park. This house was built after Sarah was grown. It is believed she grew up in a small shack.

Grandfather Charles Price

for his grandmother) felt she missed as a child. The girls loved the outdoors, tramping off to fish with their father in the nearby lakes.

Sarah and Charlie were determined to give their daughters the education that they never had. The girls excelled in school: Myrtle became a teacher, then an osteopath; Mary earned a Ph.D.; and Virginia, became an attorney.

Virginia, the youngest child, displayed her mother's determination and her father's intellect. Quick to take on anyone in a debate, Virginia was the smartest student in her class and winner of the high school's history contest award. When Virginia graduated from Spirit Lake High School she worked as a secretary for attorney Harry Narey.

Meanwhile, Virginia's future husband Walter Bedell was growing up in the southern Minnesota town of Blue Earth – 60 miles east and north of Spirit Lake. Walter learned to fish in the Blue Earth River and local ponds and streams. In 1910, when Walt was in high school, his father, a railroad engineer, bought the grain elevator in Irvington, Iowa, on the Des Moines River, about 65 miles southeast of Spirit Lake. The war raged in Europe as Walt graduated from college, so he answered the call to arms. When he returned from WWI, he completed his law degree and set out to find an opportunity to practice.

He had dreamed about living in Spirit Lake all his life. How much closer to heaven could he get; than to practice law and be able to grab his fishing pole or his shotgun and go off to the lakes? In search of his dream, Walter set up his law practice in Spirit Lake.

In Harry Narey's law office, Walter found a bright young woman who would become his partner in fishing, in marriage, and eventually, in law. He soon knew Virginia Price loved to fish, and approached life with a rare vitality and determination. After they eloped to marry, Walt quickly discovered that Virginia had been paying attention to the legal practice, and had a good understanding of estates and probate work. Whether Walt was extraordinarily enlightened in an age of gender chauvinism, or merely pragmatic enough to recognize that Virginia would never sit still as a homemaker, he encouraged his wife to study for the Iowa Bar Exam. He became her tutor.

She pursued her law studies with all the determination her mother had instilled in her, and never accepted any prevailing notions that women couldn't succeed in male-dominated professions. She had often heard her mother say, "You can do almost anything within reason, if you set your mind to it." So, if she set her mind to it, why couldn't she — without ever attending college or law school — pass the state bar exam? She could, she did, and eventually earned the respect of leaders throughout Iowa.

Virginia's law license opened the door to statewide renown, pulled her family through a harrowing period of their life to come, and launched her two sons into lives of community, state, and national leadership.

Fishing boys

Berkley and Jack Bedell learned to fish at a young age. Above, Berkley displays his first fish, in a photo that would become widely known.

In an even earlier (1925) photo at right, two future fishermen - four-year-old Berkley and his two-year-old brother, Jack, are holding turtles.

Chapter Three

Growing up in Spirit Lake

"Why does she do this to me? What will the other boys think?" Berkley wondered, as his mother dressed him in fancy short pants to wear to kindergarten.

Berkley lived a childhood every boy would love. In the innocence of 1920s small town Iowa, he and his brother, Jack, just two years younger, could play with any number of children in the neighborhood. They could go to their grandparents' house, across the gravel street and through the side yards and backyards for two blocks. Their grandmother kept toys in a closet by the door, so they could play as long as they wanted — and they didn't even have to pick up after themselves. The only time they would be scolded for leaving their toys out would be when their Mother and Dad were there.

At an early age, Berkley mispronounced "Grandma" as "Mamie." She loved it and for the rest of her life she became known as Mamie to everyone: friends, relatives, and especially to the neighborhood children who would always find an open door at her home — and if they timed it right, some delicious Parker House rolls!

Virginia and Walt took the boys fishing at every opportunity. Before they were old enough to handle a fishing rod themselves, the boys would stand on the shore and watch Mother and Dad pull on hip boots and wade out into one of the lakes, just far enough that their casts' backstrokes would clear the trees on the rocky shoreline. Mother and Dad loved to cast a fly with a little bit of worm onto the calm water and watch for a bluegill to bite. They pulled in the fish, unhooked them, and tossed them onto the shore. They smiled as their young boys tried to wrap their tiny fingers around the slippery, scaly, wriggling fish flopping on the ground. When one would succeed, he held it with both hands, while the other guided the stringer through the gills. Finally, when Berkley reached five years of age, his parents decided he should try fishing by himself.

"One late afternoon, they left me on the banks of East Okoboji with a cane pole and some worms while they went down the shore with their hip boots and fly rods," Berkley recalled. Soon, Mother and Dad heard the splashing sounds of the flip-flopping struggle between fish and fisherman. They hurried back to investigate the commotion. Berkley had landed a fish that looked nearly half as long as he, a 3-pound sheep head.

"My father paraded me all over our little community with that fish," Berkley remembered. "He appeared prouder of that fish than any he had ever caught himself." Walt made sure to document the occasion with a photograph that has been seen in fishing magazines and Berkley and Company advertising for decades: A boy shyly holding his first fish.

If the goal was to help the boys enjoy fishing as much and as long as Mother and Dad did, they could not have known how wildly they would succeed. The boys were hooked.

Although their personalities were very different, Berkley and Jack loved to have fun together. Berk, as he was called, was even-tempered and obedient, like his grandfather Charlie; Jack loved an argument and mischief making, like his grandmother Mamie. Whenever he acted up as a young boy, Virginia told Jack to put a mark on the wall, as a disciplinary reminder. One day, a playmate wondered why there were so many marks under Jack's name on the wall, and almost none under Berkley's.

"Berk and I are playing a game," young Jack proudly explained, "and I'm winning!"

Still, Berkley bristled as his mother dressed him for school. Why did his mother compound the problem of his small size by dressing him up in pretty little shorts, like a …?

"I look like a sissy!" he complained to his mother.

"I think you look like a darling young boy," she marveled at her fashion sense.

"But the boys will think I'm a sissy!" Berkley never wanted to act disrespectful to his mother, but he also did not want to look like a sissy on the playground. His mother would not relent. She had grown up with little and she prayed that her son would not. She wanted him to be the best, and to look his best.

Indeed, he did want to be the best student in his class. Studies came easily to him. It never occurred to Berk, his mother, or anyone else in his family, to not try to be the best at everything. So maybe he should have been proud that his teacher thought him to be best suited for a role in the fourth-grade play, *Penrod.* But he considered the character, Little Georgie Bassett, to be a dainty character that reinforced an image he had begun to despise.

"I hated it and, more than anything else in my school years, I wanted to prove that I was not a sissy," Berkley reflected in later years.

Third-grade musicians

The third-grade band in Spirit Lake consisted of drums, bells and tambourines. Berkley is seated directly to our right of the drums.

Berk was determined to be the best fisherman, the best hunter, the best basketball player, the best football player, and, for a while, the best boxer. His grandmother Mamie had always told him, "You can do almost anything within reason if you will only set your mind to it."

At age 10, he set his mind to fly.

To furnish the leading edge of his wings, he found a couple of boards about an inch square by six feet long. He took some small, limber limbs of a tree and tied them together to form the rest of the wing frame. He covered the under side of this framework with heavy paper.

He figured Mamie's barn would be tall enough to give his wings enough time to beat gravity. But Mamie wouldn't hear of it. Walt and Virginia didn't know about Berk's plan, and she didn't want them to find it out at the hospital!

"Why don't you use our step ladder?" she offered.

Word got around about his plan and all the neighborhood children gathered to see Berk Bedell fly. Next-door neighbor Stanley Donovan, a sturdily built lad of 12, held the ladder. Stanley's sister, Pearl, who was Berk's age, and brother, Ed, a year younger, looked on. They were children of the local funeral director, who designed and machined tools as a sideline. Ed, who shared his father's passion for figuring out how to make things, was fascinated by Berk's ingenuity. As they grew older, Ed and Berk would solve many "impossible" problems together.

Berk strapped the homemade wings to his arms and climbed to the top of the ladder. When he spread his arms and imitated a swan dive, just as if he were jumping off the diving board at the local swimming pool, the ladder fell backward from the force of his jumping motion.

He fell flat on his stomach – a real belly-smacker – on the ground. For years, Berk insisted that it was all Stanley's fault for not being able to hold the ladder.

Later, Berkley said, "I should have realized right then why my grandmother put the words 'within reason' in her statement!"

Berkley learned to box from his Presbyterian Church pastor, an accomplished boxer from England. The pugilistic preacher recognized Berk's agility, focused determination, and quickness of body and mind.

Berk soon became one of the favorites at the Saturday night Muscovite Lodge boxing matches. Walt loved watching his 11-year-old son work the ring with Shorty Hearst, another skilled boy from Spirit Lake, as they fought the preliminary bouts before the featured match. Berk loved the skill of thrust and parry, action and reaction, but he and Shorty hated the thought of hurting each other. Before one match Shorty even suggested that he and Berk try to box skillfully without hurting each other. Berk couldn't bear the thought of faking or staging a fight, so he put Shorty's idea out of his mind. Still, Virginia would say that whenever Berk worked Shorty into the corner, he backed off rather than punish his partner.

Walt also loved baseball. He knew the game like he knew the law. He umpired amateur games all over northwest Iowa. Nothing bothered him and nothing swayed him, but once, after umpiring at a tournament in LeMars, Iowa, Walt's pride and his drinking almost got Berk in trouble.

Walt had a serious drinking problem. He wasn't a violent or abusive drinker, but when he had one drink he continued drinking until he couldn't think straight. On this particular night in LeMars, Walt scared Berk more by what he said than by what he did.

Walter and Berk spent the night in a hotel during the tournament. Berk tried to sleep while Walt and some local men drank liquor and talked sports. Walt bragged that Berk was the best boxer of his age and size in Spirit Lake.

"Well," the local men said, "You should see this kid from our town." The more they talked, the more Walt bragged about Berk. "Well, we should just arrange a little boxing match and see who's better." The men agreed.

As Berk, eyes closed on the bed nearby, overheard the scheduled boasting match he became scared. He knew he had skill, but he also knew he lacked strength. He had learned how to box Shorty, but with Shorty boxing had been fun. What would happen if he boxed a really good boxer, a stronger kid with a mean streak? Berk didn't sleep very well that night. He hated to disappoint his father or mother. He wanted more than anything to please them in whatever he did; that's why he had so few discipline marks on the wall at home. But he knew he had to talk to his dad before this boxing thing got out of hand.

Berk didn't want his father to think him a coward. He never let on that he had overheard the conversation from the night before.

"I've been thinking, Dad," he said the next morning. "I've learned a lot from boxing."

"You surely have, son. You're the best young boxer in northwest Iowa. I'm very proud of you."

"Thanks, Dad," Berk said. Oh, how could he tell him now? "It's been fun, but I guess I need to say… I think I've had my fill of it now. If it's okay with you, I just don't want to do it any more."

Walt looked at the earnest young man before him. He closed his eyes and thought, "Boy, will I seem like a fool to those men from last night." Berkley was never one to shirk from a challenge. Would he fight this one last fight if his Dad asked him? Berkley was wondering the same thing. Walt opened his eyes and looked again at his son's expectant face. No, Walt thought, it wouldn't be fair to ask Berk to go half-hearted into that ring against a boy who would be primed to defend his town's honor. He nodded and smiled.

"That's totally up to you, son. You have made me very proud."

Berkley breathed a sigh of relief. His father continued to be proud of him, and he didn't have to fight that tough kid! Berkley recalled later, "Telling my father that I did not want to box anymore was one of hardest things I ever had to do."

He began to see what would become clearer to him as he grew older. "The better fighter you are, the more fights you get into. Your friends will always want to see if you can beat someone else, and there will always be someone who wants to see if they're a better fighter than you."

The more Berk understood about world affairs, the more he believed that countries fell into that same trap.

Growing up in Spirit Lake in the 1920s and 1930s seemed like a dream.

Berkley awakened in the middle of some cold, winter nights to enormous sounds like thunderclaps. The huge sheets of ice in the lakes would contract and crack with a sound that boomed throughout the town.

Winter days began and ended with shoveling coal into the furnace of their two-story wooden house on Court Street. The family finally bought a stoker to automatically feed coal into the furnace, relieving Berk and Jack from their coal-filling duties, but they still had to shovel out the ashes after the coal burned down.

The ingenious boys invented ways to deal with the bitter cold of winter and the intense heat of summer. To combat the stifling summer heat, Berk and Jack built a homemade air conditioner to fit in their bedroom window. The device had water dripping down over some excelsior (stringy chips of wood) and a fan to pull air through the cool dripping water. In later years, when Jack helped to make fishing tackle, he put a block of ice in a tub and had a fan blow on him from across the ice because of the heat.

On summer mornings, Berk and Jack listened for the sound of the iceman's horse-drawn wagon coming down the dirt alley behind their house. They scurried out to the wagon so they could catch the chips that fell when the iceman shaved and cut a block of ice. Their mother would place a card in the window to tell the iceman how big a block of ice he should cut for the kitchen's wooden icebox. Each winter, crews would harvest ice from the lake with their large handsaws. Horse drawn rigs pulled up the ice, and transported it to Diebner's downtown icehouse – a large barn where they stored the ice amid sawdust. At that time, no one gave any thought to the fact that the ice chips they enjoyed in their drinks came directly from the lake.

The milkman also came daily and exchanged bottles of un-pasteurized, un-homogenized milk in exchange for the washed, empty bottles that had been put out by the back door. The cream would come to the top of the milk, and it could be taken off for use in cooking or for coffee.

For Sunday dinner, the Bedell family might go to Mamie and Grampy's house for a dinner that started with catching a rooster or hen in the chicken yard behind the house. When they chopped its head off the chicken would flop all over the yard – a childhood lesson in life, death, and the nature of the food chain.

If not at Mamie and Grampy's for dinner, their mother might make an unlikely feast out of mud hens (coots) that Walt and the boys had shot. Most people winced at the thought of eating mud hens, the black, bottom-feeding birds that were plentiful in the reedy shallows of the lakes, but Virginia had a way of cooking them with seasonings and bacon that covered the strong, gamy taste so that the boys licked their lips at the thought of it. Sunday dinner would often include homemade ice cream for desert. The mixture of cream, flavoring, and sugar would be placed in a container inside a large wooden bucket with ice between the bucket and the container of cream. Walt would turn the handle connected to a paddle inside the creamy mixture to keep it smooth until it had frozen.

Within a few blocks of the Bedell house lived enough boys to make fun a full-time occupation. By fourth grade, Berkley and Jack knew they could come home from school, change into their rough-and-ready clothes, and head off to the vacant lot next to Pete Narey's house to play football. Since Berkley's mother had worked for Pete's father, Berkley had known Pete, a year older than himself, ever since he could remember.

Soon, John Furman would arrive, then Jim Doudna, with his younger brother Dick, who was Jack's age. Jim Shelledy would be there, and Ross and Bruce, the Bennett boys. The boys called themselves the South End Gang, a seriously playful bunch bent on adventure and sport. By junior high, a boy from the north end of town, Bob LaFontaine joined the gang.

The Doudnas' grandfather helped them build a clubhouse on the back of their garage, where the gang could meet on Saturdays to eat sandwiches and plan their adventures. They wore "whoopee hats," made from their mothers' discarded felt hats, or imitation Charles Lindbergh aviator hats.

In the summer, they spent entire days swimming at Pete Narey's grandmother's beach on Big Spirit Lake, or playing on a vacant-lot baseball field that sloped so that second base was two feet higher than home plate. More than once, they had to pay to replace broken windows in a neighboring house. When the younger boys had trouble swinging the bigger bats, Berk bought Jack one that was more his size.

In order to play hockey, the gang swept the snow off the frozen lakes and fashioned flat rocks into pucks and curved branches into sticks. They rode their bicycles out to West Okoboji Lake, where John Furman's father, Rusty, had bought shoreline land for a summer cottage.

Today, to spend their summers boating and fishing, wealthy folks from the upper Midwest pay more than $1 million for prime lakefront land and install floor-to-ceiling plate-glass windows to enjoy the sunrise over West Okoboji. But in 1934, Rusty Furman, the county engineer, bought the property for the going rate of $500.

His son, John, and friends would ice skate and play on the ice before roasting hot dogs on an open fire. They would hold open their coats and let the wind blow them across the ice. In town they played a hide-and-seek team game in which they captured each other by yelling, "Bang!" on sight.

"I banged you first."

"No, I banged YOU first."

"You didn't bang me first, I banged YOU first!"

Hungry boys could count on Mamie for Parker House rolls. Mamie's baked goods were famous in Spirit Lake. She set up a table to sell them at a local grocery store once a month. As a special treat, the boys might just get some homemade honey, made from Grampy's beehives. One time, after the boys had been to Mamie's for rolls, Pete Narey told his Mother, "Jim Bob Shelledy made a pig of himself. He ate 12 rolls."

South End Gang

Gathered at their clubhouse, built by Jim and Dick Doudna's grandfather (in doorway), are (from left) Jack Bedell, John Furman, Peter Narey, Berkley Bedell and the rest of the South End Gang. At right, a few years later, enjoying a morning's catch are: (left to right) Ross Bennett, Bob Cornell, Berkley, Oliver Babcock, Bob La Fontaine, and Peter Narey.

At left are Jack, Grandpa Charles Price, and Berkley, on a 1927 fishing trip in northern Minnesota.

"How many did you eat?" she asked.

" I only ate 10," Pete replied.

Mamie loved having the boys over, and they loved being with her. She was so unlike a mother; no demands, no expectations, her mind always at work to figure out how the gang could have more good, clean fun. Mamie laughed with them, played tricks on them, and teased them. She loved to have fun as much as any boy. They would do anything for Mamie, and she would do anything for them.

"Who'd like some buckwheat pancakes?" Mamie asked, as Berkley and Jack took their newspaper bags from around their shoulders and hung their jackets on the hook by the back door.

The boys made a regular stop at their grandparents' house when they finished their morning newspaper routes. Grandpa Charles would be sipping his coffee, scanning the local weekly *Spirit Lake Beacon*, while waiting for the boys to get there with the daily *Des Moines Register*. Mamie, a short, thick woman with a twinkle in her eye, would already have the batter ready to pour on the skillet.

The boys spent almost as much time with Mamie and Grampy as they did with their own parents, who both spent a lot of time at the office or on the road with their jobs.

The boys looked up to Grandpa Charles with respect. He was a tall, solidly built man with a thick handlebar mustache. He told a story or a joke as well as anyone, but he knew how to get the boys' attention with a stern look and a serious voice if need be.

"Look here, boys," Grampy said as he showed them *The Beacon.*

"WIN A NEW CAR!" the advertisement said.

"If we had a car, we could take you boys wherever we wanted to go," Mamie said. "We could go fishing or hunting wherever we pleased and whenever we pleased. How would you boys like that?"

"What do we have to do?" they asked.

"Well, it says here that it's a contest to see who can sell the most subscriptions to *The Beacon*, and can gather the most coupons that will be in every issue of *The Beacon* during the contest. You boys would be good at that, but you're not old enough to drive yet."

"But I am," said Mamie, who was 63.

"You're plenty old enough," answered Grampy, "but you never drove a car in your life."

"I can learn," she asserted.

"Who'd have the patience to teach you?" he said, in mock disgust.

"I'll find someone, and then we'll just see if I ever give you a ride," she retorted, with a wink. "What do you say, boys? Meet me after school, and we'll win this contest hands down."

"Yeah!" the boys lit up in agreement.

When school let out that day, Mamie found Berk and Jack at her door, with Pete Narey and John Furman. They no sooner came in and helped themselves to rolls and honey, than Jim and Dick Doudna came knocking, and soon, practically the whole South End Gang was in the kitchen. They weren't about to have Mamie do this herself.

"Okay, boys, here's what we'll do, " she said, and they worked out the details around the kitchen table.

For weeks, Mamie could be seen walking the streets of Spirit Lake with her dog, Tippy, and a gang of 10 to 12-year-old boys, knocking on doors. If the resident didn't already subscribe to the newspaper, the boys tried to sell a subscription. If they were already subscribers, Mamie and the boys asked them to clip the coupons from their papers and told them they'd be back next week to collect them.

As a result of their efforts, Mamie and the boys sold many new subscriptions and collected more coupons than all the other contestants combined – and won a new Ford V-8!

After Mamie learned to drive, the boys knew they would always be able to get a ride to go swimming, hunting, fishing, or for delivering their newspapers when the Iowa winter turned bitter cold.

Even in her 60s, Mamie loved to traipse along with the gang on their fishing and hunting expeditions. She would pull on hip boots, navigate the rocky shorelines, and wade right into the water. The boys marveled at her fearlessness and mischievous attitude. She considered it good, clean trickery to pull a deception in a card game, for example. Grampy, on the other hand, wouldn't stand for cheating.

Once, when Mamie took Jack hunting, he bagged two hen pheasants after hours and he shot a rooster ring neck pheasant across the road in Minnesota – from the open window of the car! All of Jack's game had been shot illegally. Mamie bragged about their escapade in front of Charlie. Unfortunately, Charlie was the town's Justice of the Peace.

"Boy, I hope they arrest you and bring you into MY court," he declared. "I'll throw you in jail."

"Oh, no you won't," Mamie shot back. "I'd just get a change of venue."

Years later, she was driving Walt, Berk, and Jack to hunt in nearby Emmett County, where the pheasant season opened earlier than in Dickinson County.

"There's one!" she called out when she spotted a rooster pheasant.

"You can't shoot him," replied Walt, from the back seat. "He's in Dickinson County."

Mamie turned around in the front seat to look her son-in-law square in the eye and said, "I'll be damned if we ever take you hunting with us again!"

Hunting and fishing were sports that members of the South End Gang did primarily with their families, or in smaller groups. But when it came to football and basketball, they prepared as a team and played as a team, often against boys from the North End Gang.

The lessons they learned about competition, resourcefulness, and teamwork helped all of them to later become successful lawyers, engineers, and business managers and owners. Several members of the gang remained close friends, hunting buddies, and golf and tennis partners for more than 70 years.

Berkley appreciated and cultivated their friendships for decades. They came through for him many times throughout his life in business dealings, community involvement, and personal issues starting with his family's trials of 1935-36.

Chapter Four

Troubled Teens

Nearly everyone in Spirit Lake liked Walt Bedell and admired Virginia.

Not that Walt wasn't admirable; he was considered a good attorney by all and even brilliant by some. Folks were thankful that he helped get the American Legion post started, and that he umpired baseball games all over Iowa.

Not that Virginia wasn't likeable; she was kind and pleasant, a tender and loving mother, a good cook, a woman of grace and honor.

But the Spirit Lake community knew her to be a special leader, a persuasive speaker who always seemed to know the answer. If she joined a club or a cause, she soon became president, as she did with the local chapter of the Business and Professional Women, the American Legion Auxiliary, and the Daughters of the American Revolution. She knew how to organize and motivate people for action.

Far more schooled in the law; Walt had an uncanny ability to recall and provide the citations for legal cases he had read years before. Although lackadaisical about keeping track of files or billing clients, he enjoyed the challenge and justice of the law more than the business of it.

"Dad would rather take an interesting case from someone who didn't have a dime, than to probate an estate where his fee could be in the thousands of dollars," recalled Jack Bedell, who joined his father's law firm for a brief time in the early 1950s. "He didn't get his probate work done, because he did not see it as a challenge."

People liked Walt because they knew he liked them.

"For my father, one person was just as good as the next, and he enjoyed playing billiards with the school janitor as much as having cocktails with the Governor of the State," Berkley observed. His father's egalitarian attitude became steadily more important to Berkley as he grew older.

The boys thought of him as an ideal father, kind, and well-liked by other people in the community, eager to take the boys fishing, to take them out on Big Spirit Lake in a boat for a duck-shooting lesson, always planning another fishing vacation.

Later in life, Berkley came to the conclusion that his parents were sometimes obsessed with catching fish. Fishing became almost a chore as they worked to bring enough fish home to give to neighbors and show that the trip had been a success. It was not only important for his parents to be fishing, Berkley thought, but for them to be *successful* at fishing. Whenever Berkley caught himself becoming too wrapped up in the numbers, he reminded himself that he goes fishing for the fun of it.

But another obsession became an increasing worry to Berkley and his family: Walt's drinking.

Berkley first felt scared when he and his father were returning home from a baseball game that Walt had umpired. He could tell that his father was inebriated, but Walt seemed unfazed until he completely missed a turn and went off the edge of the road into a shallow ditch. He shrugged it off and gunned the engine, to power the car out of the shallow ditch. Berkley curled up in a ball in the back seat and prayed that they would get home safely.

Virginia began to realize Walt had a drinking problem, particularly after the end of Prohibition made alcohol more available and acceptable. When he won a trial, Walt drank to celebrate. When he lost a trial, he drank to forget.

His love of the bottle and his willingness to defend undesirables proved a tragic combination toward the end of Prohibition. Walt represented some bootleg liquor dealers who were more than willing to fill him with drink. During one of their strategizing sessions, he apparently became sufficiently intoxicated that he did not realize that the bootleggers were arranging to bribe a juror. When the crime came to light in 1935, Walt was charged along with the bootleggers with jury fixing. He denied knowing anything about it, but couldn't disprove testimony that said he was present at the time of the crime.

His conviction, a nine-month jail sentence and disbarment, became a turning point in the life of the Bedell family. None of them thought Walt had tried to fix the jury, nor did most people in the community. They were convinced of two things: 1) Walt was a man of integrity in the wrong place at the wrong time, and 2) His alcohol problem needed attention.

The first of those propositions became clear at Christmas. The owner of the local billiard parlor set out a box to give patrons the opportunity to contribute gifts for Walt.

"I remember very well going down to the jail in Des Moines with my mother and brother to visit my father," Berkley recalled, "and we took a car load of gifts to him."

The South End Gang made sure that Berkley and Jack knew they would stick by the boys and their family. The Bedell family tragedy made the gang realize the harsh realities of life, to realize how much Berk and Jack needed their companionship and support. The first time a smart-aleck teen made a wisecrack about Berkley's father was the last as far as Pete Narey was concerned.

Pete, Berkley, and the gang knew they could count on each other for the rest of their lives. Pete was a year older than Berkley (two to three years older than some of the other boys in the gang), the only son of a successful attorney, later a judge. Pete's family had more money than the rest of the gang, but you'd never know it by the way Pete treated them.

"For Pete, the poor were just as good as anyone else, and he included among his friends and playmates those from the other side of the tracks, as well as those of us who were of higher social and financial status," Berkley noticed.

Like Berkley's father, Pete's attitude served Berkley well in later life when Pete became a prominent attorney and Berkley the biggest businessman in town.

Walt struggled to cope with his alcoholism while his wife became increasingly prominent. He eventually regained his license to practice law, and became a leader in Alcoholics Anonymous. But he continued to battle the bottle and his own feelings of inadequacy.

He was a quiet, congenial drunk. His sons could remember only one incident of violence. In 1938, people in the billiard parlor above Walt's law office called to say that Walt was in no shape to drive home. Jack was just 15, but the only one at home at the time, so he walked the eight blocks downtown and found his father fumbling around his office.

"Come on and get in the car, so I can drive you home, Dad," Jack said, ignoring the fact that he had never driven a car before. Suddenly, Walt angrily lunged at Jack, throwing a wild punch that missed him completely. Walt stumbled and fell onto the corner of his desk, breaking a rib. Jack helped him up and out the back door to the car parked in the alley. The keys were dangling from the ignition – some 60 years later many folks still don't lock their cars or houses in Spirit Lake. Luckily, Jack had paid attention during Mamie's driving lessons. He pushed in the clutch, fired up the engine, and maneuvered the stick into first gear. He slowly let off the emergency brake, eased off the clutch, and carefully guided the car through the back streets to get his father safely home.

"He apologized to me the next day," Jack recalled. "I don't remember him ever getting violent with me before or since."

Berkley and Jack saw firsthand how alcoholism became the weight that their father – and their family – had to drag behind them. Walt struggled with alcoholism for the rest of his life, particularly in the early days after his bribery conviction, when he could not practice and felt insignificant in Virginia's shadow. Even after the reinstatement of his law license, Walt continued to struggle to keep commitments to his clients, to complete his work, and to keep track of the business side of his practice. He became a visible and often inspiring leader in Alcoholics Anonymous, making his occasional relapses all the more painful for him and for his family.

In his later years, he finally found serenity and was of real help to those who still suffered from alcoholism.

Walt remained one of the most popular persons to ever live in Spirit Lake. When he died in 1963, the church had to mount speakers in the basement fellowship hall to accommodate all the people who could not fit in the sanctuary for his funeral.

His father's lesson made a deep impression on Berkley. He vowed that he would never bow to the temptation of alcohol, no matter how strong the peer pressure. He never worked harder on a school project than when he created an award-winning school presentation using the letters in the word alcohol to spell out the dangers of alcohol abuse.

In high school, Berkley easily avoided alcohol because none of his close classmates drank. But he also kept his promise not to drink through college, the military, business circles, and politics.

As Walt's career seemed to be falling apart, Virginia's star shone brighter and brighter across the state.

She had helped Walt in his law practice before, but quietly in the background. When Walt went to jail, she began practicing in earnest. Her reputation grew steadily and in 1936 she campaigned to become County Attorney for Dickinson County. She had to convince voters that she could prosecute criminals and provide sound legal advice for county officials, despite her lack of experience. She had to draw upon her personal integrity and Walt's pre-conviction reputation to answer the public scrutiny that followed his imprisonment.

She won the election by 13 votes, becoming the first woman ever elected as County Attorney in Iowa. She succeeded in being re-elected in 1938. Following her county service, the governor appointed Virginia to the State Parole Board, a job that took her to prison facilities across the state and away from home 10 days and nights a month.

In her absence, the boys relied even more on Mamie and Grampy, while they became increasingly oriented to working themselves.

Chapter Five

Working Boys

Berk and Jack found all sorts of ways to scrape up a few Depression-scarce dollars. They wheeled their little red wagon over to the Coca-Cola bottling plant to pick up cases of soft drinks they could deliver to local filling stations and stores. At each stop, they picked up cases of empty bottles to return to the bottling plant for 10 cents per case.

Berk cleaned the basement of one of the downtown merchants, and burned his accumulated paper and boxes, for which he received 25 cents per week. The Iowa winters brought money from heaven for boys energetic enough to shovel snow from neighbors' driveways. During the summer, money also grew in neighbors' lawns that needed mowing, and on the trees and vines of Grampy's orchards that needed pruning. Grampy had an acreage outside of town with plums and grapes where Berk and Jack picked ripe grapes and squeezed them to juice. They also picked and sold grapes to the local grocery store, for 50 cents per bushel.

Their first foray into the fishing business came on rainy, summer nights. As soon as the rain let up a bit, the boys grabbed their flashlights and gallon cans and headed for moist ground. Large, fat worms called 'night crawlers' came out of their cozy underground homes after a rain. They squirmed to the surface and into the path of a soon-slimy hand. In a good night, the boys could fill a gallon can with enough worms to fetch $1.00 from a local bait dealer. Pretty good wages for a night of damp fun!

Berk and Jack each had newspaper routes, delivering newspapers on their bicycles with their faithful dog

Stubby trotting along behind. Later in life, after trying to operate a multi-million dollar business with limited formal business management education, Berkley valued his newspaper route experience.

"A newspaper route is great training. I had to get up and deliver the papers no matter what the weather. I had to try to get new customers to increase my route. I had to be careful to order only the proper number of papers or I would have to pay for extras. And I had to collect from my customers and pay my weekly bill. It truly is great business training."

Every one of Iowa's four seasons brought unique adventures. In the fall, opportunity literally leaped out from the sloughs and fields, as hordes of frogs migrated to the lakes to hibernate for the winter. Quick-handed boys snatched them in the fields, along the lakeshore, or under rocks along the shore – and there was no limit. An agile boy could catch six-dozen frogs in one day to make several family meals worth of batter-fried legs about the size of a person's finger.

To manage the bounty, Walt built the boys a special frog basket with a hole in the top on which he attached two overlapping pieces of rubber from a tire inner tube. The boys could push a hand through the overlapping rubber flaps, but the frogs could not jump out. One night, after a particularly successful catch, the bottom dropped out of the basket just after the boys came into the house. The Bedell kitchen became a circus of boys dodging each other as they made frantic grabs at frogs leaping from sink to countertop, table to chair, and nook to cranny. Some frog dealers in town filled burlap bags full of frogs and left them out on their lawns, waiting until they had collected enough to be trucked to Chicago. It's a wonder that townspeople got any sleep on some croak-laden autumn nights.

In the fall, the boys looked to see if ducks were flying overhead, as their morning paper route took them near the East Okoboji Bridge. They could barely wait to finish their routes, so they could go home, grab a shotgun, and hurry down to the causeway across East Okoboji to hunt ducks before going to school. Barely a quarter-mile from their home, right at the edge of town, they could sight down their barrels at flocks of ducks following the migration flyway across the lakes. On Saturdays, if not hunting ducks, they would gather a few friends for pigeon hunting, courtesy of consenting farmers. "None of the other boys wanted the pigeons, so Jack and I would pick the feathers off and clean them in our basement, and the Bedell family would have roast pigeon."

Winter blizzards often blocked the roads and railroad tracks with snow, isolating the town for days at a time. Newspapers sometimes didn't make it from Des Moines to be delivered in Spirit Lake. School buses could not reach the country children so school would close for the day. On those days, the boys from the South End Gang gathered at Pete Narey's house to play Monopoly and other games. Once a week, the South End Gang obtained permission to play basketball in the high school gym, under the tutelage of the Doudnas' older cousin.

During the summer, Berk and Jack would sometimes sleep in their yard in a tent, or they would go on weekend camping trips around the lakes. By the 1980s, expensive homes lined the lakes, but in the 1930s, many of those lots were still pastures, and the farmers didn't mind their land being used as makeshift campsites.

When they wanted to fish for walleye or perch, the boys could use Grandpa Price's boat on East Okoboji Lake. Or they would go out to Big Spirit Lake, where Pete Narey's grandparents had a summer resort on the west shore. Pete, the Bedell boys, and their teen-aged friends spent countless summer days racing Narey's hydroplane boat, swimming, and trying to get to know vacationing girls. A resort owner near John Furman's father's West Okoboji Lake cottage recognized the boys' willingness to entertain girls. He gladly enlisted the Bedell boys and their South End Gang friends to be tennis partners and dance partners for young ladies vacationing in his cottages.

For Berkley and Jack, boyhood passions and emerging teen passions sometimes overlapped.

When their mother became County Attorney, the family received a complimentary annual pass to Arnold's Park, the historic amusement park on West Okoboji. After fishing, they liked to go to the park's Roof Garden dance pavilion, where it cost 10 cents admission and 10 cents per dance.

"In spite of the odor of fish and oil of citronella, which we used as insect repellent, we had no trouble finding dance partners with our free ticket, because so few boys had the 10 cents per dance rate," Berkley recalled. The brothers, particularly Jack, studied the best dancers on the floor and became experts at the long, flowing two-step that became known throughout the area as "the Roof Garden Glide."

Berkley flirted with girls at the Roof Garden, but he flirted with death on the Arnold's Park roller coaster. As an adventurous young teen with his free park pass, Berk climbed into the front seat (before the days of safety belts) and held onto the bar on the back of the low barrier in front of him. The first peak and drop brought the exhilarating thrill of danger, only a prelude to the perils ahead.

As the coaster sped over the next peak and started down the steep incline, Berkley gripped the hand bar and pushed his feet against the inside of the car with all his might. He strained every muscle trying to hold himself into the car. He couldn't do it. His momentum had carried the top part of his body right up and over the low barrier in front of him. The next few moments remained implanted in his brain for the rest of his life.

"I held onto the hand bar on the back of the barrier with my legs in the car and my body over the front of the car with the track passing just under my head. I strained for all I was worth, but I had no leverage to get my body back into the car. Fortunately a man occupied the seat behind me. He stood up, leaned over, and pulled me back into my seat. I spent the rest of the ride on the floor with my hands and feet up against the hand bar to hold me in the car. I did not fully realize how close I had come to ending my story right then until several years later when I again rode that same roller coaster – this time in a car in the middle of the coaster, with safety belts! When I found how the car bounced around, I realized that had it not been for the man in the seat behind me, I could not have kept myself from flying out over the front of the car to my certain death. I will never know the identity of the man who saved my life that day."

Chapter Six

Student, Athlete, Entrepreneur

The high school classroom helped Berkley to both escape and to confront his family problems. He wasn't a bookworm, but Berkley found studies easy, and he relished his reputation as the smartest one in his class – 40 students who had mostly been together since kindergarten.

While his parents clearly expected it of him and Jack, Berk felt no pressure to excel in the classroom. He welcomed two equally compelling motivations. He delighted in pleasing his parents and wanted to be the best in everything he did. "It never occurred to Berk or me to try to be anything but the best in school," said Jack.

Regardless of his accomplishments in class – or maybe because of them – the smallish Berkley still dreaded one thing more than any other: that someone might think him a sissy. Athletics gave him an opportunity to prove himself. He was only 5-feet-7 and 120 pounds. But he was quick, wiry strong, and had years of experience playing football, basketball, baseball, and tennis with his neighborhood gang.

Boxing had taught him the rigors of competition and how to read and respond to an opponent's movements. Years of fishing had cultivated great hand-eye coordination. He had even placed second in a statewide casting tournament as a 16-year-old competing in the adult division (Jack won the 15-and-under division).

That combination of physical gifts and mental toughness served Berk well in high school basketball.

But when it came to high school football, Berkley still only weighed 120 pounds. To make matters worse, there were others who were faster and more adept at the skill positions. One was his next-door neighbor, Ed Donovan, a year behind Berkley in school, but one of the fastest and toughest running backs Spirit Lake High School ever had.

So when Berkley realized that he would not only be the smallest player on the team, but also would have to play defensive end, such a reality put his trademark determination to the test. Berkley remembered his grandmother: "You can accomplish almost anything within reason, if you'll only set your mind to it."

"Whoever put the phrase in the preamble of the United States Constitution that 'All men are created equal,' must not have been a 120-pound defensive end trying to push a 200-pound tackle out of the way, or a 120-pound defensive end trying to tackle a 200-pound giant of a fullback," Berkley said. "But I 'put my mind to it.'

"I remember lying awake at night in my bed on our cold porch, thinking about how I would tackle the opposing halfback." Sure enough, Berk played on the varsity football team in his junior and senior years. "I still remember one of the spectators telling me that he considered one of my tackles to be the best tackle he had ever seen."

It was the beginning of Berkley's life effort to *tackle giants.* "Football is a crazy game," Berkley reflected. "You get knocked down, so you get up as fast as you can to get knocked down again, so you get up again to get knocked down again, and on and on." But then Berk came down with an impetigo rash on his arm and the coach kept him on the bench.

"When I sat on the sidelines watching my teammates getting knocked around as they struggled together to get to the goal at the end of the field, I realized how much more fun it was to be out there getting knocked around than to be on the sidelines watching. So it is in life. I decided right there that I did not want to sit on the sidelines in life any more than in a football game."

His best sport was basketball. He teamed up as starting forwards his junior year with his senior friend, Pete Narey (barely bigger than Berkley). The team relied heavily on several juniors, and gave the town hopes of awakening Spirit Lake's dormant reputation for great basketball.

When he was in tenth grade the *Des Moines Register* had a subscription contest for its delivery boys. Berkley remembered Grandma Mamie's newspaper contest from years before. Unlike her *Spirit Lake Beacon* contest, he would have to beat carriers from all over the state of Iowa. But if Mamie could do it, he surely could.

Day after day, he knocked on doors and made his pitch. He ended the contest among the top 10 carriers in Iowa and won $50. It would normally take him six months to make that much money from his route alone. You could buy a new car for about $500 at that time.

He knew just what he wanted to do with the generous prize money. He convinced his parents that he should be permitted to use it to start his own fishing fly business that coming summer.

It was 1937. Berkley spent $10 for hooks, thread, feathers, hair, and production materials. He spent another $15 to print an eight-page 2-½ inch by 6-inch catalog. He invested $25 in a one-inch ad in *Sports Afield* magazine announcing: Berkley's Hand Tied Flies.

The Berkley Fly Company was a reality. He did not realize what an historic decision he had made.

"Each day I went to the post office to get the orders I expected to come flooding in as a result of the ad, but those orders never arrived."

His total sales that first summer were less than $100. But as Berk toiled in his bedroom at his fly-tying bench to fill orders from local bait shops, with a little kerosene heater to keep him warm as autumn cooled the nights, his hopes of making some summer cash were evolving into visions of building a business for the long haul.

"I would have made more money caddying at the local golf course, or clerking in a store for the summer," he

Berkley's first ad, for "Bucktail Streamers," lower right, June, 1937

thought. Indeed, his friends were making more money at their summer jobs. But none of them owned their own business, nor shared his dreams.

It had been more than a year since his life-changing fly tying lessons with Frank Marnette at the bait shop.

Whenever he went to another town, whether with family or high school buddies, he brought along samples of his flies and an order book. When they stopped for gas, Berkley searched out the local hardware store to make a quick sales call. When his family visited his Grandma and Grandpa Bedell in Cedar Rapids, Iowa, he worked out a deal with a local department store's sporting goods manager.

When he and friends went out on a date in the Bedell family car, Berkley unexpectedly steered to the roadside.

"What's the matter, Berk? We're only halfway to Arnold's Park,"said Jack, from the back seat with his date. "I'll just be a minute," said Berk, reaching into the glove box for a paper bag. When Berkley walked toward the woods, Jack nodded and smiled. This was no engine pit stop. He could see that Berkley felt no need to step behind a tree for relief. At the edge of the ditch, Jack could see a white tuft of fur sticking up on the underside of a dead deer's tail. Berkley pulled out his pocketknife and began to harvest his crop, carefully trimming off a cupful of future buck tail streamer material from the road-kill deer. He could reap at least two-dozen fishing flies worth of fur in two minutes.

As Berkley stopped, time after time, at the sight of a dead squirrel, skunk, dog or deer alongside the road, Jack became used to explaining these stops to their girlfriends.

"He is just doing business," Jack would chuckle, lovingly amused by his brother's enterprise and eccentricity.

The boys' bedroom had also become the Berkley Fly Company corporate headquarters and assembly plant, with flies strung from wall to wall, as orders and production increased. Berkley's summer was filled with fly-tying, his pa-

Berkley works away, tying flies. As evidenced by the shelves of shoeboxes, his bedroom became the assembly plant, inventory warehouse, distribution center, and financial headquarters.

per route, and his never-ending love of fishing. Add to that his increasing affection for going to dances with his friends, or taking turns driving Pete Narey's 1919 Dodge. The boys pitched in to paint the jalopy a different color on each panel of the car, with its nickname "Judy" on the side.

The longer Berk tied flies the more he wondered how his business could grow. He could not seem to make enough of them, and he needed the variety that other fly-fishing companies had.

How could he make something fishermen always seemed to need, more efficient, in greater quantities, with less painstaking craftsmanship? How could he make a better profit for the amount of work involved? Could he teach others to do it too?

Berkley figured out a way to make some leaders from Japanese knotless gut. The material was much like a wide, nearly transparent thread. Soaking the gut in water made it soft and flexible. He tied a fishing snap on one end, and a fishing swivel on the other end, and stretched them between two pins on special boards, which he built for the purpose. After the gut dried it became straight and stiff in lengths from six to 36 inches in length.

The summer before his senior year of high school, Berkley and Jack went on a fishing trip to Walker, Minnesota with his Aunt Myrtle and Uncle E.J. Lloyd. "I shocked myself by selling an order for more than $200 of knotless gut leaders to a Walker sport shop to be delivered the following spring."

That fall, his friend Peter Narey's parents took Pete and Berk to Minneapolis to see an Iowa-Minnesota football game. While there, Berk made a sales call on a large hardware distributor: Janney Semple Hill. Their buyer agreed to place an order and asked if Berkley wanted to wait for it, or if the buyer should send it to Berkley. "Like a fool, I told him to just send it in," Berkley later reflected. "The order never arrived. It served as a good lesson in business. Later that winter the Walker sport shop wrote me a letter requesting to cut their order in half. But I was far from discouraged."

Kautzky Sporting Goods store in Fort Dodge, Iowa ordered a number of flies made with neck feathers from rooster chickens. A chicken processing plant in Spirit Lake saved feathers for Berkley, which he dyed in a big kettle on the kitchen stove and tied into flies.

"A man put a notice in a sports magazine that the fish in his area were obviously feeding on locusts, and that he would pay $5 for a fly that most resembled a locust. I wrote him not to accept any other flies until he saw mine. My Uncle Frank had an insect collection that included a preserved locust. I had the local tinsmith solder a special hook, I fashioned a locust from balsa wood and plastic, and received the $5!"

By Berkley's senior year of high school, the need to fill a business order was sometimes enough to convince him to stay home from school for the morning.

The principal called him into the office for a chat.

"Berkley, I'm concerned about your attendance record," Mr. Mahannah said. "You are making our records look pretty bad."

"I'm sorry, Mr. Mahannah," Berkley said. "My business has become bigger than I thought it would, and I don't seem to have enough time to get it done before school. But I'm still getting straight A's and I hope I don't cause anybody any trouble."

"I'm aware of your fine grades, Berkley, even though I don't see how you do it. But I don't want other students to think they can get away with missing school, too."

"I'll keep up with my schoolwork, Mr. Mahannah, don't you worry about that. And I'll try to get my business done without missing school."

"Thank you," Mr. Mahannah smiled. He wondered if it was a promise that Berkley could keep.

Berkley's classmates didn't seem to resent his easy success in the classroom, in light of his business, and they admired his determination on the football field. The basketball team looked forward to his leadership on the courts. All of Berk's teammates voted him to be team captain.

"I had great expectations of having a championship team," said Berkley. The first big test would be East Sioux City High School, a much larger school in the biggest city in

1938-39 Spirit Lake High basketball team.
Berkley is in the front row, second from left

northwest Iowa – a two-hour bus ride from the lakes. Berkley and the team were determined to give the city boys a Spirit Lake lesson.

"The Sioux City High School gym was considerably longer than ours, and time after time they went the length of the gym for a basket. We were soundly defeated. It was a terrible shock. My bubble of expectations had burst."

That game caused Berkley to realize what his grandmother meant in her saying, 'set your mind to it.'

"To set your mind to it," he reflected, "means more than just deciding that you are going to accomplish a task, although that is the first step. It means doing what you have to do to be successful. Our basketball team had not really 'set our minds to it,' between the junior and senior years. With my extensive involvement in growing my business, and everyone's other activities, the guys had not spent the necessary time practicing together for us to be a true championship team.

However, by the time he graduated from high school, no one considered Berkley a sissy. He could thank his grandmother for that, and for his broken nose and chipped teeth.

The band director also benefited from Berkley's determined attitude. The Spirit Lake High School band had gained statewide recognition, under the leadership of Harry Mahannah, who also served as the High School Principal.

"I had no musical talent, but by much practice I became first chair among five French horn players," Berkley said. "Mr. Mahannah demanded perfection and attendance by all the band members, and we practiced and practiced every little detail of our contest piece, hour after hour."

Townspeople rallied to raise money for new band uniforms and more instruments to allow the band to play more challenging music. Parents and citizens joined a caravan of cars to the state music contest in Iowa City. The band members knew this would be a big moment in their lives.

"When we took the stage I could feel the hair on my legs stand straight up, it was so thrilling," John Furman recalled, 60 years later. The old South End Gang's Furman and Narey were in the cornet section. Jack Bedell was a clarinetist.

When the curtain rose, the band members were in their new uniforms, and Mr. Mahannah raised his baton to begin *Ballet Music from Faust* by Gounod.

"We were in complete unison and the performance went exactly as we had practiced it over and over," said Berkley. "We all had a great celebration that evening as we learned that we had received the highest rating possible in the state band competition. Our small school with only normal talent had again proven Mamie's saying true. And we proved it again my senior year by doing the same thing."

When Berkley attended Iowa State College (later to become Iowa State University), he learned that because of that performance, the Spirit Lake band had a statewide reputation.

"I went over to see the College band director, Ralph Edgar, to tell him of my interest in joining the band. He asked me what high school I came from. When I told him Spirit Lake, his interest heightened. He asked me what chair I played. I told him first chair. He said, 'Come on over this afternoon. We are having band practice.' I protested that I had not played my horn in more than a year, but he insisted, knowing the reputation of the Spirit Lake band."

Mr. Edgar put Berkley in the middle of the French horn section. The first few practices went fine, then one day Mr. Edgar cringed at a chord. He stopped the band and asked for the chord again. Another cringe. He asked the cornets to play the chord. Fine. Then the clarinets to play the chord, and so on. Each section was perfect – until he came to the French horns. Obviously something was wrong.

He went down the line, one player at a time:

'Beep.'

'Beep.'

'Beep.'

'Blaaah!'

"I had stopped the entire band, because of my inability to hit the right note. I have never been more embarrassed. It proved all the more that only because of hours of practice and determination, not because of any inherent talent of my own, that I had done so well at Spirit Lake."

Berkley's hard work in high school was harder on him than he realized. While he was filled with the excitement of doing it everything seemed fine. However, at the end of his junior year in high school, Berk became ill and wanted to sleep all the time. His parents took him to the Mayo Clinic in Rochester, Minnesota for a physical exam. There was nothing physically wrong.

"It is quite clear that with my business, athletics, band, and my studies I was simply doing more than my body could stand. It was a good lesson for me as I went forward in life."

If he learned a lesson from the episode, it may have been difficult for others to see.

When he graduated from high school, he poured himself into figuring out how to make his part-time business a full-blown enterprise. He was determined to be a success.

The decisions he made as a teen-ager prepared him and his cozy band of small-town friends to one day revolutionize an industry and change the way fishermen fish.

Chapter Seven

Graduating Business

"Successful fishermen are curious, drawn to a mystery, and hopeful. And they are motivated, powerfully motivated, by something more than catching fish."
Paul Quinnett
Pavlov's Trout, The Incomplete Psychology of Everyday Fishing

By the time he graduated from high school, Berkley's bedroom walls were lined with fishing flies, leaders, and shelves of supplies in shoeboxes. He hired two classmates to work for the Berkley Fly Company (still headquartered in his and Jack's bedroom), next door neighbor Pearl Donovan and Rachel McQuirk, whom he had known since they held hands as Sunday school toddlers.

Soon Berkley discovered that there was an even bigger business for soldered cable wire leaders than for knotless gut leaders.

He found a source for the cable wire, but he needed to figure out how to solder a loop at each end to hold a snap at one and a swivel at the other – with a minimum of labor.

Berk tried all summer, but he couldn't come up with a process he liked. He would either need another set of hands – or a mechanical process – to feed wire through the eye of the snap and solder the end of the wire loop. He set a soldering gun in the vise at his bedroom worktable, rigged a foot-feed to mechanically bring the solder to the soldering gun. He figured he could wipe the wire joint across the melting solder on the swivel end, then the snap end. It worked, but it was still an inefficient, wasteful process.

"I could not figure it out," he recalled, "but I did not let that stop me."

He had to make some sales, whether he liked his inefficient, wasteful process or not. Distributors placed their orders and set up their catalogs for the following spring during the fall. To get into the fall catalogs, Berkley had to make sales by August, or wait another year.

The moment of truth arrived. He needed to go on the road to show distributors his products.

He obtained the price lists of everyone who made leaders like his, and printed up a price list that was 10 percent lower than the lowest price anyone else charged. "That is easy," he later remarked. "If you do not know how to make something, you also do not know your costs, and can set your prices at whatever level you want." He made up a handmade sample book of the leaders he proposed to sell.

His parents never hesitated to let him convert their only car into a traveling office. He took the back off the right front seat and built a bed there instead. His little 'motor home' was ahead of its time.

"What tremendous parents," he came to realize later in life. "How many parents would be willing to go without the family car for three weeks, just so their son could try to sell some fishing leaders that he didn't know how to make?"

Before he went on the road trip, Berkley taught Jack his rudimentary leader-production process.

"Berk would write home with an order, or ask me to send a sample," Jack recalled.

"It was extremely difficult to get a smooth joint. Only about one out of every three or four would be smooth, so you sometimes had to make six or eight leaders before you got a good joint on both ends."

With Berk on the road, Walt Bedell decided he needed to show 15-year-old Jack how to do it without wasting so much material. Jack warned him that melted solder dripped onto a metal sheet below the table, put there to protect the wooden floor.

"I wouldn't wear your good pants or it will splatter all over them," Jack said. So Walt took off his pants and worked in his underwear.

"Mother and I were downstairs and we could hear him cussing, every time hot solder splashed on his bare legs," Jack recalled. "Pretty soon, he came down with a bunch of terrible-looking leaders, looked at my mother, and said, 'Well, I guess the kid's not doing so bad after all.' "

Meanwhile, on the road, the 'other kid' wasn't doing so badly, either.

As Berk rolled over in his makeshift bed, he saw the sun peeking through the windshield. He pulled on some clothes and shoes, opened the passenger door, and wandered over to the fence. He picked two apples from an overhanging bough, sat on the hood of his parents' car, and thanked God for the gas station/orchard owner. For 50 cents, Berk was permitted to park overnight and eat apples for breakfast.

Then off he went, trudging to distributor after distributor, showing his samples, making sales, recording his orders in a notebook, and writing home every few days to report to his family.

When he got to Louisville, Kentucky, a telegram awaited him.

"HURRY HOME STOP THERE ARE TOO MANY ORDERS WE DON'T KNOW HOW TO MAKE STOP."

Orders had arrived for more than 1,000 gross of leaders: 144,000 leaders of different lengths. Not just soldered-cable leaders, but also artificial gut leaders, forerunners of future nylon leaders. The road trip had shifted Berkley's company into high gear.

"My folks figured it would take Berk two years to fill the orders, so he'd better come home," recalled Jack.

As he drove his parents' converted sedan across the country highways of Indiana, Illinois, and Iowa, Berk felt as if he was floating above the green waves of summer corn stalks.

He had traveled about 3,000 miles in three weeks. He spent less than $50 the entire trip – for 20-cents-a-gallon gasoline, nickel-a-quart milk, and nickel-a-loaf bread. He had worn out maps of six states, and worn holes in two sets of socks.

But he was in business to stay.

If that's the case, he thought, from what Jack and his parents told him, he had better figure out a better production process.

"I worked to beat the dickens to fill those orders for samples," said Jack. "Mother and Dad would help a little in the evenings."

A company in South Bend, Indiana, near Chicago, made and sold soldered wire leaders. Berkley stopped there as he came through. He scouted around the city and found the machine shop that made the equipment for that company's leaders. It was a fairly simple solder pot, with a protruding pipe filled with melted solder, and a slot in it into which the wire could simply be dipped to solder the joint.

"Our soldering iron went out the window," said Jack.

With a notebook full of orders, and a new manufacturing process, the Berkley Fly Company entered a new phase. Jack and his parents had donated their time helping to launch the business, but Jack needed to go back to school and Berkley needed to hire employees.

"When he came home, he gave me a $5 bill," Jack said. "I didn't complain. Seeing him succeed was payment enough, but I ceased to be his principal employee." Jack would return to the business only to help when Berkley went to college and to the military.

Berkley looked outside the family for help.

Berkley Fly Company
(From left) Berkley Bedell, Rachel McQuirk Carpenter, Marvin Hamilton,
Thelma Hilliard, Jack Bedell, and Ruby Olson

Teen-aged business leaders

His friends had graduated into the employment hunt. The farm belt continued to struggle to escape the Great Depression and Dust Bowl disasters. Berkley needed to work before thinking about college.

Thankfully, Pearl Donovan and Rachel McQuirk were eager for more work. He also added classmates Thelma Hilliard, Ruby Olson, and Marvin Hamilton, a farm boy with a keen eye for detail.

Still, he had to have money to buy materials.

How does a teen-ager get a business loan from a bank, when the economy is, at best, struggling? The South End Gang came through again – Pete Narey's father, Harry, (Virginia's first employer) served on the board of the local bank, as did John Furman's father, Rusty, the county engineer, and Bob LaFontaine's father, the electric company's district manager. The bank manager's son, Bob Cornell, had also recently joined in with the South End Gang when he moved to town. The bank trusted Berkley, saw how he had built up his business in high school, and was impressed that he already had orders in hand. They loaned him the money to buy supplies and hire enough help to make Berkley and Company (as it was now called) a reality.

"It was not surprising that I could undersell everyone else and still make a profit: Our home became my factory. I paid no rent," Berkley recalled. "I had no overhead. I lived at home and needed very little money, and I paid my workers 15 cents per hour. As the business grew, I have always been thankful that I never had to face that kind of competition from someone else."

Soon, a new law increased his expenses.

"When the minimum wage went into effect we had to go to 30 cents an hour immediately," Marvin Hamilton laughed. "We doubled our wages! We thought we were pretty smart."

The upstairs bedroom Berkley shared with Jack was set up for production, but it could no longer be both a sleeping quarters and a factory. There was a large walk-in utility closet at the end of the upstairs hallway. Would the bunk beds fit in there? Would Jack agree to move? It took only a little persuading. Jack figured it was better than living with all that mess.

Each morning, when Walt and Virginia left for the office and Jack went to school, the humble Bedell house became Berkley and Company production headquarters. Berkley met with the production crew before going on sales calls. He soon landed two more large orders – with hardware store distributors Coast to Coast and Janney Semple Hill – so the household factory found itself producing more than half a million leaders per year.

The business spread throughout the house.

Marvin Hamilton sat in an easy chair in the living room, measuring and clipping wire to the proper length. The wire was then sent upstairs to the ladies in the bedroom-turned-soldering room. Production also spilled into the upstairs hallway, a neat row of benches with soldering pots. The knotless gut leader production took place in the basement. When large orders were ready, the living room became the shipping center.

"We took over the entire house," Berkley recalled. "It was comical."

The house became filled with the sounds of teen-aged teasing and serious production. "Berkley created production contests and the ladies loved the friendly competition," recalled Rachel Carpenter, formerly Rachel McQuirk.

They also loved the fringe benefits, she said. By that time, Virginia had hired a housekeeper/cook, Ann Fronk, who treated the employees to apple pies.

"Berk would periodically take us out for a meal and a movie," said Marvin Hamilton. "He became just one of us people in that group, and he enjoyed it as much as we did. In fact, I'm not sure who laughed more, he or the rest of us. We got pretty silly."

The workers knew they were in on the ground floor of a growing business. Whenever the "Berkley-mobile" went on a selling trip, they came to expect phone calls with orders for something they had never made before.

"That became typical. You had to invent," said Rachel McQuirk Carpenter.

Berkley, Marvin, and a local machinist developed tools and processes for everything from manufacturing the leaders to packaging them. If any part of the production or distribution bogged down, Berkley wanted to develop a machine to make the work more efficient.

"Pretty soon we outgrew the house. We were all over the place, especially Virginia's lovely dining room table," recalled Rachel McQuirk, who became a professional interior designer. "Our work just about ruined the house."

Prior to shipping, the leaders were stapled to a perforated card. This process was done on top of the dining room table – until they discovered the stapling made divots in the table.

"That's when Berk got the word," Marvin Hamilton recalled. "He had to move."

Not only had the business outgrown the house, but also Berkley was to start college in January 1941.

In the fall of 1940, the factory moved out of the Bedell house and into space above a meat market uptown,

Berkley and his brother, Jack, gather in 2001 in front of their boyhood home, where the Berkley Fly Company began. Below, the building where Berkley moved in 1940. Berkley moved his operation into the upstairs of the building, above a meat market.

across from the courthouse at Hill Avenue and 18th Street; the same space that had housed the Muscovite Lodge boxing matches of Berkley's youth.

Berkley put Hamilton in charge of managing the production. The Bedell family kept an eye on things from Walt and Virginia's law office a half block away. They let Berkley use their law secretary to take care of paperwork and billing. Mamie let Berkley take her car to college. He frequently came home from Iowa State on weekends to help at the factory.

Hamilton eventually owned his own radio and television repair business, for more than 50 years. His days with the teen-aged Berkley taught him much about managing a business. He even learned from Berkley in high school.

"In science class," Hamilton recalled, "the instructor had a college professor come in. He brought with him two sacks, one containing very tiny bits of coal, the other containing lumps of coal. He poured the coal into a couple of beakers. Then the professor said, 'Now I want you to write down on a piece of paper which one will accept the most water, the one with the large chunks or the one with the small chunks.

"Every student in there except Berkley said the one with the large chunks because of the large holes. Berkley said on his answer, 'I don't know. There may be more little holes with the little chunks than there are big holes in the big chunks.' Well, that was the correct answer because he didn't have the facts. And I have never forgotten that. It has held me in good stead ever since. We were all fooled but Berk. He didn't have the facts, so he didn't guess. That's how he thinks."

"I found him to be the greatest person to work for – the same friend always; as a classmate, a boss, a fellow businessman, a corporate executive. Just the same person. He never changes. He simply had a good way of treating us and a good way of helping us to do whatever needed to be done."

Once, Hamilton recalled, he told Berkley they needed cotton fabric for the soldering process. To get the solder to stick, they touched the wire to an acid-soaked cotton pad and the pad had to be replaced.

"Berk said, 'Come with me,' and he took me into the empty hall, took off his shirt, handed me his undershirt and said, 'Here.' Never even cracked a smile."

Fully confident that his little business would continue to be successful, Berkley prepared to study mechanical engineering at Iowa State College (later Iowa State University) in Ames, Iowa.

"I could thank both my Grandmother and my parents: Mamie for her advice – 'You can do anything within reason if you'll only set your mind to it' – and my parents for their confidence in me, for letting me completely disrupt our family home to get my business started."

Chapter Eight

College and Romance

In January 1941, Berkley started living a double life – that of a student at Iowa State College, in Ames, Iowa, and as the manager of a business in Spirit Lake. He drove his Grandma Mamie's car 160 miles each way nearly every weekend to help with the business.

Berkley and Company grew steadily, and Berk's practical engineering experience served him well: If he didn't know something, he could figure it out. He had the second-highest grades of all the freshman engineers.

On a physics test his freshman year, the professor asked the students to write out the appropriate formula and solve a problem. Berkley asked to speak with the professor. "I do not know the formula, but I can work the problem," he said. He did, and he received an A.

Berkley continued to look for ways to improve the business, not just keep it going. His boyhood friend, John Furman recalls taking a trip with Berk in the fall of 1941. They were going to visit some Spirit Lake friends at another college, but Berkley wanted to stop at a machine-making company in Muscatine, Iowa.

"Berk had brought some blueprints of a machine that he wanted the company to make for his business," Furman recalled. "I was talking to one of their people out in the lobby while Berk was presenting his case. They said they had never seen anybody so young whose knowledge of engineering was so professional."

The Phi Delta Theta float illustrated the sentiments of our nation, in the Iowa State Viesha parade in the fall of 1941

Berkley was thankful he had learned good study habits in Spirit Lake, so he could study hard and still have time for dates, handball, tennis, golf, and his fraternity.

Berkley's boyhood dreams of flying came true while attending Iowa State. Through a government program called Civilian Pilot Training, Berkley learned to fly, but this time with no cost, no ladders, and no homemade wings.

When it came time for the big Iowa State Viesha parade, World War II raged all over Europe. For his Phi Delta Theta fraternity's float, Berkley designed a red, white, and blue globe about 12-feet in diameter, covered with one-inch screen. Iowa State was identified on the globe by a model of the college campanile. The whole fraternity stuffed colored tissue paper in the screen to show blue oceans, red continents, and the North and South poles in white. Berkley's brother, Jack, visited the campus that weekend, and he and Berkley laid on their backs under the trailer, turning the globe round and round with cross bars that extended through the trailer. The float's theme was, "One bright spot in a blood-stained world." Jack never got to see the parade from under the trailer, but the float won the grand prize.

Romance at the Dance

"Do you remember that cute girl I danced with last night?" Berkley asked.

"Which one?" his roommate responded. Their dormitory had an exchange dance with a women's dorm the night before, and it seemed like all the boys had met someone new.

"The one I danced with half the night. She was about this tall, and she smiled a lot. Didn't say much. Once I danced with her, I forgot about everybody else."

"Didn't you ask her for her name? Or did you forget that, too?"

"Are you going to help me or not?"

"You know the guy in Room 212? He spent a lot of time with the girl that your girl came to the dance with."

Berk tracked down the guy in 212.

"Sure, I know her. What's it worth to you?"

"I just want her name, for gosh sakes."

"25 cents."

"25 cents?!"

"25 cents. You get her name, and I buy cigarettes for the week."

"For 25 cents, I hope you're not pulling my leg." Berkley fished a quarter from his pocket and flipped it to the extortionist.

"Elinor Healy."

It was the best 25 cents Berkley ever spent.

He called Elinor's dormitory telephone. She had been so charmingly unassuming; one who listened first, thought second, spoke last, someone who only spoke when she had something to say. Berkley discovered, however, that she could be quick and witty, especially if you seemed too full of yourself.

"Hello, Elinor. Remember me? I'm the guy you danced with last night."

"Which one?"

"The real good dancer."

"Which one?"

"The real good-looking guy."

"Which one?"

They talked gaily together for a half hour – exploring, laughing, and wondering – but Berkley never gave Elinor his name. They talked again Wednesday evening. Again the following Sunday. And the next Wednesday. Half an hour, and Elinor still didn't know his name. This game was fun!

Elinor went home for Thanksgiving. While there, she told her parents about this fellow with whom she was having a fun no-name game. Her father said, "Nice girls do not talk with boys they do not know on the telephone."

The following Sunday evening, Berkley called her again.

"I'm sorry," she responded.

"What's to be sorry about?"

"I can't talk to you any more if you're not going to tell me your name."

"Well, I don't want you to stop talking to me. My name is Berkley Bedell."

She did remember his name, but did not remember anything about him. Certainly his dancing had not impressed her.

But it didn't appear that his name meant much to her. She wasn't one to gush and giggle. They continued their telephone conversations. She joined a sorority. He joined a fraternity.

They each continued dating other people, but their telephone calls continued.

His boyhood friend, John Furman, came to Iowa State to join Berk and became a Phi Delta Theta fraternity brother. Darlene Brewster (who later married Peter Narey) invited her old Spirit Lake friends to visit her Kappa Kappa Gamma sorority house at Drake University in Des Moines, a half-hour south of Ames. John invited his steady girlfriend (later his wife), Pat. Berk would escort Darlene. They went to a movie. As they departed the movie theatre, the newsboys were shouting:

"JAPANESE ATTACK PEARL HARBOR."
"READ ALL ABOUT IT."

Life suddenly became serious.

"It was a very quiet ride from Des Moines to Ames," Pat recalled.

Berkley and his friends had wondered how and when the United States might enter the war that had spread throughout Europe, parts of Africa, and East Asia. Separated from the war by two vast oceans, what would draw the United States into it?

Now they knew.

The whole country became caught up in the horror, the anger, and the determination. Each young man had to decide how and when he would do his part.

Berkley didn't see Elinor Healy again until January 1942 when his Phi Delta Theta fraternity went to a dance at her sorority house. After getting a second look, Berkley decided that he needed to see more of her. Elinor was so cute and pleasant, never self-possessed, always interested in hearing what he and others had to say. He had dated and danced with many attractive and witty girls before at the Arnold's Park Roof Garden. But Elinor had something special: a gentleness, a kindness, a humility that connected with his deepest values, everything he thought a person should be. He felt like he already knew her essence so well, yet he didn't know much detail about her. There just seemed to be so much more to her, beautiful as a butterfly.

For her birthday in March, Berkley went to the store and purchased a half-dozen small gifts that he mailed to her, including a little broom with a note that read she had, "swept me off my feet," and a key-chain ring with the note, "I want to give you a ring."

By the end of spring term in 1942, Berkley and Elinor were practically "going steady." After a spring formal, he told her, "I would like to spend the rest of my life with you."

Berkley had to make some life-changing decisions quickly. It had become clear that there soon would not be any demand for fishing leaders, and the government had designated more materials as essential for the war effort. They would not be able to get manufacturing supplies. Marvin Hamilton was called and told to use up the stock to fill as many orders as he could, then to close the company. It was the summer of 1942.

Berkley enrolled in classes that summer. By going to college during the summer, at least he could complete two years in only one year and 8 months.

"I took the bus up to Grand Marais in northern Minnesota, where Elinor's parents had a cabin camp. We enjoyed a glorious weekend together," Berkley fondly recalled.

"Everyone knew what we needed to do next, so that summer I also enlisted in the Army Air Corps. I received my notice to report for training just as college was to begin that fall."

"When I boarded the train to start Army Air Corps service, I sent Elinor my fraternity pin and we were formally engaged."

"In two months, I had completed as much education as I could, shut down my business, joined the Army, and become engaged to be married."

Chapter Nine

Earning His Wings

Berkley looked out the window of the train en route to Maxwell Field in Montgomery, Alabama and what he saw shocked him. He sure wasn't in Iowa any more.

"Reddish brown soil greeted my eyes. I had never before seen any dirt except black dirt, and I had thought you had to have black dirt to grow anything."

It would not be the only shock of his military life.

Upon arriving at the base, Berkley got in line for a cadet haircut. The barber's clippers turned cadets' lovely locks into crew cuts in five minutes flat.

Cadets became accustomed to being hazed at every step.

"We had to walk a rat line, an imaginary line on the ground. We were not to step out of the line. We each had to be famous for something. I claimed to be famous for sawing off toilet seats for half-assed upper classmen."

Upper classmen (there were no female army pilots) would stop the cadets whenever they walked a ratline from one place to another.

"'What are you famous for, cadet?' They would yell in my face." It seemed amusing, but Berkley soon learned that he dared not smile.

"Wipe that smile off your face, cadet." He waited for Berkley to follow the order literally.

"Now throw it on the ground, and step on it. Now pick it up, and put it back."

At every turn, officers tried to emphasize the importance and urgency of the training.

"I well remember going to an outdoor movie. Before the end of the movie an officer spoke to us. He told us to look at the cadet sitting beside us. He said, 'One of you will not return from this war alive.' It seemed to be a completely unnecessary remark, and it turned out not to be true."

From Maxwell Field, Berkley went to Decatur, Alabama, to start flight training. The Stearman training planes had a propeller, an open cockpit with two wings, and fixed landing gear. The body of the plane consisted of a wooden frame covered with fabric. It had two seats, one in front of the other. The instructor sat in the front seat and the student in the back cockpit.

Because he had learned to fly in college, Berkley cruised through the first flights with confidence.

"The first couple of flights with my instructor everything I did turned out well." On his third flight the instructor decided to shake Berkley up.

"Without warning, the instructor, in the front cockpit, turned the open cockpit plane upside down. I had fastened my seat belt, but only loosely. I found myself hanging upside down, half way out of the airplane. I was trying to hold myself in the plane with my hands on the flight control stick. The air rushed past me, as I looked down at the ground."

When the instructor finally turned the plane right side up, Berkley quickly tightened his seat belt and breathed a sigh of relief. It reminded him of his roller coaster near-disaster, except that this time he was 1,000 feet above the ground.

"I had on a parachute, but I sure didn't want to use it. The instructor would have been quite surprised if he had landed and found no one in the back cockpit."

Berkley met with the local pastor at Decatur, Alabama, who agreed to find some people with whom Elinor could stay, and to serve as chaperones if she came to Alabama to visit. Berkley wrote to Elinor's parents, explaining the situation. They agreed to let her make the trip under those circumstances. Berk sent her the money for the train fare and they shared a wonderful three days together.

From Decatur, Alabama, Berkley was sent to Greenville, Mississippi to be trained in larger planes, and from Greenville to Dothan, Alabama for final flight training.

While at Dothan, the trainees went to Florida for gunnery practice. They practiced shooting at a canvas target, about 5 feet by 30 feet, dragged about 40 feet behind a tow plane. The student's airplane had a machine gun permanently mounted on the nose of the airplane that fired through the propeller. Each cadet had bullets with different colored wax on them, so the instructors could determine how many times each cadet hit the target. To hit the target, the student aimed his plane at the target and fired his machine gun as he flew by the moving target.

"After about my third pass at the target, I heard a terrible noise on my ear phones, but I could not understand the message. After my next pass I could clearly hear, "Go Home, Go Home!" So I went back to the field.

"When the tow plane landed, it had some of my bullet marks in the tail, only about 10-feet from the pilot. No one ever said anything to me about it. In fact, I was complimented, because I also had quite a number of hits on the canvas target. I decided right then that I sure did not want to be a tow pilot!"

Upon completing his flight training and receiving his wings, Berkley returned to Spirit Lake on leave, and Elinor met him there.

Upon graduation, Berkley was sent to Randolph Field in San Antonio, Texas to be trained as a flying instructor. He took the opportunity to ride a bus to Austin to see his boyhood friend, Pete Narey, an officer in an infantry unit. Pete had not been informed of Berkley's coming, and had gone to town for the weekend. So Berkley simply found Pete's barracks and slept in his bed.

"The next day, I went into town, found Pete, and surprised him." Pete returned Berk's visit by traveling to San Antonio while Berk was still at Randolph Field.

Upon completing his instructor training, Berkley was assigned to be a flying instructor at Cochran Field in Macon, Georgia. He and Elinor decided that they would be married after he completed the training of his first class of cadets. Berkley also yearned to get into the action overseas.

Taking Flight

There were three courses in learning to fly for the Army Air Corps: primary, secondary, and advanced. At Cochran Field, Berkley taught the secondary course, so his students already knew how to fly. The planes had a sliding canopy over the cockpit, with the student in the front cockpit, and the instructor in the rear. The planes were low wing, with fixed gear, radial engines, and propellers, like all planes at that time.

While teaching his first class of six cadets, Berkley lived in the barracks and looked forward to his upcoming marriage to Elinor.

At the same time, Elinor was helping her parents at their resort in Grand Marais, Minnesota. She told her mother that she would like to have the wedding at her Aunt Hazel's home in Minneapolis, but continued, "Don't tell Aunt Hazel, because I do not want to worry her."

Berk flew up to Minneapolis, and the wedding was held at Aunt Hazel's home. Elinor's sister Fran Naftalin, her cousin Janet Cooper, and friend Betty Ann Serrill were the bridesmaids, and "Hubie" Waugh from Spirit Lake was the best man. All of Berk's buddies were off fighting the war. After threatening not to attend the wedding due to their objection of getting married during such uncertain times, Berk's mother and father finally relented and joined the celebration. Reverend Lowe from Grand Marais came down to Minneapolis and performed the ceremony.

Elinor's mother made her bridal gown. When Elinor put it on at the wedding, the button loops were too small for the buttons. Her mother snipped one end of the 30 loops and Elinor was sewn into her gown. Fortunately, they were able to cut her out of it after the wedding!

**Wedding day,
August 29,
1943**

"After the wedding, we started off to Macon, Georgia in a used car that my folks had purchased for me with money from the closing of Berkley and Company. When we arrived in Macon, we moved into part of a house—bedroom, bathroom, and small kitchen—that was built by a metal contractor. It was entirely made of sheet metal: all the walls, ceilings, and exterior," Berkley recalled.

"Marrying Elinor was the luckiest happening of my life."

They lived the life of many young, married military couples – in the whirlwind of honeymooners' romance, heightened by the anxious uncertainty that war brings.

"Those were wonderful years. We knew not how long we would be together, or whether I would survive the war. Each day was a day to savor, and we had many friends in the same situation."

Berkley and Elinor endured hardship together. Gasoline and food rationing were in effect. They had to be careful what groceries they bought and had to carefully limit their driving.

They also learned to endure tragedy together. The metal home they rented had no telephone. One day, a neighbor came over to tell Elinor that she had a long distance telephone call. The phone call informed her that her father had a heart attack

Berkley in June 1943, after receiving his pilot's wings. Above, Berkley and Jack with grandmother Mamie, in July 1943

and had died at the young age of 50. What a shock! His death, and the intensifying war, made Elinor and Berkley aware that they might never see friends or family members again. They took advantage of every chance to visit loved ones.

During one break between classes, they rode a bus to Orlando, Florida to visit Elinor's grandparents. Her grandfather dabbled in real estate, buying lots for $500 and selling them for a small profit. They lived in a tiny house and did not have an automobile, but Grandfather and Grandmother Healy had set a goal to leave an inheritance to Elinor and her sister.

Berkley and Elinor also rode the bus to Camp LeJeune in North Carolina to visit Berk's boyhood friend, John Furman, in the Marines. Berkley even obtained permission to use a training plane to fly to Spirit Lake to visit his parents and go pheasant hunting. With so many hometown hunters off at war and military bases, Berkley and an Army buddy found pheasants everywhere. They bagged their limits, but found that when they returned to Georgia, the bird meat had all spoiled because of the heat in the baggage compartment of the plane.

In June 1944, Berkley learned that his brother Jack, stationed in Pecos, Texas, would soon graduate from flight training and receive his wings.

"I was shocked when he came into my barracks that morning," Jack recalled. "Berk had checked out an airplane and had flown to Texas for my graduation. That was special. My brother pinned my wings on me."

They resumed sibling rivalry on the ping-pong table at the recreation center in Pecos, where "Berk gave me a pretty good lesson."

The visit also meant a lot to Berkley.

Jack told him he was going to India, to fly supply missions to China and Burma, across the dangerous storms of the "The Hump," the Himalayan Mountains.

"I hope not," Berk said. "I understand they navigate by following the crashed airplanes all over the Hump." Jack dismissed that exaggeration, but prepared for the danger. Storms hovered at 20,000-25,000 feet in the mountains, the height of many of the peaks.

"We couldn't get to that altitude in those airplanes, so we had to fly through weather instead of over it. I made four or five trips across 'The Hump' before I ever saw it," said Jack. At one point, Jack's roommate had to bail out in a storm and was never found.

Jack survived a terrible scare as a co-pilot on a flight to Kun Ming, China. Upon landing in China, the flaps on one wing split because of a hydraulic leak. The plane crash-landed with one flap down and one flap up. "We got out of the plane and ran," Jack recalled. As soon as the crew was able to reach a safe place, "the plane blew up and was completely destroyed." On another mission, Jack found out how resourceful the Army could be. His cargo consisted of broomsticks and feminine napkins. The feminine napkins were to be used as oil filters on fighter planes. He never found out the use of the broomsticks.

At Cochran Field, Berkley prepared pilots for dangerous missions. He soon discovered some of his fellow instructors would automatically terminate one of every six cadet trainees in an effort to reduce their training workload.

"What a shame," Berkley said. "The cadets had been brainwashed to think that flying was the most important thing in the world, and it devastated those who were 'washed out.' I only washed out one cadet in all the time I taught. His name was Mayhew."

Berkley almost lost his life in the process.

The training planes' controls consisted of a "stick,"

which came up from the floor between the pilot's legs, and two rudders controlled by foot pedals. The stick primarily controlled the up and down movement of the plane, and the rudders primarily controlled the right and left movement.

Berk was teaching Mayhew how to stall, go into a tailspin, and recover.

To achieve a tailspin, the pilot would pull back on the stick to raise the nose of the plane until it lost flying speed and stalled. The plane would then fall toward the ground nose first, spinning round and round. In a tailspin, the stick is held all the way back to keep the plane in a stall as it fell, and the rudder held hard to one side with one's feet to keep the plane spinning.

All went well as Mayhew pulled the nose of the plane up, took it into a stall, and applied full rudder to put it into a spin. After a few turns, as the plane fell toward the ground, he reversed the rudder and pushed the stick forward to bring the plane out of the stall, just as he was taught. But the controls are not effective in a stall until the plane once again gained enough speed to fly. The stick must be held forward until the plane gained flying speed and came out of the stall. Mayhew became confused. He pulled back hard on the stick, before the plane had recovered from its stall. The plane went into a secondary spin, spinning twice as fast in the opposite direction.

"Mayhew, much larger and stronger than me, froze at the controls. The ground rapidly approached. I finally succeeded in getting the controls away from him, pushed the stick forward, and pulled the plane out of the spin shortly before we would have crashed. I had heard how people sometimes have superhuman strength when their life is threatened, but it had never happened to me before."

"He did not want to do it, but I made him go right back up and do a spin correctly. When we arrived back at the field, I found my flying suit all torn and my shoulder was black and blue for days. But I had survived." The same cadet also nearly killed people by taxiing in front of a landing airplane a few days later.

"Much as he hated it, I really believe it best for Mayhew that I 'washed him out.'"

Some older men, who already knew how to fly, were

Elinor and Berkley at Cochran Field in Macon, Georgia, in November 1943 (above right) and 1944.

assigned to Cochran Field to learn instrument flying. In Berkley's last few months at Cochran he taught them instrument flying. The student would be completely covered with a "hood" and have to fly the airplane without being able to see anything except the instrument panel of the airplane. That training may well have saved Berkley's life at a later date.

Berkley still longed to get into combat. He found it difficult to watch comrades and his brother go overseas to battle the enemy while he remained stateside.

"How foolish of me. Whenever an opportunity came for me to volunteer for a change that would direct me toward combat I found myself first in line to volunteer."

Finally, the Air Force found themselves with too many pilots and started accepting pilots for training as flight engineers on B-29 bombers. Berkley volunteered and was accepted.

The wonderful life he and Elinor had enjoyed at Cochran Field came to an end.

Berkley and Elinor headed off to Amarillo, Texas to begin B-29 flight engineer training. For six windblown weeks, they lived in a little garage apartment on an alley before moving to Denver, Colorado for another six weeks of training during idyllic winter weather: ice skating one day, golf the next, and skiing the next.

"When we played golf, Berk found a little kangaroo mouse right beside his ball," Elinor remembered. "We took the mouse home as a pet and kept him in a milk bottle with some cloth over the top."

When Elinor's friend Betty Ann Serrill came to visit them, she found out what sort of man Elinor had married. When the car in front of them hit and killed a pigeon, Berkley did what he would have done in Spirit Lake. He stopped, picked it up, and took it home.

"I cleaned it and we had roast pigeon," Berkley recalled. "Betty Ann did not eat any of it and she did not enjoy sleeping in the same room with our pet mouse!"

Berkley enjoyed putting his college engineering education to work in flight engineering classes, but other pilots were disgruntled because they wanted to be piloting, not engineering. Berkley had more flying time and higher rank (first lieutenant) than any of them.

"Constantly listening to them complain, I became as unhappy as they were. I would say to myself, 'You enjoy this and you enjoy engineering. There is no reason for you to be unhappy.' But the other voice said, 'They have less reason to be unhappy than you do.' And no matter how hard I tried, I could not overcome my unhappiness. It was a lesson in psychiatry and about how the attitude of others has an effect upon you."

Berkley and Elinor looked forward to a change in atmosphere when they moved to Lincoln, Nebraska. But their new landlady rationed their toilet paper and would not allow them to bring their pet mouse into the house. "The milk bottle tipped over in the car and we never saw our mouse again," Berkley lamented.

From Lincoln, they went to MacDill Field in Tampa, Florida

Elinor and Berkley in Tampa

where Berkley started training. With his B-29 crew. They worked well together: pilot, co-pilot, engineer, navigator, radar operator, bombardier, and five gunners. Berkley and Elinor had been living in sheet metal bedrooms and alley apartments. They were shocked when they opened up the Tampa newspaper to find two pages of rentals advertised because of the lack of tourist trade during the war. They rented a little cottage on the beach.

"Officers were not supposed to associate with the enlisted men, but I paid no attention to that," Berkley recalled. "Our whole crew would come to our cottage where we went fishing, swimming, gathered scallops, and had great times together."

"Airplane maintenance was terrible at MacDill Field," Berkley said. "In the three months we were there, 20 percent of the crews failed to make it, mostly from crashes because of engine problems." The saying around base was, "A plane a day in Tampa Bay."

"We went over each plane we were to fly with a fine-toothed comb before we would fly it. Every single time we would correct several oil leaks in the engines. As flight engineer, I was responsible to check out the plane before we flew it. We even refused to fly one of the planes. If they had only required the ground maintenance crews to occasionally fly in the planes they were servicing, the loss of planes to fires and engine failures would have ended," Berkley reflected.

From Tampa, Berkley, Elinor, and his B-29 crew were sent to Kearney, Nebraska – one stop before heading to the Pacific War. So, Elinor returned home, not knowing if she would ever see Berk again. From Kearney the crew went to Hamilton Field near San Francisco. Before they arrived at Hamilton, the atom bomb was dropped on Japan. Shortly after they arrived, Japan surrendered and the war ended.

"I will never forget the celebration in San Francisco the night Japan surrendered. I went into town with Grady Balthrop, who was a gunner on my crew and my assistant engineer. Neither of us drank, but everyone would have thought we were as drunk as everyone else as we started and led the snake dance down the center of San Francisco."

At Hamilton Field, crew after crew was shipped to the Pacific. But Berkley's crew did not get orders to go – the only crew in their flight group not to go. Later, they determined it

Berkley at the flight engineer's panel of a B-29, and with his B-29 flight crew in 1945 (Berkley is in the back row, far left).

must have been because their co-pilot had already served long enough to have sufficient points to be eligible for discharge.

"What a lucky break for me. Those who went to the Pacific Theater simply had to sit on one of those islands for several months. I would not have been able to return to Spirit Lake and start up my fishing tackle business again."

The crew went from Hamilton Field to March Field near Riverside, California. Elinor visited from home, and they spent a few weeks together before Berkley's discharge.

During that time, one of the crewmembers, "Moon" Mullins, was married to Barbara Feid in Riverside, California. Elinor was maid of honor (photo at right).

After the wedding, champagne flowed during the course of the sweltering hot day. Elinor had never drunk champagne before. "It was the first time, and except for one New Year's Eve party, the only time I ever saw Elinor intoxicated," Berkley recalled.

Before he left Riverside, Berkley made sure to take a written commercial flying test to receive his commercial flying license, which proved to be a great benefit later in life. He also signed up to be in the Air Force Reserves.

While at March Field, word came that Grandma Mamie had a stroke. Berkley and Elinor returned to Spirit Lake, but they could only afford for Berkley to return to California.

The stroke left Mamie paralyzed on one side of her body. She could hardly use one hand. She was unable to walk. She did, however, have a special cardholder made to place in her lap so that she could play cards with her good hand. She was not about to stop having fun!

Berkley returned to California and the army discharged him in November 1945.

Berkley and Company had been mothballed for nearly three years and he was eager to start it up again. Here is a copy of a letter he wrote at that time.

Lt. Berkley W. Bedell
Sqdn. I Section I
420th. AAF Base Unit
March Field, California
October 17, 1945

H.A. Whittemore and Company
301 Congress Street
Boston, Massachusetts
Attn: Mr. H.W. Whittemore

Dear Mr. Whittemore:

My discharge has been approved here, and sent in to Washington for their approval, so it seems quite certain that I will be released within the next few weeks. My plant is ready for operation with all equipment in place and I expect to get it into operation shortly after I am released.

I am of course very anxious to be able to start Berkley and Company enjoying the same business it had when I entered the service some three years ago, and am anxious that it should continue to expand, as it had up to that time.

In supplying my snaps and swivels, you have had, and will continue to have, more to do with the success of Berkley and Company than anyone else excepting myself. I want you to know that I appreciate everything you have done for me in the past.

Will you kindly quote me your lowest possible prices on your size S-3 and S-4 safety snaps, and size 5, and 7 barrel swivels? Could you give me any discount on 1,000 gross orders?

I realize that you probably could not ship an order of this size on immediate delivery, but we could place the order with you, and you could ship it out in smaller shipments as your production permitted. We will, of course, as in the past, also be able to use smaller quantities of your other sizes of snaps, swivels, and snap swivels. However, the above named items are the ones on which your prices mean most to me, as they are the items used in our most competitive leaders, and you can probably well realize how anxious I am to be able to meet competition.

Will you also advise me as to whether you expect your production to be such that you will be able to take care of our requirements for the coming season? Can you now supply these items in the black nickel finish?

Will you kindly send your reply to me here in camp, via airmail? In that way, I will get it much more quickly than if it were sent to Spirit Lake, and forwarded from there.

I wish to again thank you for everything you have done for me in the past. As I stated before, you probably do not realize how important a part you play in the success or failure of Berkley and Company.
Sincerely yours,
Lt. Berkley W. Bedell
Sqdn. I, Section I
420th. AAF Base Unit
March Field, California

Upon being discharged, Berkley took a bus to Seattle to visit a company that made fishing snaps and swivels that he might be able to use as he started up his fishing tackle company again.

He arrived in Seattle dead tired. He went to the USO, an organization that helped enlisted service people. Officers like Berkley were not supposed to use their facilities, but he obtained permission to lie down on a couch in their large room.

"'Do you want something to eat?' somebody asked, as I awoke to a room packed with enlisted men for whom

they were having a reception. I, an officer who was not supposed to be there, had been asleep on the couch in the middle
of it all. I made a quick retreat."

When Berk visited the snap and swivel factory, he
had no idea that years later he would purchase it and move
it to Spirit Lake.

He had begun to realize that he missed the thrill of
his business. Because of college and his military service, it
had been a long time since he had focused on it. He was
ready to throw himself back into it.

A different man boarded a train for Spirit Lake and
life as a civilian, a man with different experiences. No longer
the boy who had spent his whole life in small-town Iowa.
He had lived all over the United States. No longer a teen-
aged business whiz living in his parents' home, already
touted in *Parade of Youth* magazine. Nor was he still a college-aged engineer and executive in training.

He was now a 24-year-old man with a wife, and
hopefully soon, some children. Berkley returned to Spirit
Lake as a full-fledged adult contributor to the community,
no longer under his parents' wings or roof.

Through his travels he had come to know people
from all over the United States, from different American
cultures, from cities, and towns, and farms. He knew more
about what people liked to do and how they interacted with
each other.

Berkley saw how people in leadership positions
treated their subordinates, and how people reacted to their
superiors. If they had a choice, would people follow this
type of leader or that type of leader? Berkley knew how he
liked to be treated, how people *ought* to be treated.

He had come to appreciate the importance of sur-
vival in the face of real danger.

He knew the thrill of flying and the joy of marriage.

And yet, through it all, he had not changed from the
same determined, humble, young man who loved nothing
more than putting on his hip waders and finding fish.

Chapter Ten

Starting Over

"Fishermen are an optimistic lot … and to be optimistic in
a slow bite is to thrive on hope alone."
Paul Quinnett
Pavlov's Trout, The Incomplete Psychology of Everyday Fishing

Home for the holidays, 1945. Home for good.

Berkley could be with family and friends. Berkley
re-acquainted himself with his boyhood friends and their
wives so that they could get to know Elinor. They were a
group of young couples with little money and few worries.

He could go to church again and thank God the war
had ended. Thank God you were alive. Thank God for those
who made the supreme sacrifice. Berkley's old South End
Gang mourned the loss of their buddy, Jim Doudna, who
had been killed in the war. One could never forget the losses,
but after a decade of the Dust Bowl drought and bankrupt
farmers, the Great Depression's food lines and Hoovervilles
full of foreclosed homeowners; after a half-decade of sending millions of young men off to fight in Europe, Asia, and
the Pacific Ocean, and after 15 years of wondering whether
people could make a living, by the end of 1945 the future
finally looked bright.

Berkley could get a job, start a family, buy a house,
buy a car – heck, he could buy whatever he could afford. No
more rations. No more limits.

Berkley and Elinor moved into a little two-bedroom house at the north end of Spirit Lake. His parents made a down payment on it with money from closing Berkley and Company. It was the last house built in Spirit Lake before the war. Cost: $4,800.

Berkley could fish again and play again.

Practically everybody needed practically everything. An honest businessman could make things people needed and things people wanted.

"After the war, you could sell anything you could make: There was a shortage of everything," Berkley recalled.

He busied himself rebuilding his operation and training a new workforce. Jack had gone to college to become a lawyer, like his parents. Marvin Hamilton had gone into the radio sales and repair business. Rachel McQuirk had married Leonard Carpenter and started a family, so she could only work out of her home. His other employees had gone different directions.

Berkley re-opened the fishing tackle factory uptown. His previous equipment had been stored in the old factory space (30 feet by 40 feet) above the meat market for $15 a month, thanks to "Doc" Beverly who rented the entire top floor of the building and ran the government agriculture office in only a part of it.

People hungered for fishing products. Scarcity had built up demand. Berkley could barely keep up with orders, selling his leaders as fast as he could get production materials to make them.

Rather than expand his product line, Berkley decided to concentrate on fishing leaders – to be the lowest-priced and most efficient producer in the market. His decision proved to be a good one. In later years, when the boom days ended and markets tightened, some manufacturers who had expanded into too many product lines could no longer compete.

Berkley knew he had a great cost advantage over competitors.

"They gave me a terribly difficult time at the American Fishing Tackle Manufacturer's Association meeting in New York. My prices were about half the price of some items."

Berkley stood his ground, insisting that he knew his costs and profit margin. At the conclusion of the meeting, he and Elinor boarded a propeller plane to return home. They flew at night to save money.

But gone were the days of sleeping in the car next to apple orchards. For his annual autumn selling trips Berkley and Elinor took four weeks and drove around the eastern half of the United States, staying in $8 a night motels.

He paid himself $30 a week and poured any other profits back into the business.

As Berkley and Company grew, Berk encouraged his employees to profit from sharing in responsibility and commitment.

"Leaders are people who are willing to make decisions," he said. "But if you are a good leader, you also make all the people a part of what's being done. It just seemed natural to me. I did not learn that philosophy at management school. I simply found that working in concert was effective, and the right thing to do."

Long after the company expanded tenfold, Berkley would leave his business office and work right along with his employees when they needed to get orders packed. He tried to build an atmosphere in which managers shared in the work and each worker shared responsibility for the product.

Every time an order was shipped, Berkley tallied the income, computed the profit, and tacked it up on a bulletin board for all 20 employees to see. He set aside 10 percent of all profits for company vacations and outings – a recreation fund.

"The employees did not pay much attention to the figures, but it was a good exercise for me," he said.

The recreation fund began to pay dividends for the company and for employees: weekend trips to college football games in Minneapolis, Omaha, or Des Moines; a yearly vacation for employees and their spouses, sometimes fishing in northern Minnesota or to Yellowstone National Park.

Home workers became an important part of the production process. The company kept growing, but Berkley didn't want to expand the full-time workforce in peak times only to lay off workers during slow periods. A great number of housewives were eager to work part-time or full-time, but needed a flexible schedule. So Berkley developed a production network. The company would deliver materials to women in their homes, pick up the finished products, and pay them according to the number of leaders they produced.

"Women loved it," said former employee Marvin Hamilton. Long after Marvin had stopped working for the company, Hamilton's wife became a Berkley home worker.

When one of the employees was not at work, Berkley would frequently fill in. One time, when the person who handled the home worker route was ill, Berkley substituted. One of the home workers had rented a bedroom in a home and lived and worked in that bedroom. Berkley entered the unlocked house and bounded up the stairs to the bedroom, as he had done on previous occasions, only to find that the home worker had moved. He made a hasty retreat before being found in the family's bedroom!

"There were as many as 50 women in Spirit Lake who were assembling snaps and swivels on a piece of wire and shipping them back for finishing," Marvin Hamilton recalled. "They did that much work, day in and day out, at their own choosing. It was a beautiful setup for women who wanted to work in the home."

The U.S. Wage and Hour Division was skeptical. Concerned about minimum wage compliance, investigators spent two days interviewing all the workers and home workers.

"When home workers first started, they would be paid the minimum wage. It would take them a couple of weeks to become sufficiently proficient to earn more than the minimum wage," said Berkley. "Then they would be paid by their production and start earning more than the minimum wage." The inspectors said the practice was illegal and told Berkley that he would have to pay a fine or they would file charges in district court. They noted a previous case on which they were basing their ruling.

The record of the case was only available in a larger city. Berkley's father had to go to Sioux City, Iowa on another matter. While there, he checked the record on the cited case. It was a case where the railroad hired people on a trial basis. If they didn't work out the railroad did not pay them anything! The court ruled in favor of the railroad.

"How much would it cost to defend us in district court, Dad?" Berkley asked.

"Five times as much as this fine," Walt Bedell replied. "They figure you'll pay the fine to save the legal costs. What's most important to you: the money or the principle?"

"Can we beat them in court?"

"You bet."

"They're just trying to bully innocent people. Why don't you, as my attorney, send them a letter? Tell them: 'Go ahead and sue.'"

"My pleasure."

Berkley never heard another word from the U.S. Wage and Hour Division. "What a shock: Here was a government agency that was trying to bluff us into paying a fine that we did not owe, presumably just to improve the record of the investigators."

From time to time, Berkley could still act like the 120-pound defensive end tackling the 200-pound fullback. It would take a lot more than an empty threat to beat Berkley Bedell – no matter how big the opponent.

He came off as soft, humble, and polite.

But he never thought that a government agency, a competitor, or a Fortune 500 supplier was too big to tackle, if necessary.

He soon showed competitors he had a heart of steel.

Chapter Eleven

Heart of Steel

"Fishing tackle manufacturers do not sell things that catch
fish. They sell hope, and they should."
Paul Quinnett
Pavlov's Trout, The Incomplete Psychology of Everyday Fishing

Berkley laid the *Popular Mechanics* magazine down
in his lap and looked up at the ceiling.

"Aren't you about ready to go to sleep, Berk?" asked
Elinor, beside him in bed.

"I was just thinking about this ... See this article?
This guy in Connecticut is making new rigging lines for sail
boats – steel cable coated with nylon."

"That's nice," Elinor rolled over and closed her eyes.
Did Berkley ever think about anything but his business?
"Good night, honey."

"Well, we're making steel cable leaders and we're
making leaders out of nylon," he thought out loud. "What if
we could coat our cable leaders with nylon?"

"Mmm-hmm."

"This would make wonderful leaders. My cable wire
leaders are tough, but they kink and rust and I'll bet fish see
and smell them ten yards away. My nylon leaders can be
cut by the big, saw-toothed fish. This would be the best of
both worlds."

Silence.

"I wonder if this could be made small enough for fishing leaders?"

Silence.

"I'm going to call this guy in the morning."

"Good night, honey."

"Good night, honey." He turned out the light, but lay awake thinking for another hour.

The next morning, Berkley called the Danielson Company in Danielson, Connecticut.

"Hello, Berkley Bedell here in Spirit Lake, Iowa. I was reading about your sailboat rigging in *Popular Mechanics*."

"You have a sailboat in Iowa?"

"No, I'm a businessman."

"You sell sailboats in Iowa?"

"No, I make fishing leaders. That's what I wanted to talk to you about. I'm wondering if you thought you could make your coated wire small enough for fishing leaders."

"I hadn't thought about that. I suppose we could make it just about as small as you could want it. Why don't you come on out and we could give it a try?"

Berkley packed a suitcase with spools of small stranded stainless steel wire and flew to Danielson, Connecticut. It didn't take long to help Danielson figure out how to coat the small wire with nylon. Berkley knew he had a new product – something no one had ever seen before.

"Fishermen are going to love this," he said. "Would you agree not to sell this material to anyone else? These leaders are my idea, after all."

"It's a deal."

An excited young man flew home with his new nylon-covered wire.

On his lunch break Monday, Berk took two small paper bags: one with his peanut butter sandwich and the other with the new nylon-coated cable leaders. He drove to East Okoboji Lake, eight blocks away, parked near the bridge at the edge of town, took his hip waders, fishing rod, and tackle from their customary place in the trunk. He attached one of the new leaders and a lure. He waded out 10 feet from shore.

Berkley always felt most at home when he was hip-deep in cool water, rod in hand, soft breeze against his face. He took in a deep breath and let it out slowly. He could feel his heart rate slowing. No more worrying about business, about costs and suppliers, and work schedules and meeting payroll. Time to have fun doing his job.

Cast after cast gracefully arced above the gentle ripples that came to rest against his boots. He didn't expect to catch much in the middle of the day, but sought out different depths and lake-bottom surfaces. Any leader will handle the sandy-bottom middle, but what happens up against the rocks on the west shore, or the stumps and logs and roots where bass like to gather? He could feel his leader bouncing and sliding off the irregular shapes. He felt a twitch in his line. A nibble? Another. A strike! He set the hook and played the tug and give and reeling game of bringing in his prey. Nothing big, but a fun little fighter, he thought. Bluegill? Crappie? Feels more like a bluegill. Berkley smiled. He didn't care what other fishermen said. His father always looked for bass. The big-time fishermen went to deep water for northern pike and muskellunge. Berkley was just as happy with a bluegill. He held his rod high with his right hand and swung the line toward his left side. He grabbed the squirming, eight-inch bluegill, tucked his rod under his right armpit, and unhooked the wiggler. He lowered it three inches below the water surface and let it swim back home.

"This is work?" he thought to himself, smiling, and shook his head. Tomorrow would be a good day to work the deep waters in West Okoboji Lake, he thought. "After all somebody's got to test this stuff. Might as well be me."

He fell in love with fishing the new leaders. He had half the snag trouble of previous leaders. And when the big fish bit, this leader was tough. No breaking. You could see pike teeth marks in the nylon, sawing through until they got to the steel cable, then stopping dead in their tracks.

Because of his inexperience, he did not pursue getting a patent when he was told that he could not get one. He never did patent his innovation.

But he did have a name and sales pitch for this new steel and nylon leader: "Steelon: A Nylon Leader with a Heart of Steel."

Come fall of 1949, Berkley and Company would show the world a whole new leader.

Steelon Tackles the Trade Shows

Berkley pulled the car over to the curb. "Excuse me, officer. This is Grand Central Station, isn't it? Do you suppose we can stop here and unload, sir?"

"What are you, in the aquarium business?" The New York traffic cop looked at the earnest young man and his shy young wife. Definitely not New Yorkers, he thought. He noticed the license plates. "You're not going to tell me you drove all the way from Iowa with that tank on top of your car, are you?"

"We're here for the fishing tackle trade show," Berkley replied. "It should only take a minute."

"Make it quick."

Berkley un-strapped the 50-gallon tank that rode the top of their car from uptown Spirit Lake to midtown Manhattan. He and Elinor lifted the tank off the top of the car and set it on a blanket on the sidewalk. Without a New York minute's thought, pedestrians didn't seem to notice or care and automatically swerved around both sides of the tank like a school of fish around a river rock. Berkley took a box of rocks, leaders, and sinkers from the trunk.

"Thank you, officer," Berkley said. "I'll be back in a minute, Elinor." He drove off to park the car, while Elinor guarded the tank.

They attracted attention when they set up their tank on the trade show floor. Berkley attached a Steelon leader to a rod that went round and round in the water tank bouncing the leader and a sinker off piles of jagged rocks.

Clink-clank. Clink-clink.

Clink-clank. Clink-clink-clank.

Never a kink, never a snag.

Clink-clank.

Berkley sales team, from left: Dick Moulton, Jim Stevens and Jack Nelan

The racket attracted Dick Moulton and Jim Stevens, a couple of young salesmen about to form their own business selling to outdoor sports distributors.

Moulton and Stevens looked at Berkley, the manufacturer and company president, setting up his own display with his wife, acting as his own sales force while trying to supervise production and invent new products.

"This guy will never make it," Moulton thought. "How do you go out and market your product if you have to do everything else, too?"

But they could see Berkley had a great idea.

"Steelon, the name Berkley gave to his new leader, was a wonderful leader," Moulton and Stevens agreed. "It wouldn't kink and it was extremely strong." And they liked what they saw in Berkley. "He looked so damned honest and sincere. Here's a guy with dedication and enthusiasm."

Moulton and Stevens offered to sell Berkley's products. Berkley's growing business now had a great product and someone to sell it for him.

"The first check we got from Berkley was for $1.49," said Moulton. "I don't think Jim ever cashed it. He put it in a frame."

Steelon put Berkley and Company on the map. Annual sales rose to $103,000 in 1949 and doubled in 1950. Steelon was on its way to becoming the number one fishing leader. Today, nylon-covered stainless steel wire continues to be the major material used in such fishing leaders.

Steelon was not, however, alone in its market. Berkley was too naïve to recognize the need for a patent and didn't get an exclusivity agreement in writing from the Connecticut manufacturer.

"I was shocked and surprised when I found that the Danielson Company had started selling to our competitors. They had broken our agreement! This was my first disillusionment with the ethics of some people in corporate management. It would not be my last."

The great setback turned out to be a tremendous blessing. Since he had helped to produce the first Steelon at the Danielson plant, he had an idea about what he needed to do.

First, he needed to find a new building and he needed to invent some equipment.

The process required a fairly lengthy building. The town of Spirit Lake wanted to sell a long, wooden building that had been used as duplex housing after the war. It had become obsolete as housing and they wanted to move it to create a park. The city put it up for sale, through sealed bids.

Berkley put in a sealed bid for $50 – his magic number – and went to the opening of the bids. He was prepared to raise his bid if necessary, but it was the only one. The town council voted to reject his ridiculous bid of only $50. Berkley was riled. His factory wasn't big, but it was the only one in town ... and growing.

"If that's your attitude toward the only industrial employer in the town, my plant doesn't belong in Spirit Lake. Tomorrow morning I'm going to Spencer, and then to Milford, and then to Estherville, and every town within 30 miles if I have to, and I'll see what *they'll* do to get me to move my operation to their town."

He walked out of the meeting and went home.

"How did it go, Honey?" Elinor asked.

"I'd rather not talk about it until I calm down a bit, Elinor." He picked up a magazine from the rack and went off to the living room to take his mind off the matter.

The telephone rang.

"Berk, there's a Councilman on the phone for you."

"What does he want?"

Pause.

"He says he wants to see how they can work this out with you."

It had taken them less than five minutes to reconsider and accept Berkley's miniscule bid.

They could envision a new economy forming in the Spirit Lake area. Hundreds of servicemen had come home, married, and started having children. They needed real, family-supporting jobs. The town needed business growth to pay for schools, roads, and sewers. Times had changed. The community couldn't live off summer tourism forever, they had to stimulate year-round jobs.

Berkley had his building for $50 and Spirit Lake eventually had its biggest employer, for practically nothing.

Berkley talked to his boyhood neighbor, Ed Donovan, about machinery he needed. Ed's dad, an undertaker, had a small machine shop where Ed had been tinkering since boyhood, but full-time since the war ended. Berkley knew Ed to be tough and determined. Ed wouldn't give up on Berkley's ideas and drawings until they found a solution. Ed had long admired Berkley's inventiveness, from the day his older brother, Stanley, held the ladder for his homemade flying attempt, to the days when his sister, Pearl, soldered leaders in Berkley's bedroom.

Berkley had so many ideas for machines that he could use to make things. He liked to invent things, but he needed someone like Ed to make them work.

He couldn't have known it then, but when he hired Ed Donovan in 1950, he hired a co-worker who would grow with Berk and the company until he retired.

Berk and Ed built some equipment themselves. They bought a nylon-extruding machine, "a big, glorified, heated meat grinder," Donovan called it. When they figured out how to make the nylon coating they started producing their own Steelon.

"The Danielson Company had a fit," said Berkley. "I would not have done this if Danielson had lived up to our agreement, but their mistake turned out to be a wonderful break for the future growth of Berkley and Company."

Steelon gave Berkley and Company a national reputation as the leader in its market.

Steelon's "Heart of Steel" slogan inspired employee Harper Seaman to create a new logo for the company that became the identifying trademark of Berkley's ever-more-popular products – a folksy script "Berkley" on a red heart.

Berkley's new sales team helped the company become more market savvy. He used the sales team not only for its ability to sell his innovations, but also for its expertise in knowing what would sell.

"At most sales meetings, a company would call all the salesmen in to tell them what they're going to do for the next year and sell them on the products they plan to introduce." Berkley recalled. "We would call our sales people in and show them the new items we were going to introduce for the next year. But more than anything, we would ask them what we needed to do differently."

"The first sales meeting we had was just with Dick Moulton and Jim Stevens. A lot of the leaders being sold at that time were marketed hanging on little display card boards that were set up on store counters, from which they could be removed and sold. I was proud that we had made these special card boards. I thought they were great."

"I brought Dick and Jim in to look at them, and they said, 'That really stinks.' It was actually a good thing that they told us what they needed. I would take their ideas out to Ed Donovan and he would make them happen. The next day we'd have a sample of what we could do – of what Jim and Dick thought we ought to do. So it was really a team effort, more than just selling our product line."

Berkley had a heart for fly fishermen as well. They needed a different kind of leader.

"For fly fishing, you normally use a leader that is from 7½ to 9 feet in length. They would take maybe 18 inches of nylon that was a certain diameter, then 18 inches of a smaller diameter nylon, and they'd tie them together, and then 18 inches of a smaller diameter, until you got down to where the fly would be tied – probably four-pound test or two-pound test line."

Berkley learned of a place in Minnesota that started selling nylon, knotless, tapered leaders, where the leader tapered from the larger diameter down to the smaller diameter without knots.

"They took the nylon and hung it into a bath of acid, and then they slowly pulled it out. The acid would eat out the nylon to make it smaller and smaller and smaller."

From that company, Berkley bought the rights to make that type of tapered fly leaders.

"Berk went out and started to sell these leaders, even though we didn't know how to make the crazy things," Ed Donovan remembered.

After he had sold them, Berkley and Ed set their minds to developing the process and the machinery to make them.

"We obtained a bathtub to hold the acid. Then we built a frame with pulley wheels where you could wrap the nylon around the frame, with adjustments, so you could adjust how much nylon was going round the frame. Then we had a cam that would slowly drop the frame into the acid and then slowly pull it up as the line traveled around the frame. The line that first exited the acid was the largest, and the last line to exit was the smallest. The line came through a rubber wiper and onto a spool, so you would have this whole series of tapered leaders on the spool."

"It was terribly pungent. We'd wear masks to try to protect ourselves from this terrible, terrible odor. Luckily it didn't really appear to affect the health of any of us. But we made it work. And for a while, it became a very profitable product for us."

"It's not a real big market, but knotless tapered leaders became our next big step. We had a monopoly because we were the only people producing them."

The success of Steelon and tapered leaders ushered in a new future for Berkley and Company, although Berk didn't realize it at the time. It was a future that depended on innovation, not just low production costs.

The new future was more a product of a curious mind than a strategic mind, he claimed.

"We weren't thinking that deeply. It's just sort of my personality that I find it fun and challenging to try to do things differently and better than other people."

"We didn't know anything about market research, but we knew that it's a lot easier to sell something new and different than to sell something that's the same as what other people are making."

Because of Steelon and the new tapered nylon leader for fly fishermen, Berkley sales increased from $103,000 in 1949 to $526,000 in 1954. Steelon became number one in its market, then the tapered leader became number one in its market.

The best was yet to come.

Learning how to make Steelon launched Berkley into a whole new universe of manufacturing nylon products. In the next decade, the company would branch into products that caught the fancy of everyone from water skiers to hula hoopers.

More significantly, Berkley and Company had become poised to tackle one of the giant corporations in the nation, and create a product that, in the words of *Sports Afield* magazine, "rocked the outdoor world."

Chapter 12

Trilene: Tackling Giants

"We are fishermen tying to make
better fishing tackle for other fishermen.
Watch us. We have only started."
Berkley Fly Company catalog of new items, 1952

As a boy of seven, Berkley watched his father and grandfather perform the ritual of drying fishing lines.

Each day of their Minnesota fishing trip, they returned to their camp after the last cast of the day and wrapped the end of their braided silk fishing lines around a tree branch. They let out more line and wrapped it around another branch, then back to the first, weaving a web of fishing line above their heads. The day's lake water would drip or evaporate from the saturated lines during the evening. They would then rewind the dried line onto their revolving spool reels every morning. If they didn't perform the ritual, the waterlogged line would rot and lose its strength.

After World War II, tackle innovations became prominent. Fiberglass rods were introduced in 1946, replacing bamboo and steel rods.

As spinning reels began to replace revolving spool reels, DuPont developed a new monofilament fishing line.

The DuPont monofilament resembled the bristles in a toothbrush, except it was somewhat more flexible. It did not have to be dried after use. Fishing tackle manufacturers could buy this monofilament fishing line from DuPont on large drums, and spool it onto smaller spools for sale to fishermen.

Spinning reels used the nylon monofilament line, and Berkley himself began to prefer the nylon monofilament when he used a revolving spool reel. He envisioned a day when all reels would use monofilament line.

Berkley and Company spooled and sold DuPont monofilament fishing line.

But Berkley began to wonder: Now that he had figured out how to extrude nylon to make Steelon more profitable, what if Berkley and Company could learn to extrude its own nylon for fishing line? The fishing line business was, after all, a lot bigger than the leader business.

DuPont held a patent on one of the key steps in the process. Berkley asked DuPont for a license to use their patent. They invited him to Wilmington, Delaware to discuss it. Their top executives took him out for an exclusive fancy luncheon. They advised this unsophisticated young man that they would not grant him a license. Not only was he disappointed, he resented them for wasting his time and expense, when they could have told him by telephone or by mail.

So he decided to visit a former fraternity brother in nearby Washington, D.C. Since his friend was working to get a license to be a patent attorney, Berkley told him his frustrating experience. His friend researched the federal register. He found that the federal government had reached an agreement with DuPont that required them to license this process to anyone who wanted it.

Berkley was stunned.

"What a shock! These top executives at DuPont lied to me!" The innocent, idealistic, naïve young man from straight-shooting Iowa had assumed that all people at the top of the corporate ladder were honest. "This turned out to be another step in my disillusionment with corporate America."

Berk refocused his anger into determination. DuPont didn't know Berkley Bedell. They didn't know he already *knew* how to extrude nylon and didn't know his grandma's advice!

Back in Spirit Lake, Berkley bought an old, rundown building that had been used as a plant to dry eggs during the war. Now, he just had to figure out how to extrude and stretch nylon, without degrading its strength.

Berkley and Ed Donovan put together a set of used machines and spare parts. They hooked up an old washing machine to pull nylon strands through the wringer. They used bicycle wheels and three sets of rollers with heaters between the sets of rollers to make the stretching process possible.

The homemade equipment was far from perfect. They ran it 24 hours a day. Berkley and Donovan were on call all the time.They treated their plant like a newborn that needed constant care.

In the early days, Berkley and Ed were checking their tapered leader process every two hours, all night long, to be sure the nylon didn't get tangled or that the machine didn't malfunction and leave them with a night of wasted supplies. They took turns: Donovan at 8 p.m., Berkley at 10 p.m., Donovan at midnight, Berkley at 2 a.m., Donovan at 4 a.m., Berkley at 6 a.m.

"After months of that stuff, Berkley comes in one day and says, 'I figured out what one night's loss of materials would be,'" Donovan recalled.

"I asked him, 'How much?'

"He says: 'Five dollars.' "

The two-hour shifts ended right then and there.

But they needed to keep the fishing line process going around-the-clock or it would be an awful mess. So the middle-of-the-night emergency calls kept coming from the night shift crew.

"I lived like a family doctor with a telephone by my bed which would ring at all hours of the night. I would go up to the plant to try to solve the problem and try to get the production going," Berkley said.

There were two big pitfalls to overcome: the initial material and the pressure applied at the end.

"We poured nylon chips – eighth-inch cubes of nylon – into a heated barrel at the beginning of the extrusion process. A large screw pushed the melting nylon through the heated cylinder, then through a horizontal plate containing a number of holes at the other end of the cylinder, creating strands of nylon. As the melted strands dropped into a tank of water, they would cool and solidify. Then they were stretched to their maximum length – and strength – before their breaking point."

"When it solidifies, it's a lot of molecules all mixed up," Berkley explained. "When you stretch it, the molecules all line up parallel to each other. That's where the strength comes from. When you stretch a rubber band and release it, it returns to its original position. When you stretch nylon in this manner, it changes the structure of the material and it does not return. The stretched material can be as much as four times the length of the original material.

"The secret is to stretch it as far as you possibly can, but not so far that it breaks.

"We would run eight strands, maybe ten, at the same time. But if you have any dirt, or a burn on one of those chips, one of the strands will break – and if one of them breaks, it messes up the whole works and you've got to string up the entire thing again."

At one point, Berkley thought he could save on breakage – and midnight phone calls – if he eliminated the bad nylon pellets before they went into the extruder.

"I sat at home sorting those little eighth-inch cubes, to eliminate any with some burn in them, so we wouldn't be so likely to have so many problems. It was quite a learning experience for us."

They kept their process a secret from their competitors, who were still buying, packaging, and re-selling DuPont line. Competitors could not figure out how Berkley could sell monofilament line for such a low price.

Business boomed, all through the 1950s, with Steelon leaders and Triple X monofilament fishing line. Sales increased from $103,000 in 1949 to $1 million in 1957.

In time, DuPont developed a somewhat better monofilament, which they labeled Stren. They sold it to a limited number of manufacturers to be labeled and sold under the Stren label. Berkley wanted to be in on that action. He asked DuPont if he could be included among those who could spool and sell Stren.

"They refused to sell to me." It turned out to be another disappointment that became a blessing. The company would have to develop a better line itself.

Fishermen wanted strong and flexible line.

"Regular nylon tended to be stiff, especially in heavier tests, and it tended to take a set on the spool, so if it had been on the spool all winter, you'd have a bunch of coils," Berkley recalled.

Adding a chemical to soften the line made it more flexible, but caused it to lose too much strength.

"We were already making our own nylon monofilament, but nobody knew it," Berkley recalled. "I don't know if DuPont knew or not. If they did, they did not want to let it be known so that others might do the same."

Berkley eventually found a way to make a strong flexible monofilament – flexible enough to perform better and actually stronger than the plain nylon.

He obtained a patent for a fishing line that came to be known as Trilene: the strongest most flexible monofilament fishing line that had ever been made. "We named the line Trilene to confuse our competitors into thinking it was something other than nylon," Berkley said.

When Trilene came along, DuPont Stren had been on the market for a year.

How could this small-town Iowa Company compete with the giant DuPont Company and its established Stren line? Berkley and Company had $1 million in annual sales. If DuPont wanted, it could afford to spend that much in a tremendous marketing and sales program just for Stren.

"You must be crazy," one of his own sales representatives told Berkley. "What do you think you're doing?"

Berkley kept giving Trilene the East Okoboji Lake test, the Big Spirit Lake test, and the West Okoboji Lake test. He tried it in shallow water and deep water, in all kinds of weather, with all kinds of fish. He had his friends, family, and workers test it in real fishing situations.

"I had fished with it enough that I knew we had a product that would work," said Berkley. "You could use Trilene on a revolving spool reel because of its flexibility. It was easier to cast, harder to tangle, and stronger than any fishing line I had ever used."

"So off I went to the annual fishing tackle show in Chicago to announce that we were going to compete with DuPont," Berkley recalls. People at the show were skeptical. Berkley was confident.

He knew he had a stronger line because he had taken one more innovative step. He labeled his line according to its fishing strength, not just its laboratory strength.

"When you tie a knot in monofilament fishing line, it weakens considerably below what it tests in the lab," he reasoned. Berkley figured the line lost 30 percent in strength when a fisherman tied on a leader or lure. So line that broke with nine pounds of pressure in the lab he labeled as six-pound test line. DuPont labeled their Stren with the laboratory strength. Berkley's six-pound test line was as strong as nine-pound test Stren.

Berkley asked dealers to test the line themselves, and to have their best fishermen test it: "We sent two spools of 20-pound test Trilene free to 10,000 dealers and asked them to have two of their best fishermen put it on revolving spool reels and try fishing with it."

The fishermen who tried the 20,000 free spools of Trilene loved it, and those who had breakage with 10-pound test Stren did not have that problem with 10-pound test Trilene, because it actually tested 13 pounds. They found it to be more flexible than Stren and easier to fish with.

"And you can hardly break 20-pound monofilament."

Sales took off as soon as the Chicago tradeshow reviews came in, and Trilene's reputation kept growing. As sales grew, Berkley poured the revenue into advertising to feed the momentum.

"We spent every extra penny we had to run ads in sports magazines."

Before long, Trilene was outselling Stren. The company's annual sales more than doubled in three years.

Years later, Berkley would be honored as Iowa Inventor of the Year for Trilene. In 1999, *Sports Afield* magazine ranked it among "100 years of awesome gear: tools, toys, and trends that rocked our outdoor world."

It became and remains the best-selling fishing line.

"I think I'm very, very fortunate to have a creative mind. It's had more to do with the success of my business than anything else," Berkley reflected, 45 years later. "I love to develop new things and new processes."

DuPont began coloring its Stren line with a coloring that glowed in the sunlight, so that fishermen could see it, but DuPont claimed that this color disappeared under water, so the fish could not see it. It turned out to be a great sales help. Berkley and Company found that the patent had been obtained under questionable circumstances, and started to make and sell a similarly colored line.

DuPont sued Berkley for patent infringement. Berkley counter sued.

A jury trial followed in Cedar Rapids, Iowa, about 300 miles from Spirit Lake.

"The testimony indicated that DuPont had, indeed, obtained the patent under improper circumstances," Berkley recalled. "DuPont offered to settle and pay us 'in the high six figures.' I made the decision that we should not settle. I thought we had them over a barrel."

The jury ruled that DuPont did not have a suit, but also that Berkley should not be awarded anything. The trial had cost Berkley almost a million dollars. Few fishing tackle companies would have been financially able to defend themselves in such a suit.

"It made me realize that all are not equal in our legal system and that financial power gives one a tremendous advantage," Berkley observed.

Not everyone can *tackle giants.*

The Steelon and Trilene innovations reinforced Berkley's conviction that the company should try to make as much of its own supplies as possible, rather than buy them from others.

"Usually this would save us money, but more importantly, it would enable us to develop better products."

He and Ed Donovan developed a machine shop, where the company built much of its own equipment. The company also had its own print shop. Berkley found a site going out of the cable wire business. He bought their used equipment to make their own cable wire.

Nylon was a little trickier. The company was buying nylon pellets to heat and extrude through Berkley's equipment to transform it into fishing line. Berkley wanted to cut out his dependence on the nylon pellet suppliers.

"It had always been my dream to make our own nylon," Berkley said. "It's a process using a chemical called caprolactam along with polymerizing." He flew to Germany and visited a company behind the Berlin Wall in East Germany that made a polymerizing machine. Berkley came out of East Germany through the checkpoint in the Wall and spent the night at a hotel in Hamburg. The next morning, when he came to the front desk to check out the attendant said, "Have you heard the news? You are at war!" The clerk showed Berkley a newspaper. Although it was in German, Berkley saw that it did indeed say that the United States and the Soviet Union had gone to war. It had just been discovered that the Soviet Union had installed missiles in Cuba from which they could reach anywhere in the United States. President Kennedy had issued a warning that unless they were removed, the U.S. would take military action. From Hamburg, Berkley flew to London to catch a plane for the United States. While in London, he went to a bank to cash some travelers checks. The talk everywhere was about the Cuban Missile Crisis.

The teller at the bank said, "I hope you do not get us into it."

"Why shouldn't we?" Berkley replied. "You got us into the last one."

The teller did not appreciate his remark. "As we took off from London for New York, I did not know whether there would be an airport there for us to land on or not. I had a strange feeling on that flight. I do not think I have ever before or since had such a strong feeling. I really had no concern for my own safety. All I could think about was getting back to be with my family. I realized that a nuclear war would possibly blow up the planet, but above all, I wanted to be with my family. I cannot properly describe my relief at arriving home. Much to my surprise, Russian ships arrived in Cuba, the missiles were dismantled, and returned to the Soviet Union." It averted a nuclear war, which had seemed imminent. And the planet survived.

After the worries of the Cuban Missile crisis, Berkley realized that it would not be easy to purchase equipment from East Germany behind the Iron Curtain. So he found a company called Industrial Rayon Corporation that was going out of the nylon yarn business. They had a small polymerizer, which they used for research. "I flew out to visit them and we bought their research polymerizer, which was large enough to supply our needs," Berkley recalled.

"We moved the polymerizer back to Spirit Lake, remodeled our building to make room for it, installed a chemical research laboratory, hired a chemist, and proceeded to learn how to make nylon.

"At that time, low-cost nylon fishing line made up a large part of the market. The chemical cost much less than the nylon chips, which we had been using. Since we were making our own nylon, this gave us a huge cost advantage. In fact, I believe our little fishing tackle company became the first company west of the Mississippi River to make nylon from the basic chemicals."

Ironically, that became a problem when the Arab oil embargo of 1973 limited the supply of the petroleum-based chemical used in making nylon.

"The company from which we purchased our chemicals informed us that because of the shortage they would no longer supply us. The supplier had cut us off to supply their larger customers."

Berkley flew out to meet with the supplier. It turned out to be a disaster. "There is no compassion in corporate business and the executives could not have been more rude," Berkley reported.

What a disaster! "Our entire efforts to build a successful company depended entirely upon our nylon fishing line business. Without supplies for our nylon fishing line, all our efforts would have been in vain. We were in a panic."

"We knew that a large amount of nylon yarn went into the production of textiles and carpets. We found a firm that sold nylon waste, hoping that we might be able to find some way to reprocess it. However, during that search we learned of some equipment for sale in Israel that could turn nylon yarn back into the chemical from which we made our nylon."

Ed Donovan was on his way to Israel. He purchased the equipment and had it shipped to Spirit Lake. The company purchased tons of waste nylon yarn and successfully converted it into caprolactam, the chemical that the oil embargo had made unavailable. Berkley and Company took the caprolactam and ran it through its polymerizer to make nylon, and then through its extruder to come out with nylon fishing line.

"We were going the long way around. We were starting with something that's the waste of a finished product and converting it back to the basic chemical. Then we ran the basic chemical through the polymerizer and extruder to produce a new finished product," Berkley explained.

"We wouldn't accept defeat," Berkley said.

"First, there wouldn't be many companies that would try to make their own nylon. Second, there wouldn't be many companies that would search the world for a way to make the chemical needed to produce nylon. Third, most companies would not fly to Israel to buy equipment in order to try to convert scrap into a much-needed chemical. We knew of no one else that was doing it. We had truly saved the company.

"If we had not been able to get the money to send Ed to Israel and purchase the equipment; and if I had not listened to Mamie when she said, 'You can do almost anything within reason if you will only put your mind to it,' the Berkley and Company story would have been very different."

The refusal to accept defeat, and the determination to jump hurdles, were the defining characteristics of Berkley and Company and its founder.

Berkley and Company found itself on its way to becoming the biggest fishing tackle company in the United States. Much of its success came because a former 120-pound defensive end was never afraid to tackle giants.

"I remembered the proprietor of the local hardware store telling me during my high school years that I was foolish to try to compete with the big fishing tackle manufacturing companies. But I have learned that when outside advice conflicts with that of your grandmother, trust your grandmother!"

Chapter Thirteen

Growing Family

A new spirit emerged in Spirit Lake after World War II: Young, fresh, hopeful, victorious – time to build a future, build a business, and build a family.

Elinor and Berkley suffered the heartache of a still-born baby in 1946. Shortly thereafter, Berk's brother Jack and his wife, Marcia, suffered a miscarriage. The joy of children became especially meaningful to both families.

Berkley and Elinor soon had a healthy son. Kenneth, named after Elinor's father, was born in October 1947, followed by Thomas in 1950, and Joanne in 1952. Berkley was glad to be in the hospital delivery room for all three births. They had cousins to play with nearby, as Jack and Marcia also had a daughter Ken's age and twin boys the same age as Tom.

These post-World War II children shared much of the same carefree optimism of the 1950s that their parents had experienced in the post-World War I 1920s. They had the same innocence, but more prosperity.

Their parents embodied and nourished a sense of professional opportunity, personal responsibility, and fun. Berkley worked night and day to build the business during the late 1940s and 1950s, but he remained a child of the lakes. Berkley and Company not only reflected his values, but also produced things that he wanted as a fisherman. His best market research came straight from his own experience as a fisherman.

Children in 1953: (Left to right) Joanne, 1; Tom, 3, and Ken, 5

He never lost sight of his need to feed his own recreational passion and to pass that legacy on to his children.

"Can you watch Kenny while I run some errands, Berk?" asked Elinor. Ken was two years old. Elinor was pregnant with Tom.

"Sure, honey. But it is Saturday morning. I had thought I'd go fishing."

"I just need to get some things. Can you drop me off downtown?"

"Well, all right, honey," he said. He drove downtown and let Elinor off at the drug store, and then he and Ken headed for the bridge across the middle of East Okoboji Lake. He parked near Miller's boathouse, south of the bridge, and took his hip waders, his fishing rod, and tackle from their ever-ready place in the trunk.

"Oh, you'll like this," he told the curious tot on the car seat, while he pulled on his waders. "We'll figure out how to do this. Just you wait and see." He snapped a lure onto one of his new leaders, picked Ken up and cradled him in his left arm.

"I have this clear memory of him holding me up like this and wading out at this specific place," Ken recalled. "There he was, fishing and carrying me out to fish."

Berkley sometimes came home for a quick lunch, grabbed his shotgun, and walked down the street to hunt in the weed patches and cornfields for pheasants.

He hunted wild ducks in the fall. Bad weather made the hunting even better. Jack, who had obtained his law degree from the University of Iowa and moved back to Spirit Lake to practice with Walt and Virginia, became Berkley's main hunting partner. Jack had a dog, Daisy, who swam out in the icy water to retrieve the ducks they shot.

In 1949, Berkley and his old friend Peter Narey got a group of six local young men together for a fall duck-hunting trip to northern Minnesota. Jack Bedell and Daisy soon joined the group. With a few changes in participants and destination the group continued to go every year for 52 years.

"As we became older, we spent more time taking naps and playing cards, but the trip and camaraderie became an important event in all of our lives," Berkley reflected.

In the fall of 1952, the annual trip caused a real dilemma for Berkley.

By then, Berkley and Elinor had two boys. They decided to try one last time to have a girl and were anxious when Elinor became pregnant – even more anxious when the due date was during the first week of October: the week of the big annual hunting trip.

"This caused major turmoil, because the guys needed to go hunting and I hadn't been born yet," Joanne said. "Gratefully, I was born on October 5.

"In church, they'd have a little flower on the podium when there had been a birth, and then the pastor announced to the church that so-and-so had such-and-such. So Grandma Bedell was in church that Sunday and they announced that Berkley and Elinor had had a girl. The whole church gave a huge sigh of relief. They knew how much Mom and Dad had wanted to have a girl.

"By the time they announced it, Dad had gone on his annual hunting trip."

Born into the outdoor life like all three children, Joanne most eagerly embraced it.

"I ended up being more of a tomboy than Ken and Tom." Joanne preferred getting a football for her birthday instead of a doll, and going fishing instead of playing house.

Part of that personality was having two older brothers who needed someone – anyone – to fill in as a third baseman or something. But part of it also was that the family did a lot of outdoor activities together. Whatever the factors, Joanne relished the outdoor life.

"I loved hip waders. I thought they were so cool and I loved fishing."

She also had the benefit of being the only child at home for a time. "By the time I was old enough to do things with Dad, like go pheasant hunting and stuff, Ken and Tom were busy with other things, so I would go with him."

Berkley later remarked, "Some of my happiest memories are of the times I spent with Joanne; fishing or hunting, gathering wild asparagus along the roadside ditches, or catching frogs for a frog leg dinner."

But as youngsters, Joanne and Ken both had to overcome allergies. That posed a problem for Berkley the outdoorsman.

Berkley came home from a successful morning of duck hunting one day, when Joanne was two-and-a-half years old. Elinor was waiting to use the car.

"Berk, can you watch Joanne while I run some errands?" Elinor asked.

"I'd love to, honey, but look at all these ducks I brought home."

"Those are very nice, but you need to keep them away from Joanne. You know she's terribly allergic to feathers."

"I'm certainly aware of that, but I have all these ducks and I'm afraid they'll spoil if I don't get them cleaned and into a tub of cold water."

"Can't that wait until I get home, Berk? I really need to get these errands done."

"We'll find a way to make things work, dear."

"No matter what you do, don't let her go down to the basement where you clean those ducks. You know how sick she gets. I've had a terrible time just finding food she can eat without getting sick."

How could he get those ducks cleaned? He couldn't leave a two-and-a-half-year-old alone. But the house would smell terrible if he left the ducks too long before cleaning them. He had an idea.

"How would you like to watch Daddy clean his ducks, Joanne?" He picked up his daughter and sat her on the landing at the top of the stairs to the basement. He went down the stairs and started cleaning his ducks, chatting with her all the while. "No, honey, you can't come down here, or you'll get sick. You just watch Daddy from up there."

"I thought it was great to get to sit there and watch him," Joanne recalled. "Then I was sick for a month after that! Mom never forgave him."

Elinor and Berkley never fought, however. They wanted their children to learn how to resolve conflicts peacefully. They had their share of sibling arguments, but all of their children remember the family as a place of peace.

"Ken was always very kind to me," said Joanne. "When Ken would go for walks at night, he'd ask me to come with him. He would include me at times when other kids wouldn't have done that. Tom teased me, which seemed pretty normal. But when we were in high school, we were best friends. In fact, we double dated all the time. We did almost everything together."

The desire for peace began in the home.

"My mom's a total, total, unconditionally loving mother," Tom recalled. "She spent her life doing whatever she could to make our lives special. She was always there, never judgmental."

Whether a product of personality and family traits, the strong influence of the churches in the Iowa-Minnesota area, the teachings of Jesus, or a rational reaction to the Vietnam debacle, by the 1970s working for peace became a passion for the entire Bedell family.

"Mom was always a peacemaker," said Joanne, who became actively involved with her mother in the Peace Links organization as an adult. Peace Links was an organization founded by Betty Bumpers, wife of Senator Dale Bumpers of Arkansas. Many of the early members were wives of Congressmen. They gave speeches pointing out the dangers of a nuclear war. They called themselves, 'Women against nuclear war.'

"Conflict didn't happen at our house. I don't ever remember Mom and Dad having an argument," Joanne recalled.

Ken, who also made peace a focus of his adult vocation, credits his parents with creating a climate of peace in the home.

"Mom is extremely even-tempered around the house," he said. "Looking back now, it doesn't seem at all surprising that peacefulness is something that would be a theme in her life. She's not a conflict sort of person."

That Ken became a leading advocate for peace issues at an Ivy League university and at a United Methodist seminary is a testament to his parents' example and persistence, as well as his own. When Ken had pneumonia at age seven, the family went to Florida for three weeks so Ken could recover. They discovered that Ken could not read, so they had him tutored. He went on to become an honors student, graduate from Cornell University, earn a Ph.D. degree, teach in graduate schools, and graduate from Rochester-Colgate Seminary.

When Ken was in junior high, he started to think about what he wanted to do in his adult life. Although his family went to the Methodist Church, he stopped to see the Catholic Priest. He wanted to find out how one becomes a saint. The Priest advised him that one of the requirements is for the person to be deceased. Ken lost all interest in becoming a saint!

Tom, who came back to live in Spirit Lake as an adult, after living in Washington D.C. and traveling around the world, thinks the entire town fostered a sense of community and harmony.

"I grew up where there was absolutely no fear. The lectures about 'don't talk to strangers' would have been odd, because you just talked to everybody. You could walk into the grocery store and pick up a quart of milk if your mom asked you to, without any money, and they knew you'd come by and pay them. We never locked our door. I never remember coming home and being locked out of my house. My keys are in my car sitting out there now. When I moved back to Spirit Lake in 1979, I bought a house, but never received a key. When I sold it, I didn't have a key to give to the people who bought it. Now I know how different that is, but I grew up where you trusted people and you told the truth. Everybody supported you. Your family wasn't just your relatives. It was the entire town. Still is.

"It's not a 'me' environment; it's a 'we' environment."

Joanne said Spirit Lake was more supportive than restrictive. "I knew if I did something wrong everyone would know about it quicker than my parents, so I just never did. I found that environment great, not stifling. It seemed like a guiding hand. You knew your friends. The same kids you know in kindergarten are with you through high school. I'm sure it isn't always a good thing, but it worked really well for me. I felt like people were pulling for me.

"I also thought everybody loved Dad and Mom; that they genuinely cared about them. And I felt like they genuinely cared about me too. It was a really wonderful community."

Tom said that Berkley carried into his family the same sense of order, discipline, and prioritizing that helped him succeed in business. No matter how busy his work schedule, the family had dinner together, even if he had to return to the office afterward.

"Dad would plan Sunday, family activities, because that fit his schedule," said Tom. "If my buddies wanted to play basketball on Sunday afternoon, my Dad would say, 'No, you're going to be with the family.' Mom and Dad would find stuff we could do as a family, which my own kids now call 'forced family fun.'"

The town of Spirit Lake, about 2,500 people, continued to be an outdoor playground. In 1955, as the children grew older and the business prospered so the family could afford a bigger place, Berkley looked for a way to combine the convenience of living in town with his own desire for an outdoor life.

"I had always wanted to live on the lake," said Berkley. Many of the town's upper-income professionals and businessmen were building homes on expensive waterfront property on West Okoboji Lake, three miles south-west of Spirit Lake.

"But Elinor wanted to live in town. We only had one car. By living in town she could walk to visit her friends and go shopping, but if we lived on the lake she would be stranded."

One evening when he walked four blocks to East Okoboji Lake to fish, the answer stared him in the face. He saw a break in the line of development along the west shore of the banana-shaped lake.

"There, right in town, was a city block of woods right on the lake. It was grown up like a jungle. A light bulb again went off in my head. Here I could live on the lake and Elinor could live in town. I called a local realtor and asked if a lot could be purchased. He said no, the owner did not want to break it up into lots. I had him find out what the owner wanted for the whole block. The answer was $2,800. We bought it."

For another $30,000, the Bedells built a house over-looking the lake; at the same time Trilene was becoming a huge success.

"It became a great place to grow up," said Joanne. "You had small town in the winter and you had way too much fun in the summer."

A lake full of fun bordered the front yard. As the children grew older, they could walk out the front door and go fishing, swimming, or boating from spring through fall. Elinor spent hour after hour driving the boat up and down the lake, with her water skiing children in tow.

"She took us water skiing, I bet, every day of the summer," Joanne recalled. "She was there for us, even though she could not swim. She sinks like a stone. She tried to take swimming lessons, but it just doesn't work for her. She's very good-natured about it."

The back yard became a recreation center, too. They built a lighted tennis and basketball court in the back yard, which became a gathering place for all the neighborhood children, Berkley included.

"Dad loved to get out and play basketball with us and he was good," Tom said. "He wanted everybody to call him Berk. He didn't want to be Mr. Bedell. He was obnoxious about it. 'My name's Berk!' But the kids loved him. We'd be in there pushing and shoving. He'd be right in there with us. He did that all the time."

The shallow East Okoboji Lake would freeze over before Christmas.

"Dad welded shovels from pieces of steel – wide shovels – to get the snow off," said Ken. "So in front of our house, there was a place where we and our friends could ice skate." Berkley also hooked up some floodlights on the bank to light the rink for night skating.

To make the lake perfect, Berkley and Jack hooked up a hose to the water heater in Berkley's house, so they could flood the rink with hot water that would freeze more slowly and smoothly than with cold water. The kids would skate and play hockey after school. No matter how many kids were there, they'd come inside, take off their snowy, sweaty clothes, and Elinor would serve hot chocolate.

"I could have had 15 kids down there playing hockey, after which we'd all be down in the basement, and there she'd be with her hot chocolate," said Tom. "We'd play all the time. We had hockey leagues. I remember East Okoboji kids, our group, challenging West Okoboji kids. That was a brutal deal." Ken, a deft puck handler and skater, has a dead front tooth as a reminder of being hit in the mouth with a hockey stick.

"But then on Sunday afternoons, Dad and some of the other dads would come down," said Tom. "Dad's really athletic. In basketball, he always could whip us, and in tennis too. He was pretty good in hockey."

Berkley believed the games helped draw the neighborhood together.

"We had some great Sundays when all our friends and their families would gather at our house for a big hockey game followed by hot cider and cookies," said Berkley. "We would laugh until our sides ached, watching the little children pursuing the hockey puck with their hockey sticks swinging." They would knock each other off their feet as often as they would hit the puck.

"We had an awful good time," said Jack. "We grew up that way. We wanted to show our kids that you could have good fun without money."

It had its costs, however.

Berkley and Jack were in their mid-30s at the time, young enough to feel like playing the way they did 25 years before, not quite old enough to know better.

One Sunday, Berkley skated speedily toward the goal with the puck. His sibling rival lay in wait and upended him. Berkley flew through the air. He landed with a thud and a crack.

"Are you all right?" Jack asked.

He knew it must be serious. Berkley, who never swears, said:

"Hell, no, I'm not all right!"

"Jack seemed real proud of being responsible for my two broken ribs," Berkley now chuckles.

"Oh, no. I didn't want to hurt him," Jack said. "But it *was* a helluva good play."

Berk and Jack recalled making an iceboat – a sailboat with runners to slide across the ice – when they were young teens. They built it out of scrap lumber. For runners, they went to the town dump and salvaged side rails from a bed.

Their scrap iceboat had been so much fun in those days, why not make another for the next generation?

They spent Thanksgiving Day and two Saturdays building the boat with their children. They went to the wood shop at the company and cut boards, and to another shop to weld the runners. Ken and Tom wondered how the fathers found time to do it.

"That boat was just a kick: It flew across the lake," Tom said.

One time, it flew out of control.

While in junior high, Tom and his friend Paul Hatch took the iceboat out.

"We got halfway across the lake in front of our house and the wind came up. Some of the slats from the sail blew out, so we turned the boat into the wind," Tom recalled.

Paul crawled out over the runner on the windward side to try to hold the boat down and keep it from tipping, but neither of them was heavy enough to hold it down against the fierce wind. Tom tried to walk back across the lake to get the detached slats. "I couldn't stand up on the ice. The wind was blowing me across the lake." He went down on his hands and knees to crawl back to the iceboat.

Adults on shore had seen the boat tip over. When Tom fell to his hands and knees, they thought he had fallen through the ice. They called the emergency squad and the minister. The minister feared Tom had drowned. He knocked on the front door to find that Elinor was completely unaware of the problem. The minister tried to console Elinor.

Unaware of the scene at the house, the freezing, panic-stricken youths desperately fought to rescue the boat and themselves.

"We finally got it back and parked, and we got the sail down and put away. It took us about 30 minutes," Tom recalled. They didn't know anyone noticed, so they prepared to tell their thrilling story. Meanwhile, the emergency squad had seen that the trouble had ended and returned to the station.

"I came inside the house and Mom sees me and starts screaming. She's so relieved, but she's so emotional about what I've just put her through." When the minister arrived at the front door, Elinor had thought Tom had drowned in the icy water.

As much as Berkley inherited the determination and focus of his mother, Virginia, Elinor reflected the loving care of her mother, known to the family as Gram Healy.

"My Gram was just sweet and loving and warm," said Joanne. "I don't know if many people are lucky enough to have the bond I had with my Gram Healy. When you were with her, you were her total focus."

Elinor's older sister, Fran, a brilliant student who went to college at age 16, married Arthur Naftalin, who became the mayor of Minneapolis. Arthur, a liberal Democrat, was a good friend of Hubert Humphrey and at one time served as Humphrey's Secretary. "Dad and Art didn't talk about politics," said Joanne. "Dad was just a business-man and a registered Republican." A trip to Minneapolis "seemed like kind of a culture shock because things were so different there," recalled Joanne. She depended on her spe-cial cousin Gail to show her around. "She exposed me to the reality of living in a city and going to a huge high school."

Elinor seemed so emotionally steady that her chil-dren were shocked to ever see her upset. Ken remembered a time when Berkley came home ready to leave for a family camping trip. Elinor had been packing the gear and meticu-lously measuring and individually packing each of the well-planned ingredients of the week's meals, wondering when he would be home to help. When he became impatient to leave, Ken said, it was one of the few times that he recalled his mother being openly upset with his father.

"I cannot remember any other time I saw her express her frustration with him."

Berkley and Elinor placed high value on their vacation time as time to get to know each other and get to know the world outside of Spirit Lake. In 1962, the thrifty Bedells went to Europe with Elinor's mother on $5 a day. They rented a car and drove through England, France, Denmark, Germany, and Switzerland. Berkley made business calls each day.

"We stayed at little low-cost hotels and bed-and-breakfast homes. One of my great memories is climbing to the very top of a small mountain in Switzerland with our three children and having a picnic on a little eight-foot square piece of land on top of the mountain," Berkley reminisced.

"The boys had butch haircuts, and in Europe all the boys had long hair, so everyone kept coming up and rub-bing Tom's head," said Joanne. "He hated it."

Elinor spent her summers as a girl in the little town of Grand Marais, Minnesota, on the north shore of Lake Supe-rior. Berkley's family had often gone on fishing trips in Minne-sota. So when Berkley and Elinor's children were young, fam-ily vacations almost always centered on family visits to Gram Healy's home in Grand Marais, or on canoeing and fishing trips in the wilderness along the Minnesota-Canada border.

They packed all their own gear and food. They would drive as far as they could with a little car top boat or canoe, then unload the gear and the boat or canoe, and paddle back into the wilderness to set up camp. As soon as each child became five years of age, they were allowed to come along. They would trudge along the portages, each carrying part of the gear. They slept in tents and cooked over open fires.

One time, they arrived deep in the wilderness to find Berkley had left his fishing tackle kit, containing all of the lures, back in the car. As disappointing as it appeared, they were soon glad they had a fishing tackle manufacturer with them.

Berkley found a fishing fly in his jacket pocket, found a tin can, and made a spinner from it. He cut a weight from a minnow net they had with them.

They had fish for breakfast.

One Labor Day weekend, Berkley rented a tent that was set up on a wilderness lake near Ely, Minnesota. The lake could only be reached by boat. The outfitters led them to their campsite, but it had been ripped apart by bears. It had been a very dry year and bears were hungry. The next campsite, however, turned out to be in fine shape. The outfitters provided food and left them a boat. The kids called it "Camp Hilton," because it was a two-room tent with a wooden floor. A curtain separated the cot-filled sleeping section from the front kitchen. The only exit from the sleeping area was through the curtain and out the kitchen. The kitchen had a table and a propane-stove on a cabinet. They might have become too comfortable too quickly because they didn't put away all the food that night.

In the middle of the night, Elinor shook Berkley awake and whispered, "Berk, there is a bear." As he climbed out of bed, they heard a crash in the kitchen section of the tent. The cabinet and stove were toppled.

"Dad, save us!" the children screamed.

He opened the curtain and a huge black bear stared him right in the face.

Berkley mustered all his courage, but he was so scared that his voice was two octaves higher than normal.

"Shoo, bear! Get out of here!" he shrieked in boy-soprano fear. "Shoo! Shoo!"

The children howled in laughter, through their own helpless fear. "That's really going to scare him off," they giggled. The bear just stood there. If he had come past Berkley into the bedroom, they would have had to climb over cots and past the beast to the only exit through the kitchen. The frightened bear, however, turned and slowly lumbered off through the woods. It was then that the campers discovered they were on a peninsula. The bear would have to return by the same route past their campsite. How soon would that be? They hustled to put away all the food they could repackage. They put the destroyed containers in the campfire area. An hour later, the bear returned and salvaged the leftovers they had discarded near the campfire, then moved on.

"Our tent had been destroyed," Joanne recalled. "We were lucky that nothing worse happened."

The children became Boy Scouts and Girl Scouts, although Joanne preferred family camping experiences to Girl Scout camps.

"Mom and I were totally inseparable," Joanne said. "I was pretty clingy, I think."

As shy as she was in public, Elinor felt comfortable working with the Girl Scouts. It was a place where she could provide meaningful leadership. She helped with Cub Scouts and then focused her attention on Brownies and Girl Scouts. Even after Joanne completed First Class, the Girl Scout equivalent of the boys' Eagle Scout, Elinor continued to provide leadership in the Girl Scouts.

The boys both became Eagle Scouts, diligent about earning merit badges and enjoying the camping trips. Berkley became an assistant Scoutmaster.

Each summer, the Boy Scouts would go on a camping canoe trip in the wilderness boundary waters of northern Minnesota or southern Canada, to have fun portaging, camping, catching fish, and cooking over open fires.

"That was my first memory of being with dads where they acted like kids," said Tom. "The dads wouldn't shave and they'd play games with us. The Boy Scout trips to Minnesota were the first time I remember feeling a one-ness or friendship with the dads, instead of just a parent-child deal. I remember Boy Scouts as a lot of fun."

The Bedells liked to go on similar trips with other Spirit Lake families. They would leave Spirit Lake at 4:00 p.m. on Friday, as soon as Berk was through work, and get to Ely, Minnesota about 1:00 a.m. Saturday. After a short night in a hotel, they would be paddling and portaging into the wilderness. After camping Saturday, Sunday, and Monday they would drive back to Spirit Lake Monday night, so Berk could be back at work Tuesday morning. One summer Berkley went on seven such camping and canoe trips.

Ken and Tom fished with Walt and Virginia in Yellowstone National Park. They made it a tradition to take their grandchildren, two at a time, at age 12 to 14, for such a fishing trip.

"We stayed in cabins and we'd hike a mile to the Yellowstone River," Ken said. "We'd wade into Yellowstone River, which must have been 30 or 40 degrees, and fish for cutthroat trout. Grandpa would clean them, we'd take them up to the Fishing Bridge Cafeteria and they would cook them for us. They were in their 60s at the time. It was a pretty serious pursuit." When it became Joanne's turn, Walt had become deathly ill. He died in 1963.

"After Grandpa was gone," Joanne said. "Grandma and I would go fishing in Spirit Lake. She wasn't a young woman then, in her 60s, but she would get the motorboat going."

"Grandma Bedell was incredible," said Joanne. "She'd make dozens and dozens of cookies of all different kinds and give them to us. She seemed to always be busy. She spoke her mind. I used to love the conversations that went on, but I'd never want to have to participate, because I didn't want to try to keep up with her. She was good, really good. She could win any argument. But she really helped me. I got pretty good at being able to be in situations like

The family airplane

that, think on my feet, and deal with an argument. I sat back and I learned a lot from just watching Grandma operate."

The family continued to go on wilderness fishing vacations, although as time went on they graduated to fly-in trips where there were cabins and motorboats.

Berkley's pilot's license came in handy.

In 1960, Berkley purchased a used, single-engine Piper Comanche 250 airplane for $12,400. It held four people and flew 180 miles per hour. He used it for business to fly to Des Moines, Minneapolis, or Chicago.

"We could crowd the family into it. It proved to be a wonderful addition to our lives."

When the children became old enough, the family also used the airplane to fly to Colorado or northern Wisconsin to ski in the winter.

"I will never forget the great thrill of arriving at the top of a mountain for the first time with my children on skis. Nor the thrill of again finding myself at the top of the mountain ski slopes with my grandchildren when I was 70 years old," said Berk.

When he tried to go down the back side of the mountain on an expert trail at Vail, Colorado, Berk tumbled down the mountain. At the bottom, Tom told him, "You'd make a great ski clown, Dad."

"I did not need that kind of encouragement," Berkley reflected.

Family Values

Confidence and humility were both highly valued and emphasized in the family.

"We were all coming out of the motel room," Ken recalled. "We said, 'How do we get to the restaurant?' My mother says, 'Oh, I know, it's this way,' and she takes us down a hall. We go out a door and we're out on a roof. I don't know who said, 'Oh, Magoo, you've done it again,' but from that moment on we have fondly referred to Mom as Magoo – after the famous near-sighted cartoon character. She has continued to entertain us with Magoo-isms of various sorts."

The children knew their parents made human mistakes, but respected them as morally consistent.

"Dad always supported us and lived by example," said Tom. "You just didn't break the rules. He was fair and strong in his example, and in his guidance and in his expectations."

He remembers that lesson vividly, from a vacation episode as a nine-year-old.

"Oh, Jesus, what's going on?" Tom said.

"You're swearing," his Father reprimanded him.

"No, I'm not."

"Yes, you are. You're taking the name of Jesus in vain. If you ever say that again, I'm going to spank you."

"Oh, Jesus, what's going on?" Tom baited his father.

Berkley waited until they arrived at the motel that night. He came in, reminded Tom of the warning and consequences, and then spanked him. Tom cried like crazy until his father left the room. He heard his father return to his own room and tell Elinor how terrible he felt about it. "I felt like I had to spank him after I said I would, but did I do the right thing, Elinor?" He decided to go back and make sure Tom had not been hurt.

Tom had already moved into his "too-tough-to-admit-I'm-hurt" image. He joked about it with his roommate, brother Ken. He licked the tip of his finger and touched it to his backside. "Sssssssssss," Tom mimicked steam. They laughed hysterically – as Berkley arrived at the door.

"Then he really became mad," Tom recalled. He doesn't remember what his father did next. Rather, Tom remembers how terrible he felt that he had mocked his father. "I deserved it. I respect him for showing how much he cared, and how much he loved, and how much he worried about it."

"He is true to himself. You have to admire him and you have to say, 'Wow. This guy is totally real to what he says and what he does.' He's a human being; I'm sure there are places he's been contradicted, but I can't tell you any of them. He didn't tell you not to swear and then swear. I never ever heard him swear. He didn't tell you not to drink and then drink. He simply didn't drink."

When they returned after World War II, Berkley and Elinor joined the Spirit Lake Methodist Church and have been faithful members ever since. At that time, the church became the place where they could meet other young couples, as they were all building their new lives.

"Church became more than just a place to worship. It became a real family for us," Berkley said.

It was the place where their pre-school children came to know each other; where they cared for each other. As he saw the need for his children to learn a faith, Berkley chaired a fund drive to build an education wing for the church.

Berkley came to see the church as the teacher and constant reminder of the values that had ultimate meaning. He considered it his responsibility to serve faithfully in the church and to live faithfully in the world.

"Sunday was church," said Joanne. "We went every Sunday and we always went to Sunday school. Mom and Dad were active in the church and prayer was an important part of our lives; always a prayer before dinner." It went beyond that, however.

"I'd see Dad make decisions as a result of what God would want him to do, and to live as Jesus would want us to live," Joanne said. "It's a common phrase that he says all the time. I know that it plays a huge part in his decision-making. I didn't feel as though we talked a whole lot about faith, but my parents lived it. In my family it was just a part of your being; that you would be a good person and that you would try to do things for others."

"I'm not sure how good a Christian I am," Berkley said. "I'm not sure how much I really believe that I'm going to heaven. I do not much care whether or not Christ was born of a virgin, or that he was the only Son of God. To me what matters are His teachings.

"I mainly believe that we urgently need proper values as individuals. My Christian religion gives me my values, interpreted from what Christ had to say. 'It's harder to be wealthy and enter the kingdom of God than for a camel to get through the eye of the needle.' What he really said is that wealth isn't worth a darn to anybody. You should care for each other. If somebody steals from you, you ought to give them something more.

"I interpret what is in the New Testament as a message of how people should live. I have a problem with the competitiveness of religions. I have a problem with any religion that says, 'Our religion is the only true religion and only if you believe as we tell you to, will you be rewarded by going to heaven.' I have a particular problem when anyone is taught to believe that they will be rewarded by going to a paradise for killing non-believers, as is true today of some of the Extremist Muslims, and was true of some Christians in previous times. When we sing in church, 'Trust and obey for there is no other way,' I want to sing 'To question and pray is the other way.'

"For ages, the religious institutions have been the guardians of the values of societies. I have tried to model my life after the teachings of Jesus, just as I have modeled my life after the examples of some of my teachers and friends.

"My problem comes from the fact that so often different religions focus on their differences rather than their agreements. Both Muslims and Christians believe in 'One God Almighty.' Both believe that Mohammed and Christ were great prophets. For us to fight wars and kill millions in disputes over which of the two prophets was holy seems to me to be the height of folly. Both the Bible and the Koran contain passages urging love and caring, as well as containing passages on war and violence. The world can take from each whatever it wants. When we worship Christ instead of God, we make our religion exclusive, rather than inclusive, and such belief has brought on war after war and devastation after devastation. One of the clearest examples of fighting over details is the fighting between Catholics and Protestants in Ireland.

"I had thought that the world was moving toward religious inclusiveness until the World Trade disaster where some extremist Muslims martyred themselves, thinking they would be rewarded in paradise for killing thousands of New Yorkers. I hope we will not let this action cause major conflict between the people of these two major religions.

"The Roman Catholic Church officially embraces an inclusive theology. An official document under Pope Paul VI in 1965 said this about Muslims, 'The Church also has high regard for Muslims. They worship God who is One, living and subsistent, merciful and mighty.'

"Make no mistake, my Christian religion has been extremely important to me. I have tried to live by the teachings of Christ. For us to go to church on Sunday, and be reminded of these values, is an important part of our lives.

"Prayer is important to me. I believe there are things that we do not understand about religion and spiritualism. It has been documented that praying for people, even when those people are not aware that prayers are being offered for them, has an effect. I have friends who went to a class and learned to be able to see auras on people, just as the halo is shown on pictures of Christ. The National Foundation for Alternative Medicine, that Elinor and I founded, has reports of people who have brought about healing by simply using their hands without touching the person, just as Christ is reported to have brought about healing without the use of medications. I know of people who are completely sane and sincere who claim to have communicated with deceased spouses or friends.

"I believe religion and the values it preaches are important and I pray that the religions of the world might again move toward inclusiveness and away from strife and violence.

"As I dig deeper into medicine and how our bodies work, I believe that there are some spiritual things that we do not understand. I believe faith is an important need. My concern comes when the leaders of any religion try to turn that faith to undesirable ends."

As the family's income and influence in the community rose, Berkley and Elinor's children saw no difference in their parents' expectations of them or themselves. They didn't give lavish parties with expensive caterers.

"They'd have all the salesmen come into town and Mom would host a big dinner at our house," said Joanne. "Mom would cook. The table stretched from one end of the dining room across the living room."

More important than expensive restaurants were times spent together hunting wild asparagus along the roadways, frog catching expeditions, or Sunday picnics.

Berkley's grandmother and mother taught: "Nobody's any better than you, but you're no better than anyone else."

The children had little idea that the fishing business had been making them one of the more wealthy families in town.

"One rule my folks had was that you fit in," said Tom. "You don't show off. You don't spend money. My dad drove these old crappy cars until they were going to die. He didn't 'keep up with the Joneses.' He 'stayed behind the Joneses.' He felt it important to not be showy in any way. You just don't stand out. I grew up not realizing that he'd accomplished the business and financial success that he had achieved. I didn't feel any different than anybody else ... ever. I'm sure I had things that other kids didn't have, but I don't remember feeling like that.

"They never influenced whom we associated with. They never picked friends by status or money or religion. Whenever businesspeople came to town and came to dinner, it became a fun celebration, but we did not act any different than when they were not there. Pomp and circumstance did not exist."

They were even one of the last families in town to get a television set, in 1960 – a decision that had more to do with philosophy than frugality: Berkley thought it better to live life than to watch it. He continues to think that children would be better off exploring life and relating to people, rather than entertaining themselves by watching people on television.

Frugality and humility were virtues.

"Mom made all my clothes," Joanne said. "Dad drove cars that hardly worked. I never considered myself any better off than anybody else. I never thought that people considered me one of the rich kids. When we went on vacation, we went camping. We never went without, but we never went with extra. Excess never occurred."

Car dealer Bob Boettcher recalls Berkley driving an old Plymouth Valiant, with cardboard to cover a hole in the floor. He sold Berkley a new station wagon.

"They put gray shutters on our house, because they believed gray shutters would make it look less ostentatious, would make a house look smaller," Ken said. "Both my parents, but particularly my mother, were very concerned about fitting in and not standing out. We had no yacht and we didn't join the yacht club. Mom and Dad would talk about figuring out about whether Dad should give Mom more money for groceries. They'd stew about whether they should buy a new car and whether they could afford this one. As far as I knew, we were no different from anyone else."

Berkley and Elinor were providing a normal Spirit Lake experience for raising their family.

They both felt comfortable with the fact that they could travel and go as a family to Mexico and Europe and other places.

They encouraged the children to work. Tom, a born salesman, tried to re-sell his parents' used office paper. He also started a guitar business while in high school. Joanne worked as a waitress and pumped gasoline at a local service station.

Ken had a paper route, just as his father had. As a newspaper carrier, Ken not only learned how to operate a business, but he also learned about the world. While delivering newspapers as a 13-year-old, he learned a secret about his humble parents.

"I delivered the *Des Moines Register*. It was five in the morning and I usually read the newspaper as I walked my route. I saw an ad for debentures that Berkley and Company had put on the market – one of those public notices they had to do – to raise money for the business."

"It said 'Berkley and Company in Spirit Lake, Iowa; debenture offer; net value of the company, $3,000,000; current debt of the company, $1.8 million dollars.'"

"I subtracted those and I thought, 'my gosh, my dad's a millionaire.' Reading that newspaper made me realize for the first time that Dad was wealthy. I didn't know it otherwise."

Chapter Fourteen

Growing
in the Community
and the Nation

An eager young man walked into the plant and looked around for someone, anyone. He saw grease-stained pants and workboots extending from behind the machinery.

"Sorry to interrupt, but am I in the right place?"

"Well, this is a pretty good place," the mechanic answered. "What place are you looking for?"

"They tell me that Berkley and Company is really growing," he replied. "I just can't support a family on the job I have now. I guess I shouldn't have come on a Saturday, but I was hoping to find out when I could make an appointment with the personnel manager."

"Well, if you can give me a minute to finish with this, we can talk about it some more." The mechanic applied another twist with his wrench. He came out from behind the machine, wiped his hand off with a rag, and offered it to the stranger. "My name is Berkley Bedell."

While trying not to seem too big for his greasy britches, Berkley had steadily worked his way into the public consciousness in the 1950s. He expanded production all over town and expanded sales all over the country.

By the time his son Ken had read about the company in the newspaper, people in Spirit Lake and surrounding communities realized that the company had become a major player in the fishing tackle business. In 1958, when Berk publicly advertised that he needed the community's help to take the next big step, local folks started to get an idea of how big Berkley and Company had become.

The company had expanded throughout the community with each innovation:

• To produce Steelon leaders, Berkley bought the abandoned city building in 1949. The success of Steelon and tapered leaders meant he had to keep renting more space for production and distribution.

• Berkley decided to build his own, two-story production plant in the middle of town in 1952.

• In 1953, when he decided to test the growing market for nylon ski rope, Berkley expanded into a large two-story cement block building that had been used during World War II to dry eggs for the military. He renamed it the Industrial Wire Building.

He started selling snelled hooks, saltwater rigs, Triple X fishing line, Dew Flex line, and Seastrand wire.

Bit by bit, Berkley expanded into 11 buildings in Spirit Lake by 1958. The fishing line business had grown so fast, he knew he would have to expand even more. It became a logistical problem to keep up with production and distribution in so many places, not to mention an efficiency problem.

He needed to bring it all under one roof, but he didn't think he had enough money to build a major manufacturing center. He didn't want to borrow that much money, so how could he finance such a project? How could he attract investors without giving up control?

A development consultant came up with the answer, the one Ken read about in the paper that day. Berkley could ask the public to invest in debenture bonds. Anyone could buy a bond that would provide capital for the company. The bonds would provide a return for the investor, out of company profits.

Berkley could go public without giving up control.

Increasingly, Berkley became a public figure, sometimes a controversial one. Community service became important to him. Being a leader in Boy Scouts, Kiwanis Club, and the Methodist Church had been one thing, but the school board became his first taste of what it meant to be an elected official who takes an unpopular stand.

In 1957, he and some other young parents in the community decided to deal with problems in the schools. Berkley and three others were elected to the five-member school board. Berkley was the oldest, at age 36. When they thought the superintendent refused to work with them to correct some problems in the school, they were prepared to fire him. It became messy.

The local newspaper and a significant segment of Spirit Lake's high society backed the superintendent. Some people tried to intimidate the four young board members, particularly Berkley, viewed as the leader.

"When my wife took our children to school, they saw me hanging in effigy in the school house yard. One night, while the four of us were meeting, Elinor called in panic. Someone had thrown a rock through our bedroom window. Fortunately, it did not hurt anyone." Whether it was a deliberate act by the opposition, or the act of an opportunistic vandal (as JackBedell believed), the board steeled itself for conflict.

"We stood our ground. I will always remember it as one of the most traumatic times of my life, but the problems were solved." The superintendent resigned. Berkley and the three young board members were easily re-elected at a later date.

"It introduced me to, and prepared me for, the problems of a political career," Berkley said. "I had learned the power of the press. I also learned, that if you have the people on your side in politics, you need not worry that the upper crust is not with you. And no matter how difficult the road, do not let the difficulties stop you from doing what you believe is right. It would have been easier to decide to have nothing more to do with public life.

"One of my greatest blessings in my later years has been that the superintendent whom we replaced became a good friend. He certainly had every right to hate me for the rest of his life. I believe the fact that he forgave and forgot was beneficial to both of us."

Berkley and Elinor tried to keep the controversy from frightening their children.

"I remember getting up one morning and going into my parents' bedroom and they'd moved the bed," Ken recalled. "Before, it had the head to the west, but they had turned the bed around so the head was at the south of the room. No one told me why it had been moved.

"Later in the day, I learned from some friends that some people had thrown a rock with a threatening note on it through the bedroom window. They just cleaned up the glass and rearranged the bedroom while I was sleeping." The two younger children said they didn't learn about the controversy until they were adults.

A new building, a new era

So Berkley and the business were well known by the time he asked people in the community to help finance a new building to house the entire corporate operations under one roof.

The approach was two-fold:
• To sell debenture bonds, and
• To apply for a federal Small Business Administration loan.

People in the community stepped forth to buy "Berkley Bonds."

"I would suspect that Berkley had 100 percent backing of the community," said Blaine Hoien, a realtor. "This is not a wealthy community, so there weren't a lot of people who could say, 'Here's $100,000.' People bought $100 bonds. That's one of the great things about it. Berkley has always been positive for the community and the community has always been positive for Berkley. Pretty nice way to have it."

The bond offering gave Rachel McQuirk Carpenter a chance to help out her first boss. Berkley had given her that first real job. Now that she had a successful interior design shop, she wanted to help.

"I know that we bought a $100 bond," she said. "Everybody wanted to help, because they looked at it as a community project. The community liked the whole family."

If Berkley were seen as a rich, exploitative industrialist, plainspoken Iowans would have spoken plainly with their silence. People invested in their good faith in Berkley Bedell's integrity and commitment to the community.

"Industry can sometimes build a negative attitude in the community, but not with Berkley. No matter whom you talked to, you'd find very positive feelings toward Berkley and Company. They've been a good steward in the community in every way," continued Rachel Carpenter.

"The community wanted to support a company and a leader they trusted and admired," said Jack Bedell. "Berk's a likable guy. I had a number of clients who invested in those bonds. One of them told me he was not only pleased with the return on the bonds, but also tickled to death that he could have a part in helping the company grow. And that feeling generally prevailed across the community. They made good money on them and helped a company improve the situation of Spirit Lake. They had a part in helping."

Berkley built the company through hard work, a desire to provide a good life for employees, and a sense of fun.

To build the new headquarters and manufacturing center, Berkley wanted enough land to allow for expansion. Blaine Hoien helped him explore land near Big Spirit Lake and also near Arnolds Park. But he settled on farmland that was just west of the town of Spirit lake, property owned by horse trader Mott Miller, from whom the Hoiens and Bedells had already purchased farm land on East Okoboji.

With the money from the debenture bonds purchased by the community and a loan from the Small Business Administration, Berkley and Company went to work on building new headquarters along the highway just west of town.

"For me, it made the difference of whether I stayed here and lived and raised my family," said Hoien. "The fact is, that in the late 1950s and 1960s, several communities probably tried to get Berkley to move to their town.

"This is a beautiful community in which to live and work, but the economics in this area had not been promising. The area has never been a heavy farm community. Everything in Iowa has always been based on the farm community.

"Before Berkley and Company, Spirit Lake had been a resort community. Fellows would put in docks and their wives would clean the cottages. That's subsistence, that isn't making money. For three or four months of the year, the town was a busy place – and at the end of that, hardly anything. When autumn came, it all ended. The town did not have many good jobs – especially jobs with salaries enough to raise and provide for a family. Berkley and Company provided good jobs for the people."

Company employees did much of the construction work on the new 64,000-square-foot building, so construction costs were less than $5 per square foot – about $300,000 total.

When the time came to open the plant in 1961, the company invited the whole community.

Berkley gave tours, showed slides of the company's 20-year history, set up displays of all the company's products, and served food. He hired a band and set aside a big area for dancing.

Employees presented him with a pair of gold-painted roller skates, so that he could roam the new building.

When Berkley and Company built its plant west of town it became recognized as *the* industry of Spirit Lake.

Some in the community said the new building signaled a new era for the company and lighted a large sign for the future of the community.

"The plant fit the community perfectly," said Jack Bedell. It was a successful employer of a number of people, a clean industry without bad side effects. It fit in well with the resort community of Spirit Lake. It employed many women, providing a second income for many families in town, so they could buy Mercurys instead of Fords or Oldsmobiles instead of Chevys. Each family had more income and it raised the standard of living for the entire area.

"Every farmer from miles around came to that open house," recalled Richard Moulton, a sales representative for

Berkley. Moulton had worked with Berkley for ten years, since the early days of $1.49 commission checks, when he wondered if the guy with the great ideas would ever make it. When he saw the new plant and the town's response, he thought, "We've struck a gold mine."

The affection of the community for Berkley impressed Elinor.

"It seemed wonderful to have all these people come and be interested in it," she said. "They wouldn't have come unless they considered it an important thing in town. But we kept a rather low profile. People came from communities all around to work there. We were right on the Minnesota border and people came from Minnesota, and close by towns all around. I think they all appreciated the fact that it made jobs available."

Neither Berkley nor his right-hand man Ed Donovan saw the opening of the new plant as any signal that the company had arrived. They considered it just another step in the growth of the company, one that helped the company to operate better.

"I think we just feel good if we're honored and recognized for our work," Berkley reflected. "I've had more than my share of that sort of thing. But I revel in it. Maybe that's why I'm a politician."

The new building gave Berkley room to work and play.

"We've added at least three times to the original building now, and we have a warehouse that used to be a tennis court," said Berkley.

"We built an indoor tennis court in 1967. There weren't any indoor tennis courts in our area of northwest Iowa when we built it. We put a box by the door and people would put quarters in a slot to pay for the heat and light. We finally set it up so that people would have to sign up at the plant, and we'd give them a key. There are other indoor tennis courts now, so it's used as a warehouse."

The success of Trilene, and the increased production capability, launched Berkley and Company into a new era.

Berkley receives Small Businessman of the Year award from President Lyndon Johnson, flanked by Elinor, Joanne, Tom, and Ken.

Company sales increased from $1.4 million in 1958 to $4.1 million in 1964. Net earnings increased from $103,000 to $378,000 during the same six-year period.

The federal Small Business Administration (SBA) paid attention to Berkley's growth during the next few years. The SBA wanted to measure the impact of its loans to small businesses and sought to recognize outstanding small companies. The SBA established the Small Businessman of the Year award in 1964.

Iowa's SBA office nominated Berkley Bedell, so the national office of SBA invited him to come to Washington, D.C. as one of the finalists. He and the family boarded their little airplane for Chicago, where they caught a commercial plane to Washington.

"They hadn't yet decided who they were going to select," said Berkley, "but I was the only person they had invited to Washington. They couldn't do it until they had their board meeting, or something, to formally select me."

With a big battery of reporters and photographers, Berkley proudly received the 1964 Small Businessman of the Year award from President Lyndon Baines Johnson, on a platform in the Rose Garden of the White House. Elinor, Joanne, Tom, and Ken stood right behind him.

Welcomed at home in Spirit Lake.

"A newspaper person called to do an interview. He asked me how I figured out what to wear," said Joanne, who was 12 at the time. "I told him I only had two dresses and only one was clean. What an exciting time, getting to meet President Johnson." She was surprised to see President Johnson, 6-feet-4-inches tall, towering over their family. "What an honor that Dad had been chosen out of all the people in the country."

A bigger surprise awaited them back home. They flew back to Chicago and then boarded their own plane to fly to Estherville, Iowa where they kept the plane at the community airport, about 15 miles east of Spirit Lake.

As the plane circled to land, Berkley could faintly see movement on the ground, in the twilight of dusk. He was not accustomed to seeing crowds of people at the Estherville airport.

"What do you suppose is happening there, Elinor?"

As he landed and taxied toward the hangar, the children started yelling from the back of the plane.

"There's the high school band!"

"There's the mayor!"

"There's Uncle Jack!"

"There's Grandma. Hold on, Dad! She's running toward the plane!"

Jack tried to restrain Virginia, but she could not be denied.

"Mother ran out to greet the plane and the engine had not yet been shut off. I was concerned that she was going to run right into the prop," Jack remembered.

Walt Bedell did not get to see the celebration. He died the year before, but he lived to see Berkley and Company succeed in making products for the sport he loved.

"It was kind of overwhelming," Joanne recalled. When Elinor came down the steps and saw the crowd cheering and the light bulbs flashing, she disappeared from view.

"Elinor? Where's Elinor?" Berkley looked all around. Finally, she emerged from her hiding place: behind the wing of the plane.

"I want you to be in these pictures with me, honey."

The spontaneous celebration warmed their hearts.

"It had been one thing to be in Washington, but it was quite another to come home and see all these people who were so kind to come out and meet us," said Joanne.

The crowd rode back to Spirit Lake in a caravan of car horns and band music.

The award brought Berkley and Company even more into the spotlight locally and nationally.

Berkley even appeared as a mystery contestant on the television game show "To Tell the Truth" in 1965.

But more meaningful to Berkley, the community held a surprise party to celebrate his being named Small Businessman of the Year. He had become a national figure, but continued to be a child of the lakes.

At the party, Berk's old friend, attorney Peter Narey, served as the master of ceremonies. Narey recounted some of Berkley's personal and business history.

"Washington merely confirmed what we knew," Narey said.

"It is interesting to know that there are approximately 146,000 small business concerns in the United States. There are two things we know this selection was <u>not</u>:

"1. It was <u>not</u> because of your politics (Berkley, a solid Republican from a staunch Republican family, was honored by Democrat Lyndon Johnson).

"2. It was <u>not</u> a mistake.

"I wrote a theme back in college 25 years ago," Narey said. "I don't know whether you ever knew it or not, but you were the topic of the theme. It ended something like this:

"Give me the heart of a Berkley Bedell, Life;

"Don't let me cower and die;

"Let me grin without flinching when failure is looking me smack in the eye;

" Whatever my part in the picture, whatever my part in the plan,

"Let me, like Berk Bedell, step forward bringing the heart of a man."

Chapter Fifteen

Company Growing Pains, Growing Values

By age 19, Berkley surpassed his first mentor in the business, a great fisherman who let his bait shop rot out from underneath him.

By age 28, he figured out how to become number one in fishing leaders. No big deal, according to Berkley. "So you're number one in something that the total gross sales were, what, about $2 million? It isn't the same as being big in computers or something."

By age 37, he tackled DuPont in the larger market of fishing line. With Trilene, he proved he could play with the big boys in the fishing industry.

Could he be one of them? What would it take?

Berk no longer had a small, family operation – because of the astonishing success of Trilene fishing line – but he didn't know how to manage such a big business.

"I realized that I had a sizeable fishing tackle manufacturing business on my hands, and that everything I knew about management I had learned from my newspaper route. That's not a bad teacher, as far as management is concerned: You have to satisfy your customers, collect your bills, pay your bills, and do everything that is important in any other business."

As a fisherman and executive, Berk took a Golden Rule approach: Treat others as you would like to be treated and offer customers what you would like to have.

"Businesses fail when people look narrow-mindedly at a goal of profit making and do not look hard enough at how to get there. The way you ensure profits is by treating your customers and potential customers well and by providing better services or products."

But the business had, indeed, grown and Berkley knew he would have to grow as a manager in order to lead it.

So he went off to a Management Course for Presidents held by the American Management Association in Hamilton, New York. There were 18 presidents in the class. Besides Berkley, there were two others from the Midwest: the President of General Mills and the President of Minneapolis Honeywell. The average annual sales of the group amounted to more than $100 million per company.

"It would have been higher if I had not been there to bring down the average," Berkley realized. His company had sales of about $2 million per year at the time. "I decided if leaders of such companies considered it important to take time from their busy life to study management, then I had better listen too.

"Thank God I did, because it started to change my life."

Berkley learned that the first thing a president needed to do was to determine what he wanted to accomplish with the operation and to write it down.

"They pointed out that one's goal can't be just to make a profit, because profits are of no value unless they serve a particular purpose."

He wrestled with company goals for nearly a year. As the only investor, self-serving goals of providing a financial reward for investors did not motivate him. He owned the company. He could sell the business and retire comfortably at age 40 if financial reward was the goal.

"If Berkley and Company existed to simply make more money for me, it seemed a rather worthless goal. I had no real need for more money."

Berkley determined that the primary goal of his fishing tackle business should be:

"To contribute toward a better life for our employees and their families."

"This primary objective gave me something very worthwhile to strive for," said Berkley. "I went to work with a renewed sense of purpose."

The management course also taught Berkley that he had to follow certain steps to develop a strategy for attaining the agreed goals and objectives, based on the company's strengths, the market, and the competition.

What kind of manager looks at employees' lives as more important than company profits? Berkley thought that belief to be an effective management policy, a personal core value and a community responsibility. Profit became important, for the sake of the employees.

"If the company goes broke, that's not very good for the employees. The more profitable you are, the more you can do for your people."

Berkley had a long history of trying to work for the betterment of employees, so the goal (besides being heartfelt) rang true with the workers.

He also tried several ways to provide services that employees might not be able to afford on their own.

He offered free health care.

"I decided we should hire a full-time doctor, and set up a clinic in the plant where this doctor would take care of the needs of all of our employees and their families, without charge. So we brought it up with our employees for a vote, which we always did … and they didn't want it! It shocked me. But they knew their own doctor and they didn't want another doctor to come in and take care of their needs. Of course medical care did not cost so much back in those days."

In the mid-1960s, long-distance calls were fairly expensive. Berkley let employees sign up for 15-30 minutes of use of the plant's WATTS line on the weekends, so employees could call their families, or whomever, for free.

Helping to make life better for employees is part of a larger value.

"I never put a particularly high value on wealth. My son, Ken, puts an even lower value on wealth than I do. He and I have both been smart enough to recognize that wealth does not necessarily bring happiness. Among those with whom we associate, I cannot see that those who have more wealth are happier than those who have less wealth. Our society tries to sell people on how important it is for people to have wealth. I think that's too bad. Sure as heck Christ didn't say that, did he?"

Berkley set other goals and objectives too, such as furnishing better equipment for fishermen and taking good care of customers. Berkley and Company always tried to provide improved equipment: stronger, tangle-free leaders and fishing lines.

"When I started, my success depended upon making items for less money than competitors," said Berkley. "But with the development of Steelon leaders and Trilene line, that evolved to the point that we were not necessarily making things that were less expensive, but were making things that performed better than other products."

As time went on, Berkley and Company devoted increasing resources to research. The company hired chemists and biologists, retained professional fishermen to do field testing, and encouraged employees to report on their personal experiences with the products.

The company could always count on its founder to test its equipment. Berkley fished every chance he had. He would sometimes leave the office in the afternoon, carrying a small paper sack of tackle for research.

Eventually, the company installed test tanks in the plant. The company now keeps 60 varieties of fish at the plant in order to test lines, lures, and baits under different circumstances of light, temperature, and depth. A casting tank has a window with measurements, to enable researchers and customers to observe and measure the movement and depth of a lure or bait.

"Nobody else has anything like that," Berkley said.

"The research that Berkley and Company does on fishing tackle is much more than the rest of the industry combined," Berkley said. "There is no comparison.

"The success of Berkley and Company is that we produce better fishing tackle that we can sell for a high profit margin."

The nature of people who fish, the company's workers, and wise management made it possible for Berkley to invest in innovation and still make a profit (before taxes) of 10-21 percent through the 1950s, then four to nine percent during the 1960s.

"People who fish don't care about the price for terminal tackle that costs less than $10. They only care if it works better. After World War II, a braided fishing line company colored its line two different colors and sold it at different prices. The higher priced one sold substantially more than the lower-priced line of a different color, even though it was the same item, same manufacturing cost."

"So if you make something that works better than anybody else's, and you can sell it for $9, you can sell it for $9 no matter how low the production costs or how low-priced the competition."

Berkley admits to setting one goal that he later called crazy: To be one of the top three fishing tackle companies."

"I don't know why I did that, it was stupid. What matters is not how large you are. What matters is what you do with an operation and the example you set for others."

But the company was continuing to grow.

Three more additions to the facility expanded the production plant to 160,000-square feet, making the building two-and-a-half times its original size by 1965.

To attain Berkley's goal to be one of the top three fishing tackle companies would require even more expansion of the product line. Merely selling fishing line and leaders would not be enough. He would need to sell rods, reels, and lures to get there.

Berkley and Company bought a California fishing tackle company named Rodac Equipment Company (Roddy) that made rods and imported reels from Japan. One Roddy asset was their connection with a Japanese reel manufacturer.

The supply of employees in the Spirit Lake area had reached its limit, so in 1966, Berkley built a fishing rod factory in Emmetsburg, Iowa about 30 miles from Spirit Lake.

After Berkley purchased the Roddy operation, the brothers who had owned it went with him to Japan to meet the reel supplier. Each evening, they would go out to a nightclub where pretty Japanese girls would sit and dance with the patrons. After a couple of nights, Berkley did not care to participate in the nightclub scene. He had heard about Japanese baths and suggested that he would like to experience the tradition. The gentlemen sent Berkley to a bath with Mr. Inamura, the Japanese reel supplier, who did not speak English.

When they arrived at the bathhouse, a young Japanese lady wearing a white halter and skimpy white shorts ushered him into a small room where she proceeded to take off all his clothes. Then she ushered him into another room, which had a sweatbox in it. Once in the sweatbox, Berkley relaxed, as only his head protruded. However, he did not know what to expect next. Pretty soon the lady opened the sweatbox. Since she could not speak any English, she pointed to a little stool. "I went over and stood up on the stool like a naked statue. I had stage fright. She even burst out laughing. I am sure she had never before had anyone pose like that. I then realized that I was to sit down on the stool and she washed off the sweat with soap and water. I think the sweat came from my nervousness as much as from the sweatbox! Then she had me lie down on a makeshift bench. I was lying on my stomach when I realized that she was on top of me. She was walking on my back with her bare feet. It was most uncomfortable. When I finally finished, got dressed and left with Mr. Inamura, I felt the same type of relief one has upon leaving a dentist office."

He experienced more culture shock in his deals with Roddy. "It turned out that the two brothers who owned Roddy were not our type of people. They had no loyalty to me at all. They were very close to the Japanese supplier and, together with the Japanese supplier, worked against me after the sale. With all the players working against me, I faced a difficult time."

Although Berkley did not have a signed contract, it had been understood in the sale that the Japanese supplier would not sell to any other U.S. fishing tackle company.

"We were one-third of Mr. Inamura's total business; his only customer in the United States. In one of my early meetings with him, I wanted his permission to ship his reels to Australia, where we had some connections. He did not speak English, so all of our negotiations were through an interpreter. As we were negotiating, I looked at him. He had fallen asleep! He sat right across the table from me and fell asleep during our discussions!

"I later found out that he had a contract with an Australian firm that prevented him from shipping our reels to Australia. But due to Japanese custom, he could not tell me that. He went to sleep so he wouldn't have to tell me no. What a frustrating experience.

"One thing I have learned: In any business dealings, do not get involved with anyone you cannot trust, no matter how attractive the other considerations may be."

To add to the frustration, Berkley couldn't make the Emmetsburg plant competitive with the low cost of Asian labor. "We had really, really good employees, a well-managed, well-run plant," Berkley said, "but we couldn't compete, price-wise. Rods were made in Japan and Korea with much lower labor rates."

So in 1968, Elinor and Berk took a plane to Taiwan.

"At that time, there were oxcarts in downtown Taipei and few automobiles. We rode a train to Kaochung at the southern tip of the island to visit a free trade zone where manufacturers could rent factory space. The train-ride proved to be the dirtiest one we had ever experienced. Because of the heat, the windows were open, and the soot from the steam engine came in and coated everything. However, it was an interesting ride as we saw water buffalo tilling the little plots of land and pulling carts on the highways. The government had several programs to help provide work for the Taiwanese people. The going wage was 15 cents per hour."

Elinor and Berkley returned to Iowa and hired Mike Binder, a young man with managerial experience to go to Kaochung and set up a fishing rod factory. The venture proved to be sufficiently successful that in 1970 Berkley purchased land and built a factory in Taichung, in the center of Taiwan. The company proceeded to install a complete machine shop on site to build the necessary equipment. Berkley planned to become the most efficient fishing rod and reel company in the world. The factory employed 400 workers.

Berkley and Company soon became a major producer of fishing rods, and proceeded to install and build the equipment to become a major reel producer. The company's Lightning Rod became one of the most popular fishing rods in the nation – but that all changed when Berkley went to Congress and Don Porter was hired to run the company. Porter closed the reel plant. He was not one to tackle giants.

Berkley also made golf shafts and fishing rods in Taiwan. A graphite golf shaft is made very similar to the way a fishing rod is made, just bigger.

In later years, labor rates increased so much in Taiwan that the company could no longer compete. Tom moved the production to China.

Back in Spirit Lake, a firm approached Berkley about making grain elevator cables.

The grain elevator business had been expanding in the 1960s. Two companies made equipment that required a cable that went up and down in the grain elevator, with thermocouples at every ten feet of cable. The entire cable was coated with nylon, so it could withstand the grain coming in. The companies had an instrument that would read the temperature at each of those thermocouples. Heat at the thermocouple would indicate spoilage and they could take action to take care of it.

The companies wondered if Berkley could make the cables for them: something like a whale-sized Steelon leader!

"We had everything needed: the extruders, the wires, and the strander. We knew how to strip and solder. We knew how to coat with nylon. So for several years we made a good profit making cables for grain elevators," said Berkley.

In the 1960s, the company had moved out of its relatively small niche by adding product lines to become a total fishing tackle company.

It had fallen short of being a "Top 3" fishing tackle company, although it would finally reach that goal in the 1980s.

The company continued to innovate, particularly with the development of its fishing lines.

"I think it would be fair to say, that our company was always looked at as the innovator in the fishing tackle business. We would always have some sort of new innovation in the market each year. We deliberately planned to have some kind of improvement for the annual fishing tackle show."

It became fun for people to wonder, "What's Berkley going to come up with next?"

By 1972, Berkley and Company was no longer a small town Iowa business, but a major player with international operations and products that were used throughout the world.

"Wherever I am, I check out the fishing shops to see if they have Berkley leaders," said Rachel McQuirk Carpenter. "When I visited Casper, Wyoming they had a small shop that had Berkley's stuff. I told the owner I started soldering leaders in Berkley's home back in the beginning. I do that wherever I see Berkley products."

The company built plants in Taiwan and in Winnipeg, Manitoba, Canada. A research and development addition to the Spirit Lake plant made it more than three times its original size.

The company grew from less than $1 million sales in 1957 to $15 million in 1972, with net earnings of more than $1 million per year.

"But as the 1970s approached, it became apparent that Berkley would not be content to just build a profitable fishing tackle company," said fellow businessman Cabell Brand.

Berkley had met Brand, president of Orthovent Shoe Company, at the American Management Association training session. The two businessmen felt connected because they were the smaller businesses learning how to organize for growth. But as they came to know each other, they discovered they both had larger goals in mind.

"I learned that he had bigger dreams than just being successful in business," said Brand. "He and I learned that having a successful business is a means to an end, and not the end itself."

Berkley Bedell had discovered how to make a difference in the fishing tackle industry. He now wanted to tackle new ways to make a difference in the world.

Chapter Sixteen

Goals for Living

When Berkley saw how it helped the company to write goals and objectives, he said to himself, "Surely my life is as important as my company. Surely it is important for me to do the same for my life."

So he wrote out personal goals and objectives: "How I want to live my life." Here is what he wrote:

My personal goals and objectives

A.   To have a good time and bring fun, happiness and joy to others.

Methods to accomplish this will include:

1. Try to make fun out of whatever I'm doing.

2. Be enthusiastic about my tasks.

3. Develop as wide a range of interests as possible and guard against getting in a rut in recreational activities and interests.

4. Include others, whenever possible, particularly those who might not otherwise get to enjoy the activities. Examples would include: taking children, employees, relatives, and friends fishing, camping, traveling, and the like.

5. Share my recreational facilities with others. This would include ice skating rink, tennis court, boats, beach, dock, etc.

6. Have a complete physical at least once a year, so that I know how actively I may engage in athletic sports without danger to my health.

7. Always place fun ahead of winning in competitive contests.

8. Try to always be cheerful and wear a smile regardless of the problems.

9. Do an average of at least one deed a day, which will bring happiness to someone. Keep a diary as a scorecard to be sure that this is done.

10. Try to be understanding of others whose views may differ from mine.

11. Try to keep engaged in work that I enjoy.

B.   To raise a well-adjusted family, helping them develop so that they will live happy lives and contribute toward making the world a better place in which to live.

Methods to accomplish this will include:

1. Always set a good example for my family by being honest, ambitious, conscientious, friendly, humble, and fun.

2. Encourage them in whatever they want to do and have confidence in their abilities.

3. Spend time having fun with my family, even when business matters are pressing, or I do not have the ambition for play.

4. Administer discipline when necessary, but try to teach them, so they need a minimum of discipline.

5. Take an active interest in their activities.

6. Take an active interest in, and participate in, community youth activities such as school, scouts, etc.

7. Attend church and Sunday school together.

8. Pray together.

9. Teach my family to work.

10. Encourage my family to get a good education and provide them with the necessary financial assistance to enable them to get a college education.

11. Direct my recreational activities toward family activities as much as possible, including family travel, picnics, fishing, hunting, swimming, skating, boating, and the like.

12. Show them as much of the world as possible, to broaden their future and help them plan their lives.

C.   To live in such manner as to cause the world to be a little better because of my being here.

Methods to accomplish this will include the following:

1. Try to live in such a manner as to set a good example for others.

2. Use the profits of my labor to bring about community and social improvements, and to help others.

3. Give at least ten percent of my income each year to the church and other charitable projects.

4. Lead others into giving more of their wealth and time for charity and worthwhile projects.

5. Share the profits of my business with my fellow employees and encourage them to be good citizens.

6. See that the youth of my community, and any community where I locate a plant, are not denied a college education because of lack of money.

7. Direct my hours of labor so that I am of the most service in trying to accomplish this objective. These hours should be divided between the management of my business ventures, service in public office, or work in charitable or service projects as the need appears, and my contribution would be the greatest.

8. Do not be afraid to speak out, or work for, what I think is right. Always give consideration to the feelings and views of others, and realize that reform and improvement do not always come as rapidly as I might like.

9. Preserve my health, as the amount of service I can render is dependent upon my health.

10. Work for self-improvement through study and attendance at schools and seminars, so that I may be of more value to my company and humanity.

"Writing out these objectives for my personal life had a significant influence on how I have lived since that time. I do not pretend that I have lived a perfect life, but my life has been more rewarding because I went to the trouble of writing out how I wanted to live it."

After writing these objectives, Elinor and Berkley set up a special checking account.

"This was our charity account. Ten percent of every salary check went into that account and the money was only used for charity. It was a wonderful way to handle charitable giving. Whenever a request for giving came to us, we did not have to wrestle with whether we would give or keep the money for ourselves, and we could judge each opportunity, as compared to the others available, without guilt if we said no.

"I have not been successful in doing something that would bring happiness to someone each day. From time to time, I have kept a diary and tried to keep it up, but I have not yet succeeded in completely meeting this goal. But having that as a goal has caused me to do some things I might not otherwise have done."

For example, now that Berkley winters in Naples, Florida he sends more than 70 boxes of Florida citrus fruit to northern friends in January. A diverse group of women receive a mailing from him each Valentine's Day. These ladies range from granddaughters, to former classmates and co-workers like Rachel McQuirk Carpenter, to relatively newer associates like Sue Richter, with whom Berkley has worked on a number of community improvement campaigns.

"I'm in love with Berkley Bedell," smiled Sue Richter, a happily married woman who went through school with Berkley's son, Tom, "and I know that Berkley Bedell is in love with me. I can prove it." She proudly displayed a Valentine card that Berkley sent her, like the other 70 he sent, a modest penny Valentine of the sort that elementary school children give to their classmates. But grown women giggle like schoolgirls, delighted to receive a personal note and expression of appreciation. In 2001, Berkley also included a gift with each Valentine card, after buying 70 aprons during a visit to France.

Writing his goals affected the way the Bedell family lived its daily life, Berkley said.

Previously, the family had not been having a prayer before meals, and Berkley and Elinor had not been going to Sunday school with the children.

"After writing out my goals and objectives we started to do both. I believe church and prayer are important for the values they teach. I do not know how much this has had to do with the values of our children, or the fact that one of them became a United Methodist pastor, but it has been an important factor in my life and has contributed to our whole family. I could not have wished for our children to turn out any differently. I am extremely proud of the values they have each set for themselves and the lives they live."

Berkley began to give speeches, urging people to get out a pencil and paper and start to write out their personal goals for their lives. Through the American Management Association, he conducted seminars for business executives.

He also gave Sunday sermons in various churches.

One Sunday, he had agreed to give an early sermon at a little church in Excelsior Township, near Spirit Lake, and then give the 11 a.m. sermon at the United Methodist Church in the nearby town of Lake Park. After staying too long in Excelsior, he arrived a little late in Lake Park. He walked in as the congregation was singing a hymn. He stood at the back of the church trying to decide what to do. He decided to wait until the hymn ended, walk down the aisle to the front of the church, and announce that he apologized for being late. As the hymn went on for some time, something did not seem right.

"All of a sudden, I realized that I had come to the wrong church! In Lake Park, there were two nearly identical churches on the same corner only one block apart. The Lord had rescued me from what would have been one of the most embarrassing moments of my life."

Our Island

What would be a perfect day together if you could have whatever you wished?

What would you do if you were told that you only had one year to live?

Berkley and Elinor pondered these questions as part of a Life Planning Course for Couples at a weeklong University for Presidents held by the Young Presidents Organization in Honolulu, Hawaii. The Young Presidents Organization existed for any person who had become president of a sizable business (at that time, $1 million in annual sales) before 40 years of age. People had to leave the organization by age 50.

Berkley's experience in business, in nature, in church, and in his hometown of Spirit Lake had taught him the importance of shared success. He worked hard with others to succeed in his business, his church, his community, and his family. He and Elinor were searching for what they should be doing with their lives, now that their business and their family had grown up.

In the Life Planning Course for Couples, they started with a group of questions like those above.

Each couple was handed a piece of paper.

"On this sheet of paper, draw a picture of an island. On this island, picture your lives together from the time you met until you will be separated by death."

Berkley and Elinor put two mountains on their island.

One mountain represented their family and the other the fishing tackle manufacturing business.

"Then we drew a number of hills, representing the Boy Scouts, the Chamber of Commerce, the church, the school board, and the like. As we sat there, we realized that the fishing tackle business had been sufficiently successful and that we could either sell it and retire, or hire others to run it. We had also completed raising of our family, as our two sons were in college and Joanne was in her last year of high school."

"We drew a line over the two mountains representing our family and the business, as we said 'we have climbed these mountains.' We also drew a line over the hills representing the Boy Scouts, church, and the like, because we realized that we had also climbed those hills."

Then they said to themselves:

"Now we have the choice, we can either retire and go to the beach and relax in the sunshine, or we can go find more mountains to climb. We decided that we were happier climbing mountains than resting on the beach. So we went back to Spirit Lake and started looking for new mountains to climb."

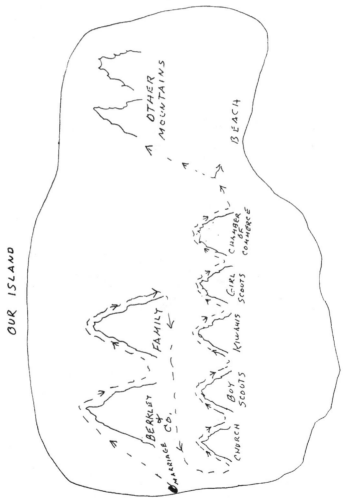

The Island that changed the life
of Berkley and Elinor Bedell

Chapter Seventeen

New Mountains to Climb

At the time Berkley was looking for new mountains to climb, his college-aged children dramatically challenged his view of the world. Their worldview – on Vietnam and politics – launched Berkley into a new, public career. He made the leap from Goldwater Republican to McGovern Democrat in a few short years.

"From about 1968 to 1972, I remember Dad going from really kind of being an old fuddy-duddy Republican establishment guy, to enjoying our conversations, to becoming a progressive, liberal thinker," recalled Tom Bedell. "That is an interesting transformation for a person at that age – 50 years old – to go through."

Berkley and Elinor raised their children to be curious, and they were. They had raised their children to try to make a difference in the world and never to shirk from challenges.

Ken, though smaller than Berkley had been, went out for football. "He had absolutely no business going out for football, but he wanted to please me," Berkley reflected. Ken quit football on his doctor's recommendation after he hurt his tailbone. Ken said he played football not just because he liked to please his father, but also because it looked like a fun thing to do.

All the Bedell children were high-achievers who took on challenges in different ways.

Ken liked a stimulating argument and didn't hesitate to raise controversial issues at the family dinner table.

"Ken was the pot-stirrer," Tom recalled. "He'd have a lot of fun with it. He'd say something outrageous, just to be provocative. He's been like that since grade school."

Ken went to Cornell University to study chemistry. While there, he met a biology student, Kathie, who shared his concerns about social justice. They participated in protest actions in the late 1960s. The first night Ken and Kathie were together, they spent the night with 1,000 other students occupying a college building in a protest movement. In 1969, while studying at Princeton Seminary, Ken became an active student leader. He and two other students organized several events and confronted the board of trustees.

Ken dove deeply into studies of economic and social systems, in a quest for justice that became a focal point of his calling into ministry in the United Methodist Church. During his pastorate in Maryland, during the 1970s, he spoke out against the Ku Klux Klan – an activity that resulted in his car being vandalized and receiving threatening notes on the door of their home. He also served as a missionary in Swaziland, Africa.

Tom was the entrepreneur.

Since the day Tom drove a wheelbarrow around the neighborhood, selling the used paper that his parents had thrown away, "everyone said he was destined to be a salesman," his sister Joanne said. "He dreamed of owning a restaurant or hotel chain, or a cabin camp like Gram Healy had."

Tom's love of music launched his first serious business career, much as his father's love of fishing had launched Berkley and Company. Tom learned to play the piano in elementary school. In eighth grade he hoped for a guitar for Christmas. As the family unwrapped gift after gift, Tom wondered why he was getting less than Ken and Joanne. Soon, all the gifts had been unwrapped and it looked like Tom had been shorted. He didn't show it, but he was crying inside. He decided to bite his tongue rather than to spoil Christmas by saying something selfish.

"Are you sure that's all the presents, honey?" Berkley asked Elinor, in near-sincerity.

"Oh, I almost forgot," she played along. "There's one other present." She went into another room and came out with … Tom's eyes widened and his heart raced … An electric guitar! He looked at the trademark.

"A Fender Stratocaster! You're kidding me! A Fender Stratocaster! The biggest rock stars in the world play Stratocasters!" From parents who only drove used cars and limited their grocery expenses they had bought their son a professional guitar!

By ninth grade, Tom had started teaching guitar lessons and playing in a band at high school dances all over northwest Iowa and eastern South Dakota. The band was called Billy Rat and the Finks. "We made a little record that wasn't very good," he said, but their record called "Little Queenie" became a lifelong favorite of his sister, Joanne.

Tom started a guitar business during his sophomore year of high school. Berkley tried not to interfere, but he did put Tom in contact with a Japanese businessperson, who put Tom in touch with guitar manufacturers. Tom invested his lawn-mowing and newspaper route money into 24 guitars that he rented to students who took lessons from him. When he needed additional cash to enter the guitar import and sales business, Berkley told him, "You're going to need to go to the bank and borrow it." Tom would have to learn how to write a plausible business plan.

"He never told me that he'd gone to the bank behind my back and said, 'Lend Tom the money.' How else would the bank loan me the money? But I never knew that then." Tom presented his business plan and the bank lent him the money to buy 300 guitars. He hired Joanne to apply "Bedell" decals on the guitars in the Bedell family garage/warehouse.

As soon as he got his driver's license, he packed guitars into the family car and drove to music stores in Iowa,

Minnesota, and Sioux Falls, South Dakota. He opened a store in the town of Okoboji, Iowa and then one in Spencer, Iowa.

"Dad never said, 'Tom, this is how you need to do it' or, 'No, that won't work.' The phrase I use now is 'investment in others' success.' I had all the responsibility. But I never could have done it without his support, his coaching, and his tolerance."

The family expanded its cultural understanding during Tom's junior year in high school, with the arrival of an exchange student from Samoa – a big, handsome young man named Moega Suesue Lutu. Several years later, when the family was vacationing in Hawaii, they were surprised to find Moega in a hospital in Hawaii. When they arrived, they found it to be a hospital for people with leprosy. The patients were to be completely isolated and a big fence surrounded the compound. In order to get into the compound, they were warned not to touch any of the patients.

"Of course, upon seeing Moega we could not restrain ourselves from big hugs," said Berkley. They then realized that Moega had the disease while he lived with them in Spirit Lake. They had been aware of his rash, but none of the Bedells came down with leprosy. Moega's treatment succeeded. He recovered and later ran for Congress from Samoa, but did not win. His relationship with the Bedells was so close, he named one of his daughters Elinor.

Like her brothers before her, Joanne excelled in school and worked. She pumped gas, worked at a restaurant, a bank, a law firm, and at Tom's guitar store. She knew the community expectations of the Bedells – from Virginia and Walt through Berkley and Jack, and Ken and Tom – and welcomed them.

"I think I was born a high-achiever," said Joanne. "I always wanted to do well. I learned a lot from Ken and Tom, so I didn't have to go through the stuff they went through. I received every bit of credit on anything I did, because they expected me to do well. I considered it a positive thing. I have Ken and Tom to thank, and I guess I have Grandma and Dad and Jack."

She saw a side of her high-powered grandmother that only a granddaughter could experience. It started when she wrote to Virginia to tell her "about how excited I was to go into environmental law studies" upon graduation from college. She thought her groundbreaking grandmother would be pleased to see her granddaughter follow in her attorney footsteps.

"She wrote back and told me that she hoped I would remember that the most important thing I could do in life was to be a good wife and mother," Joanne recalled. "I thought her reply was very interesting, because that hadn't seemed to be her focus. Her focus had been to be an attorney, to be accomplished – everything I had told her I wanted to do. For her to come back and tell me something else, said volumes about her, as she reflected on her life and what maybe she thought she had missed. That reminder of family continued in all the correspondence we had until she died. She and I really had a warm relationship when she passed away."

As the boys took care of business and college affairs, Joanne spent a lot of time alone with Berkley, as a hunting and fishing partner. She carefully watched the transformation of her father, from lifelong Republican to liberal Democrat.

Political Transformation

While Ken was in high school, Berk's friend Peter Narey formed a chapter of Young Republicans. Ken and Joanne both joined. Joanne and Narey's daughter, Sally, were the closest of friends.

"We had a group that sang, and Governor Robert Ray asked us to come down and sing for his inauguration," said Joanne. "We had a song for Congressman Wiley Mayne, 'We've Been Working Hard for Wiley.' I have a letter from Richard Nixon thanking me for helping with his campaign. We were a very active Young Republican group because of Pete's leadership and his position."

Ken and two other boys attended the Iowa State Republican convention in 1964. They elected Ken chairperson of the Sixth Congressional district Young Republicans, and they elected Grandma Bedell a Presidential elector.

All the while, Berkley had become increasingly disenchanted with the Republican Party. He had been largely inactive in the party while Virginia and Jack had been elected to county office as Republicans and held various offices in the party. Virginia had risen to vice chair of the state party organization and Jack served as a delegate to the national convention.

Then Berkley took an active part in the 1964 presidential election, as chairman of the Goldwater campaign in northwest Iowa.

"I wanted to be a delegate to the state convention, but the Republicans would not let me be a delegate," said Berkley. "They were so neatly organized that they didn't want anybody else in. So when I told them that I wanted to become active, they said, 'What you have to do is start as a block worker and you can work your block in Spirit Lake and work up from there.' That was not what I had in mind. I could see I had almost no opportunity to be really involved in the Republican Party locally."

"Dad grew up as a Republican, with a dynamic mom who was really active in state Republican politics." said Tom. "Oh, man, she really had a huge influence on Dad. He just kind of played his dutiful role. All of a sudden he wanted to jump in and consider running for a leadership position in the party, and they snubbed him, because he hadn't earned his dues. They said, 'Wait a minute,' which others might have understood, but not Dad."

Berkley also had been rethinking his stand on social issues and the Vietnam War, in no small part because of conversations with Ken and Tom.

"Dad loves to talk about ideas, social philosophy, and economic philosophy, and when we were in college, kids were really into what's right and what's wrong with society and government," said Tom. "Of course, Ken had always been on the edge. He never had to realistically say,

'How do I make all that work and deal with all the other dynamics?' And you need people like him. I'm not being disparaging, but he's played that role from day one.

"Ken and Dad like to get outside the normal look at things. Dad's really attracted to magic answers. He sees the rest of the world as resistors that are holding back and if people would only join him and welcome change, the whole world would move a lot faster. That's partly his inventive nature, and that's partly how he built his company. Ken's a little bit like that, too.

"So I think Ken had a lot of influence on challenging Dad's thinking. Maybe more than I did, although I had some experiences that I was able to share with him."

Both Ken and Tom decided they couldn't serve in the military during the Vietnam War. Their father – son of a World War I veteran and a man who desperately sought combat duty during World War II and admired his brother's service overseas – had to confront the issue and the reality of the Vietnam War.

When Ken went to take his exam for the draft, one of the questions on the exam was, "Have you ever read *The Communist Manifesto*?" Ken told the sergeant giving the exam that he had, indeed, read *The Communist Manifesto* and asked the sergeant how he should answer the question.

The sergeant told him that he should answer that he had not read *The Communist Manifesto*. Ken followed the sergeant's instructions and wrote at the bottom of the page, "I have read *The Communist Manifesto*, but the sergeant advised me that I should answer that I have not done so."

"Not long after that exam, a secret service agent appeared at our front door in Spirit Lake, investigating this young honor student who went on to become a Christian pastor with a Ph.D.," Berkley recalled. "What a paranoid government we had at the time!"

Ken became a "non-cooperator."

"I resigned from the selective service and mailed them my draft card," Ken said. "I wouldn't comply with the law that I had to inform them about my address in the future, and if called wouldn't serve."

Tom took a different approach.

Upon graduating from high school, Tom closed his guitar stores, sold his inventory, and went to the University of Colorado.

Tom registered as a conscientious objector and appeared, respectfully in a coat and tie, before the draft board in 1970. He thought he was the first conscientious objector in Dickinson County.

"I said, 'From everything that I've studied and learned, I do not believe that it's appropriate for me to kill somebody.' This wasn't something where suddenly I showed up and said, 'I don't want to go to Vietnam.' I had never hunted. When the family would go out hunting, I wouldn't carry a gun. I was a strict vegetarian."

"I had studied the regulations. I knew the law inside and out. The draft board said, 'We don't believe there is such a thing as a conscientious objector. How can you not support your country?' I said, 'I agree. I totally support my country. I'll be delighted to do alternative service.' Which wasn't really true. I'm glad I didn't have to. They said, 'How do you know that you don't believe in a war if you've never seen one?'

"I said, 'Fair enough. I'll go to Vietnam and check it out.' I'm an experiential learner. My whole experience in life, with a lot of nurture and support from my folks, had been that you could do anything you set your mind to. It never occurred to me that there would be any reason I couldn't do that." Grandma's Mamie's saying, "You can do almost anything within reason if you will only put your mind to it," must have been echoing from her grave.

"When I told my parents I was going to visit Vietnam, Dad warned me, 'It's going to ruin the rest of your life if you don't finish school.' Mom and Dad were upset that I was going to drop out of college." Berkley, who had personally succeeded after dropping out of college, said he and Elinor were even more concerned with Tom's personal safety.

"I pleaded with Tom not to go to Vietnam where the war was raging," said Berkley. They provided no financial support.

"I always made my own money anyway," Tom remarked. He ran an advertisement in *The Denver Post*, saying he would be traveling throughout Asia. Anyone who had a project he could do for them should contact him. Several people asked him to do projects, and he left with $500 in his pocket. He packed his backpack and hitchhiked from Denver to San Francisco to catch a flight to Tokyo, then to Taiwan.

In Taiwan, Tom stayed with the family of the manager of the fishing rod and reel plant Berkley had established in 1968. His arrival coincided with the Chinese New Year, a weeklong holiday celebration. "One of the things you do during that holiday is get all cleaned up and your hair cut." So Tom and the factory manager went to the barber. "The next thing I know, I'm getting my pretty long hair turned into a buzz haircut."

The GI-style haircut helped him when he arrived in Vietnam. In Saigon, a man told him that if he wanted to get anywhere in Vietnam, he should go to Ton Son Nut Air Force Base, tell them he was a civilian engineer, and they would take him anywhere, via helicopter. So he went to Ton Sun Nut and got on a helicopter to Da Nang. Tom stayed with a medic there for two nights.

"We were shelled one night by the Viet Cong. I saw a guy shoot up on heroin. One guy had taken so much speed (amphetamine) that he was skin and bones. Guys were mentally berserk. They had jars of body parts of Vietnamese that they'd killed and saved as relics. Just disgusting."

He hitchhiked from Da Nang across Vietnam to Saigon, riding with different convoys. "The stories I heard and the stuff I saw were unbelievable, just awful. This little girl, maybe five years old, comes running down this road, asking if anyone wants to have sex with her sister. I'm thinking, 'What have we done to these people that their society has gotten to where a five-year-old is pimping for her sister?' It was awful.

"When I got back home and went before my draft board, I said, 'Do you want to hear what I learned?' This stuff had just started to come out in the media. They did not want to hear."

Tom Bedell may have been the first and only American to visit a war zone to decide whether or not he would fight. As he said, "It never occurred to me that there would be any reason I couldn't do that."

The draft board gave him a hearing, but one of the board members did not attend. They voted two to two. When contacted, the absent member voted that Tom should be drafted. Tom appealed to the state authorities, arguing that it was unfair for the absent member to cast the deciding vote without hearing Tom's presentation.

The state authorities agreed and Tom escaped having to serve.

Berkley, Elinor, and Joanne supported Tom and Ken through the struggle.

Berkley had started to change his mind about the war: "Ken gave me a book to read about Vietnam and I became convinced that we were wrong in what we were doing in Vietnam." A group of college students from Spirit Lake, came to the Kiwanis Club and spoke against the war. The Kiwanians were not very kind to the college students. "Do you think you know more about the war than the President?" a Kiwanian asked. "The Kiwanians did not appreciate my speaking up in support of the stand of the students. They felt that in order to be patriotic we had to support the President."

Word that he supported the student protestors got out, and Berkley's mother asked him about growing rumors that Berkley Bedell had become a Communist. He told her no, but she continued to be disturbed by his stand. Berkley's father had been in World War I and Berkley had been in World War II, but this was different.

"Elinor and I attended a conference in Washington, D.C. One of the young men at the conference made a passionate plea that we needed to stop the Vietnam Communists before they landed in California. I could not believe it. Hitler wanted to conquer the world. If we had not become involved, he might have succeeded. We were justified in doing what we did in World War II. I don't know what else you could have done with Hitler except to defeat him."

But Berkley came to believe that comparing Hitler's expansion to the Southeast Asia threat, "was baloney. That was absolutely ridiculous."

He believed that wars were self-propagating; something akin to his childhood boxing experience. "Most wars can be avoided. I don't care whether it's an individual or a country – the more you fight, the more you're inclined to continue to fight. Fighting breeds fighting."

Berkley's positions were at odds with the Republican Party. "I've been a very liberal person all through my life and that has not fit well with the society in which I have lived. I have been completely out of step with the people in my district, which is very, very conservative Republican."

Years later, Tom seemed unaware that his trip helped change his father's thinking about the war.

"He was going through a lot of changes at that time," Tom said.

After Berkley and Elinor redrew their lives as an island and a range of new mountains, Berkley decided he needed to be more involved in public life.

"I hired a person with managerial experience to take over my position as chief executive officer of Berkley and Company, and Elinor and I spent a year traveling the country 'looking for mountains.'

"We investigated a machine to convert garbage into good soil. I visited the Methodist headquarters in Washington, D.C., and offered to serve as an unpaid lobbyist in Congress. They would have no part of it."

He decided to become involved in the political process.

"I went to a Young Presidents Organization meeting in Washington, D.C., and what I heard from top officials in the Nixon Administration shocked me. Their values were not mine. I had always been a Republican, but after listening to the Nixon Administration, I began to question my Republican registration."

"I joined a group of other Republicans who went to Sioux City to meet with our Congressman, Wiley Mayne. It was a very, very, very unsatisfactory meeting. He told us that he was not going to submit to a sixth-grade quiz on

Vietnam. So the Vietnam War had a significant impact on my political leanings.

"I also went on a trade mission trip to Europe led by Iowa Governor Harold Hughes, a Democrat. We became friends. A group formed to encourage Hughes to run for President. I met with that group and we formed a Republicans for Hughes organization. I flew some of the group to the state Democratic convention in Madison, Wisconsin in my little Comanche airplane. Hughes gave a powerful speech. It was clear that he really had momentum going in his campaign. However, Harold did not have the stomach to run for President and he dropped out of the race. That experience caused me to become somewhat more involved with the Democratic Party."

Before then, Berkley's closest relationships with Democrats were with his car dealer and hunting buddy, Bob Boettcher, and his brother-in-law Art Naftalin, the mayor of Minneapolis and friend of Hubert Humphrey.

But the issues seemed profoundly important to him, and he had a life mission to make a difference in the world.

"I did not agree with the Vietnam War and some of the Republican policies. Our Republican Congressman supported the war. I couldn't get anybody to listen to me in the Republican Party on that issue, and I had become quite close to Harold Hughes, who was the Democratic governor of Iowa. I obtained the platforms of both parties and studied them."

When he read the platforms, he became convinced that he agreed with the Democrats on the environment, military spending, and workers' rights, and that he really should be a Democrat, not a Republican.

"The rich are getting richer and the poor are staying where they are. And we're passing more and more laws that make that all the more sure to happen."

On March 5, 1971, his 50th birthday, Berkley went to the Dickinson County Court House and asked to change his registration from Republican to Democrat.

"They tried to persuade me not to do it, but I insisted. I tell everyone I thought I should spend my first 50 years as a Republican and my second 50 years as a Democrat – and then spend the rest of my life as whichever I liked the best!"

HWY 9 & 71 SPIRIT LAKE, IOWA 51360
AREA CODE 712, TELEPHONE 336-1520
CABLE ADDRESS — BERKLEYCO

March 5, 1971

Mr. & Mrs. Mel Yager
502-22nd Street
Spirit Lake, Iowa 51360

Dear Mel and Maxine:

Today is my fiftieth birthday. I have just returned from the courthouse where I changed my registration from that of a republican to a democrat.

As you know, this has not been an easy decision because of family ties. I think it will be easier for my Mother if a big fuss is not made over this action, but I do want to be active in the party and hope you will keep me advised of party activities so that I may take part.

Your friend,

Berk

"When my mother learned what I had done, she said in all seriousness that she thought she would have to move out of town, rather than suffer the embarrassment of living in the same town with a Democratic son.

"Indeed, among all of our friends, I could only name five families in the town of Spirit Lake who publicly declared themselves Democrats. Many of the people in our community thought I had done a terrible thing to my family."

Then Berkley announced what many had suspected all along was the cause of the party switch.

"As we looked more and more at what mountains we wanted to climb, I decided that I would like to run for Congress. People will question this, but I honestly had no idea of running for office when I changed parties."

Berkley commissioned a poll to be taken by a professional firm. They reported, "Don't run. You do not have a chance." But they didn't know Berkley Bedell, and they certainly had not heard Mamie's saying, "You can do almost anything within reason if you will only set your mind to it." A popular Republican, Wiley Mayne, was the incumbent in a heavily Republican district. Berkley had a major hurdle in the Democratic Party as well: organized labor played a major part in the Democratic Party at the time, and Berkley owned a non-union plant. Not only that, the company had weathered a bitter union election in his plant where the union lost. Berkley also had been active in the Iowa Right to Work Committee, which labor organizations viewed to be their worst enemy.

Despite the obstacles, Berkley was determined to run for Congress.

He went to the district Democratic convention and announced his candidacy to run for Congress as a Democrat. "It was the first major political convention I had ever attended. You can imagine the lack of enthusiasm which followed my announcement."

His children admired him.

"I had been pretty much a follower," said Joanne. "When he explained to me the difference of what it meant, it made more sense to me to be a Democrat. As a Young Republican, I don't think I knew what Republicanism stood for. I simply joined the group. All my friends were members. I don't think we ever really studied the issues. I just remember working for candidates. When Dad and I discussed the difference in the policies and platforms, it made sense to me that he should be a Democrat."

Tom Bedell gained a new respect for his father.

"I remember going to see him, and I told him, 'You know, Dad, you're running for Congress, and I'm in this negotiation with the draft board, and it's going to be really embarrassing for you. I want to talk to you about how we handle it.' He replied to me, 'I tried to raise you to always live by your values and I'm not going to change now.' I get choked up. He was saying, 'My career in politics is not as important as you doing what you believe in.' That type of response is pretty special. That sort of stuff sticks with you when you're making decisions for the rest of your life."

Berkley's two best lifelong friends – his brother Jack Bedell and Peter Narey – were dumbfounded. They understood the political party dynamics, but couldn't fathom the changes they perceived in Berkley's philosophies and policies.

"There wasn't any room for Berkley in the Republican Party to do what he wanted to do," said Jack. "We had a Congressman who was well liked and there wasn't any way Berk was going to get the Republicans, locally or otherwise, to support him against this guy. So the only way for him to run for Congress was to run as a Democrat.

"Unfortunately, I think he became convinced that the Democratic philosophy was a better philosophy. That's always been difficult for me to understand: How he could be a businessman and a Democrat. If Berkley had his way in Congress, he would have made it impossible for anybody to do what he had done business-wise. Big business is a 'no-no' in the Democratic Party. To Democrats, businessmen are bad people. I don't know how he became that liberal."

Ken said he could sense the frustration and disappointment Uncle Jack had toward Berkley. The relationship that had been so warm and close now had some distance. Maybe the logistics of their growing families had something to do with it, but it seemed the inseparable brothers didn't make time for each other as often as they once had.

"Until Dad became a Democrat, he had no better friend than his brother, Jack," Ken reflected. "Then Jack faced embarrassment among his friends. To Jack, it felt like your brother was a traitor; a breaking of a trust. I think Jack had to make absolutely certain that no one thought him to be a co-conspirator in Dad's actions."

Jack and his wife, Marcia, served as dedicated party members. Marcia had been secretary for the local Republican Central Committee for 25 years. Jack had been a candidate, a political appointee, and a faithful worker in the party ever since he had been district chairman of the Young Republicans during the 1950s. "So we were not just 'Republicans.' We were *committed* Republicans," reflected Jack.

"Berk and I just tried to avoid political discussions," said Jack. "You have to remember, that Berk befriended and supported the people whom I had opposed and worked hard against. People who were out campaigning for him were campaigning *against* me. That was a little hard to swallow, especially when I had depended on a career in politics to make my livelihood.

"People used to ask me why I couldn't support Berkley and his candidacy. And I said, 'If Berkley needed the job to support his family, I'd be out working for him, but he doesn't need the job and I don't agree with his philosophy, therefore I don't think I should support him.'

"I have a number of other friends who are not as conservative as I am, and they don't agree with me, I'm sure. I guess we accept that. It's a little tougher to take when it's your brother. Both Pete Narey and I had talked about this: Wouldn't it have been fun had Berkley been a Republican candidate for Congress that we could have worked for and reveled in his election? But it didn't come that way. It was awkward."

Narey found himself in a similarly awkward position: He was the Republican Chairman for the Congressional District in which Berkley ran.

"Jack and I both discussed it with him. I went down to his house one day to talk to him about it, but he was determined to do it, so there was no point in talking about it."

As much as he hated to be in a campaign against his best friend, Narey understood the catalyst for Berkley's party switch. As years went on, he came to agree more with Berkley on Vietnam.

"Vietnam had been a turning point for Berk. And, of course, it was a terrible thing," Narey said. "I remember that, initially, I opposed getting involved with Vietnam. But when we had a half-a-million men over there, I thought we had to support them. Now, I'm not sure I was right about that. Probably getting them out was the best thing to do. But I knew it would be a bloodbath for those people we left behind. And it was."

"Berk had become more vehemently opposed than most people. The tide shifted during that time period; it shifted with my daughters and it shifted with me."

Berkley had *tackled giants* before, as an athlete, as a teen-age businessman, as a small-town industrialist taking on international mega-corporations.

He knew that no one expected an anti-war Democrat, perceived as an enemy to labor union Democrats, to beat an incumbent Republican Congressman, in a conservative Republican district, in a year in which Republican Richard Nixon would win a landslide victory over Democrat George McGovern.

Berkley knew his chances of election were slim. He was facing a scarier opponent than the boy boxer from LeMars that Berkley had evaded so many years ago. But this fight was different. This fight wasn't about macho pride and bragging rights, it was about making a difference in the world; about saving people from war and about helping the common man. Berkley believed in this cause even more than when he took on giant DuPont in the marketplace and the courtroom.

But in 1972, for the first time in his life, Berkley would have to climb a mountain without the support of his mother, his brother, and his best friend.

Chapter Eighteen

Running for Congress

Why would the Democratic Party let Berkley run for Congress?

He did not fit, after all. He had no political experience beyond the Spirit Lake School Board. He had name recognition among Republicans and Spirit Lake area voters, but he was not well known in the nearby, urban, Democratic Sioux City area.

On virtually every major issue, Berkley did not agree with his conservative Republican district. His tax policies alienated the wealthy. He offended organized labor with his right-to-work stand. The majority did not agree with his opposition to the Vietnam War. He favored gun control and opposed the National Rifle Association. He opposed the death penalty and held a middle of the road position on abortion.

He did favor agricultural price supports, the one issue on which he agreed with the majority in a corn-driven economy.

How could the Democratic Party put up a candidate with such unpopular views? And how could the party welcome him as a Johnny-come-lately candidate for the highest office in northwest Iowa even though he had never worked for other party candidates?

The answer: Democrats were desperate. Nobody wanted to run against the popular, longtime incumbent Wiley Mayne in a district so heavily Republican.

"At the district convention one lady said to me, 'I am glad you are running. I was afraid we would not have a candidate,'" said Berkley. "That did not seem to be the greatest of encouragement. It was so hopeless to run as a Democrat in the district that I did not have any opposition in the primary."

He had many friends with experience running campaigns, but almost all of them were Republicans: his mother, his brother, Pete Narey, and Ed Donovan, whose wife became the Republican Party's Dickinson County Chairman.

Berkley drew upon a few big assets.

He had built up a 50-year reservoir of local goodwill. Among many voters, party affiliation couldn't compete with his personal reputation.

"I didn't care about his party," said Marvin Hamilton, one of Berkley's first employees and owner of a Spirit Lake business. "I cared about the man and I didn't hesitate to recommend him." Marvin knew Berkley as a person who would "give you the shirt off his back."

"Berk was simply a down-to-earth person who wanted to do the right thing, and I could tell it. He was well known, not only in this town but in surrounding towns, because people drove here from other places to work in his plants."

He had the reputation of a man who could buck the odds and get things done – a man who would fearlessly *tackle giants* of industry.

Berkley also had the benefits of time and money. In 1970, he had hired Don Porter as President of Berkley and Company, allowing him more time to work for causes important to him.

Berkley and Elinor worked the campaign trail as tirelessly as Berk had worked on his newspaper subscription contests as a teen; as determinedly as he had worked his traveling automobile office selling trips in the early days; and as earnestly as he and Elinor had made the rounds of fishing tackle trade shows. He knew how to make a sales pitch with conviction.

"Elinor and I spent months traveling the district, shaking hands with everyone we could meet," said Berkley.

He did not have to depend on endless fundraising efforts, which might have been futile anyway. "People were reluctant to give me money because they didn't think I had a chance." So Berkley spent about $25,000 of his own money to finance the campaign.

Berkley trusted his instincts and attempted to remain true to himself. He wanted to show voters that this successful businessman was a down-to-earth family man who cared about common people.

During a fundraiser in Hartley, Iowa, he discovered a quirky asset that no marketing expert would have recommended. The Everly Kitchen Band – comprised of people playing kazoos and pounding on pots and pans with kitchen utensils – played a song they had set to the tune of "Pennsylvania Polka."

> *"Berkley, Oh Berkley, Oh Berkley Bedell,*
> *"He is our man for Congress ...*
> *"Everybody vote for Berkley.*
> *"He is our man for Congress."*

"So I adopted it as my campaign song," Berkley laughed. "It may have been kind of hokey. But it fit the rural area I represented."

"People hated the song," Elinor recalled.

"Do you think they hated the song?" Berkley wondered. "I'd be in places in my district and the radio would be playing, 'Berkley, Oh Berkley, Oh Berkley Bedell' and I would hear people singing along."

It portrayed Berkley as he wanted to be seen: a regular, just-like-you-and-me person who didn't take himself too seriously. He had sort of a stuffed-shirt lawyer as an opponent. Although about the same age, the incumbent seemed much older.

The experts expected Berkley to get trampled by Wiley Mayne.

Pete Narey warned his Republican friends they would have a fight on their hands.

"I had known the incumbent Congressman since high school. He was a decent, nice, solid guy," said Narey. "When Berk inserted himself into the race, well, I had to stay on (as district chairman of the Republican Party)."

As for campaigning against his lifelong best friend, "I hated it, of course," Narey said, "but I didn't want Berk to think he was going to push me out." Narey had been looking at the prospects of running for the office himself, if and when Wiley Mayne would step down. (Berkley later said he had no idea that his friend had hopes of sometime running for Congress.) "So I stayed on for one more term as district chairman, but I felt the hot breath coming on the Republicans' neck. I told these folks, 'don't sell him short. He sells fishing leaders and he'll sell himself to the voters.'"

Berkley surprised everyone – including himself – by getting 49 percent of the vote. Far from being disappointed by his defeat, he looked forward to his prospects for 1974.

"The first thing that struck me was his energy," recalled Tom Harkin, who also lost his first Congressional election in the adjoining Iowa district in 1972, before serving more than 30 years in the House and Senate.

"We met once or twice in 1973, or early 1974 at a meeting where we were going to talk about running again. Berkley had boundless energy. He was very enthusiastic, very positive, always up.

"I remember him saying, 'I hardly expected to win the first time out, but you know, people have to get to know me. I'm going to stay out there.' Berkley was bound and determined to win the next time. He had a lot of energy and commitment and knew what he was doing. He was going to win. That was all there was to it. I was very taken by him."

Working for 1974

Berkley had a few advantages for the 1974 campaign.

He actively sought and received support from organized labor.

"They did not really support me the first time. If they had, I think I would have won the first election. In the 1974 campaign I courted them."

Berkley convinced many labor leaders that despite opposing unionization of Berkley and Company and supporting right-to-work laws, he supported workers' rights and would support worker-friendly policies. He would be a better friend of labor than his Republican counterpart, he assured them.

He emphasized his strong family.

"I hired some consultants to prepare my television ads," said Berkley. "I wanted one of my ads to be about my family. They didn't want to do it. They told me they had frequently been asked to do family ads, and they had not been effective.

"I insisted. They were greatly surprised when they interviewed my family. We actually prepared and ran a five-minute ad with my family. It was awfully long, but very, very effective. They told me they had never experienced a family that had that good a message." His favorite moment came when Elinor said, "I would vote for Berkley Bedell even if he were not my husband."

In 1974, Berkley's family was in a better position to help. Tom and Joanne had graduated from college and they threw themselves into the campaign. Ken had become a United Methodist pastor in upstate New York.

Tom found it invigorating to pour his energy into working with his father to change the world. The campaign also became his proving grounds for his first career, as a congressional aide and then campaign consultant in Washington.

A group of young Republican businessmen threw their support to Berkley.

"We especially got involved in the second campaign. My friend Jerry Stockdale, a banker, and Fritz Rosendahl, and I – three pretty good Republicans in the area," said Herman Richter, a clothing store co-owner. Berkley had served as a business mentor and tennis partner for the three younger men.

"Berk basically told us after he lost the first time, 'Listen, guys, I'm gonna do this again, but you guys have to get off your rear ends and help me.' Gosh, in my lifetime, Republican, Democrat, I'm not really sure it mattered. I simply wanted to vote for a businessperson. What better businessperson in our area than Berk?" Richter traveled the 22-county district seeking support for "a good friend running for Congress in this district and a fellow businessperson."

"The thing about Berk is he just crossed a lot of bridges," Richter said. "He had a heritage in the Republican Party, and, shucks, they wouldn't allow him to go ahead and run as a Republican, which, in my opinion, I think he would have done if given the opportunity. But we need leaders and if there's one word that describes Berkley Bedell, it's the word 'leader.' He's a role model. His moral values are important. He told me, 'you need to set a good example and live a good example.' God bless Berk, for being in that fishbowl. He's not perfect, but he's done a super, super job of leading the exemplary type of life that you'd want to live."

Maybe Berkley's integrity was his chief asset in 1974, as the Watergate scandal consumed President Nixon's final days with stories of deception, cover-up, and mean-spirited maneuvering. Nixon resigned in August 1974, just as the Congressional races were heating up.

"I knew him to be one guy that was incorruptible," said Hamilton, the first office manager Berkley's company had. "Berkley's word was as good as gold."

When the election rolled around, Republicans, particularly those who had loyally stood by Nixon, retreated in shock and stayed home in droves. Although not a presidential election year, Republican candidates felt as if they were painted with Nixon's brush.

"Nixon turned out to be a disgrace," Narey recalled, bitterly. "You know that helped Berk's campaign."

Even Virginia Bedell, the staunch Republican who never actively campaigned for her son, was nonetheless determined to defend his integrity.

Joanne recalled, "Somebody said something bad about Dad on television and Grandma was so angry. She had never been in his campaign headquarters, across the street from the Methodist Church in Spirit Lake, but she came storming down the sidewalk, charged in, and, oh my God, every staff member huddled around her, getting her to sit down on the couch to talk about what had happened. It was wonderful to see Grandma so angry that she finally brought herself to come in and vent her anger and object to others saying bad things about her son. Not that she would change parties, by any means, or openly support Dad, but we were all touched and impressed by her anger. It makes me smile every time I think of that time. 'How can people say this?' she wanted to know."

If the Democrats were going to use Berkley as a candidate, Virginia wanted to make sure they would do it right, one campaign worker remembered. Maybe it was a case of family pride, or maybe Virginia saw the handwriting on the wall during the Watergate fallout, but either way, she ventured into the Democratic election headquarters in Fort Dodge, Iowa two weeks before the election, recalled Nancy Payne, who later worked in Berkley's Congressional office.

"One of the office ladies came running to me and said, 'Nancy, Nancy, somebody wants to see the Bedell person.' So I hurried over and there was this very attractive older lady, and she just said, 'I wanted to make sure my son's stuff is prominently displayed,'" Payne remembered. "I told Berk and Elinor about it after the election. They found it very humorous. What a lovely lady."

Berkley won election to the United States Congress in November 1974, the first Democrat to defeat a sitting Republican Congressperson in Northwest Iowa for as long as anyone could remember. He would enter Congress at age 53.

In the wake of Watergate and Nixon's resignation, Berkley was joined in Congress by 74 newly elected Democrats. The "Watergate Class" included Tom Harkin, the young Democrat from the neighboring district. The two became lifelong political partners and friends.

Berkley won re-election in 1976 and 1978, and continued to be re-elected during the Republican Ronald Reagan victory years of 1980 and 1984, as well as 1982.

"Reagan carried my district by a landslide," Berkley recalled.

How could so many people vote for Reagan and Berkley at the same time? Berkley favored gun control and fuel economy standards, opposed tax cuts and military buildups – nearly everything Reagan fervently sought.

Berkley said people voted for him because he stayed in touch with his constituents, communicated his stance with reason and conviction, and continued to act as a common Iowan.

He started a "Host a Congressman" program.

"In our district mailings, we invited people who would like to have me stay with them when I traveled throughout in the district to send in a post card. My secretary would make telephone calls to be sure that it would not be improper for me to stay with a family, and I would then spend the night in the home of various constituents – without regard to their political party.

"The Host a Congressman program gave me a chance to get to know the people and their beliefs, and it gave them a chance to get to know me firsthand. Frequently, during my stay, they would invite neighbors or friends to their home so that we could all spend some time together before retiring."

The program also broke up the monotony of life on the road in Berkley's 22-county district – although it sometimes complicated matters, too. One night, after a lengthy dinner meeting in the district, Berkley got in his car and drove to a home to spend the night with a host family. He knocked on the door, but no one answered. There was a light on in the living room, so he assumed the resident must be out of earshot; maybe they had stepped out for a few minutes? Finding the house unlocked, and according to Iowa custom, Berkley went in and sat down on the couch to wait for the family to return.

"After I had been there awhile, I started to think that this seemed rather strange. I checked my schedule sheet. I was at the wrong house! It would have been quite a challenge for me to explain my situation if the occupants had returned! I made a hasty retreat."

Berkley's Open Door meetings became another way for him to listen to voters' concerns, and for him to form his own policy stances and present his current positions. He held an Open Door meeting in each county, twice a year. Post cards and press releases invited everyone in the county to attend. "My predecessor had never done anything like that."

At the beginning of the Open Door meeting, Berkley would ask the group – anywhere from 12 to 60 people – to share what issues they would like to discuss. If necessary,

Berkley, left, at an Open Door meeting

Berkley would add one or two issues he also wanted to discuss. An aide would write the issues down and then they would go down the list.

"Okay, who wanted to talk about Vietnam?" Berkley would ask. Whoever raised the issue would voice a position and then everyone else could discuss it. After each issue, Berkley asked for a vote, and then he would state his position. At the end of meetings in each of the 22 counties, he would tabulate the votes and report the outcomes to constituents and the news media.

A Washington, D.C. reporter flew to Iowa to witness one of Berk's Open Door meetings. Afterward, the reporter told Berkley, "This is probably the only place in the nation where anything like this is taking place, and it is one of the few places where something like this could be done. It is because you have such a unique, educated, enlightened group of constituents that you can have these fruitful, effective meetings."

Berkley welcomed the chance to discuss issues with people.

"Those who came to Open Door meetings tended to be friends rather than opponents. And people tend to agree with the guy running the meeting, because he has a little control about what happens. Most of the time, I knew more about the legislation and the issue than they did because of my involvement."

Berkley did not promise that he would vote exactly as they did, and he didn't. "They never challenged me on this, because the votes in Congress tend not to be exactly like you took them in the meeting. But the Open Door meetings told the people that I really cared about what they thought, which I really did, and to listen to their arguments and listen to what they had to say, and that I cared about them as people."

The discussions sometimes changed his thinking on issues, not so much in terms of whether to support a policy, but rather that he sometimes learned the proposed solution might be faulty.

"There were times the people brought up things I had not been aware of. For example, the way the farm program was being administered. I might not know that the farm program, which required farmers to set aside a given amount of acres where they would not grow crops, didn't work the way I had been told it would. Most of the education I obtained from those meetings consisted of learning how things really happened out in the field; things you wouldn't be aware of if you weren't there."

Berkley also discovered the effect legislation had on people. If a new law that was intended to discourage corn production would instead cause increased production, he would try to revise the legislation.

"You don't know about issues like that unless you talk to the farmers."

"He deftly sought opinions without putting himself in a box," commented his son Tom, who worked as Berkley's unpaid administrative assistant for two years.

"Dad's political skills started out awful. In fact, when we first produced television commercials, we tried to figure out how to do them without actually putting Dad in them. As time progressed, he became the absolute star. He really learned the skills. He became very, very good at it.

"When he got up in front of an Open Door meeting, and somebody confronted him on an issue that would be a little bit outrageous, he became very adept. For example, in an ongoing effort to unseat him, the radically conservative John Birch Society would challenge him on issues. Dad would look the guy in the eye and he'd say, 'With all due respect, I think there are some other values we need to think about in addition to what you're saying.' He'd give some kind of a moralistic approach without answering the issue question. Then he'd turn to the rest of the group and he'd say, 'It doesn't matter what I think. It matters what you all think. How many of you think we should do what he's saying? How many of you think we should do what I'm saying?' Of course, everybody would vote Dad's way, except for five or six people. And he'd say, 'Okay, next question.'

"He had a way of engaging people and making them feel like it was *their* meeting. It may have been crafty and manipulative, but it was totally sincere. In his mind, he wasn't playing a game. Dad never left his hometown personality."

In his campaign consulting work, Tom found that many members of Congress experience an ego enlargement within a year after being elected.

"Many Congressmen become kind of knighted and important," Tom said. "Mom and Dad never did that. For me to stay in a home and spend the evening chatting with constituents, and then get up and have breakfast with them would be too much for me, but Dad loved it. Now psychologically, he needs – he loves – gratification. He needs stroking. It's real important to him. And you wouldn't run for office if you didn't, because the burden is so huge.

"It's important to Dad that others think highly of him. That's a big problem for him. It's also a motivator. He is a humble person, but his sense of value of himself is not intrinsic, it's external."

People loved Berkley's energy and his desire to be close to people.

In a parade, he would jump in and out of a convertible while it continued to move.

The campaign trail

"I'd jump out of the car and go shake three or four hands, then run back and put my hands on the side of the moving car and vault back inside," Berkley recalled. "People really got a big bang out of that. It's so opposite from being a staid Congressman just sitting in a car riding quietly down the parade route."

Berkley kept in touch with his constituents. Nothing riled him more than to see a politician lose connection with the public, as his 1980 opponent discovered.

In 1980, Republicans targeted Berkley. Before Berkley came into office during a year that Republicans were demoralized by Watergate, the district had always voted Republican. Ronald Reagan's bid for the presidency re-energized the Republican Party and they hoped to chip away at the 20-year Democratic majority in the House of Representatives.

State Senator Clarence Carney gave him a strong challenge, with a well-financed professional campaign. Berkley's staff became curious when they read Carney's campaign materials.

"The materials said, 'My opponent, Chair of the Select Committee on Energy,'" recalled Mark Gearan. "That was weird, because that was not Berkley's committee."

Berkley chaired a Small Business sub-committee, not the Energy Committee. Gearan called Marc Rosenberg, who worked on energy issues for the Small Business Committee, "Does this ring a bell to you?" he asked. Rosenberg had previously worked for an Ohio Congressman named Ludd Ashley, who had served on the Energy Committee. Rosenberg realized the brochure did not describe Berkley's committee at all.

The staff found that Ashley's opponent had the same campaign consultant as Berkley's opponent. Ashley's opponent's brochure looked almost identical, with some of the same quotes. A third Republican candidate had the same consultant – and the same brochure!

Berkley had started to lose ground to the well-financed campaign. He wanted to expose the fraud immediately, but his staff urged him to wait for maximum effect. The right time came when they agreed to a live television debate in October. Carney insisted that the candidates stand during the debate. Berkley wanted to sit down. Finally, they agreed that Berkley could sit down and be comfortable, while Carney stood up. Standing up helped Carney become uncomfortable.

Berkley won a coin toss and elected to speak first. The staff members of his opponent were puzzled. Many candidates want to have the last word. When the debate began, Berkley immediately uncovered an easel with his challenger's brochure and the Ohio campaign brochure.

"I simply read his brochure out loud, highlighted what my opponent said, what a candidate in Ohio said, what my opponent's wife said, and what the wife of the person in Ohio said," Berkley recalled. "The quotes were identical. I followed that with 'Out here, we're used to having people speak their own mind and not having some consultant put words in their mouth. If you want to have somebody who will really represent you in Congress, you'd better have somebody that is speaking for you and for himself.'"

"Voters could clearly see the difference between Berkley and plastic, political, cynical marketing," recalled Gearan. "Berkley had always been the antithesis of that.

What you see is what you get with Berkley – a genuine guy who was in public service for all the right reasons."

Berkley steamrolled over the attempted upset. "The press loved it, and the race was no contest after that," Berkley remembered.

The debate confrontation had been more than a campaign ploy. To be a real leader, Berkley believed, he needed to listen to the people and speak for himself.

"They're not mutually exclusive, they're complementary. I know what my people told me they wanted. Whether that came about as a result of my influencing them, I don't know. But they wanted me to listen to them, to consider their views, and then vote as I thought I should. I think that's what employees want, too. Leaders are not just people willing to make decisions. If you are a good leader, you also make the people a part of what's being done."

As a Congressman, Berkley formed a bipartisan Agricultural Advisory Committee. He also formed advisory committees of Bankers, Doctors, Lawyers, and Small Business Persons – bipartisan groups of community leaders. Berkley informed them of legislation and considered their advice, and then voted as he saw fit.

Berkley believed the two-pronged style to be effective, but more importantly, he saw it as the right thing to do. He carried that style with him from his childhood days in the South End Gang through his athletic career, his military life, and into his business career.

"It's beneficial not to separate management and workers. That's one thing that always bothered me in the military. As officers, we were not supposed to associate with enlisted people. I considered that ridiculous. In our crew, we worked together to be sure we survived. It would have been a disaster if we had considered one group superior to the other."

Berkley's approach proved popular, even if he didn't vote the peoples will all the time. After his first two elections – his first a loss and the second a victory – his Republican district became a Berkley Bedell sure thing.

One election year, after the votes were counted, Berkley received calls of congratulations from two different Republicans, each of whom he had defeated in previous elections. Both men wanted Berk to know they had voted for him.

Berkley received votes from die-hard Republicans like Ed Donovan and Pete Narey, and eventually he even received his mother's blessing.

Although he was Vice President of Production of Berkley's company, Ed Donovan would never trade his vote for job security and Berkley did not expect him to.

"To me, he's easy to get along with," remarked Donovan, the boyhood neighbor who had admired Berk ever since he saw him try to fly with handmade wings. He had worked with Berkley to tackle giants in business and to build new inventions.

"My wife didn't see eye to eye with Berk politically, but if he ever thought, 'She's pushing Republicans against me all the time,' he never would have said it. He always made friendly political comments to her.

"He was always the better man; better than the Republicans running against him. Because my wife was the county chairman, I got to meet every single candidate. I'm no politician, but I could realize that most of them didn't know what they were talking about. They didn't really know what they were doing, and I ain't about to vote for somebody like that. One thing was pretty easy: I could damn near pick out a manager when I talked to him. I would talk to him for half an hour or so, and it may have been snap decisions, but I could tell whether I wanted to have anything to do with a person for a manager. Most politicians, hell, they were useless – but nobody else would run.

"I never told Berk that. He doesn't know whom I voted for, but I voted for him because he was the best man – not because I worked for him. I had no question about it."

Narey also rooted for his boyhood friend, even when he thought Berkley to be out of place both as a Democrat and a Congressman.

"I didn't think Berk would be happy in Congress – being one of 435. I thought he would be better suited as Secretary of Commerce, where he could run things. And I still think that's probably true. But Berk proved to be very successful as a Congressman. He liked it better than I thought he would.

"You know, the world isn't made up of politics. We can talk politics together dispassionately. He understands that all the good people are not necessarily Democrats. I have the same feeling about Republicans. We get along fine. We don't let that interfere in our friendship."

Still, "He was the last Democrat I ever voted for on the national level," Narey pointed out in 2001.

Berkley's son Ken sensed a family reconciliation, if not necessarily a political one, before Berkley's mother died in 1975.

"My grandmother wintered in Florida and made her spring trek from Florida back to Iowa to spend the summer," Ken recalled. "She stopped in Washington, D.C. on the way. Mom and Dad took her around to show her their life in Congress. Grandma gave every impression of being the proud mother of her son. I think, maybe for the first time, she came to realize that the values she passed on to Dad were the values that guided him as a Democratic member of Congress.

"Then Grandma came up to Newfield, New York where Kathie and I were living. Our daughter Charity had just been born on May 8 and Grandma got to meet her great-granddaughter. She traveled to Iowa City and had dinner with my cousins, Dick and Dave, Jack's twin sons. And finally she got to Spirit Lake and had dinner with Uncle Jack and Aunt Marcia. A day or two later, she had a massive heart attack and died. So that trip is seen as kind of a pilgrimage of closing things out for her."

Chapter Nineteen

Congress: Mandate for Change

President Richard Nixon resigned in August 1974, after two years of investigation into the Watergate Hotel break-in, illegal campaign activities, and the ensuing cover-up. Public indignation propelled 75 new Democrats to victory in that November's congressional election.

The "Watergate Class" came to Washington, D.C. in December 1974 to organize and work together as a class before taking office in January. A group of incoming freshman had never before organized in this manner.

"I found it a tremendously exciting meeting," Berkley recounted. "I have never been similarly impressed with a group of people. Many of them, like me, had never before held major political office. We were all dedicated to making a difference, and like my son Tom's trip to Vietnam, it never occurred to us that there was anything we could not do."

They decided they would vote as a bloc to reform the way Congress – and the U.S. government – worked. They would start by attacking the autocratic seniority system, through which the majority party's longest serving member of a committee would automatically be elected chairman. With such unquestioned job security, the chairman could act like a dictator, deciding which bills would go to the full Congress for a vote and punishing renegades who would oppose him or her.

If someone fell out of grace, the chairperson might not call on that member during the entire session, and no one could do anything about it. During the previous congressional session, the Democratic caucus took some power from committee chairpersons by adopting for the first time a policy of electing chairmen by secret ballot.

"We had the feeling that the seniority system had perpetuated some people in offices who were no longer competent to handle things well," said Paul Simon, a freshman Congressman from Illinois in 1974 and later a U.S. Senator and presidential candidate. "You had people who were beyond their prime chairing key committees, not just for the House, but for the country. Berkley was part of the group of us who wanted reforms."

At one of their first class meetings, Floyd Fithian, a new member from Indiana suggested that they invite the sitting committee chairmen to come meet with them, so they could decide whether to support them or oppose them for re-election to their chairmanship. The group agreed. Most of the incumbents could not imagine such a brash action. It shocked the sitting chairmen. One committee chair said he would not meet with them. The group informed him that was his privilege, but under such circumstances, they would all vote against him. He reconsidered and met with them.

"Some of the other chairmen who came were fuming that they had to meet with us," recalled Tom Harkin, a freshman Congressman from Iowa and later a U.S. Senator and presidential candidate. "They'd never done this before. Some were immensely arrogant: Wayne Hays, Bob Pogue, Eddie Hebert," Harkin said. "There were some really hard feelings. But we had the votes."

Berkley approached Wayne Hays privately.

"I'm told you're a son-of-a-bitch, in the way you manage your committee," Berkley challenged the crusty, longtime Ohio Congressman and committee chair, who was later exposed in a scandal with his mistress/secretary. "I don't really care if you've been a son-of-a-bitch or not. But I do care whether you're *going to be* a son-of-a-bitch."

Hays insisted that Berkley had been wrong about him. But Berkley had heard too many stories from credible sources.

"If he had said, 'Well, I have been a little bit arrogant and I'm sorry for that, but if I get a chance to reform, I'm going to try to do things better,' I probably would have voted for him," Berkley explained later. "So I decided after his response that I would vote against him. He didn't plan to change, so we kicked him out."

Harkin said some chairmen recognized the shift in power.

"Jack Brooks, a tough-talking Texan, came to the meeting chomping a cigar. He sat down and looked at us and said, 'Okay, you sons-of-bitches. You've got the power. I recognize that. What do you want me to do?' It broke the ice. Everyone laughed. His honesty disarmed us."

After the interviews, the freshmen decided they would try to unseat four committee chairmen.

"We mounted an active campaign and defeated all four. It was the first time the most senior member had not been elected chair, and it pretty well eliminated the major problem with the seniority system," Berkley recounted.

It sent a message to the rest of the Congress that the 75 freshman members must be reckoned with.

"The first thing we did was throw out Eddie Hebert, who headed the Armed Services Committee; then we threw out Wilber Mills, who was the giant of the 'Ways to Be Mean Committee,'" recalled Robert Edgar, elected in 1974 as a Congressman from Pennsylvania.

"We stayed as a bloc," said Harkin. "We might lose a couple or three, but on any given issue dealing with structure, chairmanships, or procedures in how the House ran, we had 65-70 people voting together."

The impact of the class was similar to some freshman classes of the past – the New Deal Democrats of the 1930s, the return of the Republicans in the 1950s – and the class shared some similarities with the 1994 Republican class, but The Watergate Class differed in two huge respects:

1) Their class had come from a grassroots groundswell, not spurred on or aided by a charismatic President (Roosevelt, Eisenhower) or a dynamic organizer/recruiter (Newt Gingrich in 1994).

2) They were not overthrowing the other party. Democrats already controlled the Congress. They were reforming their *own* party's majority-controlled Congress in a clash of ideals and institutional cultures.

In the wake of Watergate, the public clamored for openness and honesty in government.

"We led the charge on behalf of the public," commented Harkin. "We wanted to change the way things had been done and we were committed to changing the institutional structure to get things done faster – and we did."

"We were rebels," exclaimed Edgar, a 31-year-old who had been an urban United Methodist street minister from Philadelphia before being elected in 1974. "We were anti-war people who dropped in, rather than dropped out."

At age 53, Berkley found himself to be one of the oldest in the class. Like Berkley, many of the class members came directly from other occupations, not previous political office. Edgar and Bob Cornell (a Roman Catholic priest) came directly from ministry positions. Harkin had become a Legal Aid attorney after serving in the Air Force. Fred Richmond and Berkley Bedell had been successful businessmen.

"We didn't come out of state legislatures," said Harkin. "We had a much different perspective on what government does and how it goes about doing it. We wanted the system to be open and above board.

"Today, we take all that for granted. As a Senate committee chairman, when I have a Senate conference committee meeting, like I did on the farm bill this year, it is open to the public. The press and everybody can come in. Prior to 1975, meetings like that were all closed. Nobody could get in. The chairman ran it with whomever he wanted. It is hard to think about, but that's the way it worked back then."

When the class held a retreat to organize its revolution, Edgar said, the class had many dynamic leaders but no dominant personality.

Berkley provided an experienced voice, so they elected him Secretary of the class caucus.

"I saw Berk emerge as the person in the class who a portion of us respected for his curiosity, his questions, and his innocence. He asked really good questions and he gave good advice," remarked Edgar. "He brought the World War II/Korean-era generation to a place which, for the first time, had Vietnam Era congress people. He gained respect through the years because of his steady courage, as opposed to a flashy leadership style."

By April 1975, Edgar led a floor fight to end U.S. involvement in the Vietnam War.

"Berk had an active part in shutting down the Vietnam War, saying, 'We are not going to re-impose troops in Saigon. We're going to get out of this thing,'" recalled Edgar. "I led a floor fight. It had been unheard of, for a 31-year-old Congressman to even speak during his first year, and Berk stood at my side. He gave voice and courage to his beliefs."

Harkin recalled Berkley as a fearless, unassuming interrogator. Harkin remembered him as one of, if not the most, outspoken of them all.

"Berkley did not worry about what he said to anyone, about changing these systems. I had spent a lot of my former life in the military, so I was used to chain of command. But Berkley had been the general in his company. I had been just a trooper. While I wanted to change things, maybe I didn't speak up as loudly as some others did. You sure couldn't say that about Berkley."

"If you didn't know better," Harkin continued, "you'd say, 'My Gosh that guy is naïve,' because of the way he would say and do things, but Berkley was anything but naïve. He knew exactly what he was doing. By being forward and provocative in his approach to some of the old bulls, he could strip away their façade. He'd say, 'I just don't understand how we do this.' Then they would say, 'Okay, let me tell you how we do things here.' Kind of a putdown. In relating how they did things, they exposed the fact that they ran their committees like little dictatorships and they pointed out exactly what Berkley was there to uncover. Berkley didn't seek the approval of anyone. He simply wanted to get to the bottom of things and see how they reacted."

The freshman Democrats continued to meet and act as a class. A small group of them would regularly meet at Berkley and Elinor's apartment near the Capitol, including Representatives Simon, Cornell, Edgar, and Matt McHugh of New York. They elected Berkley President of the caucus in later years.

"The group included a lot of hard-chargers and bright people," recalled Harkin. "The class consisted of a group of unique, public-minded individuals."

Harkin, Simon, and Paul Tsongas of Massachusetts, eventually ran for the Democratic nomination for President. Christopher Dodd of Connecticut became a Senator and leader in the Democratic Party. Other leaders in the class were Max Baucus of Montana, Tim Wirth of Colorado, Floyd Fithian of Indiana, Toby Moffett of Connecticut, Helen Meyner of New Jersey, George Miller and Henry Waxman of California, and Jim Oberstar of Minnesota.

The Speaker appointed Berkley to the Agriculture Committee and, because of his experience, to the Small Business Committee. He later served as chairman of various subcommittees of these committees.

Berkley was active on peace and military issues, and part of a small group of activists who met with the Democratic leadership to consider strategy on various issues.

He helped to form the Environmental Study Conference and he worked with the Farm Policy Coalition.

He helped to form the Congressional Clearinghouse on the Future.

"Berk and Elinor were very involved in that group, as we listened to Jacques Cousteau, Margaret Mead, Alvin Toffler, Dr. Jonas Salk, who invented the polio vaccine, and other speakers who would stretch our minds," remembered Edgar. "One of the tragedies of our legislative process is that members of Congress and Senators don't look beyond this year's budget and next year's election. They don't understand that the 5-10-15 year perspective is important in making law." Edgar became chairman after Congressman Al Gore left to ran for the United States Senate.

"Congress either pork barrels law, in terms of what's best for their district, or they have a corporate mentality that says, 'What's the bottom line for this year, because that what's going to affect me politically.' Most members are like television sets with somebody constantly changing the channel. They either don't take the time or have the time to view the broader picture," Edgar said.

To restore integrity in government, Berkley had to buck a system of favors and tradeoffs. He thought he should have complete freedom to vote according to his convictions, regardless of party strategy, or pressure from lobbyists and constituent groups.

Members who voted against appropriations for projects in the districts of other members risked being punished by having funds not appropriated for projects in their own districts. Berkley frequently voted, and argued, against projects that he thought were not proper expenditures of taxpayers' money.

"On one occasion, I received a call from a member of the committee staff reminding me that I had a project in the appropriations bill that was coming up for a vote and they noted that I had frequently voted against appropriations bills," Berkley recalled. "He was clearly trying to communicate to me that my project might be in jeopardy if I voted against the bill.

"I immediately went down to the floor of the House and reported exactly what had happened. Those proceedings are televised and the press is there. The members of the committee managing the bill did not know what to say. They never threatened me again! People look at me with disbelief when I tell them that in the 12 years I served in the Congress only once did another member offer to vote for one of my amendments if I would vote for his. Of course, I refused."

Berkley said that fellow freshmen Paul Simon and Bob Edgar were equally adamant about supporting issues on their merits, in contrast to the well-established system of favors.

"Bob Edgar served on the Appropriations Committee," Berkley recalled. "Even the most conscientious committee members did not dare oppose the project of another member for fear that others might retaliate by opposing the conscientious member's project. As a result, the committee approved all kinds of pork barrel projects. Bob Edgar could not accept that. He openly opposed other member's pork barrel projects, and I frequently joined him."

The Congress had a reputation of reward and punishment when it came to electing colleagues for leadership positions. Berkley found that colleagues would deal fairly with him if he treated them honestly.

When Carl Albert retired as Speaker of the House, "Tip" O'Neill of Massachusetts was in line to become Speaker. Berkley and a colleague didn't try to hide the fact that they were mounting an effort to get someone to run against O'Neill. O'Neill got wind of it and said he would like to meet with Berkley, so Berkley made an appointment.

"I understand you have been bad-mouthing me," O'Neill said.

"I haven't been bad-mouthing you," Berkley replied, "but I take this job very seriously and I believe there are others who would make a better Speaker of the House. There are those who are concerned about how you will act if you are elected. I will be glad to tell you what their concerns are if you would like to know."

"I would like to know," replied O'Neill.

Berkley responded, "They think you will keep a list of your friends and your enemies, and reward your friends and punish your enemies."

"If I get to be Speaker I will not do that," O'Neill replied. He was elected Speaker.

Not long after, an opportunity developed for two additional Democrats to be appointed temporarily to the

Foreign Affairs Committee by the Steering and Policy Committee, on which the Speaker served. There were several candidates. Berkley asked O'Neill for his support.

"I have already made one commitment, but you will be my second commitment," he told Berkley. Sure enough, he argued strongly for the appointment and Berkley won.

"This said an awful lot about the person whom I had openly opposed," Berkley recalled. O'Neill also flew out to Iowa to speak on Berkley's behalf.

"We were good friends. Tip O'Neill earned and deserved the great admiration that I had for him, and both Democrats and Republicans loved him."

Berkley had a similar experience with U.S. Rep. Kika de la Garza of Texas. When de la Garza was in line to become chairman of the Agricultural Committee, Berkley and another member mounted an open effort to defeat him.

Paul Simon refused to join Berkley's effort. Regardless of his personal friendship with Berkley, Simon thought Congress needed more Hispanics in leadership positions.

"Paul let his values overrule friendship, which I admired," said Berkley.

After de la Garza won, Berkley decided to mend fences. A more vindictive chairman could have frozen Berkley out of discussions and blocked his favorite legislation. De la Garza did neither, choosing instead to cooperate fairly with Berkley.

Berkley and Kika de la Garza, during an Agriculture Committee hearing

"When I took the handle on the plow and became committee chairman, you came over and were the first to put aside divisions and help me till the fields," de la Garza wrote in December 1986. "That meant a lot to me ... we developed a friendship that I consider to be irreplaceable ... your mark is indelible."

By the end of Berkley's tenure in Congress, de la Garza wrote to say, "Why is Berkley Bedell leaving me? Why is my best friend retiring now?"

"I give him a great deal of credit for not holding a grudge, which he could legitimately have done," said Berkley. "I had learned that you should not shrink from doing what you think is right."

The Watergate Class of 1975 not only made history, but its members became lifelong friends.

"Berkley Bedell is my hero," said Edgar. "He taught me how to stand on principle and vote your best judgment. He had a basic political commitment to do well. Berk didn't need politics to expand his ego. He needed politics to make a difference."

After his career in Congress, Edgar became President of Claremont School of Theology, in California. He then became General Secretary of the National Council of Churches of Christ in the United States.

"Berkley combines compassion – he genuinely wants to help people – with courage," said Simon. "I am sure Berkley Bedell never took a poll to decide how he should vote on anything in the House of Representatives. He wasn't there to perpetuate himself in office. His combination of compassion and courage is the combination we need in Congress today."

The Watergate Class – the 75 Democrats elected to Congress in 1974 – held gatherings in 1992 and 2000, with all the warmth of a high school class reunion.

"I think we were closer than what you would find at a high school reunion," said Berkley. "It was the greatest group of people I've ever been associated with, in almost any way you would measure things: capability, intelligence, commitment, values, fearlessness. We were a completely

The Watergate Class of 1974, at their 25th anniversary reunion.

unified group, a completely naïve, committed group, and anxious to be a major factor in what happened. Which we were!"

Their impact was more significant than any single piece of legislation they passed. The group fulfilled its mandate to make the government more accountable to the public and truer to the ideals of democracy.

What they accomplished, more than anything else was the changing of how Congress operated. They made it a democratic institution instead of an autocratic institution.

And they demonstrated that a person can continue to be elected by standing for what he or she thinks is right, regardless of the perceived consequences.

Chapter Twenty

Berkley in Congress

Mark Gearan watched Berkley eat his lunch, as they talked about billion-dollar budgets, and he realized how much he admired this millionaire Congressman.

Berkley removed a sandwich from a worn, brown paper lunch bag. Next came a plastic margarine container filled with applesauce, then a spoon, and a napkin. Berkley neatly folded the lunch bag and slipped it into his coat pocket, to use again. Berkley munched on his cheese sandwich, lubricated by spoons full of applesauce.

"He made me thirsty, just looking at him eating this lunch," Gearan recalled his first few days as Berkley's press secretary. Gearan, a Harvard graduate who grew up watching the backslapping, power-brokering politicians in his Boston hometown, was still getting used to the down home representative from Iowa.

Berkley Bedell didn't leave his home for Washington as much as he brought Spirit Lake – his Depression-era Iowa childhood, his business success, his strong faith, and determination – to Washington. His values – honesty, frugality, practicality, determination, fairness, and compassion – drove his dealings with legislators, bureaucracies, corporations, Presidents, and dictators.

"The same guy who tried to root out waste, fraud, and abuse in government brought a cheese sandwich for lunch, in a re-used paper bag, when he was one of the wealthiest men in Congress," Gearan remembered. "He wasn't caught up with any of the excesses of Washington or his own financial worth. He stayed very grounded.

"He didn't spend the people's money any more than he spent his own. He didn't go out to The Palm (a restaurant in D.C. for movers and shakers) for lunch and then complain about a $400 hammer. His actions were not stunts. It was how he led his life."

He brought his walking shoes and his fishing rod. He brought part of his family. His personal way of doing business became his personal way of being a Congressman.

Unannounced Agency Visits

Berkley's office door opened right into the production plant in Spirit Lake for two reasons: to make it easy for him to get into the plant quickly, and to make it easy for workers to visit him. If he had a question, he would go and ask someone, or vice versa.

He also liked to get up and stroll around the plant from time to time. He tried to know all of the workers by name. He wanted to know how they did their jobs, what they thought would make the job or process better, and what problems they faced.

He figured this was how government should operate. When he had spare time, he would grab his coat and go off to visit.

Sometimes it was for a specific purpose. He wandered the halls of the Agriculture Department for several days, sticking his head through doorways and asking what people did in each office. During budget hearings, he stumped Agriculture officials by asking them about obscure offices.

"I stopped and asked people what they did and they really couldn't explain," Berkley challenged the official. "You can't explain either, so maybe we don't need all of them." Several of them disappeared.

Berkley would walk into a federal building unannounced, sometimes to follow up on a problem or to research a question, sometimes just to see what was happening.

"Let's try the third floor," he said to himself. He rode up the elevator, stepped out, and walked into the passport office. He loved to see how much he could learn from chatting with secretaries and office workers before – inevitably and mysteriously – someone from top management would appear.

"Hello, I'm Berkley Bedell, Congressman from Iowa," he said to the receptionist. "Just stopping by to see how things are going for you."

"Just waiting for the repairman again," the receptionist replied, pointing to the crowd around the water cooler. "They're the production line that makes the passports. When the machine goes down, the whole line can't do a thing until the repairman comes." She told Berkley the maintenance contractor would not arrive for hours sometimes, and the agency's top management did nothing to eliminate the waiting problem.

"Congressman Bedell, so good to see you," a deputy director came up and shook his hand. "Would you like to step into my office?" Berkley stepped in and persuaded the top management to demand the maintenance company start making prompt repairs – or they would be promptly replaced. Things changed, and workers in the Passport Division were most grateful.

Some departments and agencies had employee attendance problems, but it was impossible to verify if the person had actually arrived and left work at the time he or she said. Berkley got new, one-page sign-in sheets for some of the agencies so each person was required to sign in and out. If Betty Smith signed in at 8:15 a.m., John Jones signed just below her name, and could not claim he arrived before 8:15 a.m. The same process applied upon leaving.

The headquarters of the Postal Service in Washington won the prize for being the worst of all those Berkley visited in terms of management. When he arrived, he found that every person had to sign in or out at the entrance to the building. Berkley asked the administrator why. The reply was, "to be sure that the employees are actually here."

"Can't you make the supervisors responsible for that?" Berkley asked him.

"We tried that, but it didn't work," the administrator replied.

Berkley's staff wanted to translate complaints from constituents into an agency visit "where Berkley could become the surrogate constituent," said Marc Rosenberg of the Small Business Committee's Antitrust Subcommittee staff, which Berkley chaired.

It was a classic *Mr. Smith Goes to Washington* moment. Berkley said, "I would walk into an office and look around to see how they're treating people, and I wanted to hear what they would say to me when they didn't know I'm a Congressman."

One of Berkley's constituents complained to Rosenberg that they couldn't get anyone to answer the phone at the Department of Health and Human Services in the afternoons. Rosenberg called Berkley's assistant, who said, "He's got a hole in his schedule. Can you be ready to go for a walk with him?" Berkley and Rosenberg left his office at 3:00 p.m. and walked three blocks to investigate the phone mystery. They walked in unannounced. They saw 30 or 40 desks, but only three or four people in the office. Phones were ringing everywhere.

Berkley found someone to get the Secretary of Health and Human Services, former Congresswoman Margaret Heckler, on the phone. He persuaded her to come and see the roomful of empty desks and ringing telephones.

"Peggy, I don't think this is the way this is supposed to be," Berkley said.

The office had gone to a flexible-time policy a year before. Everybody in that office had figured out that the liaison telephone calls, particularly from the district offices of the Congress, would crescendo as you got later and later in the day. Three-quarters of those offices were in other time zones. So workers would start their days early enough that they were gone in time to escape the end-of-the-day flood. Most Iowa calls after 3:00 p.m. Central Time (4:00 p.m. Eastern Time) would go unanswered. It was even worse for people in Rocky Mountain or Pacific Time states.

As a result of the visit, the department decided to stagger workers' flex times so there were always enough people to answer the phones from people in the West.

When the process was successfully completed, the Secretary of Health and Human Services, a Republican, sent out a press release acknowledging Berkley's role in calling her attention to this problem. She thanked him for his constructive approach and elaborated on what she was doing to fix the problem.

"People lived in fear of Berkley showing up at their agency," said Mark Levine, who worked in the office of the Small Business Committee. "The only way they could prepare for him showing up was to make sure everything ran well."

The Small Business Administration made the mistake of ignoring a program that Berkley had created. In 1978, he had authored a bill to create a loan program to support the creation of alternative energy businesses, through the Small Business Administration. When he became chairman of the Small Business subcommittee on Energy, Environment, and Safety, he asked Rosenberg to find out how the loan program was progressing. He contacted every person who had ever received the loan.

"More than half of the people told us in writing that nobody in the SBA had known anything about this," said Rosenberg. "They saw an article about it somewhere and brought the article to the SBA office. They had to show the loan officer that such a program existed. Only at that point did someone help them."

So Berkley and Rosenberg walked in, unannounced, to the SBA field office in Washington, D.C. The headquarters were upstairs.

"I'm here from Iowa and I thought I'd stop in at the SBA and find out about getting a loan to finance a little store with alternative energy devices," he said. "Do you have any loan program for that sort of thing?"

"Not that I know of," the SBA workers said, one after another.

"Would somebody in the regional office know?" Berkley inquired. "Could we check there?"

They walked over to another part of the building and heard the same story. "Is this a new law?" the regional representative asked.

"Actually, it's a couple of years old, so I hear," Berkley said.

"Maybe somebody in the legal department would know."

Berkley sat in the legal department while the staff rummaged through files, Rosenberg said, until the general counsel walked in and recognized the Congressman sitting in the lobby in a shabby old chair being helped by a clerk.

"Oh, Mr. Congressman, what can we do for you?" Berkley explained that he was trying to get some information about how the SBA is helping people with this program that he'd heard about, without telling them that he had been the author of it. The general counsel came back with the statute and the information.

"We're curious as to why this program is on your books, but nobody in your area office or your regional office seems to know anything about it," Rosenberg challenged the general counsel.

Soon, Berkley got a letter from the administrator of the SBA assuring the Congressman that they were quickly informing all the offices of the program.

"That's good, because now you have something to tell us when we bring you in for the hearing next week," Berkley replied.

The result, said Rosenberg, "was typical of Berkley. We could have played 'Gotcha!' with these guys, but he had no desire to catch the SBA with their pants down. He simply wanted to make the program work. So we set it up so the hearing was an opportunity for the SBA to make an announcement of the improvement and changes in their program. We gave them an opportunity to dig themselves out of the hole. And they thanked the chairman for the opportunity to inform the Congress. We dealt with the agency in private. We basically said to them, here's what we have. It's embarrassing, but we're going to give you time to tell us what you're doing to fix it."

Former U.S. Representative Tom Tauke, a Republican from northeast Iowa, described Berkley's attitude:

"It was 'Somebody needs to go in and be a watchdog to tame these bureaucracies'. I'm here to protect the little guy who's having to deal with this big agency, so I'd better go over there.' It's a hands-on, Iowa approach to things. It's Berkley's personal style and an Iowa thing, too. In a sense, you can't imagine someone from New York doing this."

Berkley wanted to fix problems, not glorify himself.

"Berkley was a workhorse, not a show horse," said Tauke's former assistant, Ed Senn. "The show horse way is to write the press release, call the cameras, show up on the steps, and wave the papers. Then when the cameras leave, you just walk out. You made your point. But a workhorse shows up, does the work, sees if there's anything there, and then does the press release stating that there needs to be reforms in X-Y-Z. In one instance, the focus is me, and in the other instance, it's a 'let's solve the problem' attitude."

Living in D.C.

It had been nearly 30 years since Berkley and Elinor lived anywhere but Spirit Lake. They had traveled all over the world, but always returned to their house on East Okoboji Lake, within four miles of where Berkley's grandparents, his mother, and he and his brother grew up. He liked living close to his work.

He and Elinor first rented a small apartment ten blocks from the Capitol. When summer arrived, they decided to move to a ground floor apartment in a town house in the same block. During Easter recess, Berk and Elinor went on a camping trip to Northern Minnesota, planning to move into the town house the following week. They arrived in Washington late at night, with their camping gear. They parked and locked the station wagon in the lot by the town house, and went up to the apartment for the night. The next morning, they found someone had thrown a piece of cement through the car window and stolen all their belongings, including personal records, camping gear, and clothing.

They went to the police station to report the theft.

"The D.C. Police Department had absolutely no interest in investigating the crime. They gave us no help, whatsoever, until they learned that I was a Congressman," said Berkley. He and Elinor learned that youths had stolen their flame-orange camping tent, had taken it across the street, erected it on a piece of property in a low-cost housing project across the street, and slept in it that very night. The police made no effort to apprehend them. The youths had thrown the things they did not want down the garbage chute of the housing building. "By sorting through the garbage, I succeeded in rescuing most of our personal records!"

Berkley and Elinor decided not to rent the ground floor town house – a place where Elinor would have to spend a significant amount of time alone while Berkley toured his district in Iowa. Instead, they moved to a larger, upstairs apartment in the same area. Within three months, there were three murders on the streets within a block of this new apartment.

Spirit Lake seemed a long way away.

Shortly before the next election, Berkley and Elinor were sufficiently confident of another election victory that they purchased a row house, three blocks from the Capitol and two blocks from Berk's Congressional office. It was a 16-foot wide house with two floors, a basement, and a garage. Because it had a large living room and was close to the Capitol, the house served as a meeting place for many activities.

When Jimmy Carter first started his campaign for the Presidency, he kicked off the campaign with a speech in Berkley's district in Northwest Iowa. His speech impressed the Iowans and the momentum he gained there pushed him into the White House. Carter never forgot it. After his election, he invited the people from Berkley's district to come to the White House to hear his State of the Union Address to

Congress. President Carter joined them after the speech. Elinor thought it would be nice to invite the group to their new home for a dinner before they went to the White House. She expected 25 people. The invitations were mailed and people started to reply. The number attending grew larger and larger. When the time finally came for the dinner, Elinor cooked for 125 people in their new, little row house. They borrowed chairs from a nearby church and people ate sitting on beds and in hallways. The dinner proved to be a great housewarming for their new home, and the people appreciated it.

Family grows

During part of Berkley's tenure in Congress, their children lived close by. Tom came to Washington to be Berkley's administrative assistant and political adviser.

"I set up and ran his office," said Tom. "So Dad and I were intimately involved for a little over a year and a half, day-to-day on issues important to the district. I became the political guy and Dad was the issue guy, as well as the personality. My job was to organize his office and his work so that he could get re-elected and do whatever it was that he believed in. We had that open contract."

Ken Bedell moved from New York to become pastor of a United Methodist Church on Maryland's Eastern Shore. He was invited to lead the Congress in prayer at the beginning of one of its morning sessions.

Here is the prayer Ken gave and Berkley's following remarks, taken from the Congressional Record, June 26, 1980:

The Lord says, "I will condemn the person who turns away from Me, and puts his trust in man, in the trust of mortal man."— Jeremiah 17:5.

"O God, who makes all things possible, we pray today for all the people of the world. We especially pray for those who suffer because of the greed or selfishness of other people.

"We remember those living in this Nation who suffer because of unemployment, inadequate housing, and discrimination.

Speaker of the House Tip O'Neill (center) recognizes the Rev. Ken Bedell after he delivered the prayer on June 26, 1980. From left, Majority Leader Jim Wright, Rep. Berkley Bedell, O'Neill, Ken Bedell, Rep. Bob Bauman (Congressman from Ken's district), and House Chaplain Jim Ford

"Be with those who gather in this room today to write the laws of the United States, that their work would truly be to Your glory. Give them the wisdom to know Your perfect will and the courage to put aside their personal needs to work for the good of all and the coming of Your kingdom. Amen"

BERKLEY BEDELL: Mr. Speaker. This has been a proud and happy morning for me, as my son, Rev. Ken Bedell gave the prayer.

"I believe that so frequently here in the House, as we hurry about our legislative activities, we fail to take time to look at what is really important in life. I want to tell this body that when this young man was born in the Bedell household, some 32 years ago, it was a happy moment, and as he has grown, his life has been one of the most important things to his mother and me.

"Ken Bedell graduated as a chemist from college, and as he looked at his life he wanted to do something that he thought would be more meaningful and be of more help to people, even though certainly it was not nearly as rewarding to him financially. I am extremely pleased he decided he wanted to go into the ministry. I am extremely pleased and proud of what a great family he has, all of whom have brought great joy to his mother and me. I cannot tell you the pride that it gives me, as a tear welled up in my eye, as he spoke to us this morning with the prayer he gave."

Ken Bedell and his wife, Kathie, raised two wonderful daughters. He continued his crusade for justice and compassion. This article appeared in *The Baltimore Sun* in 1981:

If the little town of Preston in Caroline County, Maryland seems an unlikely international center for the United Methodist Church's advocacy of racial justice and human rights, including those of gays in this country and the poor in El Salvador, the answer lies with a modest 33 year-old Eastern Shore pastor, the Rev. Kenneth Bedell.

"I just think it's an important part of my ministry to raise Christian concerns that go beyond providing for our immediate needs," Mr. Bedell said yesterday.

Bedell is pastor of two of Preston's four Methodist churches, Bethesda and Grove. Both have white congregations, as does a third in town. The fourth is black.

"We have segregated churches here," Mr. Bedell said matter-of-factly.

But Preston also has an active Race and Religion Committee, of which Bedell and other townspeople are proud. It draws members from all four congregations.

Last Sunday, Mr. Bedell's parishioners prayed for all who were afflicted by the tragedy of the murdered black children in Atlanta. "And we remembered El Salvador in our worship service too," he said.

At a national conference in Louisville last month, Mr. Bedell was one of the first five signers of a letter calling on the United Methodist Church to develop a denomination-wide council on "the gospel and human rights."

He signed on behalf of the Coalition for the Whole Gospel, a liberal caucus within United Methodism that was formed two years ago.

Other signers of the letter represented Black Methodists for Church Renewal, the Affirmation Organization, the Women's Caucus, and the Methodist Federation for Social Action.

"We are deeply concerned about the rising tide of human rights violations both across our land and throughout the world," Mr. Bedell and his colleagues at the Louisville meeting wrote to the United Methodist leadership, including the Council of Bishops.

They recognized that Methodists have 'a positive record of involvement,' including recent 'support of the church and human rights victims in El Salvador.' But they added:

"We feel that in the present climate, the time has come for our church to mobilize the broadest possible constituency to counter human right violations."

They formally asked for the establishment of a "denomination-wide consultation" to address human rights violations "perpetrated against the following groups: the poor, ethnic and racial minorities, victims of repressive regimes, lesbians and gay men, undocumented workers, disabled persons, political dissenters, unemployed and underemployed women."

Mr. Bedell, a former missionary volunteer in Africa, was called to Maryland's Eastern Shore after eight years of rural parish duties in New York State. He grew up in Iowa and did his seminary work at Colgate-Rochester, in Rochester, New York.

His religious and social service work in southern Africa, from 1976 to 1978, was as a volunteer supervised by the Mennonites' Central Committee. He was stationed in Swaziland.

Mr. Bedell is modest about his own insights into the international-and local-questions that he thinks are so important for Christian churchgoers to think about. "I'm a local pastor, primarily," he said, "but all of these things are related."

On what Preston's Methodists think, or should think, about the current conflict in El Salvador, for example, Mr. Bedell said, "We really don't have a clear way to express that at this point."

The Bedells' youngest child, Joanne, and her husband, Mike Quinn, moved to Virginia in 1984. Joanne and Elinor were both active in Peace Links (Joanne established the Colorado chapter when she lived there in 1981).

Betty Bumpers, wife of Senator Dale Bumpers, established Peace Links. Wives of members of Congress dominated the Washington, D.C. chapter. The chapter called themselves, Women Against Nuclear War, and gave speeches encouraging women to realize that they could, and should, have a voice in the consequences of nuclear war.

Moving to the Washington area also made it possible for Joanne, Mike, and their two young sons to go fishing and camping with Berkley and Elinor.

Elinor blossoms

Elinor Bedell continued to blossom in Washington as the wife of, and assistant to, a Congressman. Here is an article that appeared in some of the Iowa newspapers in 1976.

Women in Politics

By Anne Marty

The saying, "Behind every successful man there is a woman," may have described Elinor Bedell a few years ago, but through politics her place is now beside him.

In 1974, when her husband Berkley became Sixth District Congressman from Iowa, the couple's lifestyle changed drastically. Politics was responsible for uprooting them, forcing them to make new friends, and making their lives hectic. But politics also was responsible for changing her life in a much more drastic way: For the first time in her marriage, she has a full-time job.

The petite, stylishly dressed mother of three traces her initial interest in politics back to 1972 when her husband first ran for Congress. "I really didn't want him to go into politics," she admitted on a recent visit to Iowa. But she became heavily involved when the first campaign began.

"I was his driver during the campaign. Berk found that it was totally impossible to drive throughout the 22 counties in the district, while also having time to prepare what he was going to say. Other than that, I was terribly low key.

"I guess that, basically, I am quite shy and I just didn't feel comfortable," she said. "Fortunately, my husband didn't ask me to do anything that I did not feel comfortable doing. This was a very difficult thing. I was not into politics and I was not too eager for him to get involved either."

Representative Bedell lost the first election, but his wife learned a lot in her first brush with politics. "I learned that I could get out and do things, and be more independent. The interesting thing," she added, "is that it has made Berk realize that I can do these things, too."

Losing an election is a political reality for all candidates. Remembering her husband's defeat in 1972, she said, "You always hate to lose and yet I don't think it was all bad. We didn't feel bitter, because we came very close to winning, but I think it shocked him how hard it is to lose. When it came to making the decision to run again, I really didn't want him to do it, but I see now that it was the right thing to do."

In 1974, when he again ran for Congress, his wife began to take a more active role in his eventually successful campaign. "I again did all the driving, but I also took pictures and wrote press releases. I felt much more a part of the whole situation and wanted to be part of it," she said.

Representative Bedell and his wife made the decision that, if he were elected, she would work in his office in Washington.

"The time was right," she explained. She had spent 20 years raising their children and being active in volunteer work. But now, with the children gone from home, she wanted to do something that was important – not just stuffing envelopes. She hadn't been involved in his fishing equipment business in Spirit Lake, but now she had the time to work with him.

Her job involves working with constituents. "I help people when they write to Berkley for copies of bills, or some material from the federal department," she explained. She also gives tours of the Capitol and arranges visits to the While House.

"I find my work totally consuming. The only thing I don't like about it is that I am interested in so many other things like art and music, and I don't have time for them," she added.

The best part she feels is, "working together toward a single purpose. I have come to believe that it is really worthwhile to have really good people in government – people who are dedicated, hard working, and who are there to try to improve things."

With the 1974 election won, and prospects of a new job in Washington, D.C., the wife of the freshman Congressman has some busy months ahead of her.

"We had to close down our house in Spirit Lake and find a new place to live in Washington. Not having children at home made quite a difference. Originally, we rented an apartment, but later we moved to a town house. We knew that it would bother us to spend a great deal of time commuting and our house is just a 15-minute drive from the Capitol," she added.

"Leaving our friends has been the hardest part. It is hard to make close friends and it took me awhile to learn that I could not quickly make friends like the ones I had known for 20 years. It was a saving grace that I was working."

Being married to a politician is not the easiest job in the world. But Bedell feels that by working with her husband everyday, "I know what he has gone through that day. I see it. He puts in long hours and gets tired, but I get tired too, and for the same reasons."

One of the things the couple's busy schedule does not include is the hectic social life of Washington, D.C.

"I hate to disillusion people," she laughed, "but for us, the wild social life of Washington just doesn't exist. There are receptions and functions that we attend, but my husband comes back to Iowa on many weekends and we are busy with our work."

When they do have a spare evening at home, they enjoy entertaining other Congressmen and their wives. "We certainly do not attend every function that we are invited to," she added.

But there are exciting things that come along. They have attended an embassy reception and the Christmas Ball at the White House this year

Congressman Bedell is currently seeking re-election. His opponent is a woman. How does his wife feel about women in politics?

She insists that being a candidate is not for her. "I have never considered running for public office on my own. I just don't think I'm the type. But in general, I think women should run for office. There is definitely a place for women at all levels of government."

If her husband wins this election, Bedell says, "We want to stay in Congress for a few years to accomplish some things, but certainly not forever. I personally think men and women should not stay there forever. And when this part of our lives is over, I'd like to travel."

Perhaps the hardest aspect of politics that Bedell is still not accustomed to is criticism of her husband. "After all, people do criticize him, and a lot of the time it is unfair." She laughingly admits that it still makes her angry.

Elinor Bedell can now be termed a seasoned campaigner. She still doesn't make speeches, but politics has made her an independent woman.

Fishing Congressman

Berkley became famous as the fishing Congressman. His exploits spawned stories, tall tales, legends, and myths, some of which were true.

Legend: Berkley Bedell could catch fish in the ponds on the Washington Mall.

Fact: Berkley and Company made a film. When the cameraman filmed Berkley fishing in the pools by the Washington Monument, Berkley caught a number of small fish during the filming. "Is fishing allowed in those pools? Allowed or not, I did it," he laughed.

Legend: Berkley Bedell could out-fish any Congressman alive. "He is an incredible fisherman," said Congressman Bob Edgar. "He can sneeze in a puddle of water and catch a fish."

Fact: "Early on, the class of 1974 had a gathering at Airlee House, a retreat center outside of Washington. I can remember Berkley fishing in the pond at Airlee House and catching fish. No one else was catching fish!" Edgar recalled.

Legend: Berkley Bedell got up and went fishing in the morning before going to the floor of Congress.

Berkley's response: "At times, yes, but not several times a week or even several times a month. It just wasn't all the time, like some articles made it sound."

Stories from the staff:

1) "At times I'd get a phone call from his office, 'Is Berk down there?'" said Mark Levine, who worked in the Small Business Committee office. "'No, I haven't seen him.' I had to go to the airport that day, and I looked off to the right. On the way to National Airport, the river comes right up to the George Washington Parkway and there's Berkley fishing! The next time I saw Berkley I said, 'I saw you fishing the other day.' 'Where?' I told him and he looks at me and he says, 'Don't you ever tell anybody.' 'No, I won't.' Then his office calls me up, 'You know what Berk did?' 'Yeah, but I can't tell you.' I think he did it a little more than he let on."

2) "He got up early in the morning and went to some of these streams in the Shenandoah and fished for a bit and still made it to the office by the time the House comes in in the morning," said Tim Galvin, Berkley's staff agricultural expert. "It amazed me that he could get out and do that. I don't know how often, but definitely more than once a month. It became clear that probably more than anything, fishing made him kind of a little kid all over again. You could just tell that fishing was in his blood, and that it refreshed him. It seemed to be central to his life. He's probably defensive about it now, for fear it sounds like he fished more than he showed up in Congress, but he never did that. Fishing never infringed on his work hours."

Berkley's story: "It was not unusual for my work week to only be three days, in terms of actual activity, Tuesday, Wednesday and Thursday, so members could be back in their district, spending time with their people. So there was free weekend time for fishing.

"There were times we didn't start sessions until Noon, so I could go out in the morning and fish early. We didn't have to travel far. I came to know a man named Ed Smith who managed farm ponds. He would catch fish and take them from one pond to another. I still know Ed (as of

2002) and once a year we go fishing together. We never catch less than 50 fish per trip."

Berkley kept a demanding schedule of hearings and meetings. He tried to return to Iowa frequently, and took informational research trips elsewhere. He and Elinor entertained people in their home, both for business and entertainment. They dreaded attending cocktail parties, but suffered as many as two or three in a night, for the sake of courtesy and political advantage. Neither liked alcohol, and Berkley hated small talk, so he found the backdoor at each party. He greeted the host, had brief conversation with some honored guests and friends, and then he would leave through a side or back door so the host wouldn't notice.

During summers, about once a month, Berkley and Elinor took weekend camping/fishing trips in Virginia or West Virginia. They drifted the rivers in a cozy, little inflatable boat that they put in Berkley's backpack for the hike. Berkley would fish and Elinor would either fish or read. When their daughter Joanne and her family moved to the D.C. area, Joanne would sometimes drift the rivers and fish with Berkley, while Elinor waited down river at their destination spot. They camped in a small pickup truck with a fold-down camper.

"It amazed us, coming from Iowa, that two hours from D.C. we could really be in the wilderness," said Berkley. "In drifting a river for two hours, we frequently did not see another person."

He asked the Maryland Department of Fish and Game whether it would be safe to eat the small mouth bass he caught at Great Falls on the Potomac River, 30 minutes from the Capitol. They said it must be safe, because they didn't have reports of problems. Berkley thought he should have a better answer, so he called the Virginia Department of Fish and Game, which manages the other side of the river. They gave him a similar answer, but suggested that he call the Washington, D.C. water department, which takes water from that section of the river. He called.

"The D.C. water department told me that the water in the Potomac River near the city was as clean as any water on the Eastern Seaboard, and that it would compare with the water in some of our finest Western Mountain trout streams."

Berkley discovered that photographers liked a Congressman in fishing gear more than a Congressman in a business suit.

In the fall of 1979, Berkley scheduled a Small Business subcommittee hearing in Bangor, Maine to hold a hearing for Republican Congresswoman Olympia Snowe. Berkley held hearings for committee members regardless of political party. Rosenberg got a call from the Bangor newspaper's sports editor, who had read about the hearing.

"Is he the same Berkley Bedell with the fishing tackle business?"

"Sure is."

The Congressional delegation flew to Maine together and held the public hearing – a big event for the host, Congresswoman Snowe. Berkley made sure the hearing ended by 11:30 a.m. and told an unsuspecting Rosenberg that he had informed Snowe he wouldn't be able to stay for lunch.

"Some guy is sitting in this beat up, old Jeep in the parking lot, looking like he's just driven in from the outback, in a pair of waders and all the gear," said Rosenberg. "Berkley disappears around the corner and, like Superman, returns in his fishing outfit. The two men disappear into the distance. Nobody knows to where. I'm shouting behind him, 'Remember, the plane leaves at 2:30!'" At 2:25, the Jeep rolled up and Berkley reappeared.

Berkley had met the Maine fisherman/sports editor in his early days of selling fishing tackle from town to town. They had gone fishing together 30 years before and had kept in touch. The following day, the newspaper ran a six-paragraph story about the hearing.

On Sunday, the front page of the sports section was covered with photos and a full-page feature story: "Famous Fisherman Comes to Maine."

Berkley with a pirhana he caught in Guyana, South America, in 1983

Inc. Magazine also did a profile of Berkley, as the Congressional champion of small business people. They reached Berkley in Colorado while he was visiting Joanne and her family. They flew a photographer to Colorado to get pictures. Since Joanne lived in the mountains, and since the photographer was not to arrive until afternoon, Berkley took his fly rod and went fishing in the mountain streams. When he started back down the mountain, he took a wrong turn. He became lost. The photographer arrived and the family panicked. They didn't know what had happened. Had he fallen and broken a leg? Had some other accident occurred? Had he become lost? It was not like Berkley to miss an appointment. Finally, Berkley arrived at a road several miles from where he had started. He hitched a ride back to Joanne's and the photos were taken of the fishing Congressman. The magazine recounted his career in business, his Small Businessman of the Year award, and illustrated the story with two pages of fishing photos.

"He had a life outside of politics and he had accomplishments for which he had already been recognized," said

Rosenberg. "He was one of those few members of Congress where ego never seem to be an issue, because he knew who he was. It gave him a perspective and a freedom that career politicians lack, because he could be honest not only with me and with himself, but with his voters. There were certain issues where he could say, 'This issue is a matter of principle. If you don't agree with me, so be it. Find yourself another representative.' He was still Small Businessman of the Year. He was still a great fisherman. He was still Berkley Bedell."

His independent spirit sometimes unnerved his opponents and made his staff anxious – they didn't want to lose him – and he gained the respect of his colleagues.

"One time, Berkley was one of only three people to vote against a nuclear issue," said Pete Rouse, Berkley's legislative director in 1975-76. When the staff worried about the voters and colleagues, "Berkley said, 'We are not here to do things according to the political consequences, we are here to do what's right.'

"Berkley is a non-politician," said Rouse, who became Chief of Staff for Senator Tom Daschle, D-South Dakota, the Senate Majority Leader in 2001. "He is outside the mold of Congresspersons who are aspiring politicians. He held the progressive views I supported, he had tremendous integrity, and he had a passion for making a difference in the world. He was universally respected by his colleagues."

"A lot of hearings on the Hill are pro forma," said Tom Tauke, Republican Congressman from Iowa. "You bring in people and listen to what people have to say. It's a show. This is what you have to do. But Berkley really listened; he would listen to discussions. Because of his intellectual curiosity, he really wanted to learn. He would argue with people. He could be very feisty in discussions."

What he heard sometimes affected his vote.

"He had one remarkable quality," said Edgar. "He would change his mind if somebody could give him the evidence that he should go the other way. That's unheard of."

"In those ways," said Tauke, "he was acting like an Iowan. Iowans are very civically engaged. They're interested in issues and knowledgeable about the world. From a character standpoint, Iowans are open and honest people, but there is also skepticism of bigness. There is a heavy church orientation and significant pacifist sentiments. You have to work hard. Don't bring too much attention to yourself. Berkley reflects all of that."

Because of his interest in foreign affairs, Berkley asked to be appointed as a Congressional advisor to the United Nations. The Speaker granted his request. He became interested in the Law of the Sea Treaty that represented an effort to get all nations to agree on how the oceans of the world would be handled. It involved issues such as pollution, control of fishing, rights of passage through straits, and similar issues. The major controversy had to do with the minerals at the bottom of the sea in the middle of the ocean. American mining companies wanted to have free access to mine these minerals, without regard for the rest of the world. Practically all the nations insisted that such minerals should be considered "the common heritage of mankind," and the entire world should benefit if they were mined. Not surprisingly, Berkley agreed with the rest of the world. The mining companies were powerful lobbyists with other members of the delegation, the Administration, and Congress. There was a bill in Congress that would give the mining companies authority to go ahead and mine, regardless of the attitude of the United Nations and the rest of the world.

Berkley argued that the world had become sufficiently small, and that in the interest of world peace the U.S. needed to learn to work together. The United States could no longer simply ignore everyone else and do what it wished.

Elliott Richardson, a Republican, the chief negotiator appointed under the Carter Administration, tended to agree with Berkley, but he finally became discouraged and issued orders to let Congress go ahead and pass the legislation to give authority to the mining companies to mine, regardless of the United Nations debate. With big lobbying efforts of the mining companies, the passage of the legislation became a certainty. It was near the end of the session and Richardson was so confident of passage he went on a trip to England.

Richardson did not know Berkley's willingness to *tackle giants.*

There is a little-known rule in the Senate that provides for any Senator, near the end of a session, to put a hold on legislation, and the bill will not come up while the hold is in place.

Berkley flew to South Dakota to meet with Senator James Abourezk to try to convince the Senator to put a hold on the bill. He succeeded and the bill died. Richardson was livid. It is reported that Richardson later stated, "Bedell was right."

Finally, all of the issues were settled and all the nations of the world were on their way to the United Nations to agree to the final wording when President Reagan was elected. Reagan issued an ultimatum that the U.S. would no longer agree to the treaty. The ultimatum was a heartbreaker for both Republican Richardson and Democrat Bedell, and for all those who had worked so hard to get a treaty. The treaty was eventually passed and nearly all the countries of the world, except the U.S, signed it. It is one of many such treaties – such as controlling global warming and land mine usage – that the U.S. has refused to sign.

"I think it is a crime the way the lobbying efforts of special interests are able to get the U.S. government to not be a responsible world citizen, but rather do whatever special interests demand, regardless of the rest of the world," Berkley lamented.

When a television reporter challenged Berkley in a live interview in Mason City, Iowa as to why he would spend time as an Iowan in the Law of the Sea negotiations, Berkley replied that he thought peace was just as important to Iowans as agricultural policy, and to build a more peaceful world was important for all the nations of the world to learn to get along, and not simply pursue their own selfish interests.

After an article by Emmett Tyrell, Jr., criticizing the Law of the Sea Treaty, appeared in *The Washington Post*, the following rebuttal by Berkley was published in *The Post*:

E. Emmett Tyrell Jr., in criticizing the Law of the Sea Treaty (op-ed, May 17) does more to explain what is wrong with current U.S. foreign policy than most writers could do if they tried.

Most of the criticisms address deep seabed mining and the controls that the treaty would impose upon those activities. Tyrell is particularly critical of the fact that these minerals have been recognized as "the common heritage of mankind." He writes: 'In this case, a few ragamuffin nations, some snoozing in the last century, some snoozing nearer the Middle Ages, simply declared that the planet's resources are 'the common heritage of mankind.'

The fact is, the United Nations passed a resolution in 1970, in which these minerals were recognized as 'the common heritage of mankind.' The United States supported this resolution and there were no dissenting votes on its passage. To renege on that resolution today is to say that we refuse to live by previous commitments and resolutions.

As a Congressional adviser to the Law of the Sea negotiations, I have been shocked to see firsthand the power of special interests in shaping foreign policy. There would be few problems in fashioning an acceptable treaty if some nodules resembling potatoes in size that have high mineral content had not been discovered on the seabed floor. But four large mining consortia, led primarily by U.S. firms, are interested in exploiting these resources. Their representatives sit on Law of the Sea advisory boards. They attend negotiating sessions and meet regularly with our negotiators.

At one briefing, one of our top negotiators advised us: 'we cannot get a treaty approved by the Senate unless it is acceptable to the mining companies.' If four mining companies, through their campaign contributions and lobbying efforts, can dictate foreign policy, I believe we must ask ourselves whether or not there is something dreadfully wrong with our political system.

The Law of the Sea Treaty is not a perfect document. Few treaties are. Certainly the rights of the industrial nations should be preserved in such a treaty. But of all the nations involved, only four—the United States, Venezuela, Turkey, and Israel—thought that the treaty was sufficiently flawed to vote against it.

The real issue is whether all nations should participate in determining how to share the wealth of the sea beyond all national boundaries, or whether this policy should be determined by mini-treaties between large developed countries. It is no secret that the United States is pushing the mini-treaty concept—which brings me to the insight Tyrell's article lends toward the attitude that shapes much of our foreign policy.

Four times in his article, Tyrell refers to "backward countries." Certainly, the implication is that "backward countries" should not participate in world discussions and because they are "backward" they should be relegated to second-class world citizenship. Well, the time was not long ago when Japan was considered a "backward" nation. I hardly think our automobile, steel, television, and camera industries would describe Japan as "backward" today. History is replete with similar examples of society's thinking another society backward.

In this regard, however, we owe Tyrell a debt of thanks. While I do not agree with his analysis of the Law of the Sea Treaty, the arrogant elitism evident in his article should alert everyone that the United States is pursuing a policy of arrogance in the conduct of our foreign affairs that may serve to build up our ego in the short run. But in the past, it has spelled disaster for all whose who have pursued it.

Berkley Bedell
The writer is a Democratic Representative from Iowa

Berkley had a major interest in peace, as did Elinor and the rest of the family. He strongly objected to the U.S. stand on the Law of the Sea Treaty, and many other international issues. He argued that the world has become so much smaller that we now face a situation similar to that which the original American colonies faced.

"Thankfully, America's founders decided that each state could not simply pursue its own interests, but they should join together to form a nation where states would lose some of their independence, but in the end, the results would be a more peaceful nation and each state would benefit."

Berkley realized that the United States was not yet ready for world government, but he strongly felt it to be in our own self-interest to be a responsible world citizen and build cooperation among the world's nations. He saw the United States as the one power that could bring cooperation and world peace, and it disturbed him that the United States so often acted like a spoiled child demanding its own way, refusing to help build a world of peace and cooperation. He particularly objected to the power of special interest lobbyists that caused the U.S. government to act in such a short sighted selfish manner, as he thought was true in the outcome of the Law of the Sea treaty and the global warming negotiations.

According to a Small Business staff member, Mark Levine, Berkley's controversial military spare parts legislation created havoc for some members of the Small Business subcommittee – especially those who also served on the Armed Services Committee that opposed the bill.

Levine recalled, "There was incredible pressure on the Congressional members that weren't as strong as Berkley. Armed Services put all kinds of pressure on these guys. They said things like, 'you've got bases in your district. You've got procurement going to your district. You have military people in your district.' There were so many people beating on the members not to support the legislation.

"Yet, Berkley Bedell said, 'Make up your mind. Then do what's right.' Some of the members would come in and try to cut deals, but Berkley wasn't interested. I would say to them, 'don't bother. You don't want to talk to him. You're just going to make him more solid in his position.' If a member came in to deal with him, it signaled to Berk that they were weak, or that they were trying to get away with something. He wouldn't let anybody get away with anything. He would try to find what else was happening."

By the same token, Berkley figured that if the attitude of dishonest favors and punishment was contagious, so might an attitude of integrity also be contagious. He found people would respect him for being true to his values, even if he opposed them.

When it appeared that Berkley was going to have a close re-election, three Republican Congressmen appeared in television ads for him. He later made a television ad for a Republican Congressman running for re-election.

"Congress was not as partisan when I arrived in 1978 as when I left in 1990," said Tauke. "Berkley really helped me when I came to Congress. I was 28 years old, a young, green member of Congress, from a district that had been represented by a Democrat – clearly a target of the Democrats in a subsequent election. Berkley had no particular reason to reach out to me, but he did. He is a very kind and generous person."

Berkley believed that the Reagan Administration demonized and shunned liberal Democrats.

"The partisanship became bitter and at times nasty," he recalled.

Berkley had to work at the politics of getting things done in Congress. In his company, he and his workers would identify a problem and solve it. He proved to be a master Congressman at visiting a department or agency, identifying a problem, and working toward a solution.

He then had to learn how to work with groups of people to gather the votes necessary to achieve the goal.

"Dad has what I think of as a World War II mentality," said his son, Ken. "You identify a problem and you use as much creativity, technology, and resources as are required to solve it. That is the thing that's really been the core – the belief that's made it possible for him to accomplish things.

Berkley was recognized as one of two Congressmen who have received patents for their inventions, at the National Inventors Hall of Fame, 1986.

But like with all of us, that is also the thing that imprisons us, because he can't think out of that kind of a box."

"Dad thought there would be a way to figure out how to fix America. He could go to Congress and if he just figured out the answers, then people would see: 'Aha!' You could have Congressional committees that would listen to what the evidence was and figure it out, and then you'd solve it."

Driven by values

As much as Berkley worked to achieve results, he placed values over pragmatism in the way he operated as a legislator, a colleague, an administrator, and a friend.

His staff and colleagues recognized a tremendous determination to do well.

"He combines compassion – he genuinely wants to help people – with courage," said Paul Simon, Berkley's colleague in the House.

Berkley and Elinor tried to establish an atmosphere of teamwork and caring concern for constituents, colleagues, and staff. They not only worked with staff on issues, but also tried to help the staff advance professionally. Their office and committee staffs remain intensely loyal: Gearan, Rouse, Galvin, Dave Hallberg, Marilyn Yager, Nancy Payne, Cindy Yaworski, Levine, and Rosenberg.

"Working for him was my MBA in Management," said Gearan. "Systems of accountability. Checkpoints. Choke points."

Gearan later worked on the presidential campaigns of Michael Dukakis and Bill Clinton. He served in the White House as communications director for President Clinton, then was appointed as Executive Director of the Peace Corps. He later became President of Hobart and William Smith Colleges in New York.

Berkley had difficulty when his strongly held values came into conflict. For example, he believed in equal rights for women, but he had also worked to reform Congressional processes.

"You have procedures that you have to go through in the House, where it goes through committee before it comes to the floor.

"Lo and behold, Tip O'Neill somehow caused us suddenly to get a vote on the Equal Rights Amendment without going through the committee process and debate – completely contrary to the way Congress is supposed to operate."

For Berkley, it was a matter of the integrity of democracy. No one's rights have any value in a democratic society if those rights are gained by ignoring democracy.

"Under normal circumstances, there would be no question that I'd vote for the Equal Rights Amendment. But I voted against it because I thought we needed to abide by the rules that caused us to function properly. If you start to ignore them, you're in awful trouble for all sorts of things."

The staff was aware of how he had voted.

When he returned to the office, Elinor, who did not know how he had voted, came into his private office. He told her.

"YOU WHAT?!" she shouted. The whole staff had their ears to the door listening.

"That vote caused me considerable trouble with my liberal friends back in the district."

He sometimes had to choose between family, friendship, and principle. He disagreed with his brother, Jack, and his boyhood friend, Peter Narey, on nearly every major policy.

One year, he had to choose between Congressional responsibility and his responsibility to family and friends. In October 1986, he wasn't running for re-election and it was time to go on his 37th annual duck-hunting trip to Canada with Jack and their Spirit Lake friends.

"He said that he didn't think he'd dare go on our hunting trip because the farm bill was coming up and he should be there to vote," said Jack. "And I said, 'Berk, it isn't going to matter because you'll stay there and vote wrong anyhow. You might just as well come along with us.'"

Rev. Bob Edgar, a clergyman and fellow member of Congress, said Berkley lived out his faith in personal interaction and in acting on social policy.

"Berkley's faith was displayed in his caring concern for creation and his selfless concern for others," remarked Edgar. "He had an intense pastoral care component to his life. It would not be unusual for him to sit next to a Republican colleague, or a conservative Democratic colleague, and put his arm around them and say, 'What's happening in your life? Tell me about it.' That behavior grew out of his spiritual life, which included the prayer breakfasts."

What most impressed Berkley's friends and colleagues, however much they liked or disliked his policies, was his authenticity. "Berkley is Berkley: Berkley is the same inside or outside of Congress," said Edgar. "Berkley is just plain Berkley."

Chapter Twenty-One

Business on the Brink

Berkley walked into the small-town Iowa restaurant prepared to shake hands with diners. This was just his kind of audience: concerned Iowans reading the newspaper. It was 1978 re-election time, time to tell Iowans how he was representing them as their man in Washington.

In the wake of Watergate, his Congressional class had worked hard to restore integrity in government, to bury the seniority system, and revive people's trust in the legislative process. Fellow members had begun to recognize him as the "conscience of the Congress."

What he saw in the restaurant stunned him.

"I will never forget campaigning in the restaurant and seeing people reading a newspaper with these headlines, as I shook their hands."

Bedell Denies Bribe

His heart sank. As his father had done, 43 years before, Berkley would have to rely on his longstanding record of honesty in order to defend his honor and reputation. In a lengthy article, the newspaper pointed out that a former manager of Berkley's Taiwan plant charged that Berkley and Company personnel had bribed Taiwanese officials to enable it to export products at less than production costs.

It was not easy for Berkley to campaign as his constituents were reading headlines such as the above, but both his constituents and the press tended to stand by him, and they felt Berkley should be considered innocent until proven guilty.

Here is an editorial from *The Cherokee Times* published September 5, 1980, typical of the reaction of the press.

"Editorial Notebook"
— PERFORMANCE AND ACCUSATIONS

Almost six years of outstanding service to those who live in northwest Iowa may be overshadowed on election day in the minds of some voters because of allegations that have been made against the character of incumbent Sixth District Congressman Berkley Bedell.

The founder of Berkley and Company is a bystander in an investigation of his Spirit Lake firm. The probe seeks to determine the validity of charges that officials of the fishing tackle business conspired to defraud the government of a quarter of a million dollars in import duties by manipulating the value of products produced at the Berkley plant located in Taiwan.

Information about the case now is being presented to a grand jury. Whether there is enough evidence to warrant prosecution will not be known until the jury files its report. Since Election Day is less than two months away, there is little likelihood that the case will be decided by then.

So it appears that voters will be faced with making judgments when they cast ballots on November 4. They can dismiss the reports and speculation that have been carried in news media and vote for or against Bedell's record as an officeholder … or they can make their own determination of his innocence or guilt and, with his public service in mind, support him for re-election or oppose his candidacy for a fourth term in Congress.

Bedell says that, since his election in 1974, he has not participated in management decisions of his company. He further states that he has not attended any management meetings where import duties of Taiwan-produced products might have been discussed.

We have found Bedell to be highly principled. If he denies involvement in the purported defrauding scheme, we believe him. He has worked harder than any Congressman with whom we have had experience. He has retained close contact with his constituents and, at penalty to his private life, has used every spare moment when Congress was not in session to meet with and listen to the viewpoints of the people he is representing.

We do not agree with Bedell's every vote, but we do applaud his efforts to determine the thinking of northwest Iowans and to reflect the sentiments in our nation's capital. We encourage voters to judge him on his posture as a public official —not on unproven accusations.

Much like 1936, when local voters elected Virginia Bedell as County Attorney in the aftermath of Walter Bedell's bribery conviction, voters respected Berkley Bedell well enough to re-elect him with more than 60 percent of the vote.

But there was more at stake than just his election.

This accusation didn't jeopardize Berkley's family, as it did in the 1930s. Berkley and Elinor could retire comfortably if he never made another penny. Their children were adults, primed to thrive.

But in the stagnating 1970s economy, the company struggled to stay afloat in Berkley's absence. These charges could capsize the good ship Berkley Company and drown the livelihoods of 1,000 employees in the Spirit Lake area.

The business found itself on the brink of disaster. Only Berkley and a handful of others knew what a serious problem existed.

"I didn't think anybody knew that it might go under," Berkley reflected, "but the company had lost a large amount of money and much of its market share."

Growth and profits had nearly ground to a halt. After 26 years of steady, and sometimes spectacular, sales growth, the company hit a slump from 1975 to 1980. Sales grew an average of 23 percent per year for 25 years. From 1975-1980 sales lagged well below the rate of inflation. How could the business get into such trouble after so many years of sustained growth? Did the Company suffer from:

A) Worldwide stagflation? After the national spending spree of the 1950s and 1960s, economic growth stagnated and inflation spiraled upward throughout the economy during the 1970s. Could this business outrun the avalanche of bad news?

B) The energy crisis? Did the lines at gas stations keep people from buying fishing tackle? Could anyone afford to go on a fishing trip?

C) The urbanization/sub-urbanization syndrome? The population had been shifting from rural to urban for decades. Would city/suburban people go fishing? Did children ever even *see* a fishing lake any more? Would a child recognize a bluegill if it stared him or her in the face?

D) The mediazation of America? Could fishing compete with other entertainment? How could you keep people at the pond after they've seen television?

E) Growing pains and/or bad business decisions? Did expansion decisions backfire? With a history of hometown friends with the shared values of Spirit Lake, could the business be trusted to hired professionals operating around the world?

F) Berkley Bedell leaving for Congress? Berkley had been phasing out since 1970, when he decided to climb new mountains and change the world. He had hired Don Porter to become president of the company. Porter had focused on short-term profits, rather than planning for the long term and was not one to *tackle giants*.

All may have contributed, but it seemed to Berkley that E) and F) were the major causes of the problem.

As for E), at least one decision – hiring a plant manager for the Taiwan factory – was about to cause the company major legal problems.

When problems arose with buying the Roddy operation and dealings with the Japanese supplier backfired in the late 1960s, Berkley had gone to Taiwan to set up a factory to make fishing rods and reels.

When Berkley went to Congress, the person he hired to run Berkley and Company hired a new manager to run the Taiwan factory.

"The Taiwan manager turned out to be a disaster," Berkley said.

"When we finally fired him, he called me in Washington and threatened that unless I paid him a bribe, he would report to the government that Berkley and Company had been cheating on its duty payments. Of course, I refused."

The fired manager did, indeed, go to the government, and in December 1978 the government raided Berkley and Company and confiscated a number of records – a month after Berkley had been re-elected.

"You can imagine the stir this caused in Iowa since I served in Congress. The press had a field day with it."

The prosecutor subpoenaed Berkley to testify before the grand jury in Minneapolis, Minnesota. Berkley found himself frustrated by the proceedings, where the prosecutor tries to convince the grand jury there is enough evidence to bring formal charges against the defendant. The defense does not present its side of the story in grand jury proceedings and cannot attend, or cross-examine, witnesses. Then the grand jury can issue an indictment, or formal charge, and the defendant decides how to defend himself in a full trial. "Without rebuttal of the evidence and testimony, a good prosecutor can convince a grand jury to issue an indictment in almost all cases where any evidence exists," Berkley said. Berkley's attorneys advised him to exercise his Fifth Amendment rights, so he wouldn't add any evidence to the prosecutors' case.

"I could not give any information and I had to answer every question with, 'I refuse to answer on the grounds that I might incriminate myself.' This proved to be terribly hard for me. It is not my way of operating. I believe in telling the truth and not hiding anything, but I took the advice of the attorneys. They certainly were correct." The case took so much time that the members of that grand jury completed their terms and the new ones never heard Berkley's testimony, nor the testimony of several of the witnesses.

"I worried for days, as I waited in Washington, to know whether or not I would be indicted. When the news finally came, it contained both the good and the bad. It proved to be a great relief that I had not been indicted, but a great disappointment that the company and three employees had been indicted for allegedly falsifying records to reduce import duties on products shipped from the Taiwan plant to Spirit Lake. There never had been anyone more honest and law-abiding than these good people who had been indicted. What a terrible heartbreaker."

The indictments came during the worst financial period in the company's history.

It could well have been that any manager who followed the founder would be doomed to fail in the eyes of the employees, many of whom idolized Berkley. And nearly all American businesses struggled to survive in the new global economy.

Berkley had vowed to let the professional manager he hired run the company without his interference.

"I felt I could not adequately do two jobs at one time and my main interest was in the great opportunities I had as a member of Congress."

However, he grew increasingly concerned with the new president's strategies.

Berkley observed, "The new president proceeded to try to maximize profits by cutting costs, without much regard to the welfare of employees. As he cut back on advertising, promotion, and research, Berkley's market share began to fall. Before long profits fell."

Not only profits, but morale also fell. People felt vulnerable. In the four years before going to Washington, Berkley had gradually phased himself out of the operation.

People had gradually learned how to operate the company without him and had accepted the notion that he would leave at some point. Still, they missed his innovation, energy, and attitude – Berkley was the guiding light of the company, its parental figure.

"It was truly his company. He had been the sunrise, the sunset and everything in the middle," said his son, Tom.

"I had mixed emotions," said Sharry Caskey, Berkley's one and only secretary (1965 to 1975) at the company. "Everybody knew that he would do a good job as a Congressman, but we were also sad to see him leave the company."

Times were difficult and people within Berkley and Company sensed that their professorial president could never measure up to the ingenuity and intensity of the company's founder. Suddenly, it became possible to think that Berkley and Company could fail – Spirit Lake's signature in the business world and the town's largest employer.

"For three or four months one summer, we went from a five-day work week to a four-day work week, getting paid for only 32 hours," said Caskey. "We didn't have a lot of benefits, we didn't have a summer picnic, many of our activities were postponed or cancelled. That fall we did not go to the Clay County Fair. We had always received free tickets to that or to the Summer Theater, but they cancelled all benefits like that, along with going to a 32-hour week."

Many people half hoped they would come to work one day and see their leader in the huddle, dressed for the game and ready to lead the company to victory.

"I knew Berk was aware of what was going on and he would never have let the company get to a point that it could not come back, to the point where he couldn't retrieve it and get it going again," said Caskey.

Berkley had a dilemma. He had accomplished his business goals and set out to climb new mountains. He couldn't bear to see his business fail, but he felt the need to move in other directions.

"He poured his life into building the company," said Tom. "It was his passion. It was his energy. That was his life and he loved it. He built a neat little company and he came to a point where he asked himself, 'Hey, am I going to keep doing this for the next 20 years?' He came back with a loud, screaming answer 'No!' He had no interest in passing the business on to his kids and we didn't have a particular interest in taking it over. Dad got totally focused on Congress and left the business to Don Porter. It was almost like 'I spent all these years of my life, 100 percent into this company world; I don't know how to be half way in and half way out, so I'm now going to spend 100 percent of my time being a Congressman.'"

By the time of the indictment, Berkley knew he had to find a leader who could deal with the looming legal problems, learn how to market fishing products to new generations, and restore confidence in Spirit Lake.

"Clearly, I faced the prospect of having to resign from Congress and go back to try to rescue the company and its several hundred employees. If I didn't, who would lead the business?"

Berkley had long ago discarded the idea of one of his children replacing him.

Ken Bedell worked as a chemistry intern at Berkley and Company for four years in high school and college. He had an engineer's mentality about finding a problem and fixing it, and he shared Berkley's values.

"People in the plant made a point of telling Berkley Bedell's son that they liked working for Berk and what a good person he is," Ken remembered. Some "just sort of assumed that eventually I'd be the president of the company or something. They felt comfortable with the family nature of the place."

Ken already had a conversation about this with his parents while in high school.

"Dad told me that of all the people he knew, he didn't know of anyone who would be more qualified or could do a better job than I could, of taking over the business," Ken recalled. "Yet, he didn't want to impose that on me. If that was something I wanted to do, I should think what it would mean in terms of college, or how I'd prepare myself. It told

me that he didn't want me to feel like I had any responsibility to do it and that he wanted me to do with my life what I
wanted to do. And running the company just didn't seem
like what I wanted to do at the time. I don't remember it
ever coming up again. That just settled it. Now, when I look
back on that conversation, it was really a nice gift."

Ken became a chemistry major in college, then earned
a Master of Divinity degree and was ordained a minister in
the United Methodist Church.

Tom went to law school without any intent of becoming a lawyer. He loved operating campaigns, beginning
with his father's successful 1974 campaign. He worked as
administrative assistant in Berkley's office for two years and
then opened a consulting firm in Washington, D.C.

"What surprised me is that Tom didn't run for Congress himself," said Peter Rouse, an aide to Berkley Bedell
in 1975-76 before becoming Chief of Staff for U.S. Senator
Thomas Daschle. "Tom's a very sharp guy."

"In 1978, I had a year that just knocked their socks
off," recalled Tom. "I won more challenged elections than
any other consulting firm. I was at the top of my game and I
loved it. I really loved my political consulting and the campaigns and I felt good at it. Relative to my expectations, I
made a nice living. I had gained the inside of the whole power
structure. In 1980, I was literally going to get to pick whatever races I wanted to work. In 1976, I had turned down the
Carter campaign. I didn't think he had a chance to win. Being single in Washington, D.C., I had the world by the tail."

Berkley began thinking again about who could lead
the company if he didn't. It would have to be someone with
a marketing background. It would also help to have someone who could understand legal issues, and it would be extremely helpful to hire someone who intimately understood
the principles of Spirit Lake and Berkley Bedell. Most important, it had to be someone whom Berkley could trust completely. The company still bore Berkley's name. Who could
protect and preserve the family name, the family's ideals?

Berkley knew just such a person in Washington – one
of the hottest political campaign consultants in the Capital –

a young man who demonstrated a brilliant knack of identifying voters' needs and longings. He had been great at helping candidates hone a message and connect with voters. He
had been so good he could choose which presidential candidate to work with.

This energetic campaign consultant had attended
Iowa Law School. And he was a native of Spirit Lake. People
in Spirit Lake had been expecting great things of this young
man since his early days as a top student and energetic young
entrepreneur. He understood Berkley Bedell's ideals. He had
experienced those ideals all his life.

Berkley had been talking to him about the company's
troubles.

"In December 1978, somebody came storming into
Dad's office in Spirit Lake to get all his records and stuff
about the scandal," Tom recalled, "so I get a phone call from
Dad and he's in tears. This is going to the heart of his self-
image. They're accusing him of being dishonest, breaking
the law. He just didn't know how to handle such accusations. To him, it was like taking your heart out. He said, 'I
don't know what's going on.'"

Tom and Berkley were very close during that period.
Tom worked on Berkley's campaigns and on his staff. When
Tom started his own consulting firm, they still crossed paths
on a day-to-day basis. "He was real proud of what I'd accomplished and I was very proud of the job he was doing,"
said Tom. "So he calls me and he says, 'I don't know what
to do. Would you mind going to Spirit Lake and find out
what's going on?' The guy was distraught."

"He reminded me of someone who had a death in
the family," said U.S. Representative Bob Edgar. "Fortunately for him, he had the gift of a son who knew institutional development and redevelopment in a way that a lot
of people would not have understood."

Tom went back to Spirit Lake and interviewed
people, met with the attorneys in Minneapolis, then flew to
the Taiwan factory – all in one week.

"In the front end of this process I learned a lot. The
whole thing was a disaster," Tom recalled.

The Bedell family with a Chinese legislator in Beijing, China, December 1978. Berkley and Elinor flank the legislator in the front row, with Ken's wife, Kathie, at far left and Tom at far right. Joanne and her husband, Mike, are in the middle of the back row.

Berkley had organized a family trip to China in December 1978. Tom flew from Taiwan to Hong Kong to meet his parents and the rest of the family.

"Dad was still absolutely distraught, but we had a great time. We were in China before it had opened up at all. The Chinese searched our luggage and bugged our rooms. We were kind of early implementers in terms of going through and seeing all this stuff, and we actually got to go to the reception when the United States and China announced resumption of relations between our countries. We all got to meet (China Premier) Deng Xiaoping. What a big deal. What a really cool trip."

During the ten-day trip, Tom briefed Berkley about what he had learned. Berkley listened to his son's insights into the complexities and principles involved. He knew who the next leader should be.

"Your mother and I have talked, and I need to ask if you would be willing to go back and take over the company and see if you can straighten it out," Tom remembered his father saying to him. "And if you don't think you can do that, then I'll need to resign from Congress and go back and do it."

Tom knew this wasn't just about business. This was an emotional decision, not a rational decision. "It wasn't just 'How do I save the business?' but this decision was also 'How do I save my reputation? How do I clear up the accusations? Whom do I turn to that I can trust?' Dad was being challenged to the core of everything he'd spent his life to build, and it devastated him. He never used these words, but to Dad it was a 'clear the family name' issue.

"Second, my sister and my brother had no interest and no inclination to do it," he continued. "It's not what their life background had been, or their orientation, or their personalities. So it was not that I was particularly qualified. It seemed clear that I became the only choice of the three … I'd done my guitar business, I'd started my own consulting business. My relationship with my father is much more in tune with his career. My brother's relationship with my father is much more in tune with his spiritual side."

"I don't think he decided, 'Tom's the guy who can save everything.' I think he didn't have any place else to turn. I don't mean that negatively. What he spent his life building was being threatened. Whom do you turn to in times of crisis? You turn to family, you turn to people you know whose whole goal, or their whole purpose, will be for you with no question of loyalty, or agendas, or dedication, or determination, or whatever. I never saw it as though he made a selection. I think he looked at it and concluded, either Tom goes back and sees what he can do or I have to. Those were the only two alternatives he saw."

Tom had to weigh his future. He loved operating in the big leagues of national decision-making. He cherished the Washington life, the culture, and the restaurants. He enjoyed the political game, the ideas, and the competition. In his mind, he had left small-town Iowa for the bigger world. How could he leave the life he loved and the city he liked? How could he go back to Spirit Lake?

He sat in China and thought about his opportunities and his loyalties.

"There were no negotiations," he recalled. " I remember the emotions I went through."

First, he thought of his father rescuing the company he built at this stage of his life and the company's life. He saw his father as an initiator and a builder, not a reorganizer and rehabilitator. The company was in a different stage in its cycle of organizational development and there were too many messes to clean up. The company needed a fresh set of eyes.

Second, they were his parents, who selflessly gave him endless opportunities. He was in China meeting world leaders, because of his parents. They were offering him the leadership of a multimillion-dollar company at 28 years of age.

"They've both done so much for me, what am I going to do? Sit here and say I'm more important than they are?"

"Third, I've got the rest of my life to do whatever I want with my career. How do I say no?"

Tom knew what he had to do.

"Tom came to me and said, 'If you want me to go back and try to rescue Berkley and Company, I will do it for you,'" Berkley recalled.

"I will always remember it as one of the most wonderful moments of my life.

"That was not what Tom wanted to do at that time, but he did it for his parents! He did not hesitate to take a job for which he had no training."

Tears came to Berkley's eyes as he recalled those events.

Chapter Twenty-Two

Rescuing the Business

Within a week, Tom shut down his consulting business and returned to Iowa.

In Spirit Lake, some saw Tom as the returning hero, a savior.

"I didn't have any question. If he couldn't do it, nobody could," said Berkley's former secretary, Sharry Caskey.

Others expected Tom to fall flat on his face.

"Before I arrived, the executive group had a meeting behind my back," Tom recalled. "They said, 'what are we going to do with this kid? We have to make sure he doesn't mess up the company.' Well, the company's almost bankrupt, so they decided they're going to ship me off to Taiwan to try to get me out of there. They had a whole scheme of how they were going to partition me off in a corner. It was just hilarious."

On February 5, 1979 Tom attended his first Board of Directors meeting.

When it came to the financial report, one of the board members turned to him and asked, "How do you feel about these numbers?" All eyes were on Tom. Would he assert himself? Would he demonstrate a profound understanding of finances? Would he sympathize or make excuses? What was he going to do?

"I apologize to the board: I have no idea how to read a financial statement," Tom said. "I don't know the difference between an asset and a liability. One of the first assignments I'm going to have to give my chief financial officer is to teach me these numbers, then I have to sign up for a course about financing, because I don't know anything about it."

They all looked at him and they started laughing.

"How do you feel about this job?" one of them asked.

"I don't have a clue how to do it. I'm just going to have to figure it out," Tom said. "I need your help. If there's ever a reason for a Board of Directors, there's one now. I need to be able to call you. I need to be able to lean on your shoulder."

His response set a tone for his leadership: Teamwork, not power plays.

"So here I am, single, 29-years old, back in my hometown in the middle of winter, with nothing going on, and the company is in the pits. Morale was terrible. People were down, with the company almost bankrupt. We weren't paying our bills. People had their resumes out. People had no sense of future. I called Dad the first week and told him, 'you don't have a fishing business. You have a mortuary business. This thing is terrible.' I was scared to death."

Whatever made him think he could run the company?

"I couldn't," he said. "I didn't want to. Last thing in the world I wanted to do."

He decided he had three big advantages.

First, "Everybody assumed the company was going to go broke."

Second, "Everybody assumed that Tom can't run it. I had nothing to lose."

Third, "My Dad said, 'I will support any decision you make.' He actually signed a note that said, 'Any decision you make, I'll back up.'"

It was difficult for some, like Ed Donovan, who had known Berkley since childhood. Donovan had brainstormed and sweated with Berkley to build machinery from scratch, had come into the plant in the middle of the night to fix problems with the extruder, had helped make it possible to produce the company's enduring moneymaker and historic product: Trilene fishing line.

"He and Dad built this company," Tom said.

"Ed started off saying — he's so sincere — 'you're not going to blankety-blank up this company that I've worked so hard to build. I'm not going to let some pipsqueak kid come in here and mess things up.'"

Whenever a phone call came to Berkley from a trusted executive at the company, Berkley would answer: "Tom has 100 percent of my support."

"He never wavered," Tom recalled. "He was wonderful. He never wavered."

During Tom's first year, the company lost large amounts of money for the first time in its history – nearly $1 million dollars – in part because of legal fees to defend itself from the federal charges.

Tom knew he couldn't just fix the leak in the dam. He had to refill the reservoir and reshape the company.

First, Don Porter held the title of president. What would Tom be?

Porter had legal charges pending against him, as did Berkley and Company and two of its employees.

"I will 100 percent support you through all the legal stuff, keep you in position as president of the company, because it's where you need to be as we defend one another in this situation," Tom told Don Porter. "You teach me how to do the job. Then when you're acquitted and everything's done, you can retire and move on and I'll take over. But I'll be behind you all the way," Tom continued. "He's a good human being: good values, honest, not good with people, and not very intuitive, certainly not one to tackle giants, but he didn't do any of the stuff that he was accused of. What he did do involved poor management and poor follow through and poor accountability – but he didn't do anything immoral or illegal. I absolutely know that. He couldn't have done it any more than Dad could have."

"Don supported me," recalled Tom. "He said to me, 'Tell me what I can do to help you and where you need my help, and I won't make any major decisions without checking with you.' And I replied, 'I'll help you save as much face as I can as we go through the process.' He was exceptional. He included me in things. That part turned out great."

Tom had the nebulous title of executive officer and became the marketing director. Porter, as president, reported to Tom in the executive officer role, while Tom in the marketing director role reported to Porter the president.

Tom had made his name in Washington by finding out what voters thought. At Berkley and Company, he went to the people who vote with their dollars.

"Selling means understanding people, understanding their needs, and trying to meet them."

He asked the sales manager, Doc Egger, to set up appointments with the company's top 10 customers.

"Just tell them Berk Bedell's son has come back into the company, that he wants to learn about the business and he wants to meet them."

Tom and Egger took a blank pad of paper to every meeting.

"I don't know anything about the fishing business," Tom would start. "I know you can survive in your company without us, but we can't survive without you. I'm here to learn how I can become a supplier that is indispensable to you. I want to learn what I need to do with my company. I want to learn what my competition's doing well that I need to learn from, and I'm here to ask you for a chance, because I know you don't need me right now. I'm here to ask if you will hang in with the company for two years and let me show you what I can do with our business, so I can earn the right to be a key supplier to you."

It worked. "Who's going to turn that down?" Tom figured.

Then Tom invited 30 of Berkley and Company's middle and upper managers to his house. He shared his notes – what customers said they wanted.

"We're going to design the most perfect, ideal fishing tackle company we can imagine. We're going to forget about all the reasons why we can't be successful. We're going to go through it and we're going to talk about what the company looks like physically, what it feels like to work there, what it smells like, what kind of people work there, what our policies are, what our environment is, what kind of products we make, how our customers feel about us, how our suppliers feel about us." They divided into teams and brainstormed. They did this exercise for two days.

"Then, on the third day, I had papers full of ideas covering the walls and I went through each one and I said, 'Okay, I've gone through all of these and I can only find three things on all these sheets that aren't up to us, that aren't within our control. All the constraints we put on ourselves and all the reasons why we can't figure out how to turn our company around are because we chose those constraints.'

"We can create the environment we want.

"We can create the working place that we want.

"We can create the relationships among one another that we want. That's up to us, not anybody else. The fact that when I come to work I find you guys depressing as hell, that's your decision. That's the way you choose to be.

"Starting Monday, this is the company I'm going to create. Those who would like to be part of it, let's build it. Those of you who don't want to be part of it, get out of the way, because I'm going to let go anybody that gets in my way of building this company. I know we have this lovely culture where we don't fire people. I've got a group of you right here that are figuring out how to kill a company and that isn't what I came back here to do.

"So the next week, I came in and I started building that company." Reality set in. Tom had never fired anyone before. In two months he had to fire six people who refused to follow or get out of the way.

People were shocked, not offended. People knew those who had been in the way, and Tom tried to fire people with care and concern, not humiliation. Everyone knew "this guy is serious."

"Things started to turn around, but I had to deal with the emotional attitudes, the things going on internally before we could get behavior to change, before we could start to relate differently to the market and build a business."

Ed Donovan, one of the key company leaders, believed Tom was serious about listening, about putting employee expertise to work, and marketing their products to meet customer demands.

"Once we got this thing turned around and going, Ed became my biggest champion and me his," recalled Tom. "He's one of these smart guys that's not very cultured in his speech and in his style and his behavior, but, intuitively, he can run a factory like … we've never been able to replace him. The guy was just absolutely fabulous at what he did.

"Ed was as core to this company's success, I would say, almost as much as Dad. The two of them complemented each other. Ed's one of these guys who gets the job done. He never set foot in an engineering class, but he is bright! He delivers, day in and day out. You don't get excuses. You don't get explanations. He delivers results and you always know where you are with the guy. He's somebody who'd look me right in the face and tell me I was full of it. Other people are working behind your back, but I have complete respect for him."

The marketplace may have been different than when Berkley and Donovan moved the company forward in the 1950s, but Tom saw the principles the same.

"Dad is a product guy. He's an inventor. He likes to be in the lab. He likes to go fishing. He designed and built and made a better product.

"But you can make the same case for him being a people-driven guy. He motivated people. He helped in shipping and packing. He helped build equipment.

"Then let's take the market. Nobody worked harder for their customers and our salesmen and staff to meet their needs than Dad did. If a phone call came and we were doing something wrong—I've heard stories. They're legend about what he did. So although you may say invention of products built the company, you also have to say that the way he handled and motivated and trained people contributed too. You'd also have to say the way he marketed and sold and worked the market helped. I don't know how you take any of that away. He's everything."

However, Tom said the most important thing he learned from his father about operating a company was his values. "If you walk around this company and ask people, 'What's the thing you like most about Tom?' I would hope that they'd say, besides the fact that I'm passionate about what I do, is 'He cares about me.' That was Dad – honestly caring about the people. The reason you're in business is for the co-workers and their careers and their lives.

"At the end of the day, on the tombstone, is it really cool to say, 'This guy made a lot of money?' I don't think so. I think he made a difference in other people's lives. He created opportunities for people. He lived life consistent with his values. Dad not only ingrained that in me and Ken and Jo, but he also ingrained it in his company, in his culture. That has served us so well. I hope I haven't broken that trust in any way in my stewardship here.

"Second, work ethic. I love what I do. Dad loves what he does. I don't do it for the money. I want to be successful because … why wouldn't you want to be successful? I want to be the best at what I do.

"Third, I don't ever look at life with fear. It's not self-confidence in an arrogant way. It's self-confidence in a 'if we work hard enough and we try enough and we are willing to learn enough' we need not fear the obstacles.

"If I do more pushups than the other guy, eventually I'm going to be stronger than he is, right? If I just rely on my innate strength, some day somebody's going to come along who will do more pushups than I will. Our whole mission is to be the world's best fishing tackle company. I hope that doesn't come across as arrogant. What I want is for it to be motivating. We want to know what it takes to be the best and we want to figure out how to get there. To me, that's a value."

Tom needed strong values, because he felt so ill equipped to operate the company. Work had been different as a campaign consultant. As a consultant he had his firm and the candidate. He took candidates who had been successful enough in life to be elected and he tried to sell them to the voters. If they lost, the firm lost some of its reputation and the candidate went back to being successful in other ways.

If Berkley and Company failed, 1,000 people could lose their jobs in a county of 20,000 people. The company had lost market share, sales had stagnated and for the first time in company history, it lost money: $1.73 million during Tom's turnaround years of 1979 and 1980.

"There was a toughness that I never had to deal with before. I went through a year and a half, maybe two, that I remember as being … I didn't have enough experience to have the confidence of being sure of what I should do. I wanted to help everybody be part of a winning company and to do that, I had to do some tough love stuff. Then I'd go home and I'd say to myself, 'Oh, man.'

"It may have been exacerbated by outside influences, but inside actions and attitudes were the biggest problem. We had been responsible for most of our own downturn. It had been poor marketing, poor new product execution, lack of a motivated work organization, and lack of creativity in how we pushed the market. You can look at markets going up or down or economies going up or down and you can always find companies that somehow know how to excel."

Tom brought election campaign competitiveness and creativity to the industry.

Tom's career mirrored his father's. Berkley learned how to compare his stronger fishing line to other fishing lines, then learned how to compare the candidate (himself) to other candidates. He brought business savvy to Congress. Tom learned it the other way around.

"I brought to this industry a very combative, competitive environment that they weren't used to. In a campaign, it's A or B. It's not just A or nothing, its A or B. Either you're going to vote for Gore or you're going to vote for Bush.

"If Trilene is our fishing line and Stren is our competitor, not only are we going to build Trilene, but we're going to kill *them*. I mean, we're not going to give them the option of killing us. We had a stronger product, but they had twice or three times the market share we did."

Berkley recalls, "Tom decided the company would live or die with Trilene. He took all the money he could borrow and invested it in advertising, promotion, and research." Employees held their collective breath for about 18 months, without seeing profitability return.

"Tom had a lot of hurdles, a rocky road," said Sharry Caskey. "We all were anxious and everybody still feared for their jobs, but we could see the light at the end of the tunnel."

Still, "deep within me, I didn't know how long it would take, but I had a lot of confidence in Tom and I just thought he would turn it around and the company would again be successful."

The company needed a victory to restore its confidence. Tom decided to take bold action.

Something like his father had done 20 years earlier, Tom wanted to tackle the giant DuPont's Stren – and any other fishing line – in head-to-head competition. So, in 1980 he ran an advertisement for a $100,000 challenge:

"If any of these competitors can prove that their fishing line is as strong as ours, we'll send them a check for $100,000."

Tom knew he had put it all on the line.

"We didn't have that hundred grand, because we were close to being broke. If we'd been challenged and lost the money, that could have been our business.

"My executive group was livid."

But Tom had decided to go for broke.

"I had confidence. I hadn't personally run the tests, but I knew we were stronger."

When the $100,000 challenge succeeded, he tried a $10 challenge. This time, Tom went straight to consumers. At consumer outdoor product shows, at convention centers, or arenas throughout the United States, Berkley and Company placed this ad in the local newspaper:

"If you can bring us a fishing line stronger than Trilene, we will give you a $10 bill."

People believed in the strength of Stren. They lined up at the shows, with Stren line in hand, to collect their $10 bills.

"We went from show to show to show, running this test. We would have people lined up for hours on this testing machine. Over the course of that year, we did thousands of tests. We lost five times – when the machine malfunctioned or something."

Each time Trilene won the test, Tom envisioned people lining up in their local bait shop or discount store ready to plunk down their cash for a spool of Trilene.

The company made line-testing machines for all of their salesmen. "Wherever our salesmen were they could make the comparison test," recalled sales representative Dick Moulton. "Their 10-pound test line would test 10 pounds. Trilene would test 14. Then we would tie a knot in each line. Theirs would test eight pounds and Trilene would test 12. It really worked."

"This kind of confrontational, in your face, 'we'll put our money where our mouth is,' 'we've got a better product and we'll prove it to you,' attitude broke through the normal 'Please try me, I'm a good fishing line,' sales technique and it got people's attention." Tom recounted.

Trilene was on its way to regaining its position as the number one fishing line and the company was on its way back to profitability.

In 1981, the Trilene challenge year:

• Sales increased by $3.6 million, 13.7 percent from 1980

• Net earnings were a company record $2.4 million: Nearly twice the company's previous best—a whopping 369 percent increase in earnings.

By 1984, annual sales surpassed $50 million – nearly double their 1980 level – and net earnings reached $4 million.

"My son is not necessarily creative in terms of mechanical aptitude," said Berkley. "But he's bright. We had been making things that performed better than what other people made. Tom recognized that and used it to turn around the company."

However, the company had one more hurdle to cross.

The federal bribery and export duty charges were coming to trial in 1981.

"It became the most traumatic time of my life," said Berkley.

Every day, Berk would go to the prayer chapel in the Capitol building and pray that it would all work out. They actually gave him his own key. He thinks he is probably the only member of Congress to ever have his own key to the prayer chapel. Finally, Berkley realized that he had to stop such praying. It was causing him to dwell all the more on

"AMERICA'S LARGEST TACKLE PLANT"

1980 post card pictures the 200,000-square foot Berkley plant

his problem. "I had known that one should not pray for a person's own wishes, but that is exactly what I was doing. I should have been praying for those facing trial and for the Lord to give me the strength to face whatever happens."

The news media reports were full of testimony by the discharged former manager of the Taiwan plant, embarrassing Berkley and his company daily.

But as the trial began, the judge dismissed the indictments of all the employees except Don Porter.

"We waited in Washington terribly, terribly nervous, day after day, as the trial dragged on," Berkley said. "I was lying in bed, worrying, when Tom telephoned that the jury had found everyone and the company, NOT GUILTY.

"What a relief! My prayers had been answered!"

Berkley had received an education about the legal system. "We had spent more than $1 million defending ourselves in this case and we had a brilliant defense attorney, Roger Magnuson from Minneapolis. A federal prosecuting attorney has the funds of the federal government behind him. Many companies would not have been in a financial position to defend themselves with the excellent attorneys we had used. A prosecuting attorney can literally bankrupt an individual or firm simply by bringing charges. I had also learned what an ambitious prosecuting attorney and a dishonest employee can do to the lives of innocent people.

"You have to learn to navigate difficult waters as you go through life without compromising your values."

Chapter Twenty-Three

Congressman Tackling Giants

Presidents, dictators,
and the military-industrial complex

"Who is responsible for paying $400 for a hammer?" Berkley asked.

In the hearing room, Berkley, chairman of the Anti-trust Subcommittee of the Small Business Committee, looked at representatives of the U.S. Army, Navy, and Air Force.

"That was my department," the Navy man said. "I am the one responsible."

"How did it happen?" Berkley questioned.

"We ordered a repair kit for some flight simulators and when the proposal for the repair kit came in, since it met our guidelines and seemed reasonable to the buyer, he did not check the individual items."

"How much did the repair kit cost?" Berkley asked.

"I do not know, but I will find out."

"I wish you would do that," Berkley said, "and find out what each of the individual items cost."

Berkley, a millionaire who re-used his paper lunch bags, could hardly believe it when the Navy officer returned to the subcommittee with the number: $847,000—FOR A REPAIR KIT!

THE WHITE HOUSE

WASHINGTON

August 18, 1978

AUG 2 ? 1978

To Congressman Berkley Bedell

I appreciate your support of my decision to veto
the Defense Authorization Bill. As you know, I
believe that this legislation would weaken our
national security in certain critical areas and
waste scarce defense dollars.

Thanks for your cooperation. Together we will
see this through.

Sincerely,

Jimmy Carter

The Honorable Berkley Bedell
U.S. House of Representatives
Washington, D.C. 20515

**Letter thanking Berkley for voting to sustain President Carter's veto
of a defense bill. Berkley frequently opposed such bills as wasteful.**

In 1979, Berkley began a four-year quest to reform
the military's purchasing practices. He and his staff uncovered mind-boggling purchases that led to public outcry and
long-term changes. Known as the "spare parts" or "military
procurement" issue, Berkley's toolbox became the most famous effort of his career in Congress, a culmination of quali-
ties he brought to the office and developed while in office.

Early during his tenure in Congress, Berkley gained
respect as an articulate and principled spokesman on issues of
peace, energy, agriculture, and small business. He helped reform the way Congress operated. When he rose to the chair-

On Air Force One (left to right) Sen. Dick Clark, Rep. Michael Blouin, unidentified aide, Berkley, President Carter, Rep. Tom Harkin, Neal Smith.

manship of congressional subcommittees, he gained more power to introduce legislation. His staff pushed him to narrow his focus to a few issues so he could effect real change.

"He would discuss his goals and they were as broad as stopping nuclear proliferation and solving the energy crisis," said Mark Levine. Levine worked closely with Berkley on the staff of the Antitrust Subcommittee of the Small Business Committee. "Berkley is great and wonderful, but his goals were probably beyond the capabilities of either him or his staff."

The former 120-pound defensive end was ready to *tackle giants*. He continued to join efforts as diverse as promoting alternative energy sources (from wind power to solar to ethanol) and opposing the National Rifle Association (a lifelong hunter who saw no justification for street weapons).

So he focused his growing influence on:

- Confronting a pompous Asian dictator
- Opposing nuclear weapons proliferation
- Supporting farmers
- Advocating for small businesses
- Battling huge oil companies
- Tackling the giant military-industrial complex
- Fighting a popular U.S. President over taxes and foreign policy.

Deflating Imelda Marcos

In 1975, each member of Berkley's freshman class took the responsibility for researching and developing policy concerning a different country. Berkley took the Philippines. He became increasingly disturbed with America's relationship with the Ferdinand Marcos regime and the presence of U.S. military bases in the country. Marcos declared martial law in 1972 and imprisoned his chief political opponent, Benigno Aquino.

When Marcos' wife, Imelda, came to Washington in 1978, at her request, the Administration asked Berkley to arrange a meeting for her with members of Congress. It would be several years before stories of her extravagance – thousands of pairs of shoes – became well known in the United States. So her grand entrance into the meeting room, with her entourage, caught members by surprise.

"I've never seen anyone in all my life so perfectly groomed," Berkley recalled. "You'd think she had been prepared to be in a movie." Her attempt to dazzle may have backfired.

"Evidently, she thought she could be charming and we'd be obsequious," said Tom Harkin, then a U.S. Representative and later a U.S. Senator from Iowa.

"She starts talking about the Communists in the Philippines: 'They've won Vietnam, but their target is the Philippines.' She played the Red Scare thing."

Berkley chaired the meeting and waited his turn while members started asking probing questions. "She had never experienced that," Berkley recalled.

"Then Berkley said, 'Well, now, Mrs. Marcos, let me understand this correctly,'" Harkin recounted.

"I can still picture him," recalled former U.S. Representative Bob Edgar, "He wasn't afraid of anybody. He wasn't awed by anybody. Berkley Bedell is genetically nice. He is not going to question people for the purpose of embarrassing them, but he is going to ask that question that will make the sweat appear on your brow."

Berkley began to ask about Marcos' imprisoning political opponents, said Harkin.

"Every time he'd ask her about Aquino ... you could see the anger in her coming out," said Harkin. "Berkley had all the data. He wouldn't let up. She'd try to give an answer and he'd say, 'With all due respect, Mrs. Marcos, you didn't really answer this.' Berkley was getting to her. Finally, she stands up in a huff, and says, 'I can see you're all just biased against the Philippines. You'll be sorry. The Communists are your enemy and ours, and that's whom you're playing to. You're going to live to regret this.' And she storms out of the room with her entourage.

"Maybe some of us were willing to be a little more gentle with her. She's the wife of the President of the Philippines, regardless of how bad she is. Not Berkley. He didn't give one inch, and in doing so, exposed to all the rest of us who she really was. Berkley had her number early on."

Republican Congressman Paul Findley of Illinois turned to Berkley as they both stood together on the floor of the House of Representatives.

"I have it all arranged," said Findley.

"What are you talking about?" Berkley inquired.

"Your trip to China," Findley replied.

Some time previously, Paul Findley had visited China and had discussed the trip with Berkley. During the conversation, Berkley had mentioned he would like to take his family on such a trip. He then forgot about it, as it was nearly impossible to go to China at that time. After careful consideration of the cost – it would be a personal trip – Berkley decided to go and to take his family.

In December 1978, with Congress in recess, Elinor and Berk, Joanne and her husband Mike, and Ken's wife Kathie (Ken had Christmas season duties at church) boarded a plane for China. Tom joined them from Taiwan. China had not yet completely opened up. People wore Mao suits and gathered in crowds to watch the American family wherever they went.

"It proved to be an unbelievable trip," Berkley recalled. "We were assigned a special guide. Each day we would tell the guide what we wanted to see the following day and usually it would be arranged. The only thing they would not let us visit was a prison. They permitted us to witness an operation performed with acupuncture anesthesia. They removed a tumor the size of a grapefruit in a barren operating room with almost no special equipment in sight. The patient remained completely conscious during the operation and waved to us as they wheeled her out of the operating room. We were impressed because, at that time, acupuncture had not been accepted in the United States.

"I also met with a member of the Chinese Diet. A whole bank of photographers photographed the event. They told us that never before had a U.S. legislator met with a Chinese of the same rank. The following night, Elinor and I were walking around the city when we saw a large group staring at a big poster. It turned out that, since people could not afford to get their own newspapers, the newspaper would be posted on a big signboard and people would gather around to read the news. 'We should look at it, Elinor,' I said. 'Maybe my picture will be there.' Sure enough, the front page contained a picture of the Chinese legislator and me – the only picture on the page. I tapped the side of the Chinese man standing beside me in the crowd. I pointed at myself and at the picture. He could have cared less. I had come all the way to China to experience one of the best put-downs of my life.

"We also happened to be there at the time of the normalization ceremonies between the U.S. and China. Because I was a Congressman, our family attended the ceremonial reception acknowledging normalization. In China, they apparently conduct such receptions in a much more formal way than in America. Elinor and I each had assigned chairs and we had to sit in them during the entire affair. The rest of the family did not even get into the main room, which only held about 30 people. We all found it to be one of the major thrills of the trip."

When the rest of the family returned to the United States, Berkley and Elinor returned by way of the Philippines.

Tom had stopped in the Philippines when he went on his trip to Vietnam and around the world. He had met with, and paved the way for them to meet with, church leaders and opponents of the Marcos regime.

The opposition arranged for Berkley and Elinor to meet with prisoners who were under house arrest. They were political prisoners that had been confined for more than a year with no charges brought against them.

It surprised Berk to find the Philippine prisons much more humane than U.S. prisons. Each 15-20 prisoners lived together in the equivalent of a home. Although confined by a big fence, they cooked their own meals and were able live somewhat normal lives.

"We met with government officials who agreed to let me visit Mr. Aquino, the most popular opponent of Marcos. He had been held for some time as a political prisoner.

"I met with Mr. Aquino in his cell. It was more like a tiny apartment than a cell. He had a small private bathroom and sitting room. Mr. Aquino impressed me tremendously." A group of nuns arranged for Elinor to have dinner with Aquino's wife, Corazon, while Berkley was secretly meeting with some of the opposition to Marcos.

Berkley and Elinor then met with President Marcos, who pontificated for 30 minutes.

"Why is it that you're keeping Mr. Aquino in prison?" Berkley finally asked.

"Well, what would he like?" Marcos replied.

"I don't know," Berkley replied. "Would you like to know?"

"Yes, I would."

"Can I go visit him again?" Berkley asked.

"Yes, you can."

"May I take my wife?"

"Yes, you can."

As they were leaving, the U.S. ambassador who had accompanied them cautioned Berkley.

"Since you are a U.S. Congressman, I cannot tell you what you can do, but you are getting too involved with Philippine politics. I plead with you not to go back to see Mr. Aquino." Elinor was worried, too. Berkley agreed to back off. He regretted it.

"I made a terrible mistake not going back to see him. Marcos may have wanted to get him out of the country. If I had gone back to see Aquino and said to Marcos, 'What he'd like is to get out of prison and leave the country,' Marcos might have done it." Marcos let Aquino come to the United States in 1980 for heart surgery. Berkley met with him while they were both in Washington.

But when Aquino returned to the Philippines in 1983, he was shot and killed as he stepped off his airplane. Filipinos believed that Marcos had Aquino assassinated. They elected Aquino's wife, Corazon, as president in 1986 and the Marcos family went into exile.

Nuclear proliferation

After his opposition to the Vietnam War in the late 1960s, Berkley, the former army pilot, became increasingly committed to peace issues. His family had become intensely involved in peace groups. Elinor and their daughter, Joanne, joined and became active in Peace Links. Along with Betty Bumpers, wife of Senator Dale Bumpers of Arkansas, Elinor had helped to start the Washington, D.C. chapter of Peace Links, "Women against Nuclear War."

When Jo Oberstar, wife of Congressman Jim Oberstar of Minnesota died of cancer, Peace Links established the annual Jo Oberstar Memorial Award.

In 1991, Elinor was the first recipient of this award, presented at the Peace Links annual "Peace on Earth Gala" in Washington, D.C. before a large group of government dignitaries ... "For Her Tireless Dedication to Peace."

As the Cold War dragged on, and President Ronald Reagan insisted on military buildup, Berkley worked toward reducing the threat of nuclear war.

"Iowa is a fairly pacifist state," said former U.S. Representative Thomas Tauke, a Republican from northeast Iowa whose 1978-1990 Congressional tenure overlapped Berkley's. "Iowa was the only state in the union that didn't have a military base. Historically, it had Midwest progressive Christian, peace-oriented, pacifist-oriented churches. There was a lot of support in Iowa for things like the nuclear freeze."

Berkley introduced a resolution that called upon the President to negotiate a treaty to end the testing of nuclear weapons if the Soviet Union would also continue not to test nuclear weapons.

"We rejoiced when the House passed my Comprehensive Test Ban legislation (H.J. Res. 3)," said Berkley.

At the beginning of a congressional session in January, the bills first introduced are numbered according to their importance. Hundreds of bills are introduced. Berkley took pride in the fact that his resolution had been designated H.J. Res. 3. When the House and the Senate pass bills on the same subject, a conference committee is appointed to work out differences before both houses vote on the revised bill. Then it is sent to the President. Usually, only senior members of the assigned committee are appointed to the conference committee, but because of his involvement in military and peace issues, Congress made the rare decision to appoint Berkley to Armed Services conference committees, even though he was not even a member of the committee – and they made such a decision not once, but twice. In the conference committee, Berkley was able to keep his resolution in the final bill.

Although his resolution called upon the President to negotiate a treaty, Congress could not force him to do so. And he did not.

"This is the first President since Eisenhower that has not tried to negotiate such a treaty with the Soviets," Berkley noted in 1986. "Now the Soviets have said, 'we will stop if you will just stop.'" But Reagan still refused and continued to pursue a military buildup that Berkley opposed throughout his time in office. During all his terms in Congress, Berkley opposed the expansion of the military. He had not forgotten his observation as a youth that, "Good fighters seem to get in the most fights and fighting breeds fighting." The little country of Switzerland seemed to prove that belief as it avoided war after war in Europe.

Martin Luther King, Jr. declared, "Darkness cannot drive out Darkness; only light can do that. Hate cannot drive out hate; only love can do that." Berkley believed, "War cannot drive out war; only peace can do that."

In the nuclear age, Berkley insisted that military might could not bring security and peace. As more and more nations obtained nuclear weapons, no nation could feel secure unless the world learned to live and work together, and control the proliferation of nuclear weapons. Berkley thought the Unites States was in a position to lead, yet it was failing to recognize and take advantage of that opportunity.

"Power tends to promote arrogance," Berkley observed. "I saw it in our actions in the Law of the Sea negotiations at the United Nations. America's arrogance breaks my heart. The United Nations has many problems, but it is a big step towards bringing world peace. Our long-term security would be enhanced if the Unites States would act like a cooperative citizen in the world community and realize that it is not to our long-term benefit to simply pursue our own selfish interests because of military strength. America is indeed a world leader. We can use that position to lead toward a world of cooperation and peace, or toward a world of continued conflict. Selfishness breeds selfishness. Cooperation breeds cooperation. Arrogance breeds arrogance. Humility breeds humility. Fighting breeds fighting. Cooperation breeds peace."

Supporting the Farmer

The economy of the 1970s and early 1980s buried farmers.

"A number of people that Berkley knew personally, farmers and small business people and others, had been sucked under by the economic crisis of that period," recalled Tim Galvin, the agriculture expert on Berkley's staff. "It devastated him to see that. People were just wiped out."

Berkley responded by trying to ensure that the new farm bills in both 1981 and 1985 provided some meaningful forms of income support to make it possible for farmers to make a living and still produce enough food.

Berkley clashed with the Reagan Administration over the government role. As a member of the Agriculture Committee, Berkley helped pass the 1981 and 1985 Farm Bill. Berkley favored production controls: paying farmers to set aside portions of farmland in order to reduce surpluses and strengthen prices.

"The Reagan Administration wanted a 'market-oriented' approach to agriculture where we wouldn't idle land, where there would be minimal price supports," said Galvin.

The economics of agriculture are not the same as the economics of industry, Berkley argued, because of U.S. farmers' capability to produce more of their major crops than they could use and sell.

"In manufactured items, such as fishing tackle, the producer only produces what the firm can sell," Berkley observed. "If inventories become excessive, production is cut back. No such controls exist in agriculture. Each farmer has a limited amount of land to generate revenue. If the farmer lets land lay idle, he or she will surely go broke, as there will be no income from it and taxes, rent and upkeep will still have to be paid.

"So every farmer plants every acre to raise as much produce as possible, resulting in large surpluses of the commodity. Prices will fall until they get to where the farmer does not plant, because the prices are less than what it costs him to plant and harvest the crop, without allowance for rent, taxes, living expenses, and other costs. Under such circumstances, the farmer would surely go broke. Land prices will plummet and there will be chaos in rural America."

Under the agricultural program in place while Berkley served in Congress, the government guaranteed the farmer a certain price for his crops, then limited the number of acres that he could plant – in order to control surpluses.

"The farmer had incentive to grow the maximum number of bushels on the acres the government permitted him to plant, so he poured on the fertilizer and did everything he could to maximize production on his allotted acres. This was both bad economics and bad for the environment," Berkley thought.

When the Farm Bill came up in 1984, Berkley put forth an amendment that would have limited the number of bushels a farmer could market, rather the number of acres he could plant.

"It gave the farmer the freedom to do what was the most economical," Berkley reasoned. "He surely would plant more acres and use less fertilizer."

The fertilizer industry opposed the amendment. The Reagan Administration opposed it. Most farm organizations were against it, but much to everyone's surprise, the committee passed the Bedell amendment.

But the Bedell amendment lost on the floor of the House primarily because of opposition by the powerful Farm Bureau organization. Berkley always thought the Farm Bureau, in its lobbying efforts, represented the large corporate farms rather than the family farmer.

But Berkley was pleased he succeeded in calling attention to a serious problem.

After Berkley left Congress, the government passed the Freedom to Farm Act that eliminated government programs to control production. Year-end surpluses increased, the cost to the government increased and prices decreased – the opposite of what had been promised.

"I don't think anybody should be surprised," Berkley reflected.

Berkley opposed government subsidizing water to irrigate surplus crops. The government furnished water to farmers, at much less than cost, to irrigate crops that were in surplus. Furthermore, each year's water legislation would authorize more dams and water projects he thought wasteful.

So each year Berkley would offer an amendment to the water bill, saying the government would not furnish subsidized water to farmers to grow crops, if at the same time the government paid other farmers not to grow those same crops.

"Because of the importance of irrigation to many of the members from some of the agricultural states, I had little help from members of the committee," Berkley recalled. Opposition from the committee, the administration, major farm organizations and members from irrigated states killed his amendment every year. After he left Congress, Berkley heard that the amendment continued to be offered.

"One of the Republican members who had been handling the water bill on the floor of the House came to me after the vote and said, 'One of the hardest things I have ever had to do was to oppose your amendment, as I knew you were right, but I had to defend the committee position.'"

Small businesses get a chance

In 1979, when Berkley became chairman of the Antitrust Subcommittee of the Small Business Committee, his business reputation brought credibility, media visibility, and clout to a previously minor subcommittee. Berkley's battles with DuPont fueled his passion for giving small businesses a chance to compete, particularly in innovation and energy.

Some of the pieces of legislation that the committee wrote and that became law were:

• The University and Small Business Patent Act that gave universities and small businesses the title to patents that they develop under government funding, which spurred innovation.

• The Small Business Innovation Resource Act, which is still in operation. The idea was to create a program through which government agencies would set aside part of their budget for funding innovation by small businesses. Berkley wrote and sponsored the bill in the House of Representatives and Senator Warren Rudman from New Hampshire, a Republican, was the sponsor in the Senate.

Departments and agencies hated to give up control of their budgets. Other Congressional committees considered it encroachment. They claimed jurisdiction.

But after months of hearings and research, Berkley showed that the government was overlooking a huge number of small businesses that could develop innovations that government agencies were seeking. The government was giving too many contracts to big companies to do work that small businesses could do better.

"This was extremely contentious," Levine recounted. "Berkley was just a tiger. He fought for this, tooth and nail." Each committee held its own hearings and its own votes. Berkley worked tirelessly to convince every single commit-

White House meeting with President Carter. Berkley is second from right.

tee that the Act was necessary. The measure went to the full House and sailed through by an overwhelming margin, a complete turnaround from the original position.

"The brief, five-page law required a simple program," said Levine. "Each year, the Small Business Administration was required to publish a booklet commonly available to all small businesses listing the projects for which the government wanted proposals. Two months later, proposals are collected and the best ones awarded. The government spends 1.5 percent of the program budget funding those proposals and then six months later, the small businesses can apply for phase two. The dollar number is like $100,000 at first and $1 million dollars at the second. It's an ongoing program that everybody loves."

At one hearing, the U.S. Chamber of Commerce testified against one of Berkley's small business bills. Berkley was upset. In their prepared remarks, the Chamber pointed out that 90 percent of their members were from small businesses.

"Who makes decisions on matters of this type?" Berkley asked them.

"Our Board of Directors," the Chamber replied.

"How many members are on your Board of Directors?"

"43."

"How many of them are from small businesses?"

They scurried around for a little bit and then replied, "three."

"Isn't it a little strange that 90 percent of your members are from small business, but only three small business representatives out of 43 members serve on your Board, which decides what your stand will be on legislation designed to help small business?" The people testifying did not know how to answer.

Later, when the Chamber of Commerce came to Washington for a convention and asked Berkley to speak, he shared the story with the members in attendance and encouraged them to demand small business be properly represented on the Chamber's Board of Directors.

Service stations vs. oil giants

By 1979, oil companies foresaw the end of the neighborhood service station.

"They were moving toward what were called superpumpers, kind of the way mom-and-pop neighborhood stores got replaced by Kmarts," said Marc Rosenberg of the Antitrust Subcommittee of the Small Business Committee. "Shell Oil could more efficiently — and they thought more profitably — sell a huge amount of gasoline through a super-pumper that they would run themselves, as opposed to three or four small dealers in the neighborhood."

The problem wasn't just that little guys had to compete with big guys. The problem was that independent franchise operators were being shoved off a tilted playing field — by their own suppliers.

"One company owned the property, provided the product, set the terms and conditions by which you could operate that property, and then that same entity opened up a store down the street and became your competitor and controlled every condition under which you did business," said Rosenberg. "In some cases, the supplier prohibited the existing franchise from changing its way of doing business. Some cases were worse.

"The larger station that opened up would be selling gasoline at retail for less than the dealer could buy it at wholesale. These guys were dropping like flies. Thirty percent of independent franchises went out of business in five years. The inequality of that relationship really offended Berkley," said Rosenberg. "The goal was to provide for more equitable competition."

At one hearing, an oil company vice-president's rationale set Berkley off.

"Berkley gave him a three-page encapsulated story of a small community and a big company," said Levine, of the Antitrust Subcommittee. "He talked about what the people need and how these people play an important role; how they're an important part of the economic chain, too."

Berkley told the executive: "They don't deserve to be run over and stomped on. They're what makes America great."

There wasn't a dry eye in the room.

"And this vice president is just sitting there stating his position, thinking he was going to stand up to Berkley," Levine said, shaking his head.

Ultimately, the legislation stalled in Congress, but a number of states picked up the issue. Berkley sent Rosenberg to share information with various state attorney generals who were bringing lawsuits. Rosenberg appeared as an expert witness in half a dozen state legislatures, presenting the evidence Berkley's subcommittee had obtained in Washington.

"We accomplished our purpose of putting a spotlight on a problem and moving it as close to a solution as was possible," said Rosenberg.

"The work we did affected every member of Congress," said Levine. "Berkley created a record of what was happening. The other members had someone they could look to and say, 'Look, we're working on this problem.'"

Tom Tauke, U.S. Representative in northeast Iowa at the time, said it was a big deal in Iowa.

"In Iowa, there has always been a concern about what Wal-Mart does to the Main Street businessman, not just to the business, but to the quality of life," said Tauke, a Republican who supported Berkley on this issue. "We thought the quality of life in communities in Iowa would be better if you had dealers who were entrepreneurs and not just working for a major oil company. Farmers are small business people and farmers are inherently skeptical. They are especially wary of large businesses that are part of the agricultural process. There are economic principles: I'm a free market kind of guy, but I had a desire to promote opportunity and to promote entrepreneurship, to give the opportunity to many people to have ownership in a business enterprise."

For Berkley, it was a basic principle.

"It was fairness – a principle he brought to the job every day," Levine said.

Tauke said the issue reflected a basic characteristic of Berkley. "He's a little bit of a crusader, more than a little bit. He sees a wrong and he wants to right it."

Researching the corner gas station led Berkley to close a loophole on the windfall profits tax. He had asked an oil company to trace the costs of getting oil from Alaska to the gas pump. In the process, he found that oil companies were taking Alaskan oil, putting it on a tanker, and sailing the tanker ten miles offshore, out of U.S. jurisdiction, claiming that this enabled them to avoid some taxes.

"You can't do that," Berkley said. The oil company tax lawyers had found a loophole. So Berkley called a hearing with the Treasury Department.

"I start getting calls from oil companies, saying 'You don't understand, you don't understand,'" Levine said.

"Often, CEOs of big corporations or oil companies would want to come in and talk to Berkley one on one and I would recommend that they not do that. I just wanted to let them know that when they went in there, everything was fair. He would find new things. Berkley's going to take you somewhere else."

Berkley had one oil executive working under the table for peanuts.

The executive came to a noon meeting to discuss offshore revenue. Levine and the well-dressed executive joined Berkley in his office.

"Do you mind if I eat my lunch while we talk?" Berkley asked.

"No, go right ahead."

Berkley reached into a previously used paper lunch bag and took out a peanut butter and jelly sandwich and a plastic margarine container of applesauce. He ate while the executive explained why Berkley's efforts with the Treasury Department were unfair. Levine took notes in the corner.

Berkley, in a three-piece suit, opened a packet of peanuts. Levine saw a peanut slip out of Berkley's hand and roll along his sleeve into his vest. Berkley looked on his lap and desk, then got down and crawled on his knees to look for the peanut.

"This guy keeps talking and finally Berkley's gone, under the desk," Levine said. "The oil company executive gets out of his chair and he's on the floor, too. They're looking like crazy for the peanut. I couldn't believe it. These guys are head to head, trying to find a peanut, while talking about billions of dollars of oil revenue."

Berkley finally gave up and sat down. "I thought: 'This is real power,' " Levine said. "I bet you that man has never crawled around on the floor with another Congressman looking for a peanut."

Berkley, the Congressman who searched for every last peanut, convinced the Treasury Department to close the offshore tax loophole.

Nailing the $436 hammer

During this same period, Berkley took an obscure subcommittee into battle with the military and their huge corporate suppliers, because of complaints that small businesses were shut out of the military's purchasing process.

Berkley discovered a purchasing system so convoluted that only a few huge corporations were qualified to bid on projects and provide supplies. The corporations claimed enormous amounts of administrative work were needed to meet government requirements, resulting in outrageous charges for simple purchases.

"As budgets got tighter, discretionary spending for small business was eaten up by big procurement — build me an F-15 rather than find me a better way to do border patrol," said Mark Levine. "One area where small businesses could have a major impact was in replacement and repair parts."

But big contractors wanted to add the after-market phase to their contracts.

"They would sell a system," said Levine. "The price would get haggled down up front in the system, but along with it would come a 10-year supply and parts contract where they were the sole source supplier of parts for replacement and repairs. They would have no competition for 10 years and could charge outrageous prices."

The investigation opened up a Pandora's box of abuses.

"When we started looking at this, the subcommittee office literally started getting phone calls from phone booths, from people who worked in these depots," said Levine. "They said, 'Guess what we have. We just paid $800 for a coffeepot.' I would get calls from all over the country. The whole committee was getting calls."

Berkley and his staff uncovered that the Navy paid a huge sum for a repair kit from the Simulation Systems Division of Gould, Incorporated. Because of the Navy's policy of only letting corporations that had been certified as "qualified bidders" submit proposals, Gould was the only firm from which the Navy could accept bids.

"Gould knew the Navy had a $1 million budget for the repair kit. Gould asked for $1,100,000. The Navy's purchasing agency got it down to $847,000, thinking this was one of the best bits of negotiation they had ever done," Berkley said.

In 1984, Berkley introduced three amendments to the full Congress. Here are excerpts from the Congressional Record account of the debate:

"This is a six-inch pair of pliers that I bought at Kmart for $3.77," Berkley said. "The Navy paid $430 for a six-inch pair of pliers.

"This is a 3/8-inch socket that I bought at Hechinger's (a local hardware store) for $1.49. The military paid $456 for this little socket.

"I have the entire list here. I went out and bought 22 tools that were included in this repair kit. I paid $92.44 total for the 22 tools I bought. The taxpayers paid Gould, Inc. $10,168.56 for these same tools.

"When we challenged them to explain how such a thing could happen, the Navy furnished us with the list you see here as to how they justified the fact that Gould could charge $436 for a $7 hammer. If you look closely, you will see quite clearly that they started with $7.

"As they added overhead to that $7 hammer, they came up with, in their opinion, a legitimate price of $436 – billed to the American taxpayers."

Berkley offered three amendments to this bill, "to open up this system so that there will be some competition, and so the taxpayers will no longer have to spend that kind of money."

Berkley and his staff had also examined the quality of the tool kit the Navy bought.

"In fact, many of the tools were not even up to what we had in our own tool kit," he told Congress. He showed Congress a tool kit that he bought at retail value.

"Here is a pair of vise grips. Their vise grips are not as big as these. The ones I bought were $3.97. The government paid $343 for their smaller ones."

Berkley challenged Congress "to move forward and say to the taxpayers: 'we are not going to sit by and let this waste continue to happen. We are going to work together to see this abuse is corrected, and this rip-off to the taxpayers no longer continues to exist.'

"With the United States facing red-ink deficits approaching $200 billion annually for years to come, I submit that it is our obligation to ensure the taxpayers' hard-earned dollars are spent as cost-effectively as possible. That is why everyone's blood boils every time it is revealed that our military spent $104 for a four-cent diode, or $9,606 for a 13-cent Allen wrench.

"Take a look at these items:

"What makes this all so absurd, is that the government *knew* they were paying these outrageous prices *before* they bought them.

"Look at this chart supplied by the Department of Defense:

Pricing example
Gould, Simulation Systems Division

Tool	Retail Price	Contractor's Price
Hammer	$7.66	$436.00
Box wrench, 1 set	$4.99	$768.00
Pliers, slip joint, 6"	$3.77	$430.00
Slip joint	$5.97	$449.00
Vise grip	$7.94	$486.00
Wrench, socket set 3/8	$12.88	$545.00
Bar extension	$1.99	$430.00
Do	$2.19	$431.00
Socket 1/2"	$1.49	$456.00
Screw drivers, square blade, 1 set	$1.69	$265.50
Jewelers, 1 set	$1.97	$232.00
Phillips, 1 set	$1.69	$258.06
Offset	$2.79	$225.00
Crimping Tool	$3.96	$729.00
Super just wrenches	$4.88	$1,150.00
Wrenches	$1.57	$234.00
Drill set	$1.69	$599.00
Hex driver	$3.99	$469.00
Feeler gauge	$4.27	$436.00
Circuit tester	$3.39	$489.00
Tool box	$11.67	$652.00
Total	**$92.44**	**$10,168.56**

"Worse," Berkley said, "The supplier provided those figures *before* the purchase was final and the government still accepted them.

"Far from an isolated case," Berkley said, "top Pentagon purchasing officials acknowledge that the problem exists and is very widespread."

Purchased item		Amount
Hammer, hand, sledge (quantity 1 each)		
Direct material		$7.00
Material packaging		$1.00
Material handling overhead at 19.8%		$2.00
Spares/repair department	(1.0 hour)	
Program support/administration	(0.4 hour)	
Program management	(1.0 hour)	
Secretarial	(0.2 hour)	
Engineering support	(2.6 hour)	$37.00
Engineering overhead at 110 percent		$42.00
Mechanical subassembly	(0.3 hour)	
Quality control	(0.9 hour)	
Operations program management	(1.5 hour)	
Program planning	(4.0 hour)	
Manufacturing project engineer	(1.0 hour)	
Q.A.	(0.1 hour)	
Manufacturing support	(7.8 hour)	$93.00
Manufacturing overhead at 110 percent		$102.00
Subtotal		**$283.00**
G & A at 31.8 percent		$90.00
Subtotal		**$374.00**
Fee		$56.00
Facilities capital cost of money		$7.00
Total price		**$436.00**

"The question remains: What do we do about this terrible problem? I ask you – if you were the chief executive of a company that had a purchasing department that operated like the U.S. government's – what would you do? I submit that you would demand changes be made immediately.

"You would demand that your purchasing department carefully examine their relationships with their sole source suppliers.

"You would demand that your purchasing agents open the doors to potential suppliers who were previously shut out of the system.

"You would demand that artificial barriers to competition in your purchasing system be lifted.

"You would demand that your company take control of rights to the technical data your business paid for, but did not control.

"If this is what you would do to return your business to the black, then this is what we need to do to reform our government's runaway spare parts procurement system.

"My amendment is the medicine we need to cure the patient."

Berkley's amendment to House Resolution 5167 would:

• Limit the use of pre-qualification criteria, such as qualified products and bidders list. Such lists were used as "screening devices to deny businesses the opportunity to even submit bids." Under the amendment, bidders would need to meet the quality standards for any purchase. The government would not have to necessarily accept the low bid.

• Allow sole source contracting of spare parts contracts only when one of five conditions would be met: 1) the existence of only one possible source; 2) an urgent need for the parts; 3) national security considerations; 4) only one party has a legitimate proprietary interest; or 5) another statute requires a specific source.

• Assure that proper pricing and overhead allocation methods are used by defense contractors when they sell spare and replacement parts to the military.

1) For items a supplier merely passes on to the military – those manufactured by another manufacturer – the supplier may charge only for direct costs, overhead costs directly attributable to the item and a reasonable profit.

2) For items the supplier manufactures itself the supplier would be required to make the products available to the military at or below their lowest commercial price, "unless there are differences in quantities, quality, delivery," or other conditions specified in the contract.

"Too many times we have found that the government paid far too much for commonly available items."

The amendment would help to open up the bidding to more businesses and "help send a message to the nation that Congress cares about how taxpayers' money is spent. Let us put some order in the spare parts procurement system."

At the beginning of each day, every member is allowed to give a one-minute speech on the floor of the House. Berkley began bringing his toolbox every day until the amendment was voted upon, pulling out a different tool each day.

"Here is a wrench set I purchased at Kmart for $12.88," he would say. "The military paid $545 for this exact same item. You can correct this waste of taxpayer's money by passing the Bedell amendment."

It might have seemed like grandstanding, if not for Berkley's reputation for frugality.

"He didn't do that simply because he wanted votes back home," said Paul Simon. "He did things because he believed in them."

When the bill finally came to the floor there was lengthy debate.

Opponents argued that the military needed pre-qualification lists to keep from having to deal with unqualified bidders.

"In my opinion, that is a restriction of competition and is a way of keeping people from being able to bid," Berkley argued.

"Bids would still have to meet the government's quality specifications," Berkley emphasized. "The government would not be required to take the low bidder."

U.S. Representative Richard Durbin of Illinois asked: "What if a company was barred from bidding government work because of its past performance, because the company had provided shoddy equipment, or was found guilty of criminal conduct? Would the amendment now say that the company would have the right to bid, regardless of that moral turpitude?"

"The government would not be required to accept the bid," Berkley replied. "The amendment was designed to allow competition with more bids to choose from. The government could apply its criteria for quality and performance, and the legislation provides that the government would not be required to accept the lowest bid."

The Pentagon was against the amendment and lobbied strongly in opposition. The Administration was against it and joined in the lobbying. Suppliers joined in opposing it. The Armed Services Committee, which was managing the bill, was against it.

Berkley's amendment carried by a vote of 324 to 75.

By the time the amendment had come to a vote, Berkley had dismantled most of the opposition with two of his favorite tactics:

1) Evidence that a practical solution was necessary; and

2) He invited the opposition to help him develop the solution.

The factor that guaranteed victory was one that Berkley didn't always worship, but welcomed when he could get it: public opinion. The hearing room was filled to overflowing with spectators, television cameras, and reporters. People lined the corridors.

"Berkley had the whole country stirred up over these hammers and everything," recalled Levine. "Every committee fought us, none harder than the Armed Services Committee, but it became clear that very strong procurement legislation was going to pass.

"The Armed Services Committee tried to stop the Small Business Subcommittee from telling the military what to do," Levine said. "The chairman of the Armed Services Committee stood up on the floor of the House of Representatives. He said, 'we have a solution to this. This is our proposal, our amendment, to reform the procurement system.'

He was trying to say, 'we're on board now. You don't have to pass this guy's legislation.'

"I remember sitting in the chamber of the House right next to Berkley, thinking 'What do we do next, now that he's done that?' But Berkley wasn't interested in defeating the enemy. He was interested in working together for mutual victory.

"Berkley got right up and said, 'I congratulate you. You know more about this than anybody else. Your committee had hearings and that's why I'm willing to accept your bill as an amendment to mine. Let's do it together. Pass mine and pass yours together instead of mine against yours.'"

"The Armed Services Committee wanted a fight between the two. They said, 'Oh, we can't do that.' Berkley said, 'Why not? Let's take a vote. That's what we're here for. Who wants to add mine to his? Say aye!' He was great."

Senator Paul Simon, D-Illinois, reflected: "He wanted to get a job done. If that meant letting a Republican or some other Democrat get a little credit for doing something, fine. Let's just get the job done. Let's not worry about who gets the credit."

The measure made an enormous impression.

Several members of Congress borrowed Berkley's tool chest to demonstrate to their constituents. They could have gone out and bought their own, but they wanted Berkley's tool chest.

"The U.S. procurement system is very, very complex," Berkley reflected. "We buy billions of dollars worth of items through this procurement system. It was amazing how it could be so easily communicated to the American public with a simple toolbox."

The issue resonated with the American people. They saw huge budget deficits and were being told that they must increase defense spending and cut back on funding for education, energy, and health and human services.

For his election campaign, Berkley produced a television commercial in which he went into the grocery store, picked up a can of coffee, some butter, and other items. The grocer rang up the prices: $539 for the coffee, $279 for the

Berkley gives President Carter a Berkley fly rod in 1980, just before Carter leaves office.

butter and so forth. Berkley's voiceover said, "That's what your groceries would cost if they had been bought by the military. If you want somebody *really* looking after what happens, send me back to Congress so I can continue to monitor these things."

The House victory could have been squandered when the House-Senate conference committee would hash out a compromise bill. The conference committee would be run by the Armed Services Committee, which might try to revoke or amend Berkley's amendment.

Because the House vote was so overwhelming, despite the Armed Services Committee, Berkley said to Speaker of the House Tip O'Neill, "I want to be appointed as a manager on behalf of the House of Representatives to support this provision in the bill." O'Neill appointed him to be a conferee and Berkley succeeded in keeping his amendment in the final bill.

Reagan tax cuts: Rich vs. poor

For six years in Congress, Berkley co-existed with Presidents that he liked personally and respected policy-wise. He didn't always agree with them and didn't always

Berkley and President Reagan

think they were effective, but he didn't think he had to fight them at virtually every turn.

The Reagan years would be different.

President Ronald Reagan was elected in 1980 by a wide margin, promising to strengthen the military, cut people's taxes, and balance the budget.

In opposing a very popular President, Berkley found himself in the minority in Congress.

"It was called a Democratic Congress, but I claim it was a Reagan Congress," said Berkley. "Although the Democrats were in the majority, there were large numbers of members who would not vote against Reagan's proposals because of his popularity. The southern Democrats tended to vote with Reagan on issue after issue after issue. That made it difficult for me.

"Shortly after his election, Reagan proposed a big tax cut that was especially large for the wealthy," Berkley said. "Dan Rostenkowski, Chairman of the Ways and Means Committee, got into a bidding war with the Reagan people as to who was going to offer the biggest tax cut."

Berkley was puzzled by tax-cut mania, in the face of 12 consecutive years of budget deficits.

"It was pretty clear to me that you do not balance the budget by cutting everyone's taxes and lowering revenues."

Berkley voted against the tax cuts.

"My constituents in Iowa had a fit. They were just livid for my having voted that way. How could I possibly vote against a bill that would lower everyone's taxes and balance the budget?"

The Sioux City Chamber of Commerce printed a flier outlining the terrible vote Berkley made. "I met with them and they were impossible to talk with. I tried to tell them why I voted as I did, what I believe, and so on, but they refused to listen," Berkley said.

As he defended his stand on tax cuts, Berk's Open Door meetings in the district became contentious.

"If there's ever a period of Berkley Bedell's profile in courage, I think it was during the early 1980s," said Tim Galvin, an Iowa native who worked on Berkley's staff in Washington.

"Reagan came in, basically in a landslide, defeated Carter, and was clearly very popular in Berkley Bedell's district, yet Berkley voted against Reaganomics. At the time, I remember being scared as a young staffer – 24 or 25 years old – thinking, 'He is definitely putting it on the line.' We were clearly going against the political grain back home, yet Berkley felt to his core that Reaganomics and the Reagan Administration policies were so fundamentally wrong that he had to oppose it all, even if it meant he was going to lose the next election. We were going against the revolution, but he had to do it. The thing I was most proud of was his standing up to the Reagan Administration in those early years."

Berkley realized he could be in trouble.

"Returning to Washington after a series of meetings in Iowa, I told Elinor that I didn't think I could possibly be re-elected in 1982."

He then voted against President Reagan's increases in military spending.

"I never considered voting differently than what I thought was right."

Berkley agreed with Reagan on virtually nothing.

"Everything about the Reagan Administration was the antithesis of what Berkley Bedell stood for," said Galvin, "whether it was huge military spending or big tax cuts that would drive us into deficits, or Reagan's position on agriculture. It seemed like much of the 1980s was about opposing the Reagan Administration."

Berkley searched for allies in his opposition to Reagan. He openly wooed a young Iowa Republican, Tom Tauke. When Tauke was elected in 1978, at age 28, to the House of Representatives, Tauke fondly remembered how Berkley helped him get settled. Both men valued bipartisan relationships, in an era when Berkley believed that the Reagan Administration ignored and demonized liberal Democrats.

"Congress wasn't as partisan when I arrived in 1978 as when I left in 1990," said Tauke. "Berkley was not a partisan and I hope I wasn't. I don't mean to suggest that he wasn't loyal to the Democratic Party – he was – but when it came to working on issues and trying to make the processes of Congress work, he reached out. I think we both had that approach to trying to get something done."

Berkley wasn't about to move Tauke from the fiscal conservative camp, but Tauke generally did not support Reagan on the military buildup and many foreign policy positions. Tauke said he was one of about 25 potential Republican swing votes that could offset the hawkish Democrats on military and foreign policy matters.

Tauke recalled, "Berkley was really opposed to the military buildup and foreign policy strategy that Reagan pursued: The Central American thing, the nuclear buildup. He thought putting money into the military was offensive and wrong."

It was bad enough that the predictable and preventable came true: During Reagan's two terms the deficit exploded, adding each year to a federal debt that tripled in eight years.

But what eventually happened was worse than that, Berkley thought.

"The greatest legacy of the Ronald Reagan's presidency was convincing the people that they should demand lower taxes, no matter how wealthy they might be.

"When our country was established, it was policy that people would be taxed according to their ability to pay. Under President Eisenhower, income tax went to 91 percent for people with very high income.

"After the Reagan tax cuts, because of loopholes, everyone was paying about the same rate," asserted Berkley.

"Worse than that, the gap widened between rich and poor, and a smaller percentage of people owned a larger portion of the wealth," he said.

"In 1964, one percent of the people owned 20 percent of the wealth in our country. In 1984, a mere 20 years later, one percent of the people owned 40 percent of the wealth.

"The problem rests not in the fact that one percent of people have such great wealth. The problem rests in the fact that the more wealth of the country that the one percent own, the less is available to the remaining 99 percent. As our society has advanced, money has become so much more important and manual labor less important. The continued concentration of wealth in America will lead to problems in the future unless something is done."

George W. Bush: Reagan renewed

As Berkley pondered the situation during the presidency of George W. Bush in 2001, Berkley grew increasingly dismayed at the renewal of Reagan's legacy.

"The rich are getting richer, and the poor are staying where they are. And we're passing more and more laws that make that all the more sure to happen. President Bush and his people are on the extreme on that issue.

"I cannot understand why most of the people in our country would favor eliminating the inheritance tax," he said. "It isn't going to help them. In fact, it is going to hurt them, because the money has to come from somewhere. If it doesn't come from inheritance tax, it's going to have to come from their pocket during their lifetime. That's life. I would have no objection to raising the exemption in the inheritance tax to five or six million dollars, but to say that billionaires do not have to pay *any* inheritance tax and that their *entire* wealth can be passed on to future generations is unconscionable."

"Millions of people have no health insurance. The U.S. is the only industrial country that does not provide health insurance to all of its people. It breaks my heart when our government adopts policies that seem to indicate tax cuts for the wealthy are more important than health care for the masses."

Berkley's legacy in Congress

People in Iowa listened to him, Berkley said.

"I was able to voice my beliefs to my people and they continued to re-elect me. I had an extremely conservative district.

" I believe that the natural values of people, particularly those who practice religious values are good. All we need is leadership that will lead us to become a nation where we care about each other and care about the rest of the world — a world where concern and cooperation replace greed, war, and the emphasis on military might. I yearn for that kind of leadership."

His supporters said Berkley left a legacy of tenacious advocacy for the oppressed, defiance of oppressors, and principled support of causes he believed in.

"Berkley didn't mind taking on someone who was powerful. That didn't bother him," said Paul Simon. "That's what America is all about. That's what we need.

"One of the things I have observed in life," Simon said, "is that most people who struggle and then make it … look back with some disdain on those who haven't made it: 'I made it, why can't you?' Berkley didn't have that attitude. That was one of the things I appreciated about him."

Bob Edgar said Berkley remained true to principles.

"When Berkley stood up to committee chairmen, the military, oil companies, the National Rifle Association, Imelda Marcos, or Ronald Reagan; or when he opposed the death penalty, or nuclear proliferation, or when he stood up for the poor and oppressed, for small businesses and farmers, even when Berkley agonized before taking a middle-of-the-road position on abortion, Berkley stood on well-grounded moral principles. He has given me courage to stay honest. He has given me the ability to stick with principle rather than the impact something might have on my career – to try to do what's right. I don't always live up to Berkley's model.

"He's probably the most courageous political leader I've ever met," Edgar said. "Berkley is one who didn't mind making a few enemies if he thought what he was doing was right.

"While he didn't wear his 'church-iness' on his front lapel, he wore it internally. It was who he was as a person. So, in his mind he was always thinking: How can I help the small farmer, how can I help the least of these, my brothers and sisters on planet earth?

"Berk is my hero."

Chapter Twenty-Four

Where Berkley Stands:

Speeches, Sermons and Writings

Berkley wrote a number of articles during his Congressional term. Here are three that were in his files, which describe some of his beliefs and stands. It is thought the first and second articles were published in *The Des Moines Register*. The publication of the third one was unidentified.

"Soviet warships are sailing between the Hawaiian Islands," Congressman Dan Akaka of Hawaii remarked to me in a worried voice, as we walked back to our offices from the floor of the House of Representatives. "I guess they think if we can challenge Libya, they can do the same to us." It was just one of the many shocks I received as I came to realize the disastrous effects of a foreign policy of arrogance and a complete lack of concern for the needs of other nations, or concern for our image in their eyes.

The first shock came as I visited the Law of the Sea negotiations in April. I found anger and disbelief among both developed and developing nations

over the announcement by the new Reagan Administration that the U.S., alone among all the nations of
the world, would not negotiate during what was expected to be the final session to conclude a treaty for all
the nations in the use of the oceans of the world.

I then shook my head in disbelief as the United
States cast the only dissenting vote on a United Nations resolution proposing some limits on the advertising of baby formula in underdeveloped countries
where it is claimed that the use of such formula frequently results in increased infant deaths.

The U.S. alone thought corporate profits more important than the lives of babies. The world's leaders
shook their heads in disbelief, just as I had.

In August, I visited Africa with a Congressional
delegation. We were shocked at what we saw in
Crossroads, a suburb of Cape Town. We watched the
black women sing together as the government tore
down the shacks they had erected. The government
would not even let in people or organizations to help
these people who were not harming anyone. They
had simply come to the area to be near their hus-
bands who had traveled to the area to find jobs. The
next day they were tear-gassed by the white government of South Africa. Our delegation sent a telegram
to Secretary of State Haig urging him to send a strong
statement to the South African government indicating our concern over these actions. His reply ignored
our request and simply said he would be glad to meet
with us when we returned. The issue is not just the
humanitarian aspects of the deplorable apartheid
policies of the South African government. The problem is, we are again joining the wrong side. By befriending a terrible government representing four
million whites, the U.S. is making enemies of the
governments of hundreds of millions of black Afri-
cans. And even the whites in South Africa admitted
that change had to come there just as it has in other

areas, and that white minority government cannot continue. So we are backing a loser.

Next, we learn that the Unites States stands alone in refusing to condemn South Africa for its military invasion of Angola. It is as if we are trying to antagonize and push all of black Africa into the Soviet sphere.

From South Africa I went to Nairobi, Kenya as a delegate to the World Conference on New and Renewable Energy Resources. There I found the United States stood alone in refusing to support a special window at the World Bank to help the developing world finance new and renewable energy efforts.

If I was disappointed with the damage the U.S. attitude was having on our image in Nairobi, it was nothing compared to what I found at my next stop at the Law of the Sea negotiations in Geneva, Switzerland. In its second session since the election of Ronald Reagan, the United States was still refusing to negotiate. The antagonism towards the United States position was intense. As I was told by delegates, "Many countries have had changes in their government over the period of these negotiations. They have not reneged on agreements and commitments made by previous administrations. If the United States is going to do so, nobody will be able to trust you." Time and again 'arrogance' was the word used to describe the United States' attitude. The delegate from one of America's friendly nations said, "What the United States is doing in the Law of the Sea negotiations is just as damaging to your image in the world as was the Russian invasion of Afghanistan to the Soviet Union."

As I returned from Geneva, I read in the newspapers of our shooting down two Libyan airplanes as we conducted maneuvers in disputed waters. With all the oceans of the world, some people would ask why it makes sense to conduct maneuvers in disputed waters. The net result is that the Libyans have now invited the Soviets to establish military bases in their country. Most nations do not want to join the Soviet camp. The Soviets are arrogant, demanding, and have little to offer economically.

If the United States looks at the Soviet Union as a rival, as I believe we do, then I cannot understand why we would try to antagonize the nations of the world and push them into the hands of the Soviets—and then have to spend more and more on arms.

Particularly in this time of budget restraint, we cannot afford the arrogant attitude now dominating our foreign policy that alienates most of the world.

Berkley Bedell
Democratic member of Congress from Iowa

Guest Opinion

NOTE: This article was written during the U.S. bicentennial year, during the cold war when both the United States and the Soviet Union had enough bombs to destroy each other many times over. Berkley has added remarks as of 2004

By Berkley Bedell

Time was in the history of man when the strongest man with the biggest club could impose his will upon those not so strong. Might made right. With the advancement of weapons through clubs, spears, arrows, and finally guns, a small person could pull the trigger of a gun just as easily as a giant, and leadership came not from brute strength, but from one's ability to lead.

The strong men who failed to recognize this change ceased to be leaders, and those who wasted their resources on more and bigger clubs and spears were the fools of the time.

Time was when those nations with the largest armies could impose their will upon weaker nations.

The Turks and the Greeks and the Romans ruled by the power of their armies, and again … might made right. With the development of weapons through the spear, the arrow, the gun and finally the nuclear bomb, nations are now coming to the place where their ability to destroy another is no longer dependent upon the size of its army, but whether or not it possesses nuclear weapons.

The development of nuclear weapons by nations is to the family of nations what the development of the gun was to the family of man. Just as a gun enables a person to destroy another regardless of their relative power, so possession of nuclear weaponry gives one nation the power to destroy another regardless of their relative military might. One Poseidon submarine carries enough nuclear warheads to destroy more than half of Russia's industrial capability.

Dinosaurs no longer walk the earth because they could not adapt to the changes in the world. History is a record of those who have fallen because of their failure to recognize changing times and adapt to them. I pray that America will not make this mistake.

American foreign policy is still dictated by those who fail to recognize the realities of the nuclear bomb. They fail to realize that with the coming of the nuclear age, brute strength can no longer be used as a tool for persuasion.

In a gun duel, the quality of one's gun and ammunition are important, but when one loads down with so many guns and so much ammunition that he depletes his strength in carrying the load, he fools no one but himself.

Today, with the new realization of the magnitude of America's economic problems, there are those who point their finger at our generals and admirals for their insatiable appetite for more and more weaponry.

I would suggest that we point that finger at America's political leadership and, indeed, at the American people, for supporting a foreign policy that fails to recognize the new realities of the nuclear age and is based upon the outdated concept that our influence in the world of tomorrow will be dependent upon how many clubs we own, and how many times we can destroy another nation.

For the bicentennial year, I suggest a new foreign policy that recognizes the reality that once a nation has the ability to destroy any possible enemy, piling on more and more weapons only serves to weaken, rather than strengthen. This new policy must also recognize that nuclear weaponry to nations, like guns to individuals, will tend to equalize the possessors, be they weak or strong by previous standards.

Only then can we move forward with a defense policy that strengthens, rather than drains America, and a foreign policy that helps to build a better world through negotiations, leadership, and example.

Congressman Berkley Bedell

Remarks as of 2004

Nuclear missiles are a tremendous leveling tool. Just as the bow and arrow overcame the power of the club, so nuclear missiles overcome the power of armies.

The United States military may be able to invade Iraq, but we are not about to do the same to Russia and face the possibility that they would fire their nuclear missiles and destroy us.

I ask you: If you were the ruler of North Korea and saw what happened to Iraq, what would you do? You know that your military is not sufficiently powerful to repel an invasion by the United States and you cannot possibly build up such strength. The United States has hinted at such a pre-emptive strike against you. You want to preserve your position and protect your people. You can be sure that if you had nuclear bombs and the missiles to deliver them to U.S. cities, the U.S. would probably not attack and risk the destruction of some of its major cities.

I do not know what you would do, but I submit that there are surely many rulers who would feel it their duty to proceed with haste to build a capability to respond with nuclear weapons—just to prevent an invasion.

So the United States can go ahead spending billions of dollars building a more powerful military machine that can go around the world engaging in pre-emptive wars that motivate more and more countries to join the nuclear club, or we can decide that we are going to recognize the reality that military might is of little use against nuclear missiles.

As I said in our bicentennial year, "Only then can we move forward with a defense policy that strengthens, rather than drains America and a foreign policy that helps to build a better world through negotiations, leadership and example."

United States needs a road map

An article written by Berkley while he was in Congress:

America has a problem. We do not know where we are going. No, that is not the real problem. The real problem is that we do not have an image of where we want to go. We are on a trip without a description of our destination and without a road map to tell us how to get there.

Many years ago, when I attended management school, we were told, "If you are going to manage any operation you have to first determine what it is you are trying to accomplish with whatever you are managing—and you must write it out."

In the five years I have served in the United States Congress, our federal government has never had a written plan of where we wanted to go in the journey we are on—a vision of the future we might hope to achieve.

I believe President Carter sincerely wanted to see a world where human rights were respected by all, and that he truly wanted to solve the energy problem. But, if there was a real vision and plan of how to get there, as a Congressman, I was never aware of it—and such a plan cannot succeed unless not only the government, but the people as well, are aware of it and support it.

Likewise, if President Reagan has a vision he certainly has not clearly portrayed it to Congress or the people. It appears to me that he believes that by increasing our expenditure for arms; cutting taxes, especially to big corporations and the wealthy; and cutting government programs we will somehow build a wonderful society.

If his vision is one of an America dominated by a few large corporations, with a greater disparity between the wealthy and the not so wealthy, hidden behind a mighty military machine, I believe we should know that is where he wants to take us. I will have a difficult time working to get to that destination.

Students of human behavior tell us that people with visions of the future they want to achieve are likely to attain their vision. The same is true for organizations. I believe the same is true for nations. The United States needs a vision of the kind of a country and world we want to leave for future generations, and a road map on how we plan to get there.

Let me try to describe my vision of the future I would like to see, and how I would propose to reach such a destination. To do so represents two very different challenges.

In describing one's dreams, one can be most idealistic, realizing that the future may not be as wonderful as are one's dreams. But someone has said, "If you reach for a star you are not likely to come up with a handful of mud."

I would like to start with my vision of the future, which I would like to see for this great land of ours.

First and most importantly, I want a country that is at peace with the world, and which by its conduct sets an example for all the nations of the world to follow.

I want a country in which there is opportunity for all—opportunity to succeed and opportunity to fail.

I want a country where everyone has the necessities of life, including food, water, shelter, clothing, and health care, together with educational opportunities—where people can share in other luxuries according to their contribution to society.

I want a country in which there is compassion and concern for one another; where cooperation is more revered than combativeness; where business, labor, and government work together for the common good; and where new technology is used to bring about a better, cleaner, renewable world.

How do we reach this vision of the future? What will we use for a road map? Let me try to provide one. In doing so, I do not pretend that this proposal is without flaws. My argument is that today none exists, and someone better offer one, so that others can correct and improve upon it.

My map starts with a foreign policy directed towards reducing world tensions and directed towards "Peace on Earth and Good Will among Men (and women)."

In fashioning our road map, we have to be realistic. There has been strife and wars as long as there has been recorded history. Of all the species on the globe, mankind is the only race that glorifies in the killing of its own species. Some species of fish eat their own; some insects kill their mates; and there are some species that kill their offspring; but in no other species are killers of their own glorified as we glorify our war heroes.

Our nation was born through a revolution because of what the fathers of our nation considered the tyranny of King George. How can we expect that others will not act similarly when faced with what they perceive to be equal or greater tyranny? It matters not whether that tyranny comes from abroad, as in Afghanistan, or from within, as in Batista's Cuba. It is difficult to reject violence to overcome tyranny and honor George Washington for leading our forces against the British.

We need to face the world realistically. Of course, the Soviet Union wants to increase its sphere of influence in the world, just as we do. I do not doubt that their leaders may truly believe that Communism is a better route for nations to follow than capitalism. Indeed, it may be for some. Fifty years ago, there was not much difference between the life of the poor in India and China. Today there is no comparison. There is little or no starvation in China. But China is starting to realize some of the advantages of capitalism. They now permit families to have their own small plots and to sell the production from these plots. When we visited China recently they freely admitted that the production from these plots per hectare greatly exceeded that from the communal land. Except in time of crisis, self-interest is a more effective motivator than cooperative effort.

But we need to recognize that capitalism has its weaknesses too. Without some controls, capitalism provides the opportunity for the economically strong to exploit the weak, just as totalitarianism makes it possible for political leaders to exploit the masses. In some capitalist countries with totalitarian governments, much of the money is in the hands of a few wealthy families.

There are questions we need to ask ourselves before we start to determine policy and lay out our road map. Repression exists in many parts of the world today. In some cases, it is external repression such as that which exists in the Soviet countries of

Eastern Europe. In some cases, it is internal repression such as exists in South Africa, Chile, and the Philippines. As long as the people are given no political methods to correct such repression, we can expect people, sooner or later, to turn to violence, just as we did under the repression of King George.

Our policies should be policies that minimize the likelihood of such violence. When it does occur we should do what we can to understand its causes and minimize its extent and the likelihood of it spreading. But we should not support a Shah, or a Batista, or a Samoza, or a Marcos, just because we perceive them to be our friends. The world's people are not likely to turn to us for leadership if they perceive us to be on the side of repression. And repressed people will not remain repressed forever.

In fashioning a foreign policy to take us towards that peaceful vision of the future, we need to recognize that there will be internal conflicts within nations—some of which may be justified. And that there will continue to be disputes between nations. We need to determine our reaction to such conflict and to recognize some realities.

All the peoples of the world do not share the same values as we. Political freedom and the right to vote in free elections become secondary when you and your children are starving.

We must come to realize that we are part of a world family of nations. Just because we are big and powerful we cannot tell everyone else in the family what to do. When action would seem to be needed, we need to discuss possible action with the rest of the family and act together. The big bully acting alone fools no one except himself!

BERKLEY BEDELL
Is a Democratic Congressman from Iowa

Foundation of prayer

Berkley found that a group of members of Congress gathered weekly for breakfast and prayer. He became a regular member and used the Congressional prayer chapel extensively, particularly during the time Berkley and Company was struggling.

"It's soothing. We like to think there's someone to whom we can turn when we need help. It's an opportunity to reflect on something important to you. I'm well aware that prayer doesn't always work, but it feels good to be able to pray for others and to seriously try to be of help to people. The mistake we tend to make is that when we pray, we ask for things for ourselves. We're wrong more often than we're right when we do that." He had to stop himself when he found himself guilty of selfish prayer, during his business struggles.

When Berkley became president of the House breakfast prayer group, he had to give a short talk during the National Prayer Breakfast, attended by about 1,000 people. Here is his talk, given February 10, 1978:

Praise the Lord! (Praise the Lord echoed from the crowd.) I bring you greetings from the House of Representatives prayer group. Three short years ago, after my first arrival in the Congress, I started attending the weekly House of Representatives prayer breakfast. I soon came to realize how important these breakfasts were, not only to me personally, but indeed to our total government. I fear that we in Congress are so busy arguing issues that if it were not for our prayer breakfasts, almost no time would be spent examining our values and beliefs.

Let me tell you a little about our weekly House prayer breakfast. We meet at 8:00 a.m. every Thursday. After breakfast and an opening prayer, we have a short talk by a different member of the House. Usually the member tells us a little bit about his or her life, his or her religious beliefs, and the talk is followed by discussion of some of the questions raised, and a closing prayer by one of the members.

These are quite personal and frequently very moving meetings. Sincerity and candor are the rule as we try to better understand each other in our philosophical and religious beliefs. It is a thrill for me to be here as I look out across the crowd and see those people who have participated in this weekly prayer breakfast.

Two of Christ's teachings speak especially loudly to me. He said, 'Love your neighbor as yourself,' and He said, 'You cannot serve both God and mammon.' For a long time, I didn't understand that second statement. I thought it simply meant that you couldn't have two masters. Then, in Sunday school, somebody explained to me that mammon was wealth. I realized that He was saying that you cannot worship wealth and God at the same time. It seems pretty clear that Christ was saying that we should set aside our selfish worship of material wealth. We should worship God and we should love and care for one another. To do so, I believe, would solve more problems than all the laws enacted by all the legislative bodies of the world.

That's why I believe that our Congressional prayer breakfast is important. I think it is a shining light for the world and I am thankful that you would come from all across the world to join us this morning in this prayer breakfast.

There are those in Congress who question this National Prayer Breakfast, and their questioning is not without justification. For we read in Matthew that Christ admonished us, 'and when you pray, you are not to pray as the hypocrites. For they love to stand and pray in the synagogues and on the street corners in order to be seen by men. Truly, I say to you, they have their reward in full. But when you pray, go into your inner room, and when you have shut the door, pray to your Father.'

This morning's breakfast can only be worth the time if we value it not for the excitement of the crowd or the fame of the occasion, but for the opportunity it gives each of us to strengthen our own faith, and to help one another to be a little closer to his God. May this morning be a period of spiritual renewal where the presence of the Holy Spirit is more important than the presence of governmental dignitaries or the press corps. May this morning be a supplement to, rather than a replacement for, our inner room prayers.

I don't know how you people feel, but when we all sang together, 'How great Thou Art' I felt that the Holy Spirit was here with us. Lest we be carried away by our numbers, remember that Christ had only twelve apostles and He told us that we could move mountains if we only had the faith. My prayer this morning is that each of you will leave with the faith that, together, we may work to build God's world here on this spaceship Earth—a world of peace, of love, of caring, of sharing and of praying in our inner rooms.

May God bless you all. May He give you the strength and the guidance to better serve Him and your fellow human beings."

Berkley also spoke to a large group of born-again Christians:

"I told them that I felt there could be a problem with born-again Christians, because not everyone would be privileged to have the experience they had. I didn't doubt their experience for a minute and I thought their experience to be wonderful. But I feared they had a tendency to try to say they were the only ones who really had the right religion, because they had the right experience, but for some of the rest of us, it didn't come that easy. Some people might automatically be transported to the mountaintop, but some of the rest of us have to climb up there – and that there is nothing wrong with those who have to climb up there.

"The group didn't particularly appreciate my talk, but I enjoyed it, whether they did or not. It worries me when some of the born-again Christians act like the town drunk, who one evening, after a drunken binge, fell into a well. As he flailed around in the cold water, he experienced the Lord and was born-again. After being rescued, he believed it was his mission to push everyone he could into the well so that they, too, might be 'born again.' "

Berkley was asked several times to preach in various churches. Here is the last part of a sermon delivered to one of the large Washington, D.C. Methodist churches:

"While we were trying to decide what we wanted to do, I spent one night at the home of a friend, along the ocean in Connecticut.

"An astronaut was also staying at my friend's home that evening.

"The next morning, he was making a movie out on the front yard.

"I will never forget his words as he sat before the camera with a big globe of the world at his side. It was during the Cold War between the United States and the Soviet Union.

"He said, 'As the three of us were traveling toward the moon in that space ship, we realized that we had to work together with our limited space, limited resources and limited waste disposal system if we were to bring that flight through successfully.'

"He continued, 'When I looked out that little window and saw that beautiful blue and white ball we call earth, on a black velvety sky, I knew that earth was something special God put in this universe. Then a strange thing happened. All of a sudden I realized that blue and white ball was a space ship, just as surely as was the one in which we were traveling.

That it had limited space, limited resources, and a limited waste disposal system just as surely as did ours. But although the three of us were working together, recognizing these limits to try to bring our flight through successfully, the crew of three billion on spaceship earth were not doing the same.'

"How right he was.

"How successful do you think that space flight would have been if two of the three astronauts had each thought they knew the best way to govern the space ship and each was sufficiently armed so that he could blow up the space ship if their arguments escalated into armed conflict?

"Then suppose that each of the astronauts had been judged primarily by how much of the wealth of the spaceship he could gather unto himself during the flight.

"And finally, suppose there had been absolutely no planning—no vision of where they wanted to go and how they would get there. No guide for his or her actions.

"Let's consider those items one by one.

"First, supposing two of the astronauts each thought they knew the best way to govern the space ship.

"Let me make it clear I do not trust the Russians.

"But we are stuck on this spaceship journey together. We can either learn to live together or we can blow up the ship.

"I know a lot of people I do not trust, but I still try to get along with them. I do not threaten them with disciplinary action, such as embargoes, when I do not approve of what they are doing.

"Partly I don't because I know it won't do any good.

"How could we possibly believe that a grain embargo would cause Russia to withdraw its troops from Afghanistan?

"The best way to unify a nation is for it to face a perceived external threat.

"The more we bombed the German city of Dresden, the site of the German submarine plants, the more Germans showed up to build submarines. Pearl Harbor unified our people like no other action could have. Countries, like people, do not like to be pushed around.

"I truly believe that democracy and capitalism is a better system than Communism for most of the nations on our spaceship.

"But the way to sell our system is not by sending more arms to oppressive governments.

"The way for our country to build its influence in the world is by setting an example, which the world will want to follow.

"For a period of time after World War II, we seemed to be doing that. Then our image as the good guys slowly faded, just as church attendance has slowly faded.

"Other nations now see America as a rich nation, which cares more about getting oil than helping others; where tax cuts to the rich are more important than health insurance to the masses. And bombs and bombers are more important than education of the handicapped or helping the unemployed; where military aid takes preference over humanitarian aid.

"I was a delegate to the World Conference on New and Renewable Energy in Nairobi, Kenya last summer. We were the only nation in the world that opposed a special World Bank window to make loans to the developing world to help solve energy problems.

"One of the delegates said to me, "How can we expect America to be concerned about our needs when you are not even concerned about the needs of the unfortunate in your own country?"

"It matters not whether you agree with him. It is his perception that shapes his thinking.

"If we want the flight of space ship earth to make it, I suggest that we start to do our part to reduce—not escalate—tensions between ourselves and the Soviets, and that we try to win over the rest of the crew not by guns and threats, but by love and caring, and by setting an example they will want to follow.

"Secondly, we asked how successful the flight would have been if each crewmember had been judged by how much of the wealth of the ship he could gather unto himself during the flight?

"I told you, I believe capitalism is a better system than Communism. In capitalistic societies we depend upon self-motivation for individual rewards—and it is a powerful motivator.

"When I visited China two years ago, they told us that the production from private plots was much greater per acre than that from communal farms.

"Here in America we say "work hard and you will get ahead." And generally, people do. And we tend to judge them by the wealth they accumulate. The trouble is, we tend to lose sight of other values.

"Does buying that third television really give you the same satisfaction as helping with Sunday school, or singing in the choir, or working in some group for a worthwhile cause?

"If our spaceship is to be successful, we need to look to our values and start to show some love and concern for others. Like the astronauts, we have to work together to bring our flight through successfully.

"Finally, we asked ourselves how successful we thought the space flight would have been if they had just started out with no planning—no vision of where they wanted to go and how they would get there?

"I think we need a vision of where we want to go and a guide to how we get there.

"I have a vision of where I would like us to go. I want us to head toward a world where there is peace. Where nations put away some of their arrogant selfish ways and try to reduce tensions; where more effort is put into building love, concern, and friendliness than building bombs and bombers; where we provide for each other the material needs to live rewarding, comfortable, meaningful lives, but where we realize that happiness is more that just material wealth.

"And if that is our vision—what is to be our guide?

"I think it is right here—right here in the words and teachings of Jesus Christ. Listen to parts of what he had to say:

'You have heard it said, 'You shall love your neighbor and hate your enemy,' But I say to you, love your enemies, and pray for those who persecute you.'

'It is easier for a camel to go through the eye of a needle than for a rich man to enter the kingdom of God.'

'You cannot love both God and mammon (wealth)."

'Blessed are the peacemakers, for they shall be called the sons of God.'

"So my message to you today is, that we accept Christ as our guide on this space ship earth.

"Not because he will reward us for doing so by finding a place in Heaven, but because by doing so, we can try to build a heaven on earth as compared to the hell of a nuclear holocaust; that we truly try to follow His teachings and love our enemies and pray for those who persecute us; that we put aside our worship of material wealth.

"So that as individuals and as a country, we set an example for the rest of the crew on this beautiful blue and while ball called spaceship earth that will help head us towards that heaven Christ promised us when he said in Mathew 16:19 to his disciples, 'I will give you the keys of the kingdom of heaven.'

Remarks in 2004

Berkley added these remarks in 2004:

As this book and my life try to point out, in most of our experiences in life there is no need to worry about failure or to be concerned about the opinions of others. I will always regret that I did not run for President when the opportunity was presented. It was one time that I was influenced by what I thought my congressional colleagues would think. Sure, it would have been a long shot, but I had nothing to lose and it is better to try and lose than not to try at all.

However, if I had run and won, I do not believe at the time I was sufficiently aware of a major problem that only a strong President can solve. And I very possibly would have failed to address what I now consider to be one of the major problems with our society.

The problem is that with the tremendously increasing cost of running for major office, raising the money for one's next campaign becomes critical for re-election. If a politician wants to continue in office, he or she had better vote as his or her contributors demand. Those contributions come primarily from the wealthy and corporate America. They are the ones who are repaid with laws to serve their contributors' interests, rather than the interests of the common people.

Elinor and I spend our winters in Naples, Florida, where there is a large population of wealthy homeowners. Money was raised from the wealthy to build a beautiful Philharmonic Hall. Concerts and programs are conducted with the prices of admission sufficiently high that those same wealthy individuals make up most of the audience That includes Elinor and myself and many of our friends. Few young workers and their families can afford to attend. Some seats are even labeled with the name of the couple or individual who made a significant contribution. Hardly anyone, rich or poor, objects to the "Phil." It is simply accepted that those who pay the bill should enjoy the benefits and the programs should reflect the wishes of those who contribute.

SO IT IS WITH OUR FEDERAL GOVERNMENT!

Those who make the contributions get the benefits.

It is most apparent in the tax laws, and health care, but exists across the board from the dairy industry to the lumber industry.

The result is that the rich are getting richer and the common people are out of luck.

In 1982, which was about the middle of my term, the nation's richest person's wealth was $2 billion and the median family wealth was $33,500, a ratio of 60,000 to 1. By 1999, the richest person's wealth was $85 billion and the median family wealth was $60,000, for a ratio of 1,416,000 to 1. In just that 17-year period, the wealth of the richest person increased over 42 times, while the median family wealth did not quite double. And that change happened not just to the richest individual, but to most all of the super rich as well.

Using my own state as an example, in 1982 the wealth of the nation's wealthiest person was not as great as the wealth of all the households in the city of Des Moines, Iowa. By 1999, it was more than that of all the households in the entire state.

In 1960, the gap in terms of wealth between the top 20 percent and the bottom 20 percent of our people was 30-fold. Four decades later, it was more than 75-fold.

The problem is that as more of the wealth of our country is concentrated on the super rich, less is left for the remainder of the population.

So what is Washington's answer to this problem? It is to eliminate the inheritance tax, so that those giant fortunes will no longer be taxed, and they can continue to multiply generation from generation. Make no mistake. The dead do not pay taxes, buy groceries, or play golf. It is those who inherit the money who pay the taxes. So the government says that those working people who win the lottery should pay taxes on their windfall, but those who inherit billions should go tax-free. What could more clearly demonstrate that campaign contributions and the wealthy control our federal government?

I have always said that the persons with whom I served in the U.S. Congress were the finest people with whom I have ever been involved. The problem is not the people. It is the system. As long as it costs such a tremendous amount to run for office, and that money must come from the rich and powerful, the tendency to do whatever the wealthy want will be overpowering.

A University of Akron study indicated that 95 percent of congressional campaign contributions came from households with incomes of $50,000 or more.

Our founding fathers came from a society in which the privileged Nobility owned most of the wealth. When our ancestors came over here from Europe, they set up a system in which the wealth would be spread among the masses, and our country prospered beyond belief. They provided free public education, free roads, and laws to protect the environment and to protect debtors. They had seen in Europe that "power corrupts and absolute power corrupts absolutely."

They set up a tax system based upon one's ability to pay. When Eisenhower was President, our income tax rates went up to over 90 percent. That did not seem to diminish people's drive to work hard.

When I went to Congress, labor unions had found that making political contributions could give them clout in government. They set an example for corporate America and the rich, who learned it well.

Corporate America and the wealthy funded conservative think tanks - the Heritage Foundation, the Hoover Institution and the American Enterprise Institute - that churned out study after study advocating their agenda. They flooded the political arena with a deluge of dollars that made the labor unions look like pygmies.

They built alliances with the religious right – Jerry Falwell's moral majority and Pat Robertson's Christian Coalition – to hide the class war that was being waged. Like most everyone else, I was not fully aware that a class war was in progress. Indeed, most of the lower and middle class that make up over 80 percent of our people are not aware that a financial war is in progress.

Daniel Altman has written a book that describes what is happening. He describes what he calls a "neo-economy" – a place without taxes, without a safety net. He said it is coming to America. He was not up to date. "It's here," says Warren Buffet, one of the richest persons in the country. "My class won."

So today, while the top 1 percent get richer and richer, nearly 44 million Americans – eight out of ten of them in working families – have no health insurance and cannot get the basic care they need. We have the worst financial inequality among all the western nations.

In America, we say work hard and you will get ahead. It is a powerful motivator and I am an example of one who started with nothing and was financially "successful." I didn't need special tax breaks to do it and the opportunity to succeed or fail needs to be preserved, but there is a problem. In America, people get income from two sources, work (labor) and investments (capital). The problem is that most working families need most of what they earn to pay their living expenses and raise their families. They have very little left to invest. However, if you are wealthy, and get a sizeable income from investments it does not take most of your income to pay your cost of living and your wealth multiplies and multiplies – and it will continue to do so unless it is taxed during life and at death.

The veteran Washington reporter, Elizabeth Drew, says, "the greatest change in Washington over the past 25 years – has been the preoccupation with money." Jeffrey Birnbaum, who covered Washington for nearly 20 years for the *Wall Street Journal* put it more bluntly: "(Campaign cash) has flooded over the gunwales of the ship of state and threatens to sink the entire vessel. Political donations determine the course and speed of many government actions that deeply affect our lives."

During his brief campaign for President in 2000, before he was ambushed by the dirty tricks of the Religious

Right in South Carolina, Republican John McCain said that elections today are nothing less than an influence-peddling scheme in which both parties compete to stay in office by selling the country to the highest bidder."

The only answer is to take the money out of politics. We are going to have to adopt public financing for political campaigns, and reduce the cost of elections. We have to eliminate politicians' dependence upon campaign contributions. That will not be easy. Members of Congress are not likely to rush to change a system which practically assures their re-election if they only vote according to the wishes of their wealthy contributors.

The only possibility, it seems to me, is that another Teddy Roosevelt be elected with the courage to address the problem. That person could come from either party or from a new party. It will not be easy as long as a large segment of the Christian Church is on the side of the wealthy and against the masses.

One thing seems certain: The control of the government by the wealthy and powerful – as they continue to gather more and more of the wealth of our country unto themselves and leave less and less for the people – cannot continue forever.

Berkley Bedell

Chapter Twenty-Five

Presidential Politics

One evening in 1983, the Democrats in the Iowa delegation had a dinner meeting with Alan Baron. Baron came to Washington from Iowa and published a political newsletter named *The Baron Report*.

When the conversation turned to presidential politics, Baron startled the crowd. His favorite candidate for the 1984 Democratic presidential nomination, he announced, would be: "Berkley Bedell."

The crowd probed the provocative Baron. Did he really think a low-profile Representative from a low-profile state could win the nomination?

"Everybody at that meeting looked at it as sort of a joke," Berkley recalled, "but he held his ground."

The Iowa Caucuses had become the first major contest in the nomination process. An Iowa favorite son like Berkley could win Iowa even while hitting the campaign trail hard during New Hampshire primaries. A candidate like Berkley Bedell could quickly gain national prominence with two quick victories and be well on his way to the nomination. And the longer people knew Berkley, the more they liked him.

Who better to take on the incumbent Reagan than a successful businessman who knew how to balance a budget, the sort of person that Reagan idealized even while Reagan's own policies ballooned the budget deficit? Who better to argue about government waste than the guy who found the $400 hammers? Who better to argue family values than a man with impeccable integrity and a loyal family? Who better to debate Reagan than a man with more Reagan credentials than Reagan, but with solid Democratic ideals and policies?

The Democrats had few high-profile potential candidates who were ready for such a tousle. Jimmy Carter wouldn't come back. Ted Kennedy's name was always in the mix, but he was controversial. Former Vice President Walter Mondale would have to defend the Carter presidency that Reagan had so successfully attacked in 1980. Rising stars might need another four years of experience before making a run for it.

It surprised Berkley and flattered him. Should he take the proposal seriously?

"What do you think, Elinor?" he asked, as they walked home from the meeting.

"Do you really think you'd have a chance at the nomination?" she wondered.

"Probably a better chance of getting nominated than I did of being elected when I first ran for Congress, don't you think?"

"How do you figure that?"

"Well, I think we could win the Iowa Caucuses, don't you?"

"Against Fritz Mondale?"

"I wouldn't want to run against Fritz, but I sure think we could win Iowa, and don't you think Tom and Joanne and Ken could set things up in New Hampshire for us? You saw what they did when we ran for Congress. If we won Iowa and New Hampshire, we'd be off and running."

"What about money? You would have to have money to run a campaign."

"I'm sure we have enough to run the Iowa campaign. We always seem to be able to raise enough money. Don't you think we have enough money?"

"I don't think we have THAT much money."

"Well, we can always borrow some money."

"I know! That's what I'm afraid of."

Berkley and Elinor walked in silence for a moment. Could they really be thinking about running for President? Were they ready for such a life-changing experience? Was Berkley ready for the job?

"Do you think you have enough foreign policy experience?" Elinor asked.

"I have more experience than Reagan or Carter had before they became President. Besides, that's why you have a State Department, to help you know what to do regarding foreign policy. I'm a pretty quick study."

Pause.

"What would you do about the budget deficit?"

"I've balanced budgets before, Elinor. You have to either increase revenue or cut expenses or both. One thing I do know is that you can't perform like Reagan: Cut taxes and increase spending."

"How much spending can you eliminate without hurting people? Reagan's already cut out the people who need help the most. Don't you think you'd have to raise taxes?"

"There's plenty of ways to increase revenue, Elinor."

"But that's what got Reagan elected in the first place. How do you think you can beat Reagan if you're going to say you'll raise taxes?"

She's got me there, he thought. Reagan will pound and pound that issue. Who will vote to raise their taxes?

Pause.

"You really don't want me to run, do you, Elinor?"

Elinor took a deep breath and closed her eyes.

"Do you really think we could handle that big a job?" she finally asked. "That much pressure; that much media attention? This isn't like running Berkley and Company, or our little congressional office. Do you remember how hard it was for Jimmy and Rosalyn? I'm just afraid it would be such a heartbreaking experience."

"I don't know, Elinor. I just don't know."

Walking home from that meeting with Elinor is a memory that has stayed with Berkley forever.

That night, he thought about the reaction from his Iowa colleagues. Why didn't they take such a possibility seriously? Did any of them think he had a chance? What would his good friends think? Should he talk to Paul Simon about it? Tom Harkin? Bob Edgar? They would think he was crazy! If they didn't support him, who would?

"As Elinor and I talked about it we decided that I should not run," Berkley recalled. He couldn't justify running without a politically acceptable solution to the budget deficit and he refused to run on the false promise of a balanced budget without a tax increase.

He also couldn't quite get past what his fellow Representatives would think. "What a foolish concern. I hadn't let their thoughts bother me during most of my life.

"I really had a fairly decent chance, if I did run, of being elected president. You know, I'm always optimistic."

Berkley addresses the 1984 Democratic National Convention on behalf of Small Business

Berkley became more involved in presidential politics in the 1988 and 1992 elections.

Eight years of Reagan leadership was coming to an end in 1988 and Berkley believed he was in a position to help elect a president whom he could believe in.

In 1987 he and Paul Simon tried to get Senator Dale Bumpers from Arkansas to run for president. They were convinced that he would run, but he kept postponing his announcement. Finally, the call came from Paul Simon. "Dale has decided to run," Paul informed him

"I flew to Washington and met with Senator Joe Biden and Congressman Dick Gephart, both of whom were planning to run, and both of whom had solicited my support," Berkley recalled. "I informed them that Senator Bumpers had decided to run and that I would be supporting him. They both agreed that Senator Bumpers would be a good candidate and could understand why I had decided to back him. I then met with Senator Bumpers and, much to my surprise, found he had not decided for certain he would run." Then one Friday, Bumpers announced that he would NOT run.

Berkley next looked to his good friend from neighboring Illinois: Paul Simon. A Congressman from Florida, a *New York Times* columnist, and the California Democratic Party Chairman had identified Simon as a potential candidate. Simon had "pooh-poohed" the talk before, but when Bumpers opted out, Simon's telephone started ringing.

"One of the people who called me was Berkley Bedell," Simon recalled. "Berk said, 'If you'll become a candidate, I'll devote a year of my life to help get you elected.' That was one of the decisive things in my becoming a candidate."

Simon and his wife, Jeanne, went to Florida for a weekend to think it over.

"I jumped into the race later than all the candidates," said Simon. "I had no campaign staff, not even a campaign manager. I just announced I was going to be a candidate and went from there. In the first poll taken after I announced, I got one percent of the vote nationwide."

Berkley became Simon's Iowa chairman. Berkley used his statewide reputation and his knowledge of the state's people and politics to help Simon get national attention in the highly visible Iowa Caucuses.

"Berkley's presence gave muscle to my campaign," said Simon. Simon's distinctive bow tie set him apart as a unique character. Through his dulcet baritone, he spoke with a professorial wisdom and yet with a plain, goodhearted common sense that attracted attention in the Democratic scramble to find a candidate to take on Ronald Reagan's vice president, George Herbert Walker Bush.

By December the *Des Moines Register* took a poll showing Simon 24 points ahead, but before they published it, Gary Hart made it irrelevant when he announced he would re-enter the race. The *Des Moines Register* never published the poll.

"For whatever reason, he (Hart) and I appealed to much the same crowd and my vote got cut way down," recalled Simon. "I ended up losing Iowa by the slimmest of margins – so slim that two weeks later NBC on its evening broadcast said Paul Simon may have won in Iowa. By that time, the momentum was gone and had shifted in another direction.

"But the fact that I did as well as I did in Iowa is a tribute to Berkley Bedell."

Fate plays strange tricks. If not for Gary Hart, Senator Simon very well might have won Iowa with a big margin and rolled on to the nomination. "If Senator Simon had become President and had wanted me in Washington to help him, I would have done it," said Berkley. "The balance of this story would have been quite different."

Ironically, Berkley's former aide Mark Gearan worked to help Governor Michael Dukakis win the Democratic nomination that year, while he lost the November election to Bush. Gearan also worked for Senator Albert Gore in an unsuccessful bid for the 1992 nomination, but ended up working in the Clinton-Gore Administration as Executive Director of the Peace Corps. When Clinton's Administration ended, Gearan became president of Hobart and William Smith College in upstate New York.

In 1991 another good friend from Iowa, Senator Tom Harkin, decided to run for president. Berkley was again deeply involved in a presidential campaign. Senator Harkin won his home state Iowa Caucuses with a big margin, but as the campaign for the nomination proceeded, Bill Clinton from Arkansas had sufficient support and financial help to prevail.

At age 71 Berkley's heavy involvement in presidential politics appeared to have come to an end.

However, in 2003-2004, at age 82, Berkley again became heavily involved in presidential politics. Since the Iowa caucuses were the first in the nation, Iowa became very important in the nominating process.

Berk's friend, Dick Gephardt, asked Berk for his support. Berkley told Gephardt that he could not support him because he voted for the invasion of Iraq. Berkley turned to a little-known candidate at the time, former Governor of Vermont, Howard Dean, partly because he was against the war and partly because Berkley was disillusioned with the whole Washington, D.C. scene. Berkley felt that the federal government was being run for the rich and powerful and corporate America and that we needed a new face and completely new policies. The three major candidates had all been in Congress and Berkley wanted a complete change.

Berkley flew back to Iowa from his winter home in Florida several times to tour with Dean and to speak on his behalf. For a while, it looked as if Dean would upset all the seasoned politicians, but as caucus day arrived, Dean's star fell and Senator John Kerry was nominated.

Berk's brother, Jack, pointed out that every time Berkley supported a presidential candidate, that candidate lost, implying that only a fool would solicit Berk's support in the future.

Who knows what would have happened if Berkley had decided to run for president himself in 1984?

"I have always regretted that I did not try. I always thought I should have gone back and talked to Alan Baron about it. It really bothered me for some time that I didn't try."

But in a strange way, Berkley's life might have been saved by his decision not to run for president.

After a lifetime of being the little guy tackling giants, he came face to face with an enormous foe; one that was so small he could not even see it. But had he not been free to fight that next battle, he might not have found a way to save his life.

And he might not have discovered the issue that would become the great cause of his life in the 1990s and 2000s.

"I have every confidence that if I had run for president in 1984, I would not be alive today," he said, in 2001.

Chapter Twenty-Six

Perspectives on Presidents

Berkley Bedell's service in Congress from 1975 to 1986 spanned three presidents and one vice president, subsequently elected president after Berkley retired from Congress. Here are Berkley's perspectives on the presidents he came to know best.

Gerald Ford

"Gerald Ford had just come into office when I arrived in Congress. Ford had served in the Congress where both Republicans and Democrats had liked him. As president, Ford still seemed to be a Congressman at heart – not arrogant and not partisan. He was friendly, very well liked on a personal basis, certainly by me, and I think by my colleagues. I'm not sure he had any great policy commitments, so we did not have someone in office for two years whom we would be bucking or supporting. Gerald Ford had me over to the White House several times in his two years of service. In eight years, Reagan never did."

Jimmy Carter

"Carter was very bright.
"He had very good values, in terms of what should be done, and concern for those issues that I think we should have concern for: environment, education, human rights,

**Tom Bedell, President Jimmy Carter, Elinor and Berkley Bedell,
at a White House picnic in 1978**

things that affect our lives so much. His election brought great hopes to me, and my Democratic friends in Congress.

"When people get elected, they tend to hire people to be on their staff who helped them with the campaign. That's what Carter did. But people who work on your campaign tend to not be the people well suited to run a business. I considered Stu Eisenstadt to be the only competent person on Carter's top staff. The others were duds. In a meeting with members of our Congressional class, Carter told us that he would be glad to meet with any of us individually if we had problems or suggestions. I really felt bad that I didn't meet with him and tell him: 'Jimmy, you've got a real problem. You have an incompetent staff.'

"Jimmy Carter was not particularly partisan. He invited both Republicans and Democrats to the White House several times during his four years as President.

"Politics is by a big percentage, luck. I don't think he should have been blamed for the gasoline shortage or inflation, which had a great deal to do with his failure to be reelected.

"He certainly has proven himself since he was president. He is the best past president we have ever had."

Ronald Reagan

"President Reagan was one of the more popular presidents we've ever had. I didn't find him particularly likable, but obviously people did like him.

"I considered him to be a disaster for our country. The U.S. deficit absolutely exploded during his presidency. His presidency added more to our national debt than all previous administrations from George Washington through Jimmy Carter. It wasn't bad luck. It was bad policy. If you're in business, the way to get into the black isn't to cut revenues. Reagan cut taxes and increased military spending. The revenue did not increase and our deficit exploded.

"That's a whole difference in philosophy and is partly why I'm a Democrat. It's easy to convince people that we ought to cut government spending, because it's wasteful, but almost without exception, the bigger the organization, the more wasteful. And you don't have the same pressures on government to control costs that you do in industry. Government will survive whether it controls costs or not, but a business may not.

"But in terms of what's important as a society: education, preservation of the environment, adequate police and law enforcement, health insurance, decent roads, sensitivity to the poor and many other things government does – I believe are more important to our lives than are more and more material goods. When it's a question of whether to buy the third television or to properly educate children that's a pretty easy choice for me. Where we make our mistake is to say that since it's inefficient, we shouldn't spend the money needed to preserve our environment and do these other things.

"Another problem is that we have television to convince everybody they need to have the newest automobile, the newest computer, the newest radio; a whole system trying to convince us we need material goods. However, we don't effectively put out the message that it's important to take care of our environment, or educate children or do other things the government does.

"The greatest legacy of the Reagan Administration was his complete partisanship and the values he promoted. I believe his arrogant partisan conduct started the partisanship that now exists in Congress; where it appears that issues tend to be settled by what is best for the political party, rather than by what is best for the nation. And Reagan preached that taxes were wrong and that each of us should be more concerned about how much we can keep for ourselves, rather than how much we can give to society in resources and service."

George Herbert Walker Bush

"I knew George Bush reasonably well and I liked him. He is a good person. He's a fisherman. Fishermen tend to be pretty good people.

"He was not nearly as ultra-conservative as Reagan or as his son (President George W. Bush). He supported the United Nations, for example. A problem is that you don't know how much of a president's policies come from him and how much comes from the people around him. President Reagan, and the current George W. Bush, surrounded themselves with ultra-right-wing conservatives. George Herbert Walker Bush did not do that to nearly the same extent and he worked with both Democrats and Republicans. He was friendly to me.

"President Bush worked with, and personally met, my son Tom several times on various environmental issues, particularly those that had to do with fishing. Reagan would have never done that. He would never have met with the son of a Democratic Congressman. George W. Bush will not even let his environmental people meet with the son of a former Democratic member of Congress."

Chapter Twenty-Seven

The New
Berkley and Company

Berkley and Company has grown from $23 million annual sales when Berkley left for Congress to $230 million in 2001. Berkley has been most proud of *how* the company grew – while emphasizing values that are dear to him.

The company, now called Pure Fishing, has become the nation's largest fishing tackle company with 1,400 co-workers in 15 regional operating centers worldwide.

True to its founder, the company has a mission statement, goals and guidelines:

Mission Statement

At Pure Fishing, our mission is to build The World's Best Fishing Tackle Company. To achieve this goal, we are committed to delivering quality fishing products that are well designed and perform beyond expectation. We also strive to be the leading innovator in our sport, using research and new technology to improve fishing tackle performance and effectiveness. And finally, we're dedicated to the future of fishing, including the responsible stewardship of the fishing resource and the enhancement of the productivity of the world's fishable waters.

Five Strategic Principles

1. Treat Others As We Would Like to Be Treated – We must constantly remind ourselves to make decisions with the perspective of others in mind. Success depends on a true collaboration based on honesty, openness, consideration, and partnership.

2. The Angler Is Our Boss – Fishing is our business. It's all we do. Understanding what anglers really want – anticipating what will delight them and doing it better than any other company – that's how we can truly be the best.

3. Whatever We Choose to Do, We Do Outstandingly – Our priorities must define exactly what we will or will not accomplish, so that we can properly focus our time, talents, and energies for outstanding results.

4. The World Is Our Marketplace – Pure Fishing is a global company. Already we include organizations in 14 countries and offer our products in more than 50 others. Providing global technology, capability, and information with the passion for meeting local market needs throughout the world is what Pure Fishing is all about.

5. Financial Strength Creates Opportunity – To sustain our commitments to our stakeholders and nurture our passion for the joys of angling and the resource, we must never lose sight of our reliance on sound financial performance. This means offering the best value to our consumers, the best return for our trade partners, the best opportunities for our suppliers, the best benefits for our coworkers, and minimal risk with a fair return for our lenders and owner.

"They're my words, Dad's values," said Tom. "To treat others as we'd like to be treated — 100 percent the same. 'The angler is our boss.' Dad may not have worded it that way, but he would certainly be interested in providing fishermen the best possible technology and products. 'We will only choose to do what we do outstandingly.' Dad would perhaps have used the word excellence or something, but it's the same thing. 'The world is our marketplace.' Dad didn't perceive that, so that principle is different. 'And the final one: financial strength creates opportunity.' Dad has always been adverse to money being a driver, but you can't provide security for your coworkers without it which he always recognized.

"If you read the principles of Pure Fishing, and you read the objectives Dad had for Berkley and Company … new words, exactly the same concept."

Pure Fishing purchased the companies producing Abu Garcia fishing reels, Fenwick rods, Johnson reels and lures, Mitchell spinning reels, Spider Cast reels and Spider Wire fishing lines, and Red Wolf fishing tackle.

Pure Fishing continues to be an innovator in Berkley leaders, Trilene and Fire Line lines, Power Bait and Gulp scented bait, Frenzy lures, and Lightning Rods.

Pure Fishing has also become Tom Bedell's company – in ownership and leadership – during the last 20 years. Berkley Bedell sold the company to his three children, then Tom bought Ken's and Joanne's shares.

But Berkley Bedell's mark remains on the company – and his name on the products. Tom feels comfortable with the similarities and differences between himself and his father.

"Dad is more disciplined and has a lot stronger paradigms about life," Tom said. "He has a strong sense of moral behavior. My priorities are a little different.

"I spend money like a drunken sailor, compared to him, in terms of how I run the company and how I live. He is absolutely frugal and a much better financial manager than I. It is part of his very nature.

"I'm not as tied to the Spirit Lake community. Until Dad reached 50, the Spirit Lake area had been his entire world. I'm only in Spirit Lake half the time and I am much more flexible about ways to get to the same point.

"The whole complexity of the business has changed. Dad considered Berkley and Company his family. He knew everybody who worked there. He made it a very hands-on business with a somewhat less complicated product line than we have today. My job is to be the CEO, lead strategic planning, growth and acquisitions, and kind of be the inspiration to the top people, but not be down at the same level. That frustrates Dad like crazy when he comes into the plant during the summertime."

The company began using the term "coworkers" years before it became popular. Berkley didn't use that term, but initiated that concept and attitude in the company.

"Sharing the responsibility for the business and sharing the success of the business is just a core value," said Tom, "and Dad felt that totally. My job is to invest in other people's success."

Berkley drew upon others' creativity and insights, as well, Ken recalled from his chemistry intern days. Ken shared an incident that occurred 20 years before "quality teams" became popular in U.S. industries.

"I worked on a project that related to making monofilament stronger. That was always the thing—do a better job. The summer following my graduation from college as a chemist, I worked in the Berkley and Company chemistry lab. We were trying to figure out some stuff. It came down to making some decisions about what was going to happen on the factory floor. Some ideas had come out of the person I worked for in the lab.

"So Dad calls in my boss and myself, and two people who were running the machines, to discuss whether there was some way we could make the process better and whether the product the lab proposed could be taken to the floor. Dad didn't just figure, 'I've got a plant manager who'll figure out how to get this product out,' but he also valued the opinion of the people making the product as much or more than the opinion of his college graduate son who knew the chemistry."

Each generation has seen a larger vision, sometimes in ripples, sometimes in waves, than the previous generation.

Berkley saw a larger vision than Frank Marnette, his mentor who operated a local bait shop. Berkley saw the opportunity for becoming a regional supplier. When he took the seat out of his parent's car so he could sleep and drive around the country selling his leaders, he didn't see himself just tying flies and selling them to the people fishing Spirit Lake and East Okoboji.

After World War II, Berkley had an even larger vision. And true to his vision, Berkley and Company became a world leader in the production of fishing equipment.

Tom has aggressively expanded the company, taking on debt to invest in acquisitions.

"What Tom has done is absolutely phenomenal," said Berkley. "The company has grown and grown.

"Each year, the fishing tackle distributors give an award to the company they think has done the best job for that year. Berkley and Company, under Tom's leadership has won that award 11 of the last 12 years. All from a company that had been in huge financial trouble, rescued by a young man with no manufacturing experience and whose interest at the time was in political consulting – and a company that initially began with an invested capital of $50 of newspaper route money."

Berkley's admiration for his son was matched by Tom's appreciation of his father.

On the following page is a short statement Tom sent to Berkley in later years.

My Father: My Hero

I remember putting my little feet in my Father's shoes and clumsily walking about the room. And trying on his military jacket and hat, looking in the mirror, and practicing a salute.

I remember my Father's determination ... to be a great father. His mission was ME. Guiding. Coaching. Reprimanding. Encouraging. His values: specific and unbending.

I remember my Father's silliness about needing to be successful, while pretending commonness. The worn out cars and understated, if not outdated, clothes.

I remember the generosity in my Father's acts. The thoughtfulness toward others. The kind deed a day. The discipline of the charity account.

I remember the constancy of love for my Mother in my Father's heart. Giving her honor, loyalty, appreciation, and respect.

I remember the example of my Father's life. A guide. A standard. Footsteps too big for my little feet. Majestic and inspiring—always.

And now I watch my Father struggle. Discontent with the memories of so many inspiring days...determined to make more footprints...just like when he got the last mile out of his old worn out cars.

And I struggle for insight. For ways to be one of my Father's best friends. To help him grasp the path to purpose and fulfillment in his new role as a senior statesman. For all he has given to be enough to nourish his soul. For him to find contentment in the gentleness and kindness of his thoughts, words, and daily deeds.

And I so badly need my Father to celebrate the gifts he has given his children. The values, inspiration, and example that empower us to carry on so much of his heart and soul. Entrusting us with his sense of purpose and determination to make the world an ever better place for humankind.

Yes, my Father has earned the right to peace and contentment. He has planted the seeds for so many of us. It is time to let us become the gardeners and for him to celebrate the harvest. I hope we have earned his trust and confidence.

Chapter Twenty-Eight

Disease Brings
Farewell to Congress

If Berkley had made a different decision and had run for President, he would not have gone fishing at Quantico Marine Base in 1985.

On a Monday morning during the spring of 1985, with Congress not in session, Berkley drove down to the Marine base at Quantico, Virginia about 30 miles from Washington to rent a boat and go fishing. Unfortunately, the boat livery was not open on Mondays.

"As I tramped through the tall grass trying to find a place to launch my inflatable boat, I did not realize that some ticks were taking up residence on my legs. I did not discover them until after I had returned to Washington."

A few days later, Berkley noticed he had also contracted poison ivy. Strange, he thought. He had been exposed to poison ivy all his life and had never been prone to the rash before.

Berkley went to see the Navy doctor, stationed in the Capitol to serve members. The doctor gave Berkley some salve to help with the poison ivy itch. Berkley promised to come back in a week. Shortly thereafter, he and Elinor visited Ken and his family in a Philadelphia suburb.

"As I swam from one end of the swimming pool in his complex to the other, my heart pounded as it had never done before," Berkley recalled.

When he went back the next week, the doctor Berkley saw on his first visit was unavailable, so he saw another doctor. In addition to the poison ivy, the doctor looked at a large, bright red area with a white spot in the middle of it, on Berkley's leg.

"That doesn't look like poison ivy to me," the doctor said. "You haven't been bitten by a tick lately, have you?"

"Why, yes," Berkley replied.

The doctor pulled down a book from his shelf and opened to a picture of Lyme disease rash.

"It was exactly like the spot on my leg," Berkley recalled.

The doctor prescribed tetracycline (an antibiotic) and sent Berkley to the pharmacy in the Capital. The only instructions were to take three tablets a day.

In spite of the fact that he did not feel well, Berkley led a Congressional trip to Japan. On the airplane home, Berkley sat beside a doctor and related his story. The doctor informed him that tetracycline is ineffective in the presence of milk. Berkley had taken the medicine at meals and drank milk with almost every one!

Berkley went back to the Navy doctors and suggested that, under the circumstances, he should take another series of tetracycline.

"They assured me that I need not do so," Berkley said. "What a gigantic mistake."

Berkley's symptoms became worse. His joints ached. His memory became blurry. Senator Tom Harkin of Iowa, a longtime and close friend, ran into Berk in Washington near that time period and was appalled by the way Berk looked. That evening, Harkin told his wife, "I think I may have seen Berk Bedell for the last time!"

Berkley visited some of the recognized experts on Lyme disease. "I had a course of heavy doses of antibiotic dripped into my vein daily for 21 days, which helped for a short time, and then I became as sick as before.

"Finally, I realized I could not run for re-election.

"As I toured the counties of my district, the meetings were emotional and traumatic. I met with my constituents and the press and announced that I could not run for re-election."

The district was shocked. Berkley, who had made the people a part of his work in the halls of the Congress, had been winning elections with more than 60 percent of the vote in the heavily Republican district, and had not hesitated to tackle giants, would no longer be serving them.

Typical of the press in his district, the following article appeared in the March 1, 1986 issue of the Sheldon and Sibley, Iowa *Review*:

Berkley Bedell's 50-year Success Tale
From country roads to the halls of the Capitol, 'Berk' finishes a glittering career

By Jay P. Wagner, News Editor.

Regional—It's not surprising that Berkley Bedell's last year in Congress may be his finest. The energetic Iowa congressman has had a career that reads like a Hollywood movie producer crafted it.

Bedell's success story began when he was still a skinny teenager selling fishing lures out of the back seat of his family's car. And although the tale is far from over, the high point of his career could have been Wednesday, when Congress passed a Bedell bill, which limits nuclear testing.

Indeed, the Spirit Lake Democrat has had a political career that frustrated – even baffled – his political opponents. Despite repeated attempts by the national Republican Party to regain the Congressional seat it lost in 1974, Bedell has won 60 percent of the vote in each election since he first ousted Republican Wiley Mayne.

Bedell announced last Saturday that he would not seek re-election this year. An avid outdoorsman, Bedell acquired a tick bite last year on a camping trip that might have resulted in Lyme disease. Although he feels energized in the morning, by four in the afternoon Bedell often finds himself drained of strength.

When announcing his decision not to seek re-election, Bedell told Sioux City area reporters "I plainly do not have the energy to do this job for three more years the way I know it must be done. I don't believe it would be fair for me to continue in a job unless I can give it 100 percent."

Senator Tom Harkin, who worked with Bedell on the Agriculture Committee for 10 years while serving in the House of Representatives, said that even at half-speed the Sixth District Congressman would still be an effective Representative.

"You've got to remember what a high energy level Berkley has. When he said he could only go half-speed, I said to myself that half-speed for him is like full-speed for everyone else."

First District Congressman Jim Leach adds: "He has tremendous energy, but it is more than matched by the respect members of Congress have for him. His Democratic colleagues simply like him."

It has been a surplus of energy, plus the respect, that has propelled Bedell's career in both government and industry, during the last 49 years.

Early Success

Aides on Bedell's staff say their boss will achieve almost any goal once he sets his mind to it. "I don't think Berkley has ever thought he couldn't get something accomplished if he worked hard enough for it," Mark Ulven, Bedell's press secretary says, "That's how we explain his success. He has that midwestern state of mind."

That's been most true of his career, which has spanned nearly 50 years.

During the summer of 1937, when he was just 15 years old, Bedell took the back seat out of the family car and loaded it with handmade fishing lures.

With $50.00 in his pocket, the young Bedell pointed his car south, stopping at sporting goods stores and hardware stores in each town to try to hawk a handful of tackle. At night,

Bedell would park the car at the edge of the road and wedge his tired body between the boxes of merchandise.

In only a few weeks, Berkley had worked his way to Tennessee, where he received a telegram from his family.

Dozens of letters from across the Midwest had arrived at the family house in Spirit Lake. The message showed that customers loved the new fishing equipment, and retailers were anxious to renew their orders. Bedell turned his car around and drove home to start Berkley and Company— today one of the country's leading fishing tackle manufacturers.

The development of monofilament fishing line buoyed the profits of the company. The incredible story of Bedell's success has been featured in countless business journals. Today, Berkley and Company has plants in Spirit Lake and Taiwan.

But despite success in the world of industry, the role of public servant beckoned Bedell. In 1972, he challenged Mayne and lost the election by a narrow margin.

Bedell was encouraged by his following and sought the election again in 1974. Mayne had suffered from support he showed President Richard Nixon during the Watergate scandal.

But with support in the district eroded, Mayne, who had been a member of the House Agriculture Committee, criticized Bedell's lack of knowledge about farming. "We don't even know if he'll be appointed to the Ag Committee," he told a Review reporter during that campaign.

Bedell won easily and, ironically, became one of Iowa's strongest voices on agricultural issues.

Grassroots Politician

The transformation from the captain of a successful Iowa industry to a Congressman whose knowledge of agriculture policy "is unmatched in Washington," was the culmination of hours of meetings with farmers in the Sixth District.

After being elected to Congress, Bedell formed separate farm advisory committees in each county in the district

– as many as 500 farmers from across northern Iowa served on the committee at one time.

"I think that's been very instrumental in making Berk more knowledgeable about farm questions," Tim Galvin, a Sioux City native who serves as research director for an agriculture subcommittee, says.

In fact, Bedell's knowledge of farming and power in the House Ag Committee have grown to the point where his retirement will leave a huge gap in the Iowa delegation, both Republican and Democratic colleagues agree.

"It will be a very serious loss, because Berk has developed seniority on the Ag committee, but also because issues in Washington get affected by chemistry," Leach says. "Everybody liked Berk and his presence has a positive effect on what happens here."

Harkin, a member of the Ag committee for ten years says, Berkley has the ability to get to the heart of the matter. "No one could do it like he could."

Representative Cooper Evans (R-Iowa), who earlier this year was considered for the Secretary of Agriculture, adds, "He hasn't been an Ag subcommittee chairman for a long time, but he's easily the strongest chairman we have. He's been a strong critic of the Department of Agriculture for a long time. His ideas will be missed in Washington."

And Galvin says, "The big thing that's going to be lost is his willingness to speak out against the current administration. The second thing is his sense of the history of Ag policy. He understands how former policy affects farming and that's not easy to replace."

Oddly enough, it wasn't his knowledge of agriculture that first garnered Bedell national attention. Instead, it was his work to expose overspending by the defense department that won him rave reviews in the nation's daily newspapers.

Bedell and other Congressmen were grilling Pentagon officials during the spring of 1984 about why small businesses weren't given an opportunity to submit bids on defense contracts. During that time, Bedell stumbled across a tool kit for flight simulators that cost the government thousands of dollars. He visited Washington, D.C. hardware stores and purchased the same items at a small fraction of the price.

"Nobody even knew he was going," recalls Ulven. "He came into the office on Monday with all these items, explained what he had found and said, 'Don't you think we should call a press conference?'" For the next several weeks, Bedell's name appeared in major daily newspapers from coast to coast.

But it wasn't Bedell's fleeting fame that endeared him to his constituents, colleagues say. Instead, it is Bedell's earthy persona that has made him a favorite of voters in both parties.

"I think people have recognized the inherent goodness in Berkley Bedell," Harkin says. "He's just a decent individual, very forthright. He lacks any guile. What you see is what you get."

And what constituents have gotten, according to Ulven, is a Congressman who makes it a point to regularly visit every county in the Sixth District with his Open Door meetings, often with his wife Elinor or son Tom at his side. He's a Congressman who has separated himself from the flashy politicians and the fast lane of Washington living that comes with being an elected official.

"Berk is like N'West Iowa," Ulven says. "I grew up there and I know he's not unlike people I've known my entire life."

Bedell is a multi-millionaire, but he finally bought his first new car—a compact model—only a few years ago. He insists on inviting his staff to his home each Christmas for a home-cooked meal prepared by his wife. According to Evans, Bedell enjoys spending quiet weekends fishing the farm ponds that surround the Washington metro area.

"Berk lives a very austere life, a very careful, principled life," Leach says. "He couldn't be more out of step with Washington life and a key element of that is Elinor. The two belong together like hand and glove."

Indeed, when Bedell decided he wouldn't seek re-election he asked both his wife and son, Tom, to consider throwing their hat in the ring.

Both refused, and so, for now, it looks like Washington will be without a Bedell come January. Berkley and Elinor are returning to their roots—the Lakes region that was the inspiration for his first business venture during the post depression era.

He told reporters last week that he won't exit from public life altogether. He wants to stay involved in the Democratic Party, write, and continue his fight for world peace.

And that's why aides and friends said last Wednesday's 100-vote margin of victory in a delicate area like defense was such a tribute to Bedell.

"It symbolizes his career, because there is no member of the House who is more committed to arms control than Berkley Bedell," Leach says. "He's not a partisan. He's always looking for the thing that his constituents would want him to do. No one loved Congress more than he did. I can't think of anyone I admire more."

March 1, 1986
Sheldon and Sibley, Iowa *Review*

Farewell to Congress

When someone retires from Congress, another member will sometimes ask for "Special Orders." These are held after the business of the day has been concluded, and it is an opportunity for other members to come down to the floor of the House and make complimentary remarks about the retiring member.

"I have been pleased with the fact that even more Republicans came down to speak well of me than Democrats," Berkley recalled. "Several members told me that they considered me 'the conscience of the Congress.'"

Here is the speech Berkley gave to a nearly empty chamber of the House of Representatives upon his retirement from Congress, recorded in the Congressional Record.

Mr. BEDELL: "Mr. Speaker, as I come to the end of my 12 years of service here in Congress, I have asked for this special time in order to talk about my appreciation for what my colleagues have meant to me; to talk a little about my beliefs, my dreams for this Congress, my dreams for our country, and to talk a little bit about how it is that I came to be in this great body.

"Let me start by saying that I truly love it here. It is very difficult for me to leave. For those who do not know, I have suffered from a disease for more than a year, in that I was bitten by a tick and came down with a disease called Lyme disease, in which the symptoms have been very similar to mononucleosis. Under those circumstances, I felt that in spite of my love for this life and this body, it would not be right to my constituents to continue to try to serve here.

"It is great to have been here, because of the great people that serve in this body, and it breaks my heart that so many, many people talk about how terrible Congress may be. Let me say, that I have never been, in all my life, with a finer group of people than I find here in Congress.

"I am thankful to my constituents for the fact that they have permitted me to serve these 12 years even though I am a Democrat in a very Republican district. I tell everyone it really appears that I was born under a lucky star. All through my life, it has seemed as if the Lord has smiled upon me.

"The first time, God smiled upon me was when He gave me the parents that He gave me and the grandparents and the brother that I had. From them, I believe I learned family values. I had parents that, regardless of what I wanted to do, said, 'Well, Berk, why don't you go ahead and try?' Many times there were things that normal parents would have said, 'that is foolish. You cannot do it.' But my parents said, 'If you wish to try, go ahead.'

"My grandmother told me, 'You can do almost anything within reason if you will only set your mind to it.'

How right my grandmother was! My parents taught me to enjoy the great outdoors. I remember when my father and mother left me on the shores of one of our lakes when I was five years old, as they went down the lake with their fly rods. As I sat there, with my cane pole and worm and pulled in my first fish, my father was so proud that the next day he had to take me downtown and get my picture taken and parade me around to his friends!

"When I was 15 years old, I took $50.00 I had saved from my newspaper route and started a business making and selling fishing tackle. It is a very interesting story of how that business grew and developed. I will not go into all of the details at this time, except to say that if it had not been for parents who said, 'Go ahead, take our car, take the back off the front seat and build a bed, and go out to sell the fishing leaders that you do not know how to make.' If they had not said, 'Go ahead and use your bedroom and use our living room and use the rest of the house as your factory, we will get by,' my business would not have happened.

"About 15 years ago, as my wife and I looked at our lives, we decided we wanted to try to do something about some of the concerns we had, so I hired a manager to oversee the business and I spent one year traveling the country, looking at what we might want to do in order to try to help with some of the problems that concern us.

"Finally, I decided I wanted to run for Congress. I had a poll taken. The pollster said, 'Don't run, you don't have a chance.' But I remembered what my grandmother had told me and I ran anyway. Here I am. What a wonderful experience this has been.

"I came to Congress with a wonderful class, the Watergate class of the 94th Congress, along with my colleague, the gentleman from Minnesota (Mr. Oberstar).

"It was one of the great experiences of my life as we first met in that class. I have always sort of been out of step at home. I was a Democrat among a whole group of Republicans. I was one of the first to feel that the Vietnam War was wrong and spoke out in regard to it at a time when that was not a very popular thing to do.

"I came in with those members and we all agreed; we all wanted to do the same thing. We all had the same values. If there was ever a fearless group, in my opinion, that was it!

"They were articulate and unified and intelligent. They all wanted a clean environment, a peaceful world, an effective government, and concern for the underprivileged.

"When I was looking around at what I wanted to do before running for Congress, one of the things I did was to stay at the home of a friend in Connecticut along the seashore. At the time I was there, another guest was astronaut, Edgar Mitchell. The next morning, out in front of the house, they were shooting a movie with Mr. Mitchell. I will never forget what he had to say. He had a globe and he said, 'As we were traveling on that spaceship toward the moon, we realized that the three of us had to work together with our limited space and limited resources and limited waste disposal system.' He said, 'Then, as I was traveling I looked out that little window and I saw that beautiful blue and white ball that we call earth. I realized it was something special that God had put in this universe.'

"He said, 'Then all of a sudden, a strange thing happened. All of a sudden I realized that the beautiful blue and white ball that we call earth was a spaceship, just as surely as was the one in which we were traveling. It had limited space and limited resources and a limited waste disposal system, just as surely as did ours. But although the three of us were working together to do everything we could to bring that journey through safely, recognizing those limitations, the crew of three billion people back on earth were not doing the same.'

"How right he was!

"One of the activities I have participated in during my years in Congress has been a prayer breakfast group that meets every Thursday morning at 8 o'clock. During our meetings, one of the members talks about his or her faith, their belief, their life, and experiences. Only a few weeks ago, we were privileged to have our friend, the gentleman from Florida (Mr. Nelson), a member of this body talk to us about his experiences as he was on the last crew that went up in space before the Challenger disaster.

"Mr. Nelson pointed out the same thing about his realization as he was in space and looked back at our planet and how he realized how small earth has become, and how fragile it is. We realize at this time, that we now have sufficient nuclear weapons capability to make this planet uninhabitable for human life.

"It is not a cinch, but there are many scientists who would tell you that if we get into a major nuclear exchange with the Soviet Union, there is a substantial chance that we will destroy the ability of this spaceship on which we live to sustain life here on our planet.

"As we look at planet earth, I would hope we would realize that we have to either learn to live together or die together. I hope we would recognize the problems of pollution and realize that we have a limited waste disposal system, just like the spaceship.

"I am pleased to say, that I believe we are making progress in regard to pollution. It is no secret that I love to fish. Now I can fish in the Potomac River right here in Washington, D.C. and I can eat the fish that I catch.

"One of the great things that my family has enjoyed in Washington is the out-of-doors and the opportunity to enjoy it so close at hand.

"Some people came to D.C. wanting to film me fishing in Washington, and have an interview with me. They wanted to set it up so that we would be able to tell that the film had been taken in Washington. So I took them down to a pond on the mall near the Vietnam Memorial. Not only could they interview me fishing on the pond right on the mall, but also as I was talking and fishing, they could see me catching a number of fish right here in the city limits.

"I have friends who take me trout fishing, and we can walk along a stream no more than 30 minutes from Washington, fish all morning, and never see another person. So I would hope, that as I leave Congress, those who are here would continue to appreciate the importance of continuing to preserve this great outdoors in which we live.

"I am thankful, for not only the outdoor opportunity that exists here, but also for the many other opportunities that come with life in this Congress. I am thankful for the opportunities we have to learn. I know of no place where there are equivalent opportunities to learn from all the various briefings that are available, and where we can call almost anyone and they will come and meet us and try to provide information on any issue that may be of concern.

"I am thankful for the opportunity I have had to influence what happens in regard to small business, particularly with the background I had as I started in as a schoolboy with that $50.00.

"I am thankful for having been able to serve under our great chairman of the Small Business Committee, the gentleman from Maryland (Mr. Mitchell). I am thankful for the opportunity I have had to serve under the chairman of the Committee on Agriculture, the gentleman from Texas (Mr. De La Garza). I feel kind of bad about that. When the gentleman was up for chairmanship of that committee, I did not think he should be chairman and I opposed him.

"It was a mistake. I want to tell everyone that I made a mistake. The gentleman has turned out to be a great chairman of that committee. He listens and he leads us well.

"The great thing about the Committee on Agriculture is that it is not a partisan committee. The members are there to do what they can to help farmers. I happen to believe that we have serious problems in agriculture, not only now, but also into the future. I am fortunate enough to be chairman of the subcommittee that has to do with department operations, research, and foreign agriculture. On that committee I have many colleagues, but there are two in particular I want to thank. That is the gentleman from Kansas (Mr. Roberts), the leading minority member of the committee and my colleague, the gentleman from Iowa (Mr. Evans).

"I happen to believe that America's agriculture problem is not just a domestic problem. I think we have a world agriculture problem and I hope we can learn to work together to help to solve it, just as I hope we can do that with the other problems we face on this spaceship planet on which we live.

"I was very pleased with the work that has been done by our staff over many, many months on a bill that we passed here just in the last couple of weeks, regarding the regulation of pesticides. I think we broke some new ground in those negotiations, because normally we each have our opinions of what should be done and we come and fight it out to see who wins, but in that particular legislation wherein we had the farmers, the environmentalists, the big chemical companies, the small chemical companies, and all the other competing interests in disagreement, we simply got them together in a room and said, 'Now try to work out your differences and if you don't do it today, come back tomorrow.'

"And as we came to the floor, there was only one item in disagreement. I wish we would do that in our society and in our world as we try to settle our differences.

"It was my privilege to serve for a short time on the Foreign Affairs Committee. I was very active in the negotiations for a Law of the Sea Treaty. It broke my heart that the thing that killed that treaty was the attitude of the government of this country. The sad thing was that we passed an opportunity to start to move toward a more peaceful world, where we would agree upon how to use our different resources.

"It was the influence of the major American mining companies with our government that wrecked the treaty negotiations. They claimed that they should have the right to go out into the middle of the ocean and claim any minerals that are there unto themselves, and the countries of the world said, 'no, those are out in the middle of the ocean. They really should be shared by the world.'

"I believe that, indeed, we are going to have to come to a point where the world does share if we are going to preserve this great spaceship.

"It has also been my privilege to work on many defense issues. I was pleased to be able to participate in doing something about the procurement practices that took place in the military.

"I am pleased to have been the author of the resolution that said that if the Soviet Union will continue not to test nuclear weapons, we call upon the President to try to negotiate a treaty to end the testing of nuclear weapons. This is the first President since Eisenhower that has not tried to negotiate such a treaty.

"Now the Soviets have said, 'We will stop if you will.' We really don't have to negotiate. We could have an agreement.

"It breaks my heart that we have that opportunity and it is passing by.

"I am pleased that I have been able to work on some of the environmental issues that have taken place here in Congress. It is no secret that I have not been very popular for opposing some of the water projects that have been offered. My argument is that we should not have taxpayers subsidizing water to enable farmers to grow crops that are in surplus. My argument is that it does not make sense if we have too much of a crop to pay a subsidy to farmers to get water to grow more crops, while we then turn around and pay other farmers not to grow those same crops.

"I have been pleased that, in spite of the fact that most or many of the members do not agree with me on that position, at least we live in a body where we can make arguments and make them in whatever manner we wish to.

"I have mentioned previously the opportunity to learn that I value so highly. There are many special caucuses here and great opportunities. One of them I would like to mention in particular is the Congressional Clearinghouse on the Future, which was led for a long time by now Senator Al Gore. Our colleague Bob Edgar is now the head of it. This is where members meet once a month to hear from somebody regarding the problems they see coming in the future. If there is one thing I think we need to do in government, it is to try to look at the future and plan for the future, not just until the time of the next election.

"So, as I leave this body, I want to thank my colleagues. I want to thank my constituents. I want to thank God.

"I took a trip to New Zealand some time ago, and as I talked to those people who were legislators in New Zealand, I realized that even though they had these same concerns they are not on the stage. They do not have an opportunity to determine whether or not we are going to have a nuclear test ban. We are the ones, the United States and the Soviet Union, that determine that possibility.

"New Zealand is concerned about nuclear war, and they can scream about it and they can do different things, but we are the ones here, our people in this country, and the people in this body, are the ones that are on stage to make that decision.

"I thank God that I was born where I could do that; so as I said earlier, I was born, in my opinion, under a lucky star. It started with being born in this great land of ours. It came from the wonderful opportunities we have from the outdoor world around us, from the great parents and grandparents and the brother that I had, for the great family that I have been privileged to have myself. Some of my fondest memories are family trips, family picnics and family life. My children are now grown and they have children who are now our grandchildren. Within the last couple of weeks, it was great as we drifted down the Shenandoah River with our daughter and husband and our grandchildren. It was good this week to go to a baseball game in Baltimore with my daughter and her husband, my wife, and our grandchildren.

"I have to say, that I could not be prouder than I am of my family. I certainly appreciate tremendously the help that my wife, Elinor, has given me during this entire period. Many times, the life of a Congressman is not the greatest life for a wife, but she never ever has complained.

"I am thankful to my friends back in the district. I am thankful for the school friends back there, the ones who played basketball and football with me. I was on the varsity of our local high school football team. I weighed 120 pounds. Football is a crazy game, you know. You get knocked down just so you can get up and get knocked down again, so you can get up, so you can get knocked down again!

"Then I got impetigo and I had to sit on the sidelines and watch my friends getting knocked around on the football field, as they worked together trying to get to that goal, and I realized how much more fun it was to be out there getting knocked around than to be sitting on the sidelines watching.

"So it is with life!

"I am so thankful that my people have given me the opportunity to be here in this body and to be part of that game. There are lots of heartaches to this job, but it is also an opportunity for us really to be in the ballgame, so I am thankful to those friends in Congress who are part of this team.

"I am thankful to you, Chaplain. I remember coming into your office when I had legal problems. I remember crying in your office and I remember the help you gave me and I thank you very, very much for what you have done.

"So as I leave this great body, I go forth not knowing what the challenges may be that He has in store for me, but I pray and hope that indeed that challenge is there. I am confident it is, because it always has been in the past.

"I go with great memories. I go with great hopes, and I go most of all with the thankfulness for the won-

Elinor and Berkley meet the Dalai Lama in 1985

derful things that have happened to me in this body and all through my life so far."

Mr. OBERSTAR: "Mr. Speaker, will the gentleman yield?"

Mr. BEDELL: "I am glad to yield to my friend, the gentleman from Minnesota."

Mr. OBERSTAR: "Mr. Speaker, this is, in a way, an intrusion into the gentleman's special order. I happened upon the scene quite by accident to make remarks of my own, but I was compelled from the gentleman's remarks to hear and listen intently to what is, without a doubt, one of the most beautiful orations ever delivered in this body. I have heard so many parting remarks by my colleagues that have been discordant notes, sour tones, on leaving the burdens of this office. This is one of those rare upbeat moments in a member's final hours in the session. It makes me feel good about America.

"If I could add one comment about the service of Berkley Bedell in the U.S. House of Representatives, having come here together with him in that 94ᵗʰ Class, the quality that has stood out above all others, my friend, has been your uncompromising integrity that compelled you to say what you have said this afternoon so beautifully, so warmly, and with such a deep and powerful meaning and feeling.

"I join all our colleagues in that class and in this House in wishing you all the very best, continued good health, service to God and country, that you have given so beautifully in these 12 years in the House."

Mr. BEDELL: "Mr. Speaker, I thank my colleague."

So ended Berkley's 12 years in the United States House of Representatives.

It was the last time a Democrat would represent Northwest Iowa, until this writing, and marked the end of Berkley's second exciting career.

Farewell letters

The following are excerpts from letters sent by colleagues to Berkley Bedell in December 1986, as he was about to retire from Congress.

John L. Burton

Berkley Bedell is the best human being I have ever met in public office.

But most importantly he was smart enough to marry the best Carrot Cake Cook in the USA.

Best Wishes, John

Tom Daschle
House of Representatives, South Dakota
December 9, 1986

You have been one of the dearest friends I have had during my eight years in the House. I have fond memories of our "battles" together.

Linda and I wish you and Elinor the very best as you start your new life! We sincerely hope that we will have many times to share with you both in the future.

With friendship, Tom

Dennis DeConcini
Senator, Arizona

> ... You represent what is good about our political
> system. ... a model for all off us who try to make
> the system work and try to improve it. ...

Dennis

Susan Hurley DeConcini
6014 Chesterbrook Road, McLean, Va.

Dear Elinor and Berk:

> You are two of the nicest, most sincere and politi-
> cally honest people I have met since coming to
> Washington in 1977. ... You were always so hospi-
> table to others, sharing your Capitol Hill home
> with groups. ...

Affectionately, Susie

Kika de la Garza
U.S. House of Representatives
Committee on Agriculture

Dear Mr. Chairman

> ... I just cannot tell you how many times I've
> thought to myself "Why is Berkley Bedell leaving
> me? Why is my best friend retiring now?"
>
> ... You and I worked that acreage together. When I
> took the handle on the plow and became Commit-
> tee Chairman, you came over and were the first to
> put aside the divisions and help me till the fields.
> That meant a lot to me – as I said, we developed a
> friendship that I consider to be irreplaceable. ...
>
> ... your mark is indelible. ...

Sincerely, Kika de la Garza

Richard A. Gephardt
Chairman, Democratic Caucus, House of Representatives

> Jane and I will miss you greatly. Our Congress and the
> country needs decent, good people like you who
> stand tall for what is good and moral and right for
> our future. All best wishes.

Your friends, Dick and Jane

Robert J. Cornell
103 Grant Street, DePere, Wisconsin 54115

... By happy coincidence in 1974 the enlightened electorate of our respective congressional districts sent us to Washington to set things straight. ... I learned from Berk how a person could be a religious without taking the vow of celibacy. He was soon recognized as the conscience of our class – indeed of the whole House of Representatives. His colleagues did observe, however, a serious fault in his conduct as a congressman – he was straightforward and truthful.

... Berk has another distinct advantage that I did not enjoy – Elinor. If ever there was a real marriage partnership, they have it. She assisted him in his congressional work, undertook other services on and off the Hill on her own, and kept Berk (if necessary) from getting inflated with his own importance as a member of Congress. They are a pair that could serve as a model for all married couples – in and out of public life. ...

Robert Cornell

Senator Christopher J. Dodd, Connecticut

Dear Berkley:

... I wanted you to know how honored I am to have served with you. ... Those of us who were your colleagues will fondly remember your tenure. Yet the affection and respect that your constituents have shown they have for you is the true measure of the success that you have enjoyed as a Congressman. ...

Sincerely, Chris

Leon E. Panetta
16th District, California

... The farmers of this country have never had a better friend in Congress than Berkley Bedell. Perhaps no issue has better illustrated your persistence, hard work, and commitment than your efforts to pass a strong FIFRA bill. Your sense of fairness and your understanding of the complexities of the issue made you a friend to farmers, consumers, and the environment.

Sincerely, Leon

Howard M. Metzenbaum
United States Senate, Ohio

Dear Elinor and Berkley:

I can't think of any couple that has been more respected and loved than the two of you. … No person has been more straightforward, more conscientious, or more dedicated than you, Berkley. And no Congressperson's spouse has been more concerned about the kind of world in which we live than you, Elinor. …

Warm personal regards, Howard M. Metzenbaum

Don Edwards
10th District, California

Dear Berk:

I have always felt a special kinship with you for many reasons, but I believe the chief one was that each of us ran for Congress because of our concern over the threat to the world inherent in nuclear weapons. …

… you set about doing something about it during your tenure in Congress. Your effort has become the shining star in your constellation of legislative achievements, and many generations of the world's men and women will be grateful to you.

You first introduced your test ban resolution in July 1982. Eight of your colleagues joined you as cosponsors. …

… President Reagan's people fought hard to defeat you. … But when the vote came, on final passage, you prevailed by the overwhelming vote of 268 yeas to 148 nays.

In August of the same year, 1986, the Senate approved the same resolution, "to prevent nuclear explosive testing."

The building of support in the U.S. Congress for H.J. Res. 3 was testimony to your powers of persuasion, your commitment to the issue, and your clarity of vision in recognizing the need for the measure. You went about convincing your colleagues of the merits of your resolution with the quiet conviction and the firmness tempered with good nature that have made us trust you.

Despite your remarkable accomplishment in shepherding this historic resolution through the Congress you have been characteristically modest.

Sincerely, Don Edwards

P.S. I presume that, having played against you, you will now be a tennis pro. Will we see you on T.V.?

Harold E. Hughes
Harold Hughes Center, Inc., Iowa

Dear Elinor and Berk:

I find it easy to say "thank you, both" for all you have done through the years. Yours has been a Horatio Alger and storybook life of serving God, family, and your fellow human beings.

I am proud to have shared some of the time, and a few of the days along the way. Even the time fishing, laughing, and praying meant so very much to me.

I know life and the God of all creation will continue to bless your talents and gifts for all of us.

Have a great life, always!

Love and appreciation,
Harold E. Hughes, U.S. Senate, retired

Pat Roberts
1st District, Kansas

… I have always enjoyed hearing you say, "Pat, it's great to work with you." Regardless of the problems we faced, you were always optimistic and willing to work to the last minute to find the compromise.

We have correctly labeled you the conscience of the House Agriculture Committee. You have persevered and fought for Iowa and Kansas farmers, and for all of rural America, setting a splendid example. ...

Sincerely, Pat

Barney Frank
Fourth District, Massachusetts

Dear Berk and Elinor:

When young people ask me if it's possible to be an effective politician and retain your integrity and dignity, I've always cited Berk as an example. I still will. Come see us often.

Barney

Andy Ireland, Florida
Committee on Small Business

... Whenever I see mention of one of our greatest Americans, Abraham Lincoln, the name Bedell will pop into my mind. Even more so, every time I get out my toolbox to fix up something around the house, I'll think of the box Berkley fixed up and allowed me to lug around the state of Florida so that I could show citizens firsthand the military waste and fraud, we were trying to end with our legislation which has now become law.

... Unfortunately few of them (politicians) backed up their words when the interests of small business came up against big government, big labor, or big business. You not only stood up for small business, you fought until bloodied on occasion. ...

Sincerely, Andy Ireland

Morris K. Udall
2nd Congressional District, Arizona

... Berkley, I'm going to miss working with you. ... In the middle of the battle, you never lost sight of that important part of public service: that we should never take ourselves too seriously. ...

Sincerely, Mo

Chapter Twenty-Nine

Life is Giving

For the first time in 55 years, Berkley Bedell didn't have a job. But retiring from work did not mean retiring from making a difference in the world.

When he retired from Congress, Berkley refused to retire from challenges, whether it meant raising money for community improvement, advocating medical reforms, standing up for prisoners, donating land for a state park, or saving the Everglades from pollution.

Immediately after he sold his company and retired from Congress; his primary responsibility in the late 1980s was to recover from Lyme disease and then cancer.

By 1988, his physical recovery was complete. He played tennis and golf. He continued to fish every opportunity he had. He routinely went to Canada on duck hunting trips during the month of October with his brother, Jack, and the same group they started out with in 1949. Many of these friends continued to go on this annual duck-hunting trip for more than 50 years, sharing adventures and stories and penny-ante poker games. Berkley's physical condition had improved so much, that when they didn't have a retrieving dog, Berkley himself waded into the cold water to gather up the fallen fowl. He continued to be the only one in the group capable of this retrieving role until he was nearly 80 years old, when the group struck up a friendship with some younger hunters who offered the use of their dogs.

At their 49th Annual Duck Hunting trip are (left to right): Pete Narey, Blaine Hoien, Berkley and Jack Bedell, Dr. Al Klein, Ken Daniels, and Bob Boettcher, in Boissevain, Manitoba, October 2000.

But a life of leisure and travel did not satisfy Berkley.

"I knew I hadn't been put on this earth to just play golf and go swimming, or whatever. I had been sent here to do something worthwhile," Berkley reflected. "That was partly why we ran for Congress. I felt I would get more personal satisfaction by doing something I thought would contribute toward making the world a little better, than simply building a bigger and bigger fishing tackle factory."

Just as they had done nearly 20 years before, Berkley and Elinor decided, "We were happier climbing mountains than resting on the beach."

Berkley became passionate about:

- Research into alternative medicine treatments, through establishing an office in the National Institute for Health and establishing the National Foundation for Alternative Medicine.

- Improving life in his beloved town of Spirit Lake, particularly through helping to establish the 'University of Okoboji Foundation.'

- Improving life for his family.

- Standing for oppressed people.

"He supports his causes," says his son, Tom. "He's a cause guy."

University of Okoboji Foundation

Tom became determined to give shape to Berkley's vision of a community-based endowment foundation that would fund projects in the lakes region. Tom and a core group of individuals – Paul Hedberg and Chuck Maxwell – quickly enlarged their circle to include Berkley.

"This was a dream that Berk had for a long time and Tom decided to make that dream come true," said Sue Richter, one of Tom's high school classmates. Her husband, Emil, and his brother, Herman, had started a mythical University of Okoboji "for fun and frolic." Their store sold sweatshirts, banners, and window stickers with the University of Okoboji wording and insignia. They give diplomas to people all over the world. Tom asked Herman Richter if they could name the foundation the University of Okoboji Foundation. He said they could, if Berkley would agree to be the first president. Berkley agreed.

"We decided we would try to get contributions of $100,000 from people, payable $10,000 a year for ten years," said Berkley. "There were about six or eight of us who met once a week at Berkley and Company offices, and we'd go through lists of people to see, and we'd try to get those pledges."

Tom Bedell hosted a reception at his home on West Okoboji Lake to launch the University of Okoboji Foundation: "Where fun in life is your degree!" In promotional materials, they even began to form lighthearted legends about the mythical "university," with tongue-in-cheek stories of storybook football contests against the University of Iowa. Berkley enjoys people seeing his University of Okoboji decal on his car and wondering why they've never heard of his college alma mater!

The more serious implication of the name was that they would promote a collegial sense of learning how to improve the lakes region.

"The concept behind the University of Okoboji Foundation was to have a vehicle wherein everybody could work together," says Herman Richter, who is also one of Berkley's tennis partners. "It could have been the Berkley Foundation or the Bedell Foundation, but Berk wanted to reach out and call it the 'University of Okoboji Foundation.' Results and accomplishment are more important to Berk than who gets the credit. There's just no question that if it weren't for Berk, the foundation wouldn't be here."

The group fell short of its $10-million fundraising goal, but Tom's house reception uncovered the first big community improvement project. A local couple, Bud and Bev Pearson, attended the reception. They had been planning to build an arts center in Phoenix, Arizona where they wintered, as a public place to store and display their personal art collection.

After the reception, Bud Pearson told the University of Okoboji board about his art center project, which he planned to erect in Phoenix at a cost of $600,000. Bud said if the University of Okoboji Foundation would raise half of the $600,000, he would put the center in the lakes area instead.

Berkley went to work.

"In a week's time, I raised the money; from no more than eight people in pledges," reported Berkley. Today, the Lakes Arts Center not only exhibits art, but also has public classes and events to promote the arts. The Elinor Bedell pottery room promotes one of Elinor's favorite pastimes.

"I guess you wouldn't find an arts center like that one anywhere in a town of 4,000 people," says Berkley. "It's beautiful.

"The important thing about the foundation is not the amount of money raised, but it sets an example that 'We could do almost anything within reason if we only set our minds to it.'" Berkley says. "Most importantly of all, we have taught people how to give, without adversely affecting their lives.

"I have yet to find anyone who has ever had to cut back on how they lived or what they did, because of money they had given away. But I've found many who get great personal gratification out of money they have given for worthwhile projects. Elinor and I are two of them."

Berkley loved the foundation's annual meetings, to which people and organizations would submit funding requests.

"We were given a certain amount of 'play money,' and we voted with our money what projects we thought should be funded. Then, the board totaled the cost of all the projects and decided how much money should go to each project." The process has changed now that the foundation works on more and bigger projects.

Since its first venture with an arts center, the University of Okoboji Foundation has helped build a new home for a maritime museum, construct bicycle and hiking trails throughout the lakes area, improved the main highway into the lakes resort area, and built an $800,000 water quality laboratory that is a joint venture of the University of Iowa, the University of Northern Iowa, and Iowa State University.

In 1999, the University of Okoboji Foundation took on its most expensive challenge yet. Berkley became involved.

Berkley's beloved Arnold's Park – the amusement park where he hung onto the roller coaster for dear life, and the Roof Garden dance hall where he and his friends learned to dance and romance – faced extinction.

Businessman Chuck Long had bought the park, on the east side of West Okoboji Lake, and poured money into it to make it viable.

"Berk probably had his first kiss at the Roof Garden and he used to dance here," said Sue Richter. "They might be a generation apart, but by golly Berk and Chuck Long both felt passionate about the park. Your first kiss is worth a lot!"

When Long couldn't make Arnold's Park profitable, he entered into a contract to sell it to a Sioux Falls, South Dakota, developer for $5 million. "The developer had plans to pretty much cover the whole thing with condos and install 600 boat slips," said Berkley. "The maritime museum was in the park and would be surrounded by all these condos."

Berkley and a group of residents were determined to save the park and to save the lake from over-development. The developer said that if the community would pay him $5.5 million, he would drop his plans. But if they couldn't raise the money in six weeks, he would proceed.

50th-year reunion of the Spirit Lake High School Class of 1939, Berkley at right of the front row.

Berkley did not just have starry-eyed nostalgia for his adolescent romances. The lakes had been surrounded by private development that choked off much of the public access. If development kept pace as it had in the 1980s and early 1990s, West Lake Okoboji would soon become the exclusive playground of the wealthy people buying all the lakefront property. Berkley himself had bought some of the lakefront land.

In 1988, he and Elinor sold their house on East Okoboji Lake and bought a home in Naples, Florida where they spent the winters. John Furman's father built a cottage on West Okoboji in 1935. He also owned several adjacent lots. Berkley's long-time buddy, John Furman, moved into the 1935 house and then built a newer home next door. When Berkley learned that the Furmans had put the original house up for sale, he and Elinor purchased it so they could spend their summers next door to their dear friends and college chums, John and Pat Furman. Berkley and John had spent many hours as youths on the shore and water of the lake. Property like Arnold's Park needed to be preserved for public access to the lake. Berkley could not bear the thought of closing it off to future generations.

When Berkley's son, Tom, called the lake's residents together for an informational meeting to kick off the campaign to save the park, all he had to do was show the developer's plans: hundreds of condominiums and 600 boat slips. The residents could see that their playground would become even more crowded quicker than anticipated.

"The last thing people around the lake wanted was another 600 boat slips," Berkley recalled.

The community formed an organization to try to raise the money. Sue Richter agreed to chair the effort if Berkley Bedell and Mickey Landon, a businessman from Omaha, Nebraska, would serve as vice chairs.

"I had to take a trip, and when I returned to Spirit Lake there were only three weeks before our deadline and they didn't have much of the money raised," said Berkley. "I remember Sue saying, 'We didn't have a very good week.'"

Berkley pledged $100,000 and reported to Sue Richter's office every day for work.

"Who's got money around this lake?" Berkley asked her each day. "Give me some names and I'll go and see them."

"I would give him three or four names of people I thought would have the financial resources to give a nice gift," said Ms. Richter. "He didn't even know these people, but he would call them up, make an appointment to see them within the next half an hour, and come back with a check or pledge in hand. Berkley always inspires you to do more than you think you're capable of doing. The man is amazing, absolutely amazing."

The State of Iowa contributed $300,000, helping the Save the Park group raise more than $6 million in a little more than three weeks. Contributions came from every state in the union.

"Without Berk, there would be no University of Okoboji Foundation. Hence, no arts center, hence, no Lakeside Lab, hence, no Highway 71 Beautification Project, hence a lot of things," said Ms. Richter. "He contributes inspiration, vision, and financial commitment. He has always made a leadership gift, whether it is land for the Great Lakes senior citizens center, or cash for many of those projects.

"It's a domino effect and he starts the dominoes."

His son, Tom, believes in leading and setting an example.

"There's hardly a project of importance in the community that either I'm not leading and Dad supports, or Dad's not leading and I support," said Tom Bedell. "He and Mom have been very generous. They do it together. Why do we do it? In this community, if we don't, where is the money going to come from? If this is the community we grew up in, it's the community our kids are growing up in, it's the community our co-workers and their families live in, and if we don't do the things to make it a better place, we're being silly."

"As different as Berkley and Tom Bedell appear on the surface, they share a passion for making a positive difference in the world," said Tom Kuhlman. Kuhlman has known Tom since they were schoolmates, and, as executive director of the Iowa Great Lakes Chamber of Commerce, has worked with Berkley.

"Berk's far more conservative than Tom, business-wise and in personal life," said Kuhlman. "Berk never drove the shiniest, newest cars, and he was a very common dresser. Tom likes more flash and flair."

But in other ways, "Tom is a continuation of a great deal," said Kuhlman.

"The community's spirit is shaped by leaders like Berkley and Tom Bedell," said Kuhlman. "Communities are shaped by what they believe they can do. Our community has done things that other communities don't even think about. We have more can-do attitudes around than just Tom and Berk, but with that kind of leadership, others are inspired to become that way. So when you want to have a major fundraiser for a foundation, you have an attitude that comes from people like Tom and Berk and a lot of others."

Berkley and Elinor refused to retire from the life goals they had written in 1970:

    A. "To have a good time, and bring fun, happiness and joy to others.

    B. "To raise a well-adjusted family, helping them develop so that they will live happy lives, and contribute toward making the world a better place in which to live.

C. "To live in such a manner as to cause the world to be a little better place to live because of our having been here."

Cabell Brand attended the same American Management seminar that led Berkley to write out his goals. "Berk and I both learned that a successful business is a means to an end, not an end in itself," said Brand, who remains a close friend and served on the board of the National Foundation for Alternative Medicine. "I have not known anyone in my life who has had such a balanced approach."

Berkley and Elinor decided it would not be enough to give ten percent of their annual income to their special charity checking account. They needed to keep working on causes they believed in.

"I feel happiest when I'm involved in things," said Elinor. "I'm one of these strange people who enjoys going to meetings and being involved in whatever's going on. I helped found the Voluntary Action Center. I helped found the Arts Center. I worked in Girl Scouts and Cub Scouts, and had a lot of friends."

And Berkley set out, with a missionary zeal, to share two stories:

1) The joy of giving, as they had experienced it; and
2) The power of alternative medical treatments, as he had experienced it in his own healing.

Passions for Peace, Faith

Elinor continued to work for world peace through Peace Links. Berkley remained active with political causes and candidates.

Berkley said, "I made myself sick packing 70 boxes of citrus to give people in February last year, but it gave me real joy. I think they enjoyed receiving them, and part of my joy came from *knowing* they would enjoy receiving them. I don't think of giving as sacrifice versus self-gratification. I think they all fit together. It's a circle, instead of a line."

He acted on his faith when, in 1987, Ken joined the Master of Arts in Religious Communication faculty of United Theological Seminary, a United Methodist graduate school

in Dayton, Ohio. Berkley invested in the development office of United Theological Seminary to spur others' giving.

He joined the board of another United Methodist
seminary, Claremont School of Theology in California, at
the behest of his congressional friend Robert Edgar, who
had been hired as president of Claremont.

"He raised questions that were sometimes uncomfortable for me, his good friend and buddy," said Edgar, "He didn't
take on face value what the president of the Claremont School
of Theology said. He reached deeper than that.

"He had the staff, at great pains, undertake an analysis and they discovered the only profit center at the seminary was the planned giving office. Everything else lost
money. It changed the way the Board of Trustees thought
about planned giving. They recognized that for every $5
million raised, we ought to hire another planned giving spe-
cialist. Then Berk found another board member who would
put up $20,000 and he said, 'I'll put up $20,000, he'll put up
$20,000, and if the rest of you board members match this,
we'll have a second planned giving person.' He had all the
facts and figures of how planned giving would be healthy
for the school. When you're dealing with marginal budgets
and balancing budgets, you're often not hiring more staff,
which costs more money, but Berk convinced me and the
board that NOT hiring planned giving people would lose
money for the school.

"In a nice way, he looks at things differently than
most people do."

Elinor Bedell State Park

Mott Miller was an old horse trader. He owned a
120-acre farm on the shore of East Okoboji, less than a mile
north of the farm where Berkley's grandmother was born
and raised. In the 1950s when Berkley and his friend Blaine
Hoien learned that the farm was for sale, the two families
purchased it for $24,000. It was not much of a farm, but it
had nearly three-fourths of a mile of shoreline.with some
beautiful oak trees. It was one of the Berkley Bedell family's

favorite places for a Sunday afternoon picnic since they could go to it by boat from their Spirit lake home on East Okoboji.

"We'd go to Mott Miller's farm and fish," said Ken. "We'd walk across this field to get down to the water. My understanding was that within six feet of the lake it was public property, so if you came by boat, you could go in. Even before we owned it, we just saw it as a public trust."

Soon, when half of it did belong to the Bedells, they did see it as a public trust.

"It was just the worst piece of land in the whole county," Hoien said. "Lakefront was not so popular in those days. Most people would come up during the summer for a month or two, and live on the lake and then in the wintertime there was nobody there. It was vacant. It's hard to believe, but it's true. We bought it for the long haul. I thought it would educate my kids. Buy that and by the time they were ready for college, it would be worth enough to educate them."

From the mid-1950s until the mid-1990s, the East Okoboji land remained a farm that people used for fishing, picnics and hikes.

Over the years, Berkley and Elinor watched as the lakeshore became less and less accessible to the public. They knew how much they had enjoyed picnics on the lakeshore and they couldn't bear to see the experience being enjoyed by only those who could afford lakefront homes.

By the early 1990s, they knew what they had to do: They divided the land parcel with Blaine Hoien.

In 1997, Berkley and Elinor and some friends were having Sunday lunch at a local lakeshore restaurant. At the same restaurant, Iowa's governor, Terry Branstad, and his family were also having lunch. Berkley asked the governor if he would have time to look at some property he and Elinor were considering giving to the state for a park. Terry said he did not have to go back to Des Moines until later in the afternoon, and he would be glad to look at the land. Berkley went home, picked up the key to the gate, and he and the Republican governor toured the property.

"We want the land to stay in pristine condition," said Berkley. "We want trails, a shelter house, and we want some parking spots for motor homes." When the state agreed to those conditions, the Bedells donated the property to the state.

Tom Kuhlman, director of the Iowa Great Lakes Chamber of Commerce said, "Elinor Bedell State Park defines Berk and Elinor's philosophy: 'It would be better for the public than it is for us.' That's their attitude. They could have made a substantial profit with today's trend of breaking up property into buildable lots, but the higher priority for them is the public good." Elinor Bedell State Park was the first new state park to be built in Iowa in 20 years.

The fact that it had been appraised for nearly $1.3 million at the time they gave it to the state did not faze them.

"It didn't hurt us any," said Berkley. "We gave away the $12,000, which we had originally paid for our half of the farm.."

The gift became more meaningful to the community when the state allowed a playground to be installed by the local Rotary Club dedicated to the memory of a slain two-year old girl – a victim of a family caught in the throes of substance abuse. "That made the park much more useful," said Berkley.

On September 3, 2001 – the day of the park dedication – the people of Spirit Lake had the opportunity to thank Elinor Bedell. Berkley had decided that since the park had been named after her, she and Tom would give the dedication speeches. He stayed quietly in the background.

"The problem has been, all through our life together, I've been the star and Elinor has been in the background. So for the dedication, I did not want to speak. I wanted her to speak, and we asked our son Tom to speak. I think it shocked people that I didn't speak."

"Elinor had done a tremendous amount of things in her life that had gone unrecognized," said their daughter, Joanne Quinn.

"That day she stood up and gave this wonderful, from the heart, speech about how important it had always been for them to want to have a place where people could recreate, because the lakes had been so over developed.

Elinor Bedell State Park is an effort to give all people access to the land of the lakes in much the same condition as when Berkley's grandmother lived nearby in the late 19th century.

Spirit Lake was becoming a 'have and have not' community, with people who could afford to be on the water and people who couldn't. This park would include everybody. For many years, Dad and Mom had talked about how they would love to see the land become a state park. How wonderful that this had always been their goal and now to see the dream come true.

"When she finished speaking, Mom came back to the picnic bench and sat down. The people clapped and they clapped and they clapped. We finally had to nudge her and say, 'You should stand up.' And she did. It was so moving, because they were clapping for her personally, not just for the new park. They wanted to show the warmth and appreciation they had for her. It made me cry."

Berkley added, "I have heard many speeches by many important people, but in all my life I have never heard an audience applaud to the extent they did that day for Elinor. It wasn't because of what she said, or even the giving of the land for the state park. It was because of their great love and appreciation of her as an individual."

It was also a long-awaited chance for the public to recognize Elinor, the shy lady who, 36 years before, had to be coaxed from behind the airplane wing for a photo, when the town came out to recognize Berkley's Small Businessman award. A photo from the dedication event is engraved on the informational kiosk in the new park.

"It was a thank-you, not only for a Cub Scout and Girl Scout leader, for a Sunday school teacher and volunteer, but for the woman who had emerged," said Berkley.

"She is the active one in our winter home in Naples, Florida. Now that we spend our winters in Florida, she is involved in the League of Women Voters and is on the board of the Naples Council on World Affairs. She is involved in PEO, a woman's service organization. She is much more active in things in Naples than I am."

Elinor emerged as a national leader in movements like Peace Links, a passion she and Joanne shared from their days in Washington and beyond. The former Girl Scout leader had shown how you could influence discussions about nuclear arms, giving a memorable demonstration that became a Peace Links trademark.

"We'd fill a tennis ball container full of BBs. Each BB represented the total firepower of the two atom bombs dropped on Japan during World War II, then we would ask people to close their eyes and listen. We would slowly pour them into a metal pan. It would seem to go on and on forever, emphasizing how many nuclear weapons we had. It impressed everyone," Elinor recalled.

Joanne thought their discussions influenced Berkley to introduce the first comprehensive test ban treaty legislation.

A giving family

Berkley said he rejoiced that Joanne, Ken, and Tom all seemed to live with giving as part of their lifestyle.

"I hope we taught them to have values that would be beneficial to society. We did a heck of a job of that with Ken," Berkley recalled.

Ken, a United Methodist pastor, has been active in

peace and justice issues at local, national, and international levels.

"Ken is off saving the world and a whole variety of really meaningful things. He's addressing the racist problem, the poverty problems, and peace, and he has a really rich life from that," said Tom. "And you have to give Mom and Dad a lot of credit for that, too. Their example, I'm sure, has a lot to do with motivating him. Ken is really generous. He has the same attitude, a little bit, that Dad does about money. 'It's great if it comes to me. How quickly can I get it to people where I can help affect their lives?'"

Shortly before the first Gulf War with Iraq, Ken led a group of students to Iraq. The United States was already building forces to attack. Berkley and Elinor tried to convince Ken that he should cancel the trip, but to no avail. Ken was greatly moved as the group met with local students in Baghdad, realizing that they might shortly face invasion and bombing from the United States. Ken and his students escaped to Jordan just as the war clouds thickened, where they had to stay in their hotel for fear of being killed if they ventured out. They were on the last plane out of Jordan.

Berkley and Elinor were greatly relieved when Ken called upon arriving back in New York.

"I really think that the Iraq government would like to avert a war," Ken said. "Could you contact former President Jimmy Carter to see if he would be willing to try to negotiate peace?"

There were two problems, his father noted.

"First, I am not that close to Carter, and second, I do not think President Bush would be very amenable to listening to Carter. Why don't we go to Washington and see if Tom Harkin has any suggestions?" Berkley called Harkin, who was scheduled to preside over the Senate, but said he could meet with them at 5:00 p.m. Berkley flew to D.C. from Florida, and Ken came from New York. Ken explained his findings to Harkin and said he thought if someone would serve as a negotiator, war could possibly be averted.

"Who do you have in mind?" asked Harkin.

"You," replied Ken, referring to Harkin.

It was a complete shock to Berkley.

"I would do anything I could to prevent this war," said Harkin. "If your people can arrange it, I will go over." As Berkley and Ken left the office to go to their hotel and contact the people who had arranged Ken's trip, the office television announced that the United States was bombing Iraq. The war had started.

The young United Methodist minister was willing to risk his life to try to prevent a war—and a U.S. Senator was willing to do the same.

Joanne said each of the three children took to heart their parents' recommendation to put a portion of their money in a fund to be used strictly for charitable work.

And each of them lived in such a manner to try to make the world a better place.

After earning a Ph.D. degree, an associate degree as a medical assistant, and a teacher's certificate, Joanne established the Educational Learning Strategies Foundation to improve the learning and health of children. She has focused much of her resources on children with attention deficit disorder and dyslexia.

Her interest in this matter came about because of a problem her oldest son, Jason, encountered when he was in third grade. During third grade, students learn to read words with three syllables. Jason could not do it. "He simply could not put words like 'gov-ern-ment' together," said Joanne. "He could pronounce the word, but he could not put them together. The school placed him in remedial reading. It devastated this boy who wanted to do well. Hard as he tried, Jason could not keep pace with other children."

Joanne learned that Jason's right brain and left brain were probably not communicating. The right brain works with creative matters, such as art and music. The left brain works with factual matters, such as math and science. Joanne learned some exercises Jason could do to help his right and left brain communicate. She had him do the exercises and in two months he was doing well in regular class.

"Jason became a straight A-student and graduated from college summa cum laude. Jason is not the only young person to have had this problem. What a shame that the information on these exercises is not available to all who need it." Joanne became a certified instructor in Brain Gym. She trained more than 500 teachers in Colorado to use the exercises, with reports of extraordinary improvement, especially with gifted and talented students and students with attention deficit disorder (ADD).

Joanne also became interested in Sudden Infant Death Syndrome (SIDS), a condition where babies die in their cribs with no apparent cause. Research done over the past 13 years in Great Britain by Barry Richardson and real life application of Richardson's Gas Theory in New Zealand indicates that SIDS is an environmental poisoning in the crib. Richardson determined that a common household fungus, Scopulariopsis brevicaulis, gets established in the mattress from the baby's sweating, spitting up, and so on. Once established, the fungus begins to consume the flame-retardant chemicals in the mattress, arsenic and antimony. This results in a byproduct of arsine and stibine, very deadly nerve gases. A scientist in New Zealand produced a gas impermeable polyethelene mattress cover free of arsenic and antimony. Since 1996, 100,000 baby mattresses have been wrapped in New Zealand with this cover. The Minister of Health of New Zealand has reported that no babies have died on these wrapped mattresses. There are many risk factors that play a part in SIDS, but the bottom line is that if the gases cannot reach the baby, the baby does not die.

Joanne's work in these two areas had a profound influence on Berkley as he formed The National Foundation for Alternative Medicine.

Berkley is glad that his children, in the spirit of their great-grandmother, are determined to put their minds to doing "almost anything within reason," to benefit others.

"I am proud that all three of our children are living lives of giving," said Berkley.

Tom recently gave a lead gift in the drive to build a Family YMCA in Spirit Lake.

After selling part of the fishing tackle factory to some investors, Tom gave a $6 million gift to the Spirit Lake School district, which was matched by the school with $3 million to build a new 1,000-seat auditorium.

"We're by far the most aggressive company in the nation regarding fishery policy on the federal and the state level, in terms of conservation and the environment. If you were to go to the industry and say, 'Who are the leaders in helping change the quality of the outdoors and the outdoor experience for Americans?' Pure Fishing would be named. If you asked 'Who's next?' they'd say 'Pure Fishing,' and then who's next? 'Pure Fishing.' That's a sense I got from Dad, too. That's part of giving back. I want to take 20 percent of my time and spend it on causes that relate to the outdoors, fishing, and conservation. To me, Dad would be doing that if he were here. That would be a natural for him."

But Tom would like to be remembered in a different way, as well.

"Once, when the company was going through some challenges, I gave a speech to our coworkers. I said, 'I want to be remembered by all of you as someone who helped you be more and better than you would have been without me; that you had a better life than you might have had without me, that we cared about each other, that we loved each other, and were fulfilled by one another.' So it's making a difference in other peoples' lives and allowing them to make a difference in yours.

"Each person needs to give in accordance with his or her ability to give," said Tom.

"Ken lives his life giving up stuff. My Mom and Dad do. So if somebody were to say, 'Tom's going to leave a bigger legacy' … I'm going to leave a bigger company. I'm going to leave more employment. I'm going to leave more impact, because of the timing, just like if I had been first and Dad had followed, he would have. I'll be able to contribute to more buildings and causes because of our size, but to some degree I've got the easier time. Dad started and made it happen; built the values, built the foundation. I just got the chance to do something with it. I wouldn't make comparisons about that. I would hope I can take the legacy that Dad has created and do it proud."

Berkley and Elinor don't use the word sacrifice, he said, because they don't think of donating money as giving up something they need.

"He doesn't really want things he doesn't have. That's the beauty of my parents. If you don't want things, you're not giving anything up," Tom recounted.

Tom recognizes and reconciles his vocational irony: Berkley set out in life to be a businessman and Tom set out to be of political influence. At this stage in their lives, they appear to have switched places. But Tom says he can make as big a contribution in the fishing industry as he could if he were in office.

"I'm excited about the causes I'm going to be able to influence, the contribution to some community things here, certainly to my kids, because they're going to high school and college. My daughter, who's a sophomore at Colorado State University in Fort Collins, Colorado, calls me a lot. It's so much fun now, because we get to really talk and share and communicate, and be much more emotional about feelings.

"So I'm looking not at the escape to politics as the transition, but for me, I have a company in place where I can spend more of my time on causes, both family causes and do-gooder causes, and have the resources of the company and the base of the company to do them from. And I'm pretty energized by that. The difference between Dad's and my case is he needed to leave here and go do something else to fulfill that need. I think I can fulfill a very similar need in a different way here.

"I like this as my base. I like this as my platform to function from, but I have the company organized in a way where I can go off to Washington and work on a Fishable Waters Act for three days, and the company won't fall apart. At this point, I can see my ability to meet my 'make a difference' needs."

In 1984, Berkley and Elinor sold Berkley and Company to their three children.

Berkley has made it a goal to influence other people, especially people with wealth, to give away more than they ever thought they could.

"As people give and find they can give more than they thought they could, and find that it doesn't adversely affect their situation, it's really amazing how much money people can give, people of wealth, if they want to," said Berkley. "It's hard to get them going sometimes, but I contend that the *more* they give, the *easier* it is to give. It's not a question of the money ever running out. The more you get from people, the more they will give.

"The most you can deduct from your income tax is 50 percent of your income. For several years, Elinor and I have exceeded that. A large part of it has to do with the land we gave for the state park, but it has not adversely affected us. And a large part of our giving has to do with the foundation, that we're having to carry for a little while, until we get that going.

"The most important thing is not what we have given, not by a mile. We've tried to teach other people by setting an example, so they will give more. The most important thing is that we are talking to people who know that we don't have nearly as much money as they have, and yet we set an example. Then they find out they can give more, and get enjoyment from giving. It raises their sights for the next opportunity that comes along.

"The important thing is to keep trying to make the world a better place. The task becomes more urgent all the time. I get a great amount of satisfaction from the money we have given for projects, the involvement we've had in raising money for them, the example we have set for others, and what they can do. I hope that, in some small way, we will have left the world a little better for our having been here.

"I'm 80 years old. When you're 60 years old, there isn't much of a difference between 60 and 70. When you're 80 years old, there's a big difference between 80 and 90. The reality is, I have a limited time yet to be on this earth. I would like to do what I can with the time I have left."

In 2002, Berkley and Elinor rejoiced in the birth of their first great-grandchild, named Berkley Pelletier. He is the son of Ken and Kathie's daughter, Charity.

Above, Berkley and Elinor enjoy a vacation with former members of Berkley's World War II B-29 crew, in 2000.

Right, Elinor and Berkley at a meeting of the President's Circle of the National Academy of Sciences, in 2002. Berkley served on the Board of the organization.

Chapter Thirty

The Most Powerful Giant

"What did you ever do that fool thing for?" one of Berkley's constituents asked him after he had announced that he would not run for re-election because of his Lyme disease. "I will take you to someone who can fix you."

The ever-practical Bedell replied, "Well, the doctors can't fix me, so I will try most anything."

The man who could "fix" him turned out to be a dairy farmer named Herb Sanders, who lived just north of the Iowa-Minnesota border. Sanders had lost his dairy herd to disease. When he acquired a new herd, he started using a veterinary medicine made by a firm in Iowa. They make the medicine by injecting into the udder of a pregnant cow killed germs of a particular type. So, when the cow has its calf, the whey from the colostrums, or first milk, is used as medicine.

The theory is that, had the cow really been infected, the unborn calf would have contracted the disease from its mother before being born, and Mother Nature would have made in the colostrum the material needed to cure the calf. This new veterinary medicine proved to be very effective for Sanders, and he started helping other dairy farmers. Finally, he started helping other people. He had significant success with cancer, multiple sclerosis, and other diseases. Berkley served on the Board of Directors of the Lyme Disease Foundation where he worked with scientists and researchers. Berkley obtained some of the killed spirochete germs that cause Lyme disease and took them to the place in Iowa that makes the veterinary medicine. They ran the germs through a cow and gave Berkley the colostrum whey. Berkley then took the whey to the farmer who proceeded to mix it with other veterinary medicine wheys. According to Sanders' directions, Berkley carried a little bottle in one pocket and a timer in the other. He took a tablespoon of the medication every hour-and-a-half while he was awake. Before long, Berkley's symptoms disappeared and he no longer had Lyme disease.

Sanders learned he could inject the blood of a person who was ill into the udder of a pregnant cow and the colostrum would be effective in treating the person.

"Stick your leg out and twist your foot back and forth. Does that hurt?" Sanders asked. "It sure does!" Berkley replied. Berkley had asked Sanders if he could do anything for what appeared to be arthritis in his knee. He had been limping from knee pain for several weeks. Sanders mixed up some of the various veterinary wheys – the company makes several different formulations according to what they inject into the cow – and said, "Swish this around in your mouth before you swallow it." They talked for a few minutes and then went through the same procedure again. After a few minutes, Sanders said, "Now stick out your leg and twist your foot around as you did before. Does it hurt?"

"No."

Berkley stood up and walked around the room. He could hardly believe that his problem could be cured in those few short minutes.

For Berkley, this cure was another encounter with the vast and fascinating world of alternative medicine. It was a world full of wonderful therapies that have been swept under the table or outlawed because they might be "disruptive" technologies—they could upset the economic order of things. Berk wondered, "Why aren't these targeted colostrums available for everyone?" His recovery from Lyme disease and the disturbing questions it raised changed his life.

Sanders continued to help people with his colostrum whey treatment. Years later, the government sent an agent with a recorder to Sanders' farm, posing as a patient. Sanders was indicted on a number of counts, including fraud, cruelty to animals, and practicing medicine without a license. If convicted, he could have faced a prison sentence of several years. Sanders had no money with which to hire a lawyer to defend him.

The state appointed a public defender. The public defender had been unhappy with the way the doctors had treated his deceased wife and took a great interest in the case. The state fired him as public defender for spending too much time on the case. So he defended Sanders without charging him a dime. Another attorney also donated her services.

Berkley convinced some expert witnesses to also testify without charge, and he donated $20,000 to cover the cost of copying documents, travel, and other legal expenses. When the two defense attorneys went to interview the expert witnesses, the prosecutor went along. Apparently, he had his eyes opened that there really was some scientific evidence for the colostrum treatment.

Two days before the start of the trial, the state dropped all charges, except for practicing medicine without a license, which, in Minnesota is a gross misdemeanor that only carries a penalty of a short jail term and a $5,000 fine. Obviously, the state did not want the patients who had been helped to be able to tell their story to the jury and the press. When the state advised that they would drop the jail term if Sanders would agree to discontinue treating people, Sanders refused. Berkley told him he would pay the fine himself. The trial lasted three weeks. It was the longest trial ever held in the County Court House of Saint James, Minnesota. There was a hung jury. The state tried the case a second time, and again a hung jury. Finally, the state gave up.

Sanders was a farmer treating people and charging them. The fact that a jury would refuse to convict him of practicing medicine without a license speaks to how the public feels about alternative medicine, and the monopoly of allopathic medicine.

Still later, a law was passed in Minnesota that would make it possible for people such as Sanders to treat people as long as there was no harm to the patient, and the patient was fully informed of both the treatment and the fact that the practitioner was not a regular doctor.

After Sanders' colostrums cured his Lyme disease, Berkley proceeded to investigate other alternative treatments, and what he saw shocked him. While mainstream medicine branded anyone who tried something different as a quack, Berkley found many practitioners and scientists involved in research of great promise. Invariably, they were stopped at every turn by the federal Food and Drug Administration.

Federal law stipulates that no medicine can be distributed unless it is proven to be 'safe and effective' to the satisfaction of the Food and Drug Administration (FDA). Berkley found that the FDA requires so many tests that their approval process costs hundreds of millions of dollars. In addition, the FDA is relentless and without compassion in prosecuting anyone who does not fit the conventional system. The end result is almost no non-patented medicine can become FDA-approved and be administered, because without abundant profits from a patent, nobody can afford the tests.

As such, the FDA process effectively eliminates simple, cheap, non-toxic, but effective medicines that for one reason or another cannot be patented. In effect, Berkley discovered, the FDA policy gives the pharmaceutical companies a practical monopoly on what medicines are to be used in the American health system. While pharmaceutical drugs have proven to be effective against contagious infectious diseases such as pneumonia or meningitis, which once were our nation's greatest health problems, they are not as effective against degenerative diseases such as cancer, heart disease, and multiple sclerosis. Giving the drug companies a monopoly on medicines that are effective for what used to be major health problems, but are not nearly as effective for major current problems, seemed to practical Berkley Bedell to be the height of folly.

It devastated Berkley to tell Lyme disease sufferers that they could not get the treatment that cured him because of FDA regulations — a completely non-toxic whey from cow's milk. He observed to one: "Little Miss Muffet was fortunate that she could eat her curds and whey before there was an FDA!"

As this book is written in 2004, the United States has a serious problem with our health care system. The U.S. spends nearly twice as much per person on health care as any other nation. In most methods of measurement we do not rate very high, and there is a growing dissatisfaction among consumers with the lack of effectiveness of conventional treatments for many degenerative diseases. If costs continue to rise as predicted, cost will be a serious national problem. In fact, it could be argued that it already is.

We should not be surprised that this is happening. In most areas of our economy competition controls cost. The tremendously high cost of getting FDA approval prevents any non-patentable medications from getting into the system. Patents prevent competition from the exact same item, but usually similar non-patented items are able to enter the market and compete pricewise. This is not the case with pharmaceutical drugs. Non-patentable medications cannot enter the market and compete because of the tremendous cost of getting FDA approval for distribution. This gives patented pharmaceutical drugs a complete monopoly without any of the price competition that exists in almost all other areas of our society, where non-patented items compete pricewise with patented items.

The FDA even goes so far as to try to prohibit importation of identical medications from foreign countries where they are of lower cost. The argument is that the pharmaceutical industry needs their tremendous profits in order to fund research. That would be legitimate if we were getting much more effective treatments because of pharmaceutical research. But in most areas we are not.

If the U.S. is ever going to bring about better health and controlled costs, it is imperative that the public be permitted to choose for itself whatever treatment one desires. If the treatment proves to be harmful or ineffective the supplier will be subject to law suites just as is the case in other areas, and the patent will still give protection just as is the

WHAT DRUGS REALLY COST

BRAND NAME	CONSUMER PRICE (For 100 tabs/caps)	COST OF GENERIC ACTIVE INGREDIENT (For 100 tabs/caps)	PERCENT MARKUP
Celebrex 100 mg	$130.27	$0.60	21,712%
Claritin 10 mg	$215.17	$0.71	30,306%
Keflex 250 mg	$157.39	$1.88	8,372%
Lipitor 20 mg	$272.37	$5.80	4,696%
Norvasc 10 mg	$188.29	$0.14	134,493%
Paxil 20 mg	$220.27	$7.60	2,898%
Prevacid 30 mg	$344.77	$1.01	34,136%
Prilosec 20 mg	$360.97	$0.52	69,417%
Prozac 20 mg	$247.47	$0.11	224,973%
Tenormin 50 mg	$104.47	$0.13	80,362%
Vasotec 10 mg	$102.37	$0.20	51,185%
Xanax 1mg	$136.79	$0.024	569,958%
Zestril 20 mg	$89.89	$3.20	2,809%
Zithromax 600mg	$1,482.19	$18.78	7,892%
Zocor 40mg	$350.27	$8.63	4,059%
Zoloft 50mg	$206.87	$1.75	11,821%

COMPARISON OF U.S., EUROPEAN AND CANADIAN DRUG PRICES

Drug	Quantity	Potency	U.S. price	European price	Canadian price
Augmentin	12	500 mg	$55.50	$8.75	$12.00
Cipro	20	500 mg	$87.99	$40.75	$53.55
Claritin	30	10 mg	$89.00	$18.75	$37.50
Coumadin	100	5 mg	$64.88	$15.80	$24.94
Glucophage	100	850 mg	$124.65	$22.00	$26.47
Norvasc	30	10 mg	$67.00	$33.00	$46.27
Paxil	30	20 mg	$83.29	$49.00	$44.35
Pravachol	28	10 mg	$85.60	$29.00	$40.00
Premarin	100	0.625 mg	$55.42	$8.95	$22.46
Prempro	28	0.625 mg	$31.09	$5.75	$14.33
Prilosec	30	20 mg	$112.00	$49.25	$59.00
Prozac	20	20 mg	$91.08	$18.50	$20.91
Synthroid	100	0.1 mg	$33.93	$8.50	$13.22
Zestril	28	20 mg	$40.49	$20.00	$20.44
Zocor	28	10 mg	$123.43	$28.00	$45.49
Zoloft	30	100 mg	$114.56	$52.50	$47.40

cases in other areas of our economy. These charts obtained from the Life Extension Foundation, P.O. Box 229120, Hollywood, Florida, 33022, show the comparative costs of drugs in the U.S., compared to the costs of the same drugs in Canada and Europe, and the U.S. consumer price compared to the cost of the generic active ingredient in 2004 at the time this book was written.

After his recovery from Lyme disease, Berkley's heath continued to improve. Senator Tom Harkin remembers seeing Berk again at that time, and was relieved that he now looked fine.

But the respite did not last long and health again took the front seat. The diagnosis of prostate cancer hit him like a thunderbolt. Berkley's Spirit Lake doctor told him that the surgery could be done in the nearby town. Berk later regretted insisting to the doctor that he be sent to the Mayo Clinic in Rochester, Minnesota. Berkley didn't know the Mayo doctor, and somehow, he had bad feelings about the whole procedure. He even became sick the day before he was to travel to Rochester for the operation. as though his body was giving him a warning. But the Rochester doctor answered Berkley's telephone inquiry advising him he should come up for the operation even though he was ill.

After the operation, Berkley wished he had trusted his instincts. As he came out of the anesthetic, he was relieved to hear the doctor proclaiming that the operation had been a success. They had removed all the cancer. The newspapers reported the success of the operation and many of the citizens of Northwest Iowa were relieved.

"Two days later, the doctor came into my room and reported that he had been wrong. They had not succeeded in removing all the cancer. I lay there crying as I realized that the news may well have been a death sentence. I did not want to die. The procedure had also left me incontinent and I spent the rest of my life wearing a diaper."

But whenever the philosophical Berk began to feel sorry for himself, he realized he didn't have to look far to find people with far worse problems.

Two years later, in the spring of 1990, Berkley and Elinor attended a conference in Florida where they met and became friends with former New York State Assemblyman Daniel Haley, who became fascinated by the story of how a colostrum product cured Berkley of Lyme disease. Then Berkley told his new friend about his bout with prostate cancer. "As a matter of fact," Berkley remarked, "some days I just feel terribly tired and have to rest in the afternoon and that isn't normal for me. Sometimes I wonder if the cancer could be coming back."

"Well, it's easy to find out," Haley replied. "You just go up to Quebec and see the scientist Gaston Naessens. He can look at your blood with a special microscope he invented, and he can tell from the forms he sees whether or not the cancer is returning." Haley then explained 'somatids,' which Naessens discovered; tiny particles in the blood that change from one form to another depending on the internal conditions within the body. If there are pre-cancerous conditions in the body, certain patterns of somatids appear in the blood. Haley told Berkley about the trial, which Naessens had survived two years before. The Quebec Medical Corporation had tried to convict and send Naessens to prison. People from all over the world came to testify that Naessens had saved their lives and the Canadian government failed to convict him. Always interested in exploring new frontiers, Berkley had heard enough to know he wanted to meet Naessens and learn what might be in his blood. Never one to let grass grow under his feet, he asked Haley: "How soon could you set up an appointment?"

Two weeks later, Berkley flew to Montreal, Canada where he rented a car and drove east for two hours to Rock Forest, where Naessens maintains his laboratory and residence. The tall, courtly Naessens showed Berkley the special microscope he had invented that he calls his 'Somatoscope.'

"I have always been interested in blood," he said, "and the electron microscope, although a great scientific advance, can only see dead material because living material is killed in the process of preparing it to be viewed."

Berkley with Gaston Naessens, whom Berkley credits with curing him from prostate cancer. Note microscope in background. (Rock Forest, Quebec, July 2002)

Wanting to see more, Naessens invented the Somatoscope, which is much more powerful than conventional light microscopes. The conventional wisdom had been that one could not see anything smaller than the wavelength of light with a light microscope. However, Naessens had discovered a way to separate the various light wavelengths and combine them in such a manner as to enable one to see particles much smaller than the wavelength of light. With this, Naessens can view things in the living blood that could not previously be seen, and therefore not acknowledged, by conventional medicine. Naessens' bilingual wife served as translator, since Naessens speaks only French. The scientist explained the 16 forms of what he calls the 'Somatid Cycle,' and how certain organisms appearing in the blood indicate conditions inside the body that suggest a predisposition toward various degenerative illnesses.

"Somatids are carriers of some genetic information," Naessens informed Bedell. "In one of my experiments, I took somatids from the blood of a white rabbit and injected them into the blood of a black rabbit. One-half of the black rabbit's fur then turned white, making it appear gray. Similarly, when I injected somatids from a black rabbit into the blood of a white rabbit, half of the white rabbit's fur turned black, making it too appear gray. Still using the same rabbits, each containing the others' somatids, I took a patch of skin from the white rabbit and grafted it onto the back of the black rabbit. It was not rejected, as a rabbit graft normally would be."

Naessens believes that he could culture the somatids from the blood of a transplant donor and inject them into the blood of the transplant recipient prior to the operation and the recipient's body would not tend to reject the transplant. This would solve a tremendous medical problem. It is hard to see how it could in any way injure the patient. It is a shame that our system is such that it cannot be tried.

Naesens also showed Berkley a jar with a large piece of meat covering the bottom of the jar. "I injected a small piece of rat meat with somatids and placed it in this sterilized jar under a vaccum. I then put it up on this window well where the sun could shine on it. It not only didn't rot, it has grown and grown without any nourishment of any kind, except for the sunlight.

"Now, let's have a look at your blood. Bad news," he said. "Here are some of the advanced forms of the somatid cycle, which would suggest that, indeed, conditions inside your body might permit the return of a cancerous condition."

Naessens explained how the "terrain" or environment inside the body is all-important, indicating the strength of the immune system. Overall, he told Berkley his blood indicated that his body's defenses were not in a strong enough condition to fight off disease. "Perhaps you should take 714-X."

Berkley had already learned that Naessens had invented a medicine called 714-X, which consists of a molecule of nitrogen combined with a molecule of camphor. Nitrogen is included because cancer cells crave nitrogen, Naessens explained, and camphor because it has a great affinity for cancer cells, heading right for them like a homing pigeon carrying nitrogen. "We know that cancer cells tend to drain the body of nitrogen, thus starving and weakening the immune system by denying it the nitrogen it needs," said Naessens. "Therefore, our concept is that we supply the cancer cells with all the nitrogen they want – in effect, getting them drunk on it. While they receive nitrogen, they stop robbing the body's immune system of the nitrogen it needs, so that it can fight off the cancer."

The 714-X treatment is taken over a 21-day cycle via injections into the lymph system through a point in the groin. During that period, the immune system gets its needed nitrogen and recovers. By the end of the 21-day cycle, or after two such cycles, the immune system has usually recovered sufficiently to be able to handle the job on its own. It is a new type of alternative medicine in which the problem is diagnosed before symptoms appear and the defenses of the body are used to prevent the disease from developing.

"My sense is that you might do well to take two cycles of 714-X," Naessens told Berkley. "After that, it would be good if you could return so that we can look at your blood again." Presuming that his doctor in Iowa could do the injections, Bedell obtained the 714-X and returned to Spirit Lake. To his dismay, his doctor had never heard of intralymphatic injections (which is not taught in medical schools) and had no idea of how it would be done. Calling Dan Haley, who had first put him in touch with Naessens, Berkley explained his problem. Haley remembered that when he had told Mildred Nelson of the Hoxsey Clinic in Tijuana, Mexico, about Naessens she had immediately sent a doctor to visit him to learn Naessens' therapy. So, Haley figured, that doctor should know the procedure. Calling Mildred Nelson, whom he already knew, Berkley learned that Mildred's doctor did, indeed, know the procedure and would teach him. So he took a plane to San Diego, where he crossed the border and took a taxi to the Centro Biomedico, as the Hoxsey Clinic is called. Quickly learning how to inject 714-X into his lymph system, Berkley returned to Spirit Lake and proceeded to give himself two 21-day cycles of 714-X. Naessens had explained to Berkley that the lymph, the body's sewage system, is thickened and gelled in someone developing degenerative diseases, but that the lymph generally liquefies within an hour or two after the first injection of 714-X, thus allowing the body to get rid of its toxins.

"What will he see in my blood this time?" Berk wondered, as he traveled once more to Quebec. Naessens lost little time in pricking Berkley's finger and he proceeded to project onto a screen what the Somatoscope saw in the blood. "Well, that's a lot better," Naessens commented after studying the screen a moment. "Now we see only the normal first three forms of the somatid cycle, and none of the advanced stages which indicate trouble. Now you are healthy and no longer possibly pre-cancerous, and there's no further reason for you to continue taking 714-X." This was the news Berkley had hoped to hear! Just to be sure, he continued to visit Gaston Naessens every six months to make sure his blood continued to look all right.

Returning home and feeling great, Berkley pondered what would need to be done so that any American could have access to targeted colostrums or to 714-X, the things that had helped him. He had kept in close touch with his good friend Senator Tom Harkin, who was fascinated by the various breakthroughs Berkley was uncovering, and who also was wondering what might be done to make them available to the average American.

Now Berkley had a lot to live for. He had a mission. He wanted to make sure that ordinary Americans had access to the treatments that had cured him.

He was also a good friend of Dr. William Robb, acting head of the National Institutes of Health (NIH), whom he urged to send a group of researchers to investigate Naessens' microscope and his 714-X treatment. So, on his next trip to visit Naessens, Dr. Robb, one of Robb's colleagues, and a member of Senator Harkin's staff accompanied Berkley.

"According to conventional medicine," Naessens explained to his guests, "people with the 16-stage somatid cycle that I have shown you, cannot be called sick, because a degenerative disease has not yet manifested in their bodies. But if the cycle is not brought to normal, after 12-18 months, the body becomes more and more exhausted to the point where any additional stress can lead to the development of abnormal cells, with the ultimate consequence of a cancerous mass. But remember, somatids are never the cause of an illness, but rather a witness, a caution light. Somatids are an indicator of danger. They say 'slow down, take precautions.'"

Perhaps Naessens' ideas were a little too far from their orthodox medical training, perhaps it was because 714-X has long been on the American Cancer Society's "blacklist" of "unproven" therapies, or perhaps it was just too new, but nothing more was ever heard from the National Institutes of Health (NIH) after their visit to Gaston Naessens. They could have taken on the Naessens' technique for using somatids to facilitate organ transplants or skin grafts for burn victims, or at least they could have undertaken research with the Somatoscope, or the 714-X. Instead, the NIH – the pacesetters of U.S. medical research – did *nothing – absolutely nothing*. Of course, their mentality is completely different from that of Berkley Bedell. None of them ever qualified for the Young Presidents' Organization membership which signifies that someone has built a company to a very large size before reaching the age of forty. None of them ever did anything on the scale of going to Israel to buy equipment to enable the production of nylon. In short, instead of problem solvers, the NIH were 'medicrats,' accustomed to *studying* problems, not *solving* them. They were like the cardinals who refused to look through Galileo's microscope in the middle ages, for fear of what they might see.

They were not accustomed to *tackling giants*, and they had not known Berkley's grandmother.

"What is the matter, Tom?" Berk remarked. He was visiting Iowa Senator Tom Harkin in his office, and Senator Harkin was having a terrible time sneezing and had a runny nose.

"I am having a terrible time with my allergies," Harkin replied.

"I know someone who claims he can cure you of that," answered Berkley.

"What is it?"

"It is bee pollen."

"Oh, my gosh."

"Well I don't see how it could hurt you and he claims he can cure you."

"Okay, I will try it."

Mr. Royden Brown flew to D.C. from Phoenix, Arizona and came to Harkin's office for treatment. The capsules actually contain various herbs, as well as bee pollen. The treatment consists of taking 12 capsules at one time. If the symptoms have not disappeared after 15 minutes, the patient takes another 12 capsules and waits another 15 minutes. This process is continued a maximum of three times. After two cycles, it was agreed by all those present that Harkin's symptoms had disappeared. Whenever the symptoms again appear, the patient is to repeat the same process. Harkin took approximately 200 capsules over the next few days. He still occasionally takes some capsules, but he no longer suffers from allergies. Harkin was convinced. He made a statement to *USA Today* that the disappearance of his symptoms was one of the strangest things that ever happened to him.

Berkley Bedell continued his intensive investigations into alternative medicine, always taking time to keep his friend Tom Harkin fully informed of what he was finding. Together, they came up with a plan for a federal effort to research some of the innumerable promising leads that kept popping up. They would call it the Office of Alternative Medicine and they would place it at the headquarters of the NIH. At that time, in 1991, Senator Harkin was Chair of the Health Subcommittee of the Senate Appropriations Committee. In that position, he had his thumb on the NIH budget, which had to pass through his committee.

And so it came about that, in the 1992 budget, Senator Harkin put into the NIH budget a small item to appropriate two million dollars to establish an Office of Alternative Medicine (OAM), with a mission to "investigate and validate" alternative treatments for disease.

The late Senator Everett Dirksen used to say, "You take a billion here and a billion there, and pretty soon you're talking about *real money!*" Given Washington's nonchalance about billions, the reaction to the OAM proposal was startling. Never had a puny, miniscule appropriation of just $2 million dollars received so much attention. It was written up in *The New York Times*, in *The Washington Post*, and in newspapers and periodicals all across the country. It was as though a basic rumbling dissatisfaction with conventional medicine had finally found expression in contemplating the novel idea that the federal government would actually spend some money "investigating and validating" alternative medicine. Especially strong was a growing underground revolt against conventional cancer therapy, with its almost religious-like insistence that there can only be certain accepted ways to treat cancer: i.e., surgery, radiation, and chemotherapy. Indeed, in California, Caspar Weinberger (when he was an Assemblyman) succeeded in getting a law passed that outlawed any cancer therapies other than orthodox ones, and certain doctors went to jail for venturing outside that law. (It was quite immaterial that they were curing people.)

The Office of Alternative Medicine (OAM) was set up within the Office of the Director of the NIH, with an Advisory Council to which Berkley was appointed. NIH top brass had not asked for the OAM, did not want it nor like it, and hoped it would go away. NIH bureaucrats, planning to make a career within the massive NIH bureaucracy, soon sensed which way the brass were inclined, and took appropriate steps. An early initiative was to award $20,000 grants for studies of various subjects within the field of alternative medicine. It's pretty hard to study much of anything for $20,000, but when the grants were announced, it was easy to see that the NIH bureaucrats who were staffing the OAM did not take it seriously. An award was given to a hypnotist and an acupuncturist to see what common ground they might find, and another grant was given to a neurologist to study crystals – the sort of thing that tended to trivialize alternative medicine. As launched, the OAM sadly showed its determination not to "investigate and validate" any of the many therapies which the medical establishment had spent so much time stamping out.

Berkley attended every meeting of the Advisory Council and soon became completely exasperated with OAM's first Director, Dr. Joseph Jacobs. It seemed that, as a Native American, Dr. Jacobs might be expected to be fairly sensitive to alternative medicine, because of the rich native traditions in herbal medicine. Apparently, he had turned his back on those traditions. Berk later recalled, "Perhaps I was too hard on Joe. I may have blamed him for things that were not completely his fault. It may well have been that the Director of NIH and top officials simply would not let Joe investigate any alternative treatments."

Of the Advisory Council, Berkley recalls: "We tried to get the OAM to conduct what are called "outcome studies." In these trials, the OAM would first survey the field, both domestic and foreign, to find practitioners whose records indicated more success in treating disease than is seen with conventional treatments. A protocol would then be set up; incoming patients would be checked before treatment to reconfirm the diagnosis. Patients would then be treated and checked again, after treatment, to confirm the treatment's effectiveness, or lack of it.

"But the NIH and the OAM absolutely refused to conduct such investigations, or to in any way "investigate and validate" alternative treatments. It was almost as though they were afraid they might find something that would force them to change their views. In testimony I gave before a Senate committee, I said 'the Advisory Council is like a bunch of pygmies trying to get an elephant to go where it doesn't want to go.' It was a terrible eye-opener for me to find that a major federal bureaucracy charged with finding answers to the health problems of our society had absolutely no interest in doing so, unless such answers came directly from their own laboratories. They had no interest in studying other treatments, no matter how promising they might be. Between the NIH and the FDA, there was a clear policy of preventing any improved treatment from being seriously considered unless it originated with the NIH or the pharmaceutical industry. Indeed, these bureaucracies were so powerful that they would even completely ignore the instructions of the Congress and refuse to do what Congress had appropriated money for. What a heartbreak. But I remembered my grandmother's advice: 'You can accomplish almost anything within reason if you will only set your mind to it.'"

Very clearly, results-oriented Berkley Bedell did not have in mind what the NIH "medicrats" did. Dr. Harold Varmus, head of the NIH at that time, was quoted in *Politics of Cancer Revisited* by Dr. Sam Epstein, as saying, "Talking about cures is absolutely offensive to me. In our work, we never think about such a thing even for a second. You can't do experiments to see what causes cancer ... It's not the sort of things scientists can afford to do."

No interest in cures? Can't afford to look? Dr. Varmus later left NIH to become head of Memorial Sloan Kettering in New York City, an institution that is one of the basic building blocks of 'official medicine.'

It was stressful to Berkley when the OAM floundered and was driven off course. After all, this was his brainchild, the vehicle to help make alternative medicine available to the American people. When he next visited Gaston Naessens, he had an object lesson in the effects of stress on the human body: the dreaded bad forms of the somatid cycle had returned. He went back on 714-X and they were gone the next time Naessens looked at his blood.

Hearing of the opening at the OAM, Dr. Wayne Jonas, a career Army doctor stationed at the Walter Reed Army Institute of Research in Washington, asked for a transfer to the NIH to run the OAM. He was approved for the job in 1995. A competent doctor, dedicated to improving the health of the American people, Jonas soon made a difference at the Office of Alternative Medicine. He was serious about making something happen, and published his ideas about what OAM could accomplish in an article in *Natural Health* magazine. The article was not popular with the NIH top brass, who seemed to prefer to think of themselves as beyond the need for suggestions. One of Dr. Jonas' staff pointed out to him that the OAM would never accomplish much as an office, and would need to be upgraded to a CENTER for Alternative Medicine before it would have enough independence to do a job. (Center being a term of bureaucratic art that denoted more prestige, more money, and somewhat more independence.) In effect, seeing OAM as a Trojan horse, the NIH brass attempted to hamstring it at every turn, making no bones about their intention to ignore Congress' expressed intentions. Dr. Jonas began to make efforts to turn the office into a center – achieving victory in 1997.

Berkley Bedell lost no opportunity to tell people of his two escapes from disease courtesy of unapproved alternative treatments. While in the House, Berkley and Tom Harkin had both been close to Tom Daschle of South Dakota who, meanwhile, like Tom Harkin, had been elected to the Senate. Displaying his organizational skill that later led to his becoming Senate Majority Leader, Daschle chaired a monthly luncheon meeting of Senate Democrats to which important speakers were invited, usually cabinet secretaries. One day, Tom Daschle invited Berkley to come and tell the Senate Democrats about his experiences with alternative treatments. After his dramatic presentation, there was general agreement among the senators that something had to be done so that all Americans could have access to the type of treatments that had twice saved Berkley's life. As Berkley shared, "Considering that the man who saved my life from Lyme disease is likely to be put on trial and perhaps sent to jail, and that when I seemed to be having a recurrence of cancer, I had to go out of the country, it seems clear to me that SOMETHING IS WRONG!!"

Daschle assigned Peter Rouse, his administrative assistant, to work with Berkley to develop ideas for legislation. This was a happy choice of partner, because Pete Rouse had been Berkley's administrative assistant when he was in the House.

Berkley was very clear about what was needed: a mechanism to allow promising nontoxic (and probably unpatentable) therapies onto the market without FDA approval, and a way to permit licensed doctors to use the treatments for their patients. Berkley knew patients would need to be informed that they were being treated with a substance not approved by the FDA, that the patients would need to sign a consent form indicating their understanding, and it was clear that if anything went wrong, the FDA had to be informed. Protecting Americans against harmful drugs was, after all, the FDA's original purpose, so if an experimental therapy proved to be harmful, it needed to be stopped immediately. From these considerations, and after many consultations, what became known as the Access to Medical Treatment Act was born. The Act provided a method by which a manufacturer could put a medical therapy on the market and a practitioner could use a treatment without FDA approval, as long as a number of requirements were met: The treatment had to be administered by a properly licensed practitioner under the limits of his or her license; there could be no evidence that the treatment would be of danger to the patient; there could be no advertising claims made; the patient had to be completely informed of the contents of the treatment and any possible side effects; and the patient had to sign a statement that he or she had been informed of all this, and still wished to be treated. Berkley had long since learned that many promising treatments are not permitted because of the expensive FDA approval process.

Senator Tom Daschle agreed to become the bill's lead sponsor, and he quickly brought together a strong bipartisan group of co-sponsors such as Senators Bob Dole, Orrin Hatch, and Tom Harkin. In the House, Representative Peter DeFazio of Oregon introduced the bill with a large number of co-sponsors.

Then began the long and arduous march toward gathering support and more co-sponsors. Outside Congress, Dr. Julian Whitaker quickly joined ranks with Berkley and brought the organization he founded, at that time known as the APMA (American Preventive Medical Association), strongly behind the bill. Dr. Whitaker's organization's name was recently changed to American Association for Health Freedom, which more clearly explains the work of the group. The executive director of APMA, Candace Campbell, scoured the halls of Capitol Hill for co-sponsors for the bill, trying to explain to members of Congress and their staffs that all was not well in the medical field. Alternative medicine was a very new concept for many, and an unwelcome one for some. When Candace had set a series of meetings, Berkley would fly to D.C. and meet personally with doubtful or wavering legislators. Candace recalls one marginal meeting with a Congressman. She and Berk left the Congressman's office not sure whether or not they had won him over. Suddenly, he burst out of his office as they were talking in the hall and said, "I didn't realize you were 'the' Berkley Bedell who founded Berkley and Company – I always use Berkley equipment!" Then he and Berkley talked for another half hour about fishing! Finally Berk, ever the savvy businessman, closed the sale and got the man's agreement to become a co-sponsor. This fish was caught with Berkley fishing tackle!

With strong citizen support from the burgeoning health freedom movement, sometimes called the "vitamin vote," support grew. The Access Bill had the most sponsors in 1997: 13 in the Senate and 71 in the House. By 2002, the number had fallen. Legislators were not hearing a roar from their constituents demanding they pass the Access to Medical Treatment Act. As this chapter is being written, it appears that there will be a new, concentrated effort to get this legislation passed.

While finding ways to create more acceptance of alternative medicines, Berkley turned his attention in another direction. The OAM was on its way to becoming a Center, but whether it was an Office or a Center, it became more and more apparent to Berkley that the government was not very likely to do the things he had dreamed of when Tom Harkin placed the original $2 million appropriation into the 1992 budget.

So Berkley had another talk with his best advisor, his best friend, and his best counselor – his wife Elinor. With so many marriages that don't work, it's a joy and a delight to see one that does, and the Bedells' is that kind of marriage. Elinor had followed Berkley's adventures into alternative medicine with enthusiasm, even developing some expertise of her own in the field, as had their daughter Joanne. The original idea was for the OAM to "investigate and validate" – i.e., to follow up any lead, and if it looked good, to test it in some way. The Bedells finally came to the conclusion that the government was not going to do the job.

"But the job still needs to be done," Berkley would say, "so if the government won't do it, we will just have to do it ourselves." After a lot of discussion, consultation, and prayer – the Bedells decided to establish a National Foundation for Alternative Medicine (NFAM). They would launch it with their own money, but to keep it going, they would have to go out and shake the money trees. While quite comfortable, they were not multi-multi-millionaires.

The Rev. Tim Forbess, a United Methodist minister from Dayton, Ohio is a close friend of the Bedells' son Ken, also a United Methodist minister. Tim vividly remembers a call he received on New Year's Eve, 1997. He immediately recognized Berkley's voice, and, as usual, Berkley went right to the point. "Elinor and I have decided to set up a foundation to do what we'd hoped the government would do (but have realized they won't) and we'd like you to go to Washington to run it." Berkley had long been helping to support a seminary where Tim was involved and knew him quite well. He knew Tim was bright, imaginative, and a determined 'plugger' who would just keep going until the job was done. In addition, Tim had experience raising money for the seminary, and the NFAM was going to need that experience.

Berkley explained to Tim that the first order of business was to find competent and well-credentialed doctors who would be willing to travel abroad to follow up the innumerable leads Berkley was receiving. Everybody was calling him to ask, "Have you heard about such-and-such a treatment for cancer, or so-and-so's new therapy?" For instance, Berkley had already heard about two clinics in Germany that claimed to be averaging 80 percent success in all types of cancer. True? Not true? That was what he'd hoped the OAM would work to discover, and what he now wanted the NFAM to achieve.

"Somebody needs to go over there and check their records," he told Tim, "read their X-rays, look at their pathology reports to make sure that their patients really had cancer, and to see if this is true! If we find it's true, then NFAM will announce the success and provide free information on the treatment to whoever wants it."

Tim Forbess liked the challenge and breadth of Berkley's vision. He was well aware of Berkley's health experiences and knew that much was not right in American medicine. Could something be done about it? Well, why not try?

Tim Forbess hit the ground running and soon had an office and staff assembled at 1629 K Street NW, in the heart of Washington, D.C. Early on, the Foundation decided not to accept money from either the NIH or the pharmaceutical companies. While such a policy has imposed limitations, NFAM is convinced it is the right way to go, thus staying at arm's length from the two most polluting influences on the American healthcare system.

One day, the phone rang; the caller, Mark Neveu, Ph.D., said he was calling from Dulles Airport, where he was between planes on his way to Guatemala. He was going to Guatemala to undertake private cancer research, after spending eight years directing a Pfizer research lab. To get ideas for his Guatemala project, someone had suggested Mark call Tim Forbess. Impressed, Tim insisted that upon his return to the U.S., Neveu come to Washington. Six months later, Mark returned from Guatemala, called Tim again, came to Washington, and Tim hired him on the spot to be vice president of NFAM. Remarkably well qualified and talented, Mark Neveu became incessantly busy on research trips to Europe and elsewhere, leaving Tim Forbess more time to raise money.

In its first four years of operation, NFAM visited 80 clinics in 24 countries. Recalls Berkley, "In eight years, the bureaucrats of the NIH and Office of Alternative Medicine did not complete even a single field investigation. They did not "investigate or validate" even one treatment!"

NFAM soon visited the clinics purportedly running an 80 percent success rate in cancer, and they are now concluding a "best cases" study with one of the clinics. This process turned out to be considerably more complicated than expected, with the need to occasionally hunt all over Europe for documents, and then to arrange for translations.

Cancer was chosen as NFAM's first target because of the ghastly cancer epidemic in the United States, where one American dies of cancer every minute – a statistic equivalent to three fully-loaded 747 airplanes crashing and killing everyone onboard, every day, all year long. If a disaster such as that really were to happen, the country would be up in arms; no one would fly anymore and one can be certain that something would change – and fast – in the Federal Aviation Administration and the aviation industry itself. But in cancer? Nobody seems to care; nobody seems to think this holocaust rate of death is any big deal. All the more reason, people say, to spend more money on cancer research, and so billions are distributed, year in and year out, to the National Cancer Institute (NCI). But what if the drug companies heavily influence the NCI? What if effective and non-toxic (unlike chemotherapy) cancer cures have been discovered and have been overlooked, or even suppressed? Nobody in any official position with the governmental bureaucracy seems to be concerned with the cancer epidemic – at least not until he or she, or a family member, contracts cancer. The late Dr. Hans Nieper of Hamburg, Germany once startled a conference in New York City by announcing that he regularly received high officials, and their family members, of the NIH and the AMA to take treatments they would not permit in the U.S. Of course, the NIH and the AMA would denounce such treatments as quackery, prosecuting and taking the licenses of any doctors who were bold enough to use such treatments.

While the medical establishment insists on conventional therapies, their 'medicrats' are quick to pounce on anyone who steps out of their circle. Most cancer doctors are content to go with the flow. Indeed, it can be quite a comfortable one.

Part of the reason doctors insist on the use of conventional medicines is an absence of information. At medical schools, students are taught drugs, drugs, and drugs with little or no nutrition education. If students hear scuttlebutt about some successful alternative treatment, they may also learn that such treatment is on the "unproven" list published by the American Cancer Society, whose board includes a number of pharmaceutical company executives. An ambitious student who hopes to get research grants and publish his or her discoveries will soon learn that if he or she attempts to research anything on the American Cancer Society's "unproven" list, he or she will certainly not get a grant, and, indeed, may never get a grant on anything at all. Nor are respectable medical journals, most of which are heavily dependent upon pharmaceutical drug advertising, likely to publish studies showing effectiveness of anything other than pharmaceutical drugs.

Moral of the story: a conscientious young medical student would be hard pressed to come across reliable information on successful alternative cancer treatments that could be discussed with colleagues without being laughed out of the room. The power of the conventional medical community; the pharmaceutical industry; the state medical boards; medical schools; and governmental agencies is such that any practitioner who tries anything new or different does so at their own peril.

Considering the amount of chemotherapy and radiation pushed onto cancer patients, Dr. Wayne Jonas recalls the "heroic" medicine used in the early 19th century – i.e., the bloodletting to which President George Washington was subjected after he had a chill following a ride around his plantation. When the bloodletting had no favorable effect, the orthodox doctors of the time (considered the "best" doctors) resorted to their second armament: mercury. They packed Washington's mouth and other orifices with mercury (after bleeding him four times). Finally, the founder of our country expired as the only sure way of getting away from his doctors. Once, when the second First Lady, Abigail Adams, was feeling unwell, Dr. Benjamin Rush, one of the most famous doctors of the period, proposed to bleed her. The sagacious Abigail adamantly refused. Dr. Rush referred to bloodletting and mercury as "heroic" medicine, and proudly stated that he bled all his patients. He believed that if you were sick, the sickness had to be attacked and beaten out of you.

Dr. Jonas wonders if the U.S. is not living through the Second Age of Heroic Medicine, and speculates that it may meet the same fate as did the first such age. In the early 19th century, remembering how the orthodox doctors had killed George Washington, people rushed toward the gentler and far more effective treatments of homeopathy – just as today, people are rushing to alternative medical treatments, to the consternation of orthodox medical practitioners.

We no longer bleed people, as was done to George Washington. If a person has cancer, they are simply injected with a poison so powerful that one better not get it on their hands. We no longer administer mercury, one of the strongest poisons known. We simply put it in the fillings of people's teeth, so they can breath the fumes every day and every night.

This is some of the background of the situation in which NFAM proposes to make a difference and precipitate some badly needed changes in U.S. medicine today.

Change never comes from a majority, but rather from a dissatisfied minority seething with creative discontent that wants to find better ways. This group, a small but rapidly growing number of doctors, is the choir to which NFAM wants to preach. At the moment, doctors have few sources of reliable information on alternative treatments, and they will certainly find nothing about most of the successful alternative cancer treatments of the past or the present in their medical libraries.

If even a handful of the low cost, non-toxic, successful trial results NFAM is aware of were published, NFAM could cause a revolution in American healthcare. And if even a fraction of those treatments subsequently became freely available, as open competition, to frequently toxic patent medicines, U.S. healthcare costs could plummet. Healthcare costs are currently sky high only because our present system gives a virtual monopoly to the pharmaceutical industry, with no opportunity for creative alternative treatments to get into the system and compete.

When NFAM first started visiting foreign clinics they discovered some of the clinics looked at cancer treatment very differently from the prevailing conventional view in the United States. Conventional treatments concentrate exclusively on destruction of the tumor by radiation, surgery, or chemotherapy. Alternative cancer clinics view cancer much differently. They begin with the premise that something must have gone wrong in the patient's body for cancer to develop. Rather than simply concentrating exclusively on destruction of the tumor, alternative clinics treat the patient's *whole body*, in order for it to overcome cancer. Alternative treatment might consist of as many as ten different treatments given to each patient – treatments directed primarily towards strengthening the patient's immune system; detoxifying the patient; and allowing the patient's immune system to recognize and address the cancer. There is also a thought, in some circles, that cancer has an ability to hide itself, or protect itself from the patient's immune system.

Sometimes alternative clinics will surgically remove a tumor to eliminate the toxicity coming from the tumor, and sometimes they will use some chemotherapy, but only in very small doses. These clinics believe it is wrong to administer heavy doses of chemotherapy, which severely compromise the immune system.

"If you are going to administer heavy doses of radiation or chemotherapy, as we do in conventional medicine, surely it makes sense to strengthen the immune system and detoxify the body at the same time," Berkley reasoned.

JIMMY CARTER

November 16, 2002

To Berkley Bedell

Rosalynn and I are pleased to congratulate you on the 5th anniversary of the National Foundation for Alternative Medicine. As a congressman, businessman, and family man, you have employed your incredible talents to make knowledge of and access to alternative medicines more available to the general public. It is fitting that your innovative, courageous leadership and service are being recognized in this way.

You and Elinor have our warm best wishes as you look forward to many more years of success and fulfillment.

Sincerely,

Jimmy Carter

The Honorable Berkeley Bedell, Founder
The National Foundation
 for Alternative Medicine
1629 K Street, NW
Suite 402
Washington, D.C. 20006

Given budgetary restrictions resulting from its self-imposed rejection of any funding from official medicine, NFAM has had to observe the old adage that "necessity is the mother of invention."

Acceptable medical trials, as currently defined in U.S. medicine, cost millions and millions of dollars. For NFAM to carry out trials in the U.S. of successful alternatives found elsewhere, would be cost prohibitive and impossible. But NFAM has discovered that it can conduct medical trials adequately under U.S. standards in various other countries, for a fraction of the cost of an equivalent test done within the United States.

U.S. Senator Tom Harkin, D-Iowa, presents Berkley and Elinor Bedell with an award celebrating the Fifth Anniversary of the National Foundation for Alternative Medicine, in November, 2002.

To ensure tests are carried out in accordance with strict standards, NFAM created a unique plan. It has formed a close liaison with a major U.S. university. The university observes and monitors NFAM tests, which, when completed, it will then publish as a participant in the trials. Thus, at a fraction of the cost, NFAM will conduct tests abroad with the professionalism and high standards expected of such trials, and with arrangements to publish the results. As a result, the knowledge of breakthroughs in cancer, heart disease, etc., will be made available in ways that will reach the entire U.S. population. This is a major breakthrough in strategy.

As NFAM scoured more of the world, they uncovered increasingly exciting claims for alternative treatments administered abroad, outside the restricted medical environment that exists in the United States. Among such treatments are claims of effective use of energy or electro-magnetic therapies. This new type of science and treatment is based upon the findings that the body operates electrically, as well as chemically. Acupuncture, which was once ridiculed and is now widely practiced in the U.S., is based on the electrical meridians of the body. Traditional Chinese medicine has recognized electrical energy of the body for centuries.

With recent advances in technology, it is now possible to measure the electrical energy of the body's cells, and by administering the proper frequency, the energy of the cells can be enhanced. The treatment is completely non-invasive. Sometimes, the frequency is administered through pads placed on the patient and sometimes the frequency is simply beamed at the patient, as is done with a radio. This therapy is a whole new science when compared to conventional pharmaceutical medicine.

There is not much hope conventional medicine can give to Parkinson's disease patients. Some people, suffering with the disease brought information to Berkley of a doctor in Greece, Dr. Photios Anninos, who is successfully treating Parkinson's disease with an electro magnetic treatment. Dr. Anninos has a new piece of equipment called a SQUID. The equipment costs about one million dollars. A large part of the cost comes from the room in which it is housed. The walls of the room are constructed so that no electro magnetic waves of any kind, such as radio or television waves, can get inside the room. The equipment then measures the electro magnetic waves of the patient's brain to detect the frequencies at which the electric potential is weak. A helmet is then built with a battery and coils to transmit the exact weak frequency to the paient's brain. The entire treatment consists of having the patient meditate for 45 minutes each evening, and then wear the helmet with the battery and electric coils for two minutes each evening. The patient then retires for the night. That is the total treatment – no medications of any kind! The power of the electric frequency transmitted to the brain is less than a person would receive using an electric razor or watching television.

Berkley had one of Dr. Anninos' patients come to Naples to talk with a group. She told how her symptoms had been so severe that she could hardly function. She was literally housebound. After the Parkinson's disease treatment in Greece, she had hardly any symptoms and requested they play golf the next morning after her appearance at the meeting. She and her husband won 10-cents from Berkley and his partner by winning the golf game! It is claimed that Dr. Anninos' treatment has ended the progression of Parkinson's disease in 80 percent of his patients, and symptoms have been reversed or nearly eliminated in a number of patients receiving this treatment. It is also claimed that the treatment is effective for Alzheimer's and other diseases, particularly epilepsy.

A well-known physician in Mexico City, Mexico, Dr. Sodi Pallares, has been treating people with a multi-faceted treatment plan, the center of which includes an electro magnetic process. His plan consists of a low salt diet and administration of a polarizing solution, which is high in potassium and low in sodium, together with the electro magnetic treatment. The NFAM staff visited Dr. Pallares to learn more. Dr. Pallares claims his treatment is effective for both cancer and heart disease, and that in his practice he has treated 14 patients – each who were scheduled for a heart transplant and, after treatment, the surgery was not required. "I asked the person who visited his clinic whether he believed the statement in regard to the heart transplant patients," Berk reported. "He said he believed it.

"I had dinner with two heart disease patients who had been treated by another doctor with an electro magnetic frequency treatment. Each of them had been scheduled for a heart transplant. One of them was even unable to go up the stairs to get to the doctor's office prior to his treatment. Both of them have not needed a heart transplant and both are now playing golf!" Berkley reported.

NFAM is currently trying to raise money to monitor incoming heart disease patients to confirm diagnosis, and then check patients after treatment to solidify whether Dr. Pallares' claims can be confirmed. To date, $37,500 has been pledged to cover half the cost of a heart disease patient trial. NFAM is busy trying to raise the other half.

Berkley wth Dave Stetzer, one of the inventors of a device that filters out electromagnetic frequencies that pollute buildings.

As NFAM searched the world, they realized electro magnetic frequencies could have harmful, as well as beneficial, effects. An electrical engineer in Wisconsin who had diabetes, David Stetzer discovered that his diabetic symptoms were much worse in certain buildings than in others. As he pursued this oddity, he realized the increasing use of computers, televisions, printers, faxes, dimmer light switches, and the like feeds electrical pollution into the wiring of the building. This pollution is then transmitted from the building's wiring into the air space of the building, and is very damaging to some people's health. Stetzer has developed some little filters, which are simply plugged into the electrical outlets of the building to filter out this pollution.

Berkley and Elinor have installed these electro magnetic frequencies filters into their home, and notice a definite difference. Currently, they cost $25 each, and it took 20 of them to cover the Bedell house – for a total cost of $500. The items can be obtained from Stetzer Electric, 520 West Broadway Street, Blair, Wisconsin, 54616.

They were also installed in some schools in Wisconsin. Here is a copy of a letter from one of the teachers at the school:

November 30, 2003

My life changed one year ago.

The past 3.5 years of my life are filled with sad memories of serious health problems. The list of my symptoms includes fatigue, memory loss, facial flushing, headaches, numbness, loss of taste and smell, eye irritation, sleep disturbances, double vision, sinus infections, and bronchitis. These health conditions began when school started and gradually went away throughout the summer. I missed more school in one year than I had in the previous ten years of teaching. I went from doctor to doctor, searching for answers. I had two MRIs of my brain, blood tests, neurological exams and yet no answers. I went to my optometrist, chiropractor, allergist, general practitioner, and neurologist. Everyone was concerned, but no one had any answers. So my life went for the next three years. I was finally diagnosed with benign multiple sclerosis.

My students suffered. It was a fifty-fifty chance I would call them by their correct names. The days and weeks blended into a time in my life I barely remember, except for the pain of being me. I was so busy trying to not fall when I went for a walk while I had double vision that I missed the sights of spring. For years, I would go to bed by six in the evening so I could get up for school the next day. I was always exhausted. Last year, my headaches were so severe I didn't make it a complete week for the first three months of school. I was miserable. I had decided at that point I would give up teaching in hopes of getting my good health back.

The only people I let into my sad, little world were my parents and brothers. Everyone felt helpless. When I went to bed at night I would often cry in my pillow to hide the true fear I felt. I was trapped in a horrible world with no hope in sight.

One year ago, however, everything changed. My school brought in Mr. Dave Stetzer, a power quality expert. He identified problems in our electrical environment. Mr. Stetzer filtered our school to eliminate the dirty electricity riding on the line. My headaches stopped immediately and so did the exhaustion that was my life. My health from that point has been wonderful People who know me best see me as a new person. A person they used to know, but hadn't seen for years. All signs and symptoms of benign multiple sclerosis are gone. The health concerns that once consumed my life are no longer an issue. I once again enjoy life. I attribute this change in my life to the filters that surround my world. The filters that eliminated the electrical pollution we are all exposed to every day, everywhere. I have found filters to be a simple solution that changed my life and a countless number of people I know.

I am forever thankful to have my life back!

Angela Olstad,
Teacher/Principal
Olstd@mel-min.k12.wi.us

The former director of the Office of Alternative Medicine at NIH, Dr. Wayne Jonas, M.D. served in the military. Although no longer on active duty, he continues to have strong ties with the military. Because of his interest in alternative medicine, he has obtained funding from the Samuelis, a wealthy California family, for the establishment of the Samueli Institute, dedicated to the research of alternative treatments for disease. Dr. Jonas serves on the Board of NFAM and there is a very close working relationship between the two organizations.

Thanks mostly to the work of Dr. Jonas, the two groups have succeeded in getting an appropriation of $2 million dollars from Congress to investigate alternative treatments that may help the military. It is indicated that top personnel will not stall this effort, as was true of the Office of Alternative Medicine at NIH.

It appears that Berkley Bedell is again likely to prove that his grandmother was right when she said, "You can accomplish almost anything within reason if you will only set your mind to it." Just as was true when the pollster told him he did not have a chance to be elected to Congress, and when his vendor cut off his supply of the chemical needed to make nylon, Berkley has again refused to give up. If the NIH Office of Alternative Medicine thought their refusal to "investigate and validate" alternative treatments for disease would deter Berkley Bedell, they were not aware of his will-ingness to *tackle giants*, and they did not know his grand-mother.

The spectator who told 15-year old, 120-pound Berkley Bedell that his tackle of the opposing halfback was the best tackle he had ever seen, has long since died. The former Spirit Lake high school football player is now tack-ling the most formidable giant of his life, the giant medical pharmaceutical monopoly. After a lifetime of *tackling giants*, Berkley is well prepared for the challenge.

Like David as he faced Goliath, Berkley goes forth with confidence, not only that he will prevail, but that by "investigating and validating" non-toxic, low-cost alterna-tive treatments, he will bring better treatments and better health to the entire world.

As a teenager, Berkley wrote an article about his little fishing tackle business that appeared in a sporting goods magazine. It ended with the words, "Watch us. We have only started." At 82 years of age, he again echoes those words, "Watch us. We have only started."

As we come to the end of the book, we do not come to the end of the story. The story goes on as Berkley Bedell continues to tackle the strongest giant of his life. Keep posted. It may change your life and your health.

Afterword

All income from the sales of this book will be given to The National Foundation for Alternative Medicine.

Berkley and Elinor Bedell truly believe that the National Foundation for Alternative Medicine is likely to bring better health and better treatments to the entire world.

For those who would like to be a part of this exciting project, contributions can be sent to:

The National Foundation for Alternative Medicine
5 Thomas Circle, Suite 500
Washington, DC 20005
or
The National Foundation for Alternative Medicine
c/o Berkley Bedell
15712 Rusty Road
Spirit Lake, IA 51360
All contributions are tax-deductible.

Addresses

Berkley and Elinor Bedell
Summer address: 15712 Rusty Road, Spirit Lake, IA 51360
Winter address: 4815 Aston Gardens Way, B-201, Naples, FL
34109

Daniel Haley
Summer Address: P.O. Box 138, Waddington, NY 13694
Winter Address: Rt. 1, Box 175A5 Daingerfield, TX 75638

Larry Ramey
1310 Amherst Place, Dayton, OH 45406

The National Foundation for Alternative Medicine

Office: 5 Thomas Circle, Suite 500, Washington, DC 2005
Book Orders: National Foundation for Alternative Medicine %
Quick Pick
Distribution, 22167 C. Street, Winfield KS 67156

The National Foundation for Alternative Medicine publishes this book so that people may be aware of our founder and what we are doing. The mission of the National Foundation for Alternative Medicine is "To investigate and evaluate alternative medical treatments being administered around the world, and to make more effective treatments available to the people of the world." New scientific discoveries are being made daily. The health care system in the U.S. makes it extremely difficult for such discoveries to be validated and put into the system in the U.S. The National Foundation for Alternative Medicine is dedicated to bringing better health and medicine to the world by investigating and validating treatments being administered around the world.

NFAM is a not-for-profit foundation, dependent upon tax-exempt contributions for its work. Any profits from the sale of this book will help the foundation, or two books will be sent as a gift from the founder to anyone making a tax-exempt contribution of $100 or more.

Order Form

To: National Foundation for Alternative Medicine
c/o Quick Pick Distribution
Distribution, 22167 C. Street, Winfield KS 67156

I enclose $ _____ for which please send me _____ copies of
"Tackling Giants" @ $19.95 plus $4.95 postage. (The $4.95
postage applies no matter how many books are ordered.)

Name: _____

Address: _____

_____

Telephone _____

****

National Foundation for Alternative Medicine
5 Thomas Circle, Suite 500
Washington, DC 2005

I enclose a tax-deductible contribution of $ _____. I would like
1 or 2 (circle which is desired) copies of "Tackling Giants" as a
gift from Berkley and Elinor Bedell.

Name: _____

Address: _____

_____

Telephone _____